PCI DSS Made Easy

(2017 revision to the PCI DSS 3.2 edition)

by Yves B. Desharnais, MBA, CISSP, PCIP

Edited by François Desharnais

This page left intentionally blank.

Book Series Acknowledgement

Writing acknowledgements is always a tricky thing since we always forget someone. So if you were deserving of such recognition and did not get it here, my bad.

I want to thank all of those from which I have learned over the years: family, friends, colleagues, teachers... all of whom were teachers in some way, shape or form. Your support and constructive criticism have helped me learn and improve. I do want to call out a few individuals who were instrumental in my professional career.

I would have probably not felt ready to write a book had it not been for the detailed and exhaustive review of the proposals, reports and other communications that Jan Hertzberg, my boss for over 2 years, took time to review, helping me improve my communication skills in the process.

The text you're reading also reads better thanks to the help of my brother François, a literary mind to my technical and business one. François performed the role of editor and made sure that this text was proper English. Francois is also who can be thanked for the French language translation, while I reviewed the translation as the subject matter expert.

Finally, I want to mention a few of the colleagues with whom I've discussed information security and PCI DSS over last few the years: Dan Waggoner, Jamison Rock, Josh Bozarth, Vanya Okuka, Hakim Aliane, and Tom Beaupre.

Table of Contents

Foreword

I have worked for the past several years as a PCI Subject Matter Expert in the Cybersecurity technology industry. I often get laughed at, mocked, or challenged about why I keep bringing up PCI when discussing the industry, the state of security, and how to best promote various products and services within the context of "compliance". "Why are you still talking about PCI?". "It's just a checkbox exercise and has little to do with security". "PCI - Is that still a thing?" If you've picked up this book you might yourself be asking, "why another book about PCI?" Let me explain.

I got my start with PCI in late 2004 when I started a job with a new company. One day I was handed a document and was told, "Here you go. Read this. Learn this. We're going to do this." This was my introduction to the Payment Card Industry Data Security Standard (PCI DSS) Version 1.0 which turned into nearly 10 years of being a Qualified Security Assessor (QSA) performing validation assessments for many of the largest merchants and service providers in North America.

As I read through the standard for the first time I thought, "this is a fairly comprehensive overview of how you should implement an Information Security program in your organization." I had twenty years of InfoSec experience under my belt at that point, and I considered the PCI DSS to be a pretty rational approach to doing security. I approached PCI compliance with the perspective of "this is the right thing to do", and spent much of my time as an assessor providing education and awareness and context to my customers. I wasn't the typical QSA, and that mattered to my customers. I often received feedback such as, "That was the toughest assessment we've ever been through…thank you." These were assessments where I took the time to explain how the six goals of PCI DSS work together to help organizations be more secure, and would explain the meaning, or "spirit" of every requirement so that the customer understood the context and why it was so important to follow.

I have been exposed to other regulatory and compliance standards over the past several years (it's fairly common in the vendor marketing space to lump all compliance together), but the more I learned about other standards the more adamant I became that PCI stands alone as not just a compliance standard, but as a framework for implementing an Information (or Cyber) Security Program for any organization.

That is why there is a need for yet another book on PCI. I met Yves several years ago at a PCI Community Meeting where he first told me about his idea for putting together a different kind of book on PCI. We agreed that there is a need for a resource that takes the time to explain the context of every PCI DSS requirement, how they all work together, and different approaches to meeting the requirements.

PCI is too often misunderstood, and dismissed by many because of ignorance and lack of understanding. There is nothing magic about security, and there are no silver bullets. Good security takes planning, resources, work, diligence, and a healthy does of paranoia. The PCI DSS provides a comprehensive framework for building that type of program. Is it hard? Yes. Is it time consuming? Yes. Is it costly? It can be. But that is the reality of Cybersecurity in today's world. There really are no shortcuts if you want to do it right, and those responsible for providing Cybersecurity for their organizations need a framework that is grounded in history, and the collective lessons-learned from past compromises. That is security. That is PCI.

So, read this book. It is certainly useful as a reference guide for specific questions about certain requirements, but it is also important to take the big picture view of the whole standard.

- Jeff Man

Jeff is a respected Information Security expert, advisor, evangelist, and co-host on Paul's Security Weekly. With over 34 years of experience working in all aspects of computer, network, and information security, including risk management, vulnerability analysis, compliance assessment, forensic analysis and penetration testing. He previously held security research, management and product development roles with the National Security Agency, the DoD and private-sector enterprises and was part of the first penetration testing "red team" at NSA. For the past twenty years, he has been a pen tester, security architect, consultant, QSA, and PCI SME, providing consulting and advisory services to many of the nation's best known companies.

Book Series Introduction

Welcome to this book series on PCI DSS. If you're reading this book, then you must have either an interest (in the field of PCI DSS compliance) or a need (your organization must become compliant, or currently has issues with PCI DSS compliance) to gain a better understanding of PCI DSS.

The books have been updated annually from the initial version of the books covering PCI DSS 3.1 in 2015, to PCI DSS 3.2 in 2016, where a physical compilation of volumes 1 to 3 was produced. Recent communications from the PCI SSC make it appear that no revision will be forthcoming shortly, thus this 2017 release includes clarifications and new relevant information that was brought to light over the last year. But the underlying understanding of the original books remains consistent.

My goal is to provide a common understanding for business and technical people alike, and to provide a way for those people to communicate better about PCI DSS compliance, and information security in general. This is not a book for dummies. I believe that PCI DSS can be explained to laymen if properly presented. Some clients have even hinted that I'm pretty good at explaining it in a language that everyone can easily understand.

This book has been divided and broken up in 4 volumes (there were 3 initially, with the fourth released in July 2017) that address the following ideas:

- The Business Case for PCI DSS - What PCI DSS is and why it matters
- PCI DSS Scoping - How scope is defined and documented
- Building a PCI DSS Information Security Program - How organizations should approach the standard effectively and efficiently, and apply it to their in-scope environment (people, processes, and technology)
- Hypothetical Case Studies – Examples of what PCI DSS compliance looks in organizations from small to large

This book is for anyone who wants to better understand PCI DSS and its implications. I come from a strong technical background but I have also worked with many who do not. I tried to explain everything clearly without dumbing anything down while remaining true to my understanding of the standard. Some technical items are still present but will be highlighted accordingly so that the non-technical reader who wishes to do so can skip those sections (although I do hope that less technical readers might learn a few things from them should they look into these aspects).

My goal in describing PCI DSS is that a reasonable and knowledgeable person would arrive at a very similar conclusion to mine on most issues. While this book is published, it is by no means complete. The PCI SSC continues to release information based on new questions that come up and on changes in business and technology. Every such change will be documented on the associated website (www.pciresources.com) and I will issue reviews as warranted.

I believe the general approach and description in this book will stand the test of time. Links on the web however, since they are out of my control, may be more subject to change. For that reason, all links will be placed on the website for this book and updated as the standard evolves (including new information that I come across). A PDF version of the references for printing will also be available from the website.

About the author

I started doing information security work in 2001, a time when there were still limited resources out there for those learning how to get started in the field of information security.

At the time, there were mostly two ways of starting in information security. The first was through administrative studies, and focused on governance and policy. The second was for network and system administrators involved in the technical aspects of the work. I came more from the latter side and my technical background was helpful in learning the ropes. My background was more related to application and system development, and I had decent system administrator skills, mostly self-taught, on Linux, Windows and OS/2. And I had also done work on two Unixes: Solaris during my undergrad years, and AIX for an internship.

The mid-90s undergrad course in computer engineering I took really prepared us well for what was to come. Through reading on a myriad of topics, practicing my craft, discussing with colleagues, I grew as a professional.

I was a QSA for a bit over a year while I lived in Chicago, and I now perform this work for organisations of all sizes, from the large and complex to the small and simple. I've helped many clients understand, scope and assess their PCI DSS compliance.

I wrote this book because, while there are many very good but disparate sources of information online (from the PCI SSC, blogs, etc. - see www.pciresources.com for a complete list of the sources I followed and used during the writing of this book), I have not found one document (physical or online) that presents things the way I think they should be presented. I felt a need to document my own thinking. The work I did for one PCI client led me to a deep reflexion on how I should present this information. This book is the result of this process.

This book is geared towards the business side of dealing with PCI DSS but also includes technical elements required for completeness (the PCI DSS has a more technical bent itself). Technical sections are identified as such and can be skipped by the non-technical reader. My hope is that having both technical and non-technical sections in one document will help both business and technical staff have the same vocabulary and understanding, thereby helping organisations reach (achieve) and sustain over time (maintain) their PCI DSS compliance.

Throughout this book, I'll spell out PCI DSS to ensure no confusion exists with other PCI norms such as PA DSS and PCI PIN PTS. PA DSS will only be discussed briefly; PCI PIN PTS even less so.

Disclaimers

This book is the result of my experience and only represents my understanding, and is not endorsed by anyone other than myself, including previous or future employers, the PCI SSC or the card brands.

Mention of any product in the text should not be construed as an endorsement of any specific product, but only seen as examples, unless otherwise specifically mentioned.

What this book is and is not

This work is an interpretation of the standard based on my experience with it, various client experiences, conversations with peers and information security in general. I've read all that I could find on the subject including most documents from the PCI SSC and every internet post I could find.

Please confirm with your assessor (QSA or otherwise) and document any interpretation you may use within your network. Your assessor, internal or otherwise, is the ultimate arbiter in the compliance world.

So, without further ado, let's dig in.

Volume 1 - A Business Case for the PCI DSS

1.1 Volume Introduction

The goal of this volume is to explain why the PCI DSS matters, how it works, how we got here, and where it may be heading. Other volumes of the book will deal with more detailed and technical questions.

Let's start with the obvious. What exactly is the PCI DSS? It is a standard that includes over 250 mandatory requirements and whose stated goal is the protection of card information. Why does it exist? It was created because the payment card industry (PCI, often referred to as the credit card industry) sees value in protecting card information. We can easily identify two main reasons for this: the first being fraud; and fraud, in this case, means the industry makes less money (profit) in the end. The second reason is that instances of fraud may make users prefer alternative forms of payment (cash, for example), which once again implies less money for the industry as a whole, and for the card brands in particular.

Just as your neighbour may generally not care about what you do to your house until it starts affecting the neighbourhood and his house's value, the same principle applies to the payment card industry, which generates a lot of money through transaction fees and interest payments. They won't care what happens to other companies until it starts affecting their own bottom line.

The goal of PCI DSS is to protect cardholder data from theft or unauthorized disclosure. This is our gold standard, the lens through which we will look at the various PCI DSS requirements. This primary goal is always to protect data, and it is accomplished through measures on people, processes and technologies.

PCI DSS is not about compliance, it is about security. The card brands don't worry about us being "compliant", they mainly care about the information being protected. The problem is that it remains virtually impossible to prove anyone is secure (one can only prove lack of security). And a level of 100% security is unachievable anyway, so the next best thing is to do an assessment (which is a point-in-time review, not an audit) to ensure that you have basic controls in place. But why only basic controls if they are not sufficient? The problem is that there are many ways to implement security, too many technologies to consider, and risk levels that wildly vary between different industries and even similar organizations in the same industry, based on their different processes and technologies. We can only deal with standard (recognized) security best practices that should be common to any environment.

Some of the straightforward questions that the PCI DSS tries to assess are:

- Do you know where the information you need to protect is kept? (And, if you don't, how can you protect it?)
- Are only the right people/individuals accessing it (and for legitimate purposes)?
- How would you know if someone who should not access it does so?
- Would you be able to figure out how someone got access to that information should you learn about it after the fact?

This volume may be less technical than others in the series, but it serves to introduce the vocabulary used in the PCI DSS standard, so that everyone employs the same terms to describe the same things, and communicates efficiently. A full glossary is provided at the end of the book (or on the website [1]).

1.2 Why PCI DSS?

1.2.1 The value of card information

Why do we need a standard such as the PCI DSS? Simply put, because it adds minimal security requirements that organizations should reasonably put in place to protect information that is very valuable. If you don't have even these you're basically not even trying. Cardholder Data (CHD), as it is referred to in PCI lingo, is very liquid, meaning easily sold, or monetizable. We need to look no further than the evolving string of cardholder breaches of the last few years to be reminded of that fact.

Recounting just the ones that include over 1 million credit card numbers up to summer 2015 [2], we find CardSystems in 2005 (40 million), TJ stores (TJX, including TJ Max) in 2007 (100 million), Hannaford Bros. Supermarket chain in 2008 (4.2 million), Heartland Payment Systems in 2009 (130 million), Sony PlayStation Network (PSN) in 2011 (12 million), Global Payments Inc. in 2012 (7 million), Adobe in 2013 (2.9 million), and culminating with the Fall 2013 Target breach (40 million), and the Summer 2014 Home Depot breach (56 million). And these are just the ones with over 1 million cards stolen! Some attackers are now targeting smaller banks and merchants. In May 2016, thieves used around 1,600 forged cards from a South African bank to withdraw the money from 1,400 individual cash machines across Japan, netting about $13 million dollars (USD) [3]. And breaches are still happening. The 2017 Equifax breach of data on about 143 million (initial estimate) US citizens and residents (half the US adult population) is mind-boggling. This breach is said to include at least 200,000 credit card numbers, and enough data to fraudulently request many new ones.

What initially started off with local thieves or organizations stealing data has become a very professionally run operation managed by organized criminal groups with large budgets, and heavy technical expertise (while we've heard mostly of Russians and Ukrainians in 2014, we are certainly not limited to individuals from these countries).

Based on reports [4], [5] of the Target breach of 2013, it seems that a third-party that provided refrigeration services was initially/also compromised. It appears that the connection from the third-party to Target did not follow security best practices of using multi-factor authentication (renamed from two-factor authentication in PCI DSS 3.2, which requires that two of the three authentication methods be used:

something you know, such as a password or passphrase; something you have, such as a token device or smart card; something you are, such as a biometric) and/or that the Target internal systems may not have been as well segmented as required by the standard. The attackers, once inside the Target infrastructure, installed malware at the Point-of-Sale terminals (POS, the payment terminal) to grab information that flowed through memory (a type of program called a RAM-scraper).

Note that some of the most recent guidance that the PCI SSC has delivered was regarding third-parties (Third-Party Security Assurance [6]) in August 2014 (and updated in March 2016). Also note that PCI DSS 3.0 (released in November 2013) introduced a new requirement, 11.3.4, which calls for penetration testing of the network segmentation used to reduce scope. Both of those try to mitigate those risks.

Card information is considered easy to sell or monetize by criminals. The 'darknet', a series of online black markets with (mostly complete) anonymity, has made selling this type of information very easy. Brian Krebs has written extensively on the topic [7] and his reporting is worthwhile for anyone interested in learning more.

These attacks are not always crimes of opportunity. The information security industry calls many of these attacks that take a long time to organize APT, for Advanced Persistent Threat. An APT is a concerted long term attack on any target. These are generally run by either state-sponsored organizations, or by criminal groups. These are very well funded operations, and they can target cardholder data as well as other secondary/tangential information. As to why they do this, as famed American bank robber Willie Sutton is stated to have said: "*I rob banks because that's where the money is*"[8]. These criminal organizations do it for the same reason. They target organizations with the 'goods' they seek.

1.2.2 The costs of PCI DSS

Like any regulation, there are costs to implementing and maintaining compliance to the PCI DSS standard. These costs cover the triad of people, process, and technology that must be maintained as part of the business process.

As with most regulations, in order for organizations to comply with the standard, we either need a carrot (for motivation) or a stick (for sanction), or a bit of both. For PCI DSS, the carrot is often better transaction fees. This also works as the stick approach, meaning higher transaction fees for non-compliance. Other costs of non-compliance that an organization can, and should consider, include (mainly in case of a breach):

- Negative reputation/publicity
- Loss of clientele
- Financial losses (called "radiations" in financial terms)
- Financial penalties and/or fines (including increased transaction fees)
- Loss of capacity to operate as merchant, acquirer, service provider or issuer
- Health check (mandatory periodic follow-up regarding security and compliance)

While the PCI DSS is an industry regulation, that does not mean that government regulators will not also get involved. Wyndham hotels initially had cardholder data stolen in April 2008, and then again in March 2009 and later that same year. The US Federal Trade Commission (FTC) eventually fined Wyndham hotels for the failure to protect their customer's information, which lead to a repeated breach [9].

1.3 How We Got Here - An Oversimplified History of the Payment Card Industry (PCI)

To understand what the PCI DSS is and where it may be going, it is helpful to remind ourselves how we got here. The PCI DSS follows the evolution of the financial sector and information technology, and I will attempt to briefly paint you the story of its history and evolution. This section is not a full history, but it does summarize important changes that impacted the PCI DSS.

1.3.1 Credit in ancient times?

The concept of credit has existed for a very long time. Say you were a farmer growing your crops. All of a sudden, your beast of burden fell ill and died. You couldn't pull all the heavy plowing equipment across your field by yourself, now could you? So you sent your son with an offering of a basket of goods to your neighbour asking him to lend you his own animal, or even better still, to let you buy it, promising to pay him back with the receipts from your crops. This type of barter is also a basic form of credit. The concept of interest also existed, as you could pay back someone with a bigger amount of the same resource.

The history of money, or the use of a physical medium of value, has been around for thousands of years. From gems, to precious metals (often minted coins) down to more common goods, the methods used by human societies have evolved over time. Precious metals and stones, as valuable as they were, were also out of reach of the common man, requiring another form of currency accessible to all. For Aztecs, it was chocolate (the word chocolate is derived from the Aztec language Nahuatl and was originally written chocolatl). In "The History of Money", the author writes:

> *The Aztecs used chocolate for money, or more precisely, they used the cacao seeds usually called beans. With these cacao seeds, one could buy fruits and vegetables, such as corn, tomatoes, chillies, squash, chayottes, and peanuts; jewelry made of gold, silver, jade, and turquoise; manufactured goods such as sandals, clothing, feathered capes, cotton padded armor, weapons, pottery, and baskets; meats such as fish, venison, duck; and specialty goods such as alcohol and slaves.* [10]

And that was but one example: "Natives in part of India used almonds. Guatemalans used corn; the ancient Babylonians and Assyrians used barley." [11]

The use of a physical medium made trade easier. It could be hard to pay back the value of a chicken against a cow, but assigning an exchange rate to any item in balance to a specific physical medium (which is what we still do with modern currencies) allowed for easier exchanges of goods and services. And we still use goods as monetary tools in some places. Cigarettes are often portrayed as exchanged for favors in both war time and prison environments.

Money lending is probably as old as money itself. Modern banks appear to have evolved from rich north-Italian families. [12] The banks started dealing not directly with gold or silver, but with paper notes. The banks differed from previous lending institutions in that they lent to anyone (no matter their creed) and did not face the limitations placed by the Roman Catholic Church of the day, such as that which forbade usury. [13] The Christian church in medieval Europe banned the charging of interest at any rate (as well as charging a fee for the use of money [14]). "The History of Money" details this:

> The Christian prohibition against usury was based on two passages in the bible: "Take thou no usury ... or increase; but fear thy God. ... Thou shalt not give him thy money upon usury, nor lend him thy victuals for increase" (Leviticus 25:36-37); and "He that ... hath given forth usury, and hath taken increase: shall he live? he shall not live: he hath done all these abominations; he shall surely die, his blood shall be upon him" (Ezekiel 18:13). [15]

The Romans had carefully restricted interest rates, but this changed after the end of the Roman empire. Usury by Christians led to excommunication from the Church. So either Jews became lenders, or loopholes were used to get around this by not lending money directly, but using "bills of exchange", paying back a higher value in another currency [16]. And using these 'bills' made the exchange of money more portable.

What started in Italy obviously expanded to all of Europe. Ultimately the restrictions on interest were lifted. One example is: "England reintroduced the right to charge interest (particularly the 1545 Act, "An Act Against Usurie" (37 H. viii 9) of King Henry VIII of England)." [17]

Gold and silver were still the underlying asset behind every financial transaction in Europe and the new European colonies, and remained so until the 20th century when the gold standard was abolished for most currencies [18]. Indeed, this decision was fueled by all the gold taken from the Americas back to the old continent (at first from local civilizations, and later mined).

In North America, The U.S. dollar was enshrined into law on April 2, 1792, making official what was common practice by most people living in the U.S. [19] Spanish dollars and Mexican pesos (both silver coins) remained legal tender until late into the 19th century [20].

Paper money had existed for a long time, apparently originating in China in the 1st or 2nd century [21] (China is also credited for the invention of paper). Paper money had also emerged in North America, as we learn that "as early as 1690, the Massachusetts Bay Colony printed the first paper money in North America". [22] The use of paper obviously grew in both the new colonies as well as in Europe. The growth of the new colonies, with opportunities in development of the West for example, fostered the spread of paper money, but also of gold, silver and other valuables. And gold was found in the US west and the Yukon (Canada) in North America, and elsewhere.

Back in those early days, information security mostly implied physical security as everything was physical, meaning gold and silver coins, bank-issued dollar bills, letters of credits, and others (no "electronic" support was available, although postal mail was involved early on). Valuables (cash, cheques, etc.) were thus protected by physical handling procedures, safes, locked cabinets and doors, and several other physical methods.

Protection of those paper documents became important to the authorities of the time. Indeed, postal mail and wire fraud, another way to get access to this information, became a federal crime in the USA in 1872 (almost 150 years ago).

As stated earlier, gold was the underpinning of paper money for quite a while. You could exchange any bill for its equivalent in gold. But gold was much less portable. And untying paper money from gold allowed a government to print at much as it wanted (with potential consequences, mind you). Many western governments dropped the gold standard requirements for their currencies around the turn of the 20th century, though some debated returning to the gold standard (and some still do to this day). But as Weatherford states: "In 1931, Britain permanently dropped any pretense of tying the value of its currency to its deposits of gold." [23] The U.S. suspended its gold standard twice during World War I, and mostly in 1933 because of the depression [24]. A few more changes occurred post World War II, and finally in 1976 all references to the gold standard were removed [25]. However, gold is still viewed as a form of reserve currency that people flock to in times of economic trouble.

1.3.2 Development of the financial industry in the USA

Up until a few years after World War II, Americans (as well as most people in the world) used mostly cash for payments. Loans did exist, but were generally limited to assets such as property and equipment. The first modern credit card was created in 1951 by Diners Club, and used mostly by the affluent at high scale establishments, and became a "plastic" card in 1955 [26].

Credit cards have been around for well over half a century. Credit cards became a normal extension of then store credit that customers would negotiate. "We know you're good for it Joe," might have said one such general store merchant. And Joe would generally show up at the end of the month after getting paid to pay off his debt. Eventually, money lenders appeared outside of the of tacit agreements between shopper and shopkeeper, becoming the first credit lenders. These credit granting organizations have had to deal with fraud pretty much since their inception. Merchants at first provided their own credit, but banks and credit unions also provided varied (and changing) forms of credit over time.

1.3.3 The credit card era

The major card brands we know today have evolved considerably. The PCI SSC which manages the PCI DSS standard was created by 5 major card brands: Visa, MasterCard, American Express, Discover and JCB. BankAmericard, created in 1958 by Bank of America, became Visa in 1977. Master Charge was created in 1966 to compete with BankAmericard, and later became MasterCard in 1979. American Express, or Amex, is a financial company that started back in 1850 that was known for a the "traveler's checks company" [27], but only entered the credit card market in 1958. Discover was launched by Sears (the largest retailer in the USA at the time) in 1986, and later became an independent company in 2007. JCB retains the initials of the Japanese Credit Bureau, created in 1961. Many other card brands were created, merged, were acquired or died over that period.

And while card brands operated initially mostly as credit card networks, they now account for a big chunk of the debit card market as well (although in some countries, debit cards are not covered by PCI DSS but by other regulations and standards, such as Canada's Interac system).

Initially all payments were in person (called card-present in the PCI world), but at some point card-not-present (a PCI term for when payments are not made in the physical presence of the merchant) transactions were performed via phone, or via catalog order through postal mail or in person. In fact, until early in the 21st century, if you purchased many magazines in the USA or Canada, you would have found a form that you could fill in with your credit card information to subscribe.

A signature is generally used to authenticate the user (which is why we're supposed to sign our credit cards). The merchant is supposed to compare the signature we write on the paper slip with the one at the back of the card. There are multiple problems with this method. First off, it's fairly easy to fake a signature (I can't even make mine that consistent). Second, when was the last time anybody ever checked the signature on your card? Finally, there's the added issue that for card-not-present transactions, we do not have the back of the card to validate the signature (I have heard of people sending in their actual credit card through postal mail to have a payment processed, though that may just be an urban legend). That type of fraud through catalogs has existed for a long time. The card number (called PAN, or Primary Account Number in PCI terminology) was used as both a customer identifier (to know who someone is) and to authenticate a user (confirm his identity) in phone transactions. Using the same information for both is a big no-no in information security.

This is not the first time that we have been faced with such an issue. The use of Social Security Numbers (SSN) in the USA (similar to the Social Insurance Number, SIN, in Canada) in computer systems in the 1980's still rears its ugly head. The problem is that one set of data (SSN) was being used to not only identify a user, but also to authenticate him (prove his identity). There are implications from both from a security concern (think Identity fraud) and on a privacy side. Canada has mostly solved the SIN issue through legislation (Privacy Act of 1983 [28]), but the USA has not.

1.3.4 Credit card and the internet - or the automated fraud era

Forward now to the advent of the commercialization of the internet in the mid to late 1990s, and e-commerce took off. The same mechanism used for phone-based payments (card number only) started being used for online payments as signatures could not be used in this new type of card-not-present transactions. With interconnected systems available 24/7 from anywhere in the world, hacking started in earnest. And just like any maturing industries, it moved from skilled individual hackers to less sophisticated attackers often referred to as script-kiddies (since those users may not be fully technically savvy but employed scripts written by others) to, more and more nowadays, organized criminal groups.

In response, the card brands created new 'authenticators' that could be used online (as well as during in phone-based transactions) for additional security. Most of us have used that 3 or 4 digit number on our cards now for many years. These codes use different acronyms depending on the card brand. We'll use the term CVV, Card Verification Value, as the catch-all term for these (very often using the number 2, as in CVV2, to distinguish it from other verification codes in the card). MasterCard introduced its code in 1997. Amex followed in 1999,Visa in 2001.

1.3.5 Government Reaction to Accounting Scandals and Industry Reaction

By the early millennium, most accounting was now supported by IT systems. The early 2000s saw large accounting scandals emerge: Enron, Worldcom, Tyco [29]. In part due to these accounting scandals, Sarbanes Oxley (SOX) was enacted in the USA in 2002 (and similar legislation elsewhere around the world). It took the industry many years to fully comprehend that legislation (further guidance was needed and produced) and implement proper IT controls that would address SOX requirements without being overly (some would say any regulation is too much) burdensome to organizations.

With the advent of the internet, credit card brands and networks (Visa, MasterCard, American Express, Discover, JCB) were victims of increased fraud. To deal with this issue, the card brands each started issuing IT security standards for everyone operating in their network. Visa instituted the first one, the Cardholder Information Security Program (CISP), back in 1999 (but that only became mandatory to all in 2001). All others followed suit. Still, getting everyone to comply proved very difficult. A major problem was that the card brands depended on a large number of other organizations to comply, namely banks, merchants, etc. The required changes also take time to implement (and they do cost money upfront, though they may hopefully save money through reduced fraud down the road).

So the card brands, strong competitors in the marketplace, all facing the same fraud and security issues, decided to start working together to address this as an industry. Such a move would provide the added benefit of likely preventing potential government regulations (à la Sarbanes Oxley). Thus the card brands worked to create a not-for-profit umbrella organization, the PCI SSC, charged with the creation and maintenance of common security standards, the most well-known being the PCI DSS. PCI DSS 1.0 was issued in 2004 in pre PCI SSC days. More on this in section 1.8.

1.4 Who should care about the PCI DSS?

So who does PCI DSS apply to? The PCI DSS 3.2 standard states that:

PCI DSS applies to all entities involved in payment card processing-including merchants, processors, financial institutions, and service providers, as well as all other entities that store, process, or transmit cardholder data and/or sensitive authentication data. [30]

So basically, if your organization comes into contact with any cardholder data, meaning a complete card number (seeing only the last 4 digits, for example, is not a full number) with associated data (name, address) or what is called sensitive authentication data (such as the 3 or 4 digit code we all are used to entering when we buy something online), then you must comply with the PCI DSS. The only issue is how you must validate compliance (via self review or third-party) and whom you report your compliance to. More on this in section 1.7.

1.4.1 The payment card model

The world of the payment card industries involve only quite a few roles performed by different entities:

- **cardholder**: the individual person to whom a payment card is issued and who pays for products or services using that card;
- **issuer**: the entity that issues the card to the cardholder, often (but not limited to) your bank;
- **merchant**: the entity who receive payments from cardholders for products or services;
- **payment processor**: the entity that receives payment information from the merchant, authorizes, settles and clears the transaction (can be a bank, but can also be a service provider);
- **acquirer**: the entity that takes on the financial risk of the merchant transaction (sometimes the acquirer is also a payment processor and the roles are mingled - we will distinguish between these functions);
- **the card brands**: the 5 founding members of the PCI SSC that facilitate the payment and settlement (other entities may be involved- for example, in Canada, Interac fulfills that role for debit card payments);
- **service providers**: an entity that performs some functions regarding to the payment process and/or provides services that may affect the security of the cardholder data.

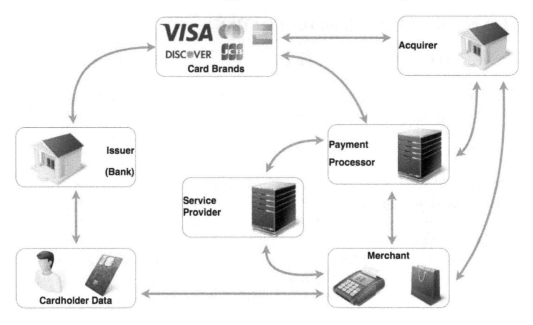

Volume 1 Figure 1 - The PCI payment model

We can now see how all these entities are involved, but what actually happens here?

We'll cover the actual data we're protecting in volume 2. For now, we'll just focus on what happens with card data itself.

1.4.2 Anatomy of payment card transactions

As stated earlier, there are 2 types of payment transactions in the PCI model: card-present and card-not-present. Card-present refer to transactions where the cardholder (the payer) is physically in the presence of the merchant (in the store) and uses his card to pay, whether through signature, chip and signature, chip and pin (also called EMV) or through some non-contact medium usually using a NFC chip on the physical card or through a phone such as Apple Pay, Google Wallet (now called Google Pay). While the payment transaction data generally follows the same path, the details of which information will be sent for validating payments will vary.

Card-not-present steps are used anytime the cardholder is not in the physical presence of the merchant. This is most often done through phone-based ordering, postal mail or fax orders (remember no email please as this is an insecure medium), or increasing online over the internet (eCommerce). The term MOTO (for Mail Order Telephone Order) is also often used to describe the non-internet card-not-present payments.

Let's say a cardholder visits a merchant. This could be a physical store where the in-person transaction would be referred to as a "card-present" transaction. For card-present transactions, the cardholder presents the card to the teller or at a payment terminal. As of the latest update of this book, most international based cards include a chip while US based cards are slowly integrating the chip. Many reasons exist for this disparity, such as personal liability limits in the USA versus other parts of the world, and higher fraud rates at certain periods in some countries. But the good news is that the chip (which provides added security) is catching on.

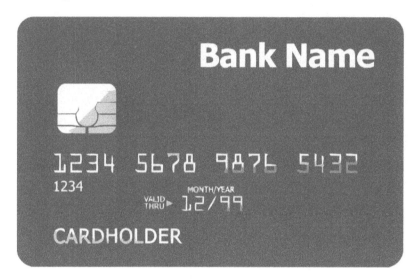

Volume 1 Figure 2 - Rendering of a chip-card

For chip-based cards in chip-supporting payment terminals, authentication of the user is done with a 4 to 5 digit PIN (Personal Information Number) that the user enters in the payment terminal. The PIN number is validated on the card's chip itself [1] (the chip is a very limited computer that performs some mathematical calculations) and then that information is sent from the merchant payment terminal to the payment processor through a network connection chain (which can involve a series of service providers). If either the card does not have a chip, or the payment terminal does not support the chip, then the assumption is that the cashier (or the client) swipes the card's magnetic stripe [1] (which includes many of the same information in the chip, although in a much less secure format), or that the user signs the receipt and that the cashier reviews the signature or asks for personal identification. This signature verification seems less common nowadays. Either way, the information from the device is sent to the payment processor [2].

The payment processor, either directly or through another service provider, sends the information to the appropriate card brand's network [3]. The card brands maintain secure networks (independently managed by each card brand, though there are interconnections) that connect all the issuers, payment processors and acquirers in their network.

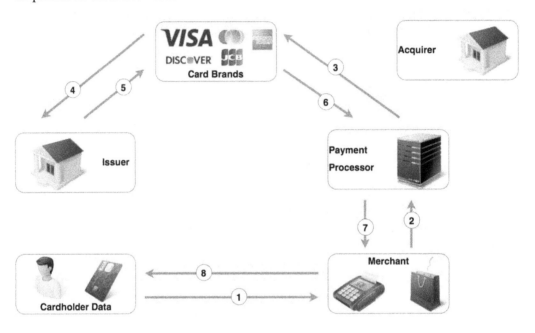

Volume 1 Figure 3 - Payment card transaction authorization

The IT data centers, at each payment processor and issuer, host systems (computers and network equipment) owned by the card brands that the organization do not control but send information to. The first 6 digits of the card number are called the IIN (Institution Identification Number) previously called the BIN (Bank Identification Number). The 6 digit IIN is assigned to a particular issuer by the card brands. Mapping tables are maintained by organizations to direct payment traffic based on a set of rules. The card brand redirects the transaction data to the issuer of the card (identified by the IIN) [4] who validates the information received, authorizes it (or does not) and returns this information

[5] along the path whence it came [6,7]. Back at the merchant's, an authorization or refusal is received and the process terminates [8].

Card-not-present transactions include (postal) mail (or even fax) order catalog, a phone-based transaction such as airline ticket reservation or very often an online store (eCommerce). For card-not-present transactions, the only difference is the authentication process which uses the card verification code or value (often called CVV2 though many acronyms exist, generally a 3 or 4 digit code printed on the back of the card; American Express has it on the front) to validate the user's identity [1]. The CVV2 is only required for authentication and should never be kept by anyone after the transaction is authorized. The one exception is that of issuers who obviously need to keep it in order to validate all card-not-present transactions, but it should be secured very well (more on what information is to be protected in volume 2).

That model, called the open loop model since many organizations are involved, happens with Visa and MasterCard payment cards. Amex, Discover and JCB are closed loop networks, meaning that they are also their own issuers, acquirers and payment processors. There are obvious advantages and disadvantages in both models (scalability, costs and security) but I will not discuss them here.

1.4.3 Clearing and Settlement

An authorized transaction does not mean that the merchant has actually been paid for it, just that a promise of payment from the issuer has been made. This is where we get into the last two parts of the payment process, invisible to the cardholder: clearing and settlement.

Clearing is the process of matching (called reconciliation in accounting terms) merchant bank (which is generally the acquirer) and issuer transactions. The merchant's bank sends the purchase information to the payment processor (then to card networks) [1], who then send this information to the issuer (often called issuing bank) [2] of the cardholder. The issuer adds this information to the cardholder's payment card statement [3]. The payment processor then provides the reconciliation information (confirmation) back to the merchant bank [4]. The clearing process generally happens within one day, but can happen much quicker than that.

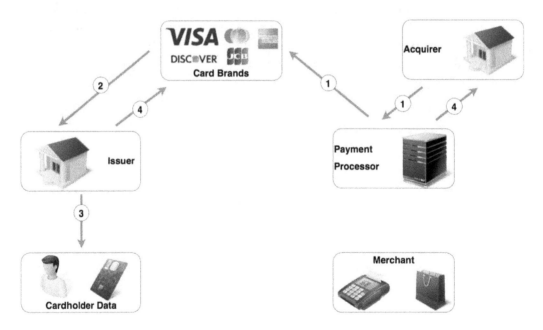

Volume 1 Figure 4 - Payment clearing

The next step is settlement, and means that the outstanding balance owed by the issuer will be paid (or eventually assumed by the issuer, acquirer, merchant or other in cases of disputes). The issuer sends the payment to the processor [1] who then sends it to the merchant bank [2]. Only then is the merchant paid for the purchase [3]. As a last step, the issuer bills the cardholder [4]. The settlement process generally takes up to two days. The length of these processes explains why you'll sometimes see in your online banking that a transaction has been authorized but not yet added to your statement (cleared and settled).

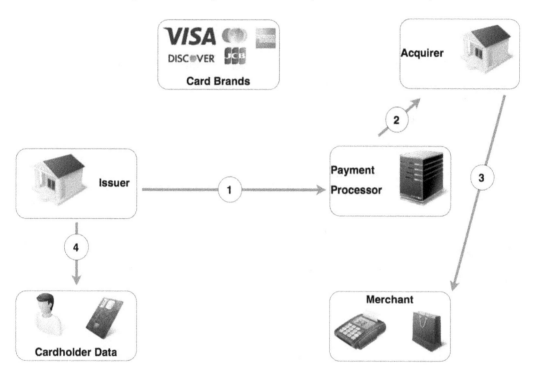

Volume 1 Figure 5 - Payment settlement

1.5 So what exactly is PCI DSS?

1.5.1 PCI DSS and the PCI SSC

The PCI DSS (Data Security Standard) is the main standard of the payment card industry. There are other standards that I'll touch upon where applicable (PA-DSS, P2PE, PIN PTS, Card Production) but will not go very much into detail. All those standards are managed by the PCI SSC (Standard Security Council). The board of the PCI SSC includes a representative from each of the 5 founding member card brands: Visa, MasterCard, American Express, Discover, and JCB.

The PCI SSC provides other information to help clarify points of the DSS standard. It provides a mechanism for anyone to ask a question on the PCI DSS and receives an answer from the council. All these questions and answers are published on a FAQ page [31].

The SSC also creates working groups that develop supplements [32] to address more complex topics. I will elaborate briefly on many of these topics as they become relevant. Some of the topics covered include telephone data (Protecting Telephone-based Payment Card Data), using virtualization (PCI DSS Virtualization Guidelines v2.0) and cloud-based services (PCI DSS 2.0 Cloud Computing Guidelines), Managing Third-party Providers (Third-Party Security Assurance), maintaining compliance (PCI DSS 3.0 Best Practices for Maintaining PCI DSS Compliance).

1.5.2 Defining the PCI DSS?

Contrary to what seems to be the common belief out there, PCI DSS is not an IT requirement; it is both a contractual requirement (for example, most merchant business agreements include language mandating compliance with PCI DSS) and an industry standard that has a (very) strong IT security focus. Most practitioners always recommend that PCI DSS be seen as an organizational (business) issue and not as an IT issue. I agree with them on this.

The goal of PCI DSS is the protection of payment card information, called cardholder data (CHD. This is a very self-serving but quite logical extension from the payment card brands to the PCI SSC, an organization created by the same payment card brands to standardize the security programs of the card brands. Massive fraud and theft are not in the interest of the Payment Card Industry (PCI) as a whole (banks, intermediaries, etc.), nor of the card brands sitting at the top of the industry. Such fraud reduces confidence in this very profitable method of payment which generates transaction fees paid by the merchants, as well as interest expenses for the unpaid balances from the cardholders themselves. In this sense, cardholders and industry are mostly aligned with the goal of protecting this information, with the onus placed on merchants and service providers.

Information Security is often described as addressing confidentiality, availability and integrity. For PCI DSS however, whose goal is the protection of cardholder data, confidentiality is really the only focus. This is also the case for patient data and its U.S. regulation, HIPAA (Health Information Privacy Accountability Act). PCI DSS is only concerned with availability (generally covered by Disaster Recovery and Business Continuity plans) and integrity in ensuring that we don't see a degradation of security controls while in Disaster Recovery/Business Continuity (DR/BC) mode. Indeed, the only reference to availability is in requirement 12.10.1, which focuses on ensuring a maintenance of the security controls (for confidentiality again) in case of incidents in a DR/BC operating mode. Other regulations such as NERC standards (North American Electric Reliability Corporation, which manages information security standards for electrical energy companies) are not focused on confidentiality but mostly on availability and integrity as there is no data to protect, but instead systems used in the production or distribution of electrical information. Sarbanes-Oxley (SOX) is concerned with ensuring the integrity of financial statements.

For many organizations, availability (or should I say lack-there-of) has direct and calculated financial costs. And so does integrity, which may prevent the business from operating. Confidentiality costs are often harder to calculate as many of its factors (fines, reputation costs) may be unknown or hard to quantify.

PCI is different from other industry and their security regulations, such as HIPAA in the USA. HIPAA is a regulation whose goal is to protect patients' health information. Protection of health information is good for the individual patients, but other than from a reputation issue, is not well aligned with the health care providers themselves (hospitals, doctors, etc.). The government can assign penalties for breaches of data, but has only barely started validating compliance. The Office for Civil Rights of the U.S. Department of Health and Services (OCR HHS) has enforced HIPAA since 2003 but as with PCI DSS, the enforcement and penalties have increased over time.

The PCI industry in this sense is more mature. The biggest constituents based on transaction volume must validate compliance, generally through an independent third-party that is certified for that purpose (a QSA company, or QSAC). There are penalties for non-compliance, as well as in cases of breach. And ultimately, an organization could have its ability to process payments removed.

Security focuses on risk reduction and risk management, as 100% security is not achievable. Some level of fraud in any industry is inevitable. The issue is keeping it within a reasonable, acceptable and controlled level.

At its most basic level, PCI DSS tries to:

- prevent breaches (to the extent possible)
- detect compromises early
- and hopefully minimize the damage

Thus, to address these goals, the generic approach for PCI DSS compliance is/should be to:

- reduce/limit scope, and isolate systems containing valuable information
- secure systems and accesses
- monitor & fix problems once identified

This aligns perfectly with the controls put in place in all organizations and referred to as the control triad that we can use to classify all PCI DSS individual requirements (more on this in volume 3):

- preventative
- detective
- corrective

This is to say that all requirements in PCI DSS (and any decent information security program) will attempt to either:

- prevent non-acceptable behavior (internal or external),
- detect this behavior,
- and correct this behavior over time.

1.5.3 PCI DSS at a high-level

The 12 PCI DSS high-level requirements are grouped in 6 different objectives. These categories and the 12 high-level requirements should be straightforward to anyone who has been involved with IT security. Other information security frameworks exists (ISO 27001/2, Cobit, etc.) which we will cover more in volume 3. PCI DSS can easily be seen as a subset of most of these security frameworks.

Build and Maintain a Secure Network	
1	Install and maintain a firewall configuration to protect cardholder data
2	Do not use vendor-supplied defaults for system passwords and other security parameters
Protect Cardholder Data	
3	Protect stored cardholder data
4	Encrypt transmission of cardholder data across open, public networks
Maintain a Vulnerability Management Program	
5	Use and regularly update anti-virus software
6	Develop and maintain secure systems and applications
Implement Strong Access Control Measures	
7	Restrict access to cardholder data by business need-to-know
8	Assign a unique ID to each person with computer access
9	Restrict physical access to cardholder data
Regularly Monitor and Test Networks	
10	Test and monitor all access to network resources and cardholder data
11	Regularly test security systems and processes
Maintain an Information Security Policy	
12	Maintain a policy that addresses information security

Volume 1 - Table 1 - PCI DSS High Level Overview [33]

Again, this is about reducing scope (requirement 1) and securing systems (requirements 2, 5, 6), limiting accesses (requirements 7, 8), protecting data (requirements 3, 4), protecting physical security (requirement 9), monitoring the environment (requirement 10 - detective controls), testing the environment for flaws (requirement 11 - corrective controls) and managing all those controls (requirement 12 - which I would rather call an "information security program" than a simple policy, which is now covered for some entities by appendix A3). Some additional requirements for shared hosting providers also exist in Appendix A1.

The ultimate goal of PCI DSS is to implement a security program that protects the payment card information that companies are a custodian of (for most organizations, the cardholder data is only entrusted to your organization). The PCI DSS requirements are considered by most a bare minimum, one that is not necessarily sufficient to keep your data safe. But it builds on a very traditional and well-respected process, and on recognized security best practices.

The goal of PCI is security, not compliance, although compliance is often what is sought (by clients) or provided (by consultants and assessors). I see compliance as a tool to force recalcitrant organizations which create risk and uncertainty for the industry (imposing an external cost to the industry, and thus called an 'externality' in economics).

1.6 How should PCI DSS compliance be addressed?

PCI DSS does not bring in anything that information security practitioners do not, or at least should not, know about. It boils down to minimal (maybe not even completely adequate) set of (mostly IT) controls, best practices really. The stated goal of the standard is to protect cardholder information. This generally starts by reducing the amount of information an organization keeps. Remember this notion: you don't have to protect what you do not have.

When trying to achieve compliance, the first recommendation is to reduce who comes in contact with this information, and to save as little data as an organization needs. That generally requires as many process changes, if not more, than IT changes. Remember, IT is not an end in itself; it is a tool that is present to help an organization achieve its (business) goals.

The basic approach that PCI DSS adopts is to concentrate all that information into a central zone (called the Cardholder Data Environment, or CDE), isolate it from the rest of the network, and heavily control all access to that information. This is very much the 'castle' approach to security (taking from how security was done in medieval times) that has permeated information security since its inception. How we document and ensure a CDE has been properly created will be covered in volume 2 of the book.

1.6.1 Fort Knox or the 'castle' metaphor

The approach presented by the PCI DSS is modeled on standard physical security notions that date back millennia. From Sun Tzu's Art of War, to medieval castles, to Fort Knox, and even recent military strategy, physical security is well understood. But instead of building high walls to keep the enemy out, we now have firewalls set up against electronic intrusion. And, instead of gold or precious stones tucked away in vaults, we have digital (and paper) information on (hopefully secure) computers.

Medieval castles were always built with the knowledge accumulated in the previous millennia, from the Greeks, Romans, Persians, Chinese (think Sun Tzu) or any other fortress builders. These holds were generally built in mountains or hills (which were easier to defend), and consisted of multiple layers of security. The leader's quarters were located at its inner core. This smaller building usually held the most valuable items, including the local leader, his family and most trusted advisors. Access to this inner sanctum was heavily guarded, with many sentries roaming the halls or watching the doors and other access points. Only the most trusted worked in these areas. They were probably also the best treated.

Protecting this inner core, there would be at least one (there were often more than one layer) high and large outer wall that surrounded and protected the inner core. This wall was equipped with strong defenses. Lookouts kept an eye out for potential trouble, ready to sound the alarm as required. Archers behind arrow slits also provided protections. Moats and drawbridges provide more security. These are just a few of the many ways the fortresses were kept safe.

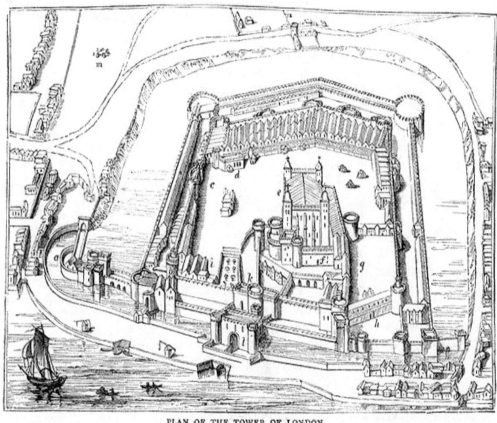

PLAN OF THE TOWER OF LONDON.

a. Lion's Tower.	*b.* The Keep, or White	*h.* Queen's Gallery and Gar-	*l.* St. Thomas' Tower, and
b. Bell Tower.	Tower.	den.	Traitor's Gate.
c. Beauchamp Tower.	*f.* Jewel House.	*i.* Lieutenant's Lodgings.	*m.* Place of Execution on
d. The Chapel.	*g.* Queen's Lodgings.	*k.* Bloody Tower.	Tower-hill.

Volume 1 Figure 6 - London tower structure in 1597 [34]

The approach for PCI DSS is very similar. We have a very restricted inner core, the CDE (Cardholder Data Environment) with strong controls that restrict access to this area. Very few people should have access to CDE. Then, we have an outside perimeter, the external firewall and DMZ(s), that restrict access to someone not "trusted", not within the organization (someone coming from the internet). Other tools such as Intrusion Preventions Systems or Intrusion Detection Systems (IPS/IDS) form part of the defenses that protect our networks.

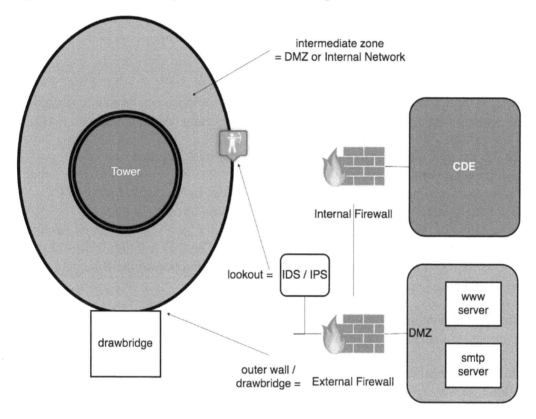

Volume 1 Figure 7 - Castle vs. Network

1.7 Demonstrating PCI DSS compliance

The programs for managing compliance with the PCI DSS is a responsibility of the payment card brands and not of the PCI SSC. How and to whom you must demonstrate compliance depends on the type entity you are in the PCI model. In the current model, there are only 2 recognized types for compliance: merchant and service provider. So if you're not a merchant, then you must be a service provider. Issuers and acquirers are covered in section 1.7.4, but are often seen as special cases of service providers.

1.7.1 RoC vs SAQ (and AoC)

The current model lists two methods by which compliance can be demonstrated: Assessment (documented in a RoC) or Self-Assessment (documented in a SAQ).

The Report on Compliance (RoC) is generally the work product of a QSA (Qualified Security Assessor) of a QSA company (QSAC) engaged to assess the organization's compliance. The QSA and QSAC are both certified by the PCI SSC. I say generally by a QSA because, in some cases (often larger organizations), this work can be performed internally by an ISA (Internal Security Assessor) who has been certified by the PCI SSC. The ISA training is almost the same as the QSA training. But in most cases, the production of the RoC is performed by a QSA.

Starting with version 3.0 of PCI DSS, the RoC format has been standardized (and a template [35] provided) and every RoC should follow the same structure.

The Self-Assessment Questionnaire (SAQ) is a series of forms that entities without the obligation to produce a RoC (though an entity can still decide to do a RoC on its own) use to report their compliance. There are many SAQ for different uses. SAQ-D contains all PCI DSS requirements and there are 2 versions. All service providers must use the service provider SAQ-D. Merchant SAQ-D is also the merchant 'catch-all', meaning that if a merchant cannot use any other of the SAQ, or would have to use more than one SAQ, then the SAQ-D is the one that must be filled out. All merchant SAQ are described in the following table (excerpted from a document from the council [36]):

SAQ	Description
A	Card-not-present merchants (e-commerce or mail/telephone-order) that have fully outsourced all cardholder data functions to PCI DSS compliant third-party service providers, with no electronic storage, processing, or transmission of any cardholder data on the merchant's systems or premises. *Not applicable to face-to-face channels.*
A-EP	E-commerce merchants who outsource all payment processing to PCI DSS validated third parties, and who have a website(s) that doesn't directly receive cardholder data but that can impact the security of the payment transaction. No electronic storage, processing, or transmission of cardholder data on the merchant's systems or premises. *Applicable only to e-commerce channels.*
B	Merchants using only: • Imprint machines with no electronic cardholder data storage; and/or • Standalone, dial-out terminals with no electronic cardholder data storage. *Not applicable to e-commerce channels.*
B-IP	Merchants using only standalone, PTS-approved payment terminals with an IP connection to the payment processor, with no electronic cardholder data storage. *Not applicable to e-commerce channels.*
C-VT	Merchants who manually enter a single transaction at a time via a keyboard into an Internet-based virtual payment terminal solution that is provided and hosted by a PCI DSS validated third-party service provider. No electronic cardholder data storage. *Not applicable to e-commerce channels.*
C	Merchants with payment application systems connected to the Internet, no electronic cardholder data storage. *Not applicable to e-commerce channels.*
P2PE	Merchants using only hardware payment terminals that are included in and managed via a validated, PCI SSC-listed P2PE solution, with no electronic cardholder data storage. *Not applicable to e-commerce channels.*
D	SAQ D for Merchants: All merchants not included in descriptions for the above SAQ types.

Volume 1 Table 2 - Merchant SAQ description

Note that multiple SAQs cannot be combined if a merchant does not meet some of the individual SAQ requirements. In such a case, a merchant must fill out a SAQ-D. I've produced an appendix ("An introduction to the Merchant Self-Assessment Questionnaire (SAQ) selection process") with volume 4 which covers merchant SAQs in more detail.

If you are unsure which SAQ applies to your organization, please see the easy-to-use selection chart at the end of the SAQ Instructions and Guidelines [37] document.

Finally, the Attestation of Compliance (or AoC) is a short-form that is signed by an officer of the entity demonstrating compliance. It accompanies either the RoC or SAQ produced. If a QSA (or ISA) was involved in the production of the RoC, then that individual also signs that document. In the case of SAQ, the signature of the QSA is generally not required (as they are often not involved in the self-assessment).

1.7.2 Merchant Compliance

Merchants must report their compliance to their acquirers (which can be the same as the payment processor). Payment card brands have defined levels of transactions (volume quantities, not monetary amounts) that will determine how merchants will demonstrate their compliance. These lists vary between card brands, but the list most often used is the one provided by Visa (see the book website for links to each of the card brands) whose levels, as of the writing of this book, can be summed up as follows [38]:

Level / Tier	Criteria	RoC or SAQ	Validation performed by	AoC
1	More than 6 million transactions	RoC	QSA or (ISA and signed by officer of the merchant)	yes
2	Between 1 and 6 million transactions	SAQ	Entity	yes
3	Between 20,000 and 1 million e-commerce transactions	SAQ	Entity	yes
4	Less than 20,000 e-commerce transactions AND all others less than 1 million transactions	SAQ	Entity	yes

Volume 1 Table 3 - Determining Visa merchant levels

These numbers represent the level of risks to the payment networks. This level of risk is proportionate to the number of individual transactions performed on the network. Note that all merchants are required to be compliant with the PCI DSS. Also note that your merchant bank, or acquirer, may require more than what is requested by the card brands. What varies is how this compliance is reported. Visa, in November 2015, demanded that its acquirers ensure that its level 4 merchants who do not meet certain exemptions (75% of transaction through chip-and-pin Point of Sale Devices) prove compliance by January 31, 2017. Prior, Visa only demanded acquirers managed their risks for those smaller merchants.

1.7.3 Service Provider Compliance

Service providers, if they are required to do so, report to the payment card brands. Depending on what role they serve in the payment process, some service providers will choose to get certified as PCI DSS compliant, while others will not. Service providers often get certified in order to get published on approved lists maintained by the card brands (see the book's website for links to card brands service provider list [39]). While an entity must ensure that the service providers it uses must be PCI DSS compliant (more on this in volume 3, requirements 12.8.*), how this is proven is more open ended. Ultimately, getting certified is a business decision that balances certification costs vs. external (client) auditing costs.

As they do for merchant levels, the payment card brands maintain a list of levels for service providers to determine the risk (based on transaction volume). For Visa, at the time of this writing, the threshold for level 1 risk evaluation is at 300,000 transactions per year, or roughly 25,000 per month. Please review the payment card brand levels in your region or country as these can vary greatly. For reporting compliance, Visa level 1 service providers must produce a RoC while level 2 can simply produce a SAQ-D (Service Provider version) (both documents must be accompanied by an AoC).

A note on shared service providers. These are generally certified providers that offer the same type of service to multiple clients. There are specific requirements for these specific providers that will be covered in volume 3. We've seen that many breaches of cardholder data that occurred in 2013 and 2014 have included targeting of (shared) service providers to breach an organization. The PCI SSC issued an information supplement in August of 2014 describing how organizations should manage service providers.

1.7.4 Other compliance - issuers, acquirers

Issuers and acquirers must report their compliance to the card brands (the next level up the payment chain). The payment card brands will dictate what requirements are incumbent on these organizations, which can include many other requirements in addition to PCI DSS. Visa, for example, has a set of regulations known as VIOR [40] (Visa International Operating Regulations) that organizations have to adhere to be part of the Visa network. Visa also has a program [41] that all its acquirers must implement to manage the risk of their merchants within the payment card industry.

1.8 Where do we go from here? The evolution of the PCI DSS standard

Now that we've explained the PCI model and a basic history of the credit payments comes the time to review the changes to the PCI DSS made over time, and then use strategy frameworks to attempt to determine where the standard might head next.

1.8.1 Early versions 1.0, 1.1, 1.2 and 1.2.1

As mentioned in section 1.3.5, Visa Inc. created its Cardholder Information Security Program (CISP) in 1999 but it only became mandatory in 2001. That standard became the basis of version 1.0 of PCI DSS in 2004 as the card brands were organizing the structure of the PCI SSC. Version 1.1 of PCI DSS came out on September 7, 2006, under control of the newly formed PCI SSC.

The overall structure of the standard (6 high-level objectives, 12 high-level requirements described in section 1.5.3) have been here since the beginning of the standard (CISP [42] in pre-PCI DSS days), or over 10 years now, although more detail has been added since. Version 1.1, for example, only ran 16 pages long. Version 1.2 increased to 72 pages, 1.2.1 to 74 pages and 2.0 to 75 pages. Version 3.0 is the only one, other than 1.2, that increased the length substantively to 112 pages. The main reason that version 3.0 increased so much is that another document that had existed to accompany each version since version 1.2, and called "Navigating the PCI DSS", was integrated with the standard. "Navigating the PCI DSS" provided a 'guidance' for each requirement. This 'guidance' detailed more of the rationale behind each requirement of the standard (the 'intent' or objective, or risk to be addressed) so that users of the standard (organizations, QSAs, etc.) may better be able to judge if the intent of the requirement were met by a specific implementation.

1.8.2 Version 2.0

Version 2.0 was released in November of 2010. Version 2.0 occurred as the PCI SSC moved the standard to a 3 year period for major revisions (unless important and unexpected changes warranted a revision). Version 2.0 came into effect on January 1, 2011 and there was a one year overlap with 1.2.1 in 2011. As of January 1, 2012 all entities were supposed to demonstrate compliance with version 2.0, which was not retired until December 31, 2014.

Version 2.0 included only 2 "evolving requirements". The PCI DSS defines "evolving requirements" (called "enhancements" in previous documents) as "[c]hanges to ensure that the standards are up to date with emerging threats and changes in the market." [43] Those changes affected risk ranking of vulnerabilities and web application vulnerabilities. The remainder of the changes were clarifications or additional guidance. Version 2.0 also added more information about the standard in the preamble.

My personal belief is that most changes to the PCI DSS over the years have been to make explicit notions that were previously implicit and well understood by experienced information security professionals, but where a loophole existed in the model since it was not specifically prescribed by the standard. Such a case is requirement 1.1.3, introduced with version 3.0, which mandates that an organization create and maintain data flow diagrams.

Version 2.0 [44] introduced the expected approach to be performed by an organization annually in determining or confirming its PCI DSS environment scope, "by identifying all locations and flows of cardholder data" and by "[d]ocumenting cardholder data flows via a dataflow diagram [to help] fully understand all cardholder data flows and [ensure] that any network segmentation is effective at isolating the cardholder data environment." [45] While not specifically mandating the production of cardholder data flow diagrams, it was made implicit. Unless you had a very simple environment, I cannot fathom how you could properly understand and manage your scope without these particular diagrams.

I started working with PCI DSS version 2.0 back in 2012, and I became a QSA in 2013. Other than information from colleagues and presentations made by others in the firm where I worked, there was not much data other than the standard available to me. The "Navigating the PCI DSS" guide was one I used often with clients to help them understand the PCI DSS.

1.8.3 Version 3.0 and 3.1

Version 3.0 was published in November of 2013. Version 3.0 changes [46] included mostly clarifications and codifications of implicit requirements. It also included, as mentioned previously, the guidance column taken from the "Navigating the PCI DSS" guide which ceased to exist as an independent document.

Version 3.0 also introduced a template for producing the RoC which all QSA must use from now on. This helped ensure consistency in the RoC produced by various QSAC firms. The PCI SSC reviews a sample of the RoC produced by QSAC firms. The template was produced to ensure a minimal baseline and to ease comparison of RoCs produced by different firms.

Version 3.0 included 19 evolving requirements, either new items or ones with major modifications:

- A new requirement, in addition to network diagrams (1.1.2), to create and maintain a set of cardholder data flow diagrams (1.1.3)
- A new requirement to maintain an inventory of everything (systems, applications) that is in scope (2.4) (for what is in scope, see volume 2)
- A new requirement that if an antivirus is not considered necessary (mostly on non-Windows systems but that I would categorize as affecting mostly Linux and potentially Apple's Mac OSX systems) to conduct and document a risk analysis of why this is not required (5.1.2)
- A new requirement that antivirus be running and not be generally disabled by end-users (5.2)
- A new requirement stemming from changes in web application security reflected in changes to the OWASP top 10 [47] to train developers on "broken authentication and session management" (6.5.10)
- Changes for more flexibility in password complexity requirements (8.2.3)
- A new requirement for service providers to use different credentials (username, passwords) for different clients (8.5.1) (meaning that if one set of passwords is stolen, not all clients are automatically endangered)
- A new requirement that other factors for authentication be tied to a single individual (8.6) (I once heard the story of a company that had placed an RSA secureid token in front of an internet facing webcam so that their employees, sharing the second factor, could all share the device - not a good idea)
- A new requirement for physical security that requires immediate authorization, but more importantly the immediate removal of access in case of termination (9.3) (generally, getting physical access to a system is "game over" in terms of security)
- A new set of requirements (4 of them) to protect payment terminals from physical tampering (9.9.*)
- Two new logging requirements for changes in authentication and administrative actions (10.2.5) and changes to the logging system (10.2.6)
- Changes to the wireless scanning (11.1) to maintain an inventory of authorized access points (11.1.1) and to ensure that identified unauthorized

wireless access points connected to the network be treated as a security incident (11.1.2)

- A new requirement to maintain a methodology for penetration testing (11.3) (note that this is for the organization performing this work, which could be a third-party)
- A new requirement to test segmentation (11.3.4) as part of the internal network penetration test
- A new requirement to implement a process to respond to changes identified by the "change detection mechanism" (11.5.1) (11.5, File Integrity Management, was modified to add more flexibility in meeting the requirement, more on this in volume 3) (review to confirm the change is correct, usually covered by some sort of change request)
- Changes to the risk assessment process (12.2) to ensure that it "be performed at least annually and after significant changes to the environment."
- Two new requirements linked to the third-party management (those affecting PCI DSS)
    - Maintain information about which PCI DSS requirements are managed by the third-party vs. the organization, or with shared responsibilities (12.8.5)
    - For service providers to provide to their clients in writing their agreements regarding requirements 12.8.*, but really focused on 12.8.5 mentioned previously (12.9)

All of these should seem reasonable to most people. They aim to increase the documentation of scope, to remove loopholes that might threaten the security of some organizations, or to address tactics used by various attackers.

There were also changes where requirements were moved. For example, all requirements for user identification are now under 8.1 and all those about user authorization fall under 8.2. Requirements from 12.1 were moved to each of the 12 high-level requirements. I personally wish they had brought requirements 9.2 and 9.4 on handling of visitors closer together, (maybe in the next version of PCI DSS).

Business-as-usual (BAU)

PCI DSS 3.0 brought in a few new ideas that were not in version 2.0. Most changes were clarifications and additions to the level of rigor required to demonstrate that the organization has properly identified what is in scope, and then applied the appropriate controls.

Security as business-as-usual (BAU) was introduced in the preambles of 3.0, so we can expect it to become a requirement in future versions of the standard.

Too many organizations see PCI DSS compliance as a check-the-box process or a once-a-year event. And very often, breaches occur because controls are not effectively and continuously executed, and attackers take advantage of that. The approach is to ensure that your security controls (including all PCI DSS requirements) are well integrated into routine (daily, weekly, monthly) processes, producing metrics which can be tracked, and are tested every so often to ensure that they are operating efficiently. Section 1.8.4 on DESV gives us insights to where the PCI SSC may be taking BAU.

Version 3.1

In January 2015, a message to assessors was distributed stating that the PCI SSC would be releasing an updated version of the standard to address weaknesses identified regarding cryptographic protocol. Indeed, 2014 was a year where many vulnerabilities were identified in SSL (Secure Sockets Layer) and its successor TLS (Transport Layer Security) or in specific implementations (often both are combined and referred to as SSL/TLS).

That update to the PCI DSS arrived on April 15, 2015 with version 3.1 and immediately replaced version 3.0. Other than changes to SSL/TLS in requirement 4.1, it also provided more clarifications but nothing that affected my understanding of the standard. The changes in requirement 4.1 call for deprecation of older versions of the SSL/TLS protocols (specifically SSL 3.0, published back in 1996, and TLS 1.0 published in 1999) and gives organizations until June 30, 2016 to move to newer versions of the protocols (TLS 1.1 and 1.2, with TLS 1.3 in advanced phases of ratification) while, in some cases, implementing risk mitigation measures. The PCI SSC published an update on December 18, 2015 [48] which modified those dates without changing the version of the standard. The date has been pushed back to July 1, 2018. More details can be found in section 3.7.4 of volume 3.

1.8.4 PCI DSS Designated Entities Supplemental Validation (DESV)

In June 2015, the PCI SSC published a new document called "PCI DSS Designated Entities Supplemental Validation" [49] or DESV for short. The document also mentions that it is to be used in conjunction with PCI DSS 3.1. This document was integrated as appendix A3 in PCI DSS 3.2 (described in the next section) and requirements DE.* are now A3.*.

This document includes a new series of requirements to be validated by QSAs for designated entities. The document states that designated entities will be identified by the card brands or acquirers (as part of the acquirer risk program, and likely in part at the request of the card brands). The document does identify categories of organizations that may be designated entities. It boils down to organizations with a large number of card information such as large merchants, large acquirers or service providers that aggregate a lot of card information. It also includes organizations that have "suffered significant or repeated breaches of cardholder data" such as the ones mentioned in section 1.2.1 (or repeat offenders) [50].

The new requirements try to ensure that an organization maintains compliance with PCI DSS over time, and that non-compliance is detected when it occurs through a continuous (if not automated) audit process. They are divided into 5 control areas that are as follows:

DE.1 Implement a PCI DSS compliance program.

DE.2 Document and validate PCI DSS scope.

DE.3 Validate PCI DSS is incorporated into business-as-usual (BAU) activities.

DE.4 Control and manage logical access to the cardholder data environment.

DE.5 Identify and respond to suspicious events.

These requirements are not required unless an organization is notified that it must implement them. It would not be surprising however to see these new requirements included in later versions of the PCI DSS, and so I would recommend that organizations perform reviews to see if these requirements can help in maturing the organization's information security program. I'll go through these more in details in volume 3, "Building a PCI DSS Information Security Program", but I do want to describe some of the changes DESV brings forward.

The bulk of the changes are within the first 3 control areas.

DE.1 establishes the governance and accountability of PCI DSS within an organization. This sets the 'tone at the top' and reinforces the requirements 12.4 and 12.5.* of PCI DSS 3.1. It also aligns very well with the "Three Lines of Defense" [51] model used by many organizations in the financial sector.

DE.2 creates explicit requirements from the implicit ones described in the section of scope identification in the standard. It links scope identification to network diagrams (1.1.3), firewall/router rules documentation (1.1.6) and firewall/router rules revision (1.1.7), review of segmentation (11.3.4), maintenance of the inventory of everything in scope (2.2.4), validation of controls of systems that are in-scope; it adds review of change control processes (6.4), mandates data-discovery (often performed using DLP tools) of CHD on systems where there should be none, and adds requirements to monitor for data exfiltration.

DE.3 is the Business-as-usual (BAU) control area, which ties back to the types of processes that internal audit generally performs in large organizations, and that some smaller organizations farm out to public accounting firms. It includes requirements to identify failing critical controls, although it does not provide much guidance on how to identify those failures. It also covers ensuring that technologies used are still secure, monitoring for end-of-life of hardware and software for example. It also calls for quarterly reviews to ensure all processes are performing as designed, also called operating effectiveness, so that detection of failures are addressed in a more timely manner. In audit terms, PCI DSS assessments are a point in time, or test of design assessment, also called type 1 reports. Audits can include type 2 reports which add test of operating effectiveness over a period. BAU is pushing us towards type 2 testing and towards ensuring we maintain compliance. And as the Verizon PCI compliance reports clearly demonstrate maintaining compliance is the biggest issue.

DE.4 on logical access reviews is a periodic review control that most organizations already have in place.

DE.5 calls for a reinforcement of monitoring (10.6.*) to include "identification of attack patterns", which is to say that log monitoring software (often provided by a Security information and event management, or SIEM, system) should be routinely reconfigured or tweaked based on organization and industry experience.

1.8.5 PCI DSS 3.2

PCI DSS 3.2 was released at the end of April 2016 and replaced version 3.1 as of November 1, 2016, although new requirements will only become mandatory on February 1, 2018. As a point release, this version did not change the DSS dramatically. The SSL/TLS changes of PCI DSS 3.1 and a subsequent revision published on December 18, 2015, were integrated in appendix A2 (and requirements using SSL/TLS now point to this appendix). As stated earlier, appendix A3 was added including the DESV requirements (applicable for designated entities only).

In terms of requirements, it introduced only two new requirements for all entities:

- 6.4.6 - a new requirement within change control aiming to ensure that the entity maintain compliance with PCI DSS. Any changes that touches on any in-scope "system components" (that list must be maintained per requirement 2.4 and the scope documentation that should be maintained) must be reviewed before approval. A change may affect the scope or the security and this needs to be evaluated before the change takes place.
- Two-factor authentication was renamed to multi-factor authentication and expanded (8.3 is now 8.3.2) and a new sub-requirement 8.3.1, was introduced to address the risk of phishing on IT administrators by requiring multi-factor authentication for access to CDE systems.

While most other changes were clarifications to the requirements, there were a few substantive changes:

- Requirement 1.3.5 (moved from 1.3.6 as 1.3.3 was removed) removed "stateful inspection" and replaced it with "permit only 'established' connections into the network." as there are stronger options available (evaluation left to the assessor)
- Requirement 1.4 for a "personal firewall" for devices changed from "mobile" to "portable" since devices that connect remotely (and/or wirelessly) no longer include laptops but smartphones and tablets (and potentially more devices). Personal firewalls in laptops, Mobile Device Management (MDM) generally provide this functionality.
- Requirement 11.5 (change detection management) had a change in its test procedures which used to imply that this requirement only applied to CDE

systems (not connected ones). It is now clear that all in-scope systems should now be covered by this requirement.

There were also a few new requirements applicable to service providers only:

- A new documentation requirement 3.5.1 mandating the documentation of the cryptographic architectures.
- A new set of requirements to monitor for failures of critical security controls (10.8) and treat failures as incidents (10.8.1); this ties back to requirement A3.3.1 in Appendix A3.
- A new requirement (11.3.4.1) for testing network segmentation every six months (instead of every year); this ties back to requirement A3.2.4 in Appendix A3.
- A new requirement (12.4.1) mandating the assignment of responsibility for the protection of cardholder data and a PCI DSS compliance program; this ties back to requirement A3.1.1 in Appendix A3.
- A new set of requirements to perform quarterly reviews to confirm personnel are following security policies and operational procedures (12.11) and treat failures as incidents (12.11.1); this ties back to requirement A3.3.3 in Appendix A3.

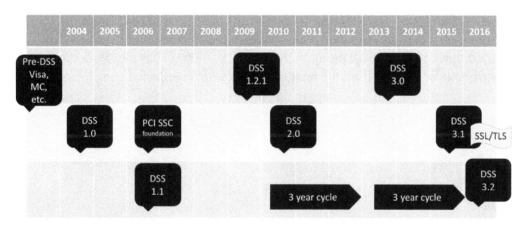

Volume 1 Figure 8 - Summary of PCI DSS versions over time

1.8.6 Next versions of PCI DSS?

This section was written in late November 2017. At the european PCI Community Meetings (PCICM) in Barcelona in October 2017 (the North American one was cancelled due to a hurricane), we got confirmation that no new version was to be expected in 2017 as this author and many others expected. It appears the council feels that version 3.2 was a major release in the 3 year release cycle. There could be a point-release in 2018 (maybe 3.2.1 or 3.3) but that the changes would be minor such as typos and small errors like those corrected in 3.1 and 3.2 (and maybe more changes on TLS 1.0). I also learned that we're back on a 3 year cycle for the next major release to be published in 2019 (maybe version 4.0, but now no one really knows). A blog entry posted on August 3, 2017 stated that "[t]he PCI Data Security Standard is a mature standard" and "we will continue to evolve the standard as needed". That blog post included mention of a new comment period. *52*

The PCI SSC opened a comment period lasting from September 6, 2017 to November 15, 2017 asking for feedback on PCI DSS and PA-DSS from stakeholders ("PCI Participating Organizations, Affiliate and Strategic Members, and Qualified Security Assessors (QSA)"). Saying that "we are working with the industry on ways to provide greater flexibility for organizations" and that "[b]ased on this feedback and market need, we will evaluate the need for changes to the standards, and/or additional guidance and resources." Whatever feedback was provided during that period, along with reports from breaches and leadership of the card brands, should drive the next editions of the standard. *53*

1.9 Where do we go from here? Learning from failures

Now that we've seen the approach proposed by PCI DSS and how the standard has evolved, it's time for us to try and see where it should be going to address its stated goal of protecting CHD. To help with this, we'll first take a look at what seems not to be working with the standard based on publicly available reports. The initial release of this volume in July 2015 looked at 2 reports published by Verizon in 2015: the 2015 Data Breach Investigation Report (referred to as DBIR from now on) and the 2015 PCI Compliance Report. Since then, the DBIR has been updated twice (2016 and 2017) and each sub-section of 1.9.1 has been updated with findings pertaining to the payment card industry. Verizon did not release a PCI compliance report in 2016 (I learned at the 2017 PCICM it was produced, just never released - internal company decisions), but it released one in late August, 2017 (which includes the information that was in the unpublished 2016 report) which has been integrated in this edition of the book as well.

1.9.1 The Verizon Data Breach Investigation Report (DBIR):2015 to 2017

This section has been almost completely rewritten in 2017 to account for changes over time. Each annual report covers the previous calendar year. Thus, the 2015 DBIR [54] covers calendar year 2014, the 2016 DBIR [55] covers calendar year 2015, and the 2017 DBIR [56] covers calendar year 2016. 2017 also marks the 10th anniversary of the DBIR.

The DBIR includes more than just the payment card industry concerns, and is biased due to breach notification laws and regulations towards the US markets and specifically the US public sector. In 2017, the addition of 65 other sources does help diminish that bias, though it likely remains. In the 2017 DBIR report, the Verizon authors acknowledge that they "have a lack of success stories" [57] that are reported (though they mention they are aware of some).

The DBIR covers both incidents ([a] security event that compromises the integrity, confidentiality or availability of an information asset) [58] and breaches ([a]n incident that results in the confirmed disclosure–not just potential exposure–of data to an unauthorized party.) [59]. One issue with the DBIR is that it is skewed towards failures (and yes, information security is often a thankless job where we are only noticed when issues occur).

My focus here is obviously the payment ecosystem and I will only touch briefly on non-related issues. For PCI DSS, our main interests are companies in either the financial sector, service providers or merchants.

The financial services companies are in multiple subsectors including traditional banking which cover mainly the issuer and acquirer functions (other subsectors tend to have limited involvement in the payment ecosystem). Merchants can be part of many reported industries such as retail, accommodation, education, healthcare, and others, though some of these industries cover more than payment data concerns in the report (education also sees cyber-espionage for PII and research information, while healthcare is targeted for patient data and PII).

Service providers range from simple document storage and physical security services to payment processing or other more technical related services.

According to the report, the top three affected industries (by breaches) are those in the public sector, information services and financial services [60]. The 2015 DBIR reminds us that "no industry is immune to security failures" [61]. Some attacks are targets of opportunity as we learn that "in 70% of the attacks where we know the motive for the attack, there's a secondary victim" [62].

In the 2016 DBIR [63] the most affected industry are financial services, followed by information services, the public sector, and retail [64]. Again, the secondary motive (or victim) is also presented [65].

In the 2017 DBIR [66] financial services are again the most affected industry (24%), but are now followed by healthcare (15%) and the public sector (12%). If combined (15%), Retail and Accommodation would share the #2 spot with healthcare [67]

1.9.1.1 Who is performing these attacks?

Threat actors, those alleged to be performing the attacks, appear to have varied only slightly over time (since the 2015 DBIR has reported on them) with external actors representing around 80% of attackers, partners less than 2%, and the remainder coming from internal actors in 2014 [68]. Organized crime is one of the main external attackers "with financial gain being the most common of the primary motives for attacking." [69] The 2016 DBIR shows that this trend is stable [70]. The 2017 table reproduced below shows this only moves slightly from year to year.

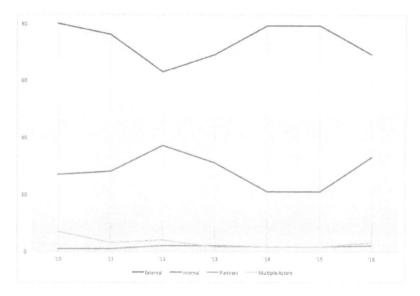

Volume 1 Figure 9 - Threat actor categories over time (Source: DBIR 2017, Figure 2) [71]

Still, we often don't exactly know who was behind an attack. The 2015 report mentions that "two-thirds of the incidents in this pattern had no attacker-attribution information whatsoever" [72]. This makes it hard to get a clear picture of the involvement of cyber-espionage (state sponsored or not) or organized crime within these attacks.

In 2016 (DBIR 2017), financial gain and espionage were still the top two motives combining to account for 93% of breaches. [73]

The authors write regarding as to how attacks are performed:

The triple threat of hacking, malware and social has been on top and trending upward for the last few years, and it does not appear to be going away any time soon. [74]

And regarding the attackers' motives:

The actions taken and assets compromised are influenced heavily by the actors and their motives. Numerous areas of concentration are quickly observable in Figure 5 (e.g., use of keylogging malware by financially motivated actors). [75]

Indeed, the 2017 report separates looks at "actors, their motives, and their modus operandi". For actors, we still see external (state-sponsored, criminal gangs, etc.), internal, partners, and multiple (a combination of previous groups).

Actor/motives are separated into 3 categories:

"FIG (Fun, Ideology, Grudge motives OR activist group threat actors), ESP (Espionage motive OR state-affiliated OR nation-state actors), FIN (Financial motivation OR organized criminal group actors)." [76]

"Modus operandi", can be divided into patterns (denial of service, crimeware, etc.), action (hacking, physical, social), and asset (server, media, person) as shown in the report's figure 9. The following figure extracts the relevant information for our discussion: When breaches occur, they generally are quick occurrences with "compromises [that] are measured in minutes or less 98% of the time" [77] ; but "[b]reaches that are taking months or longer to discover in this year's dataset are likely to fall into Point of Sale Intrusions, Privilege Misuse, Everything Else or Cyber-Espionage." [78]

The detection of breaches appears to still be mostly external, but while "[e]mployee notifications were the most common internal discovery method for the second straight year and there was also an uptick in detection through internal financial audits, associated with business email compromise (BEC)." [79]

		Accommodation	Education	Finance	Healthcare	Information	Manufacturing	Public	Retail
P a t t e r n	Denial of Service				1	2		1	
	Privilege Misuse	5	5	26	104	13	8	58	6
	Lost and Stolen Assets	4	3	2	42	2	1	7	
	Everything Else	8	14	16	28	24	4	19	3
	Point of Sale	180		3	3				8
	Miscellaneous Errors	1	16	10	6	9	2	38	12
	Web App Attacks	3	11	364	15	61		13	24
	Crimeware Payment		5	7	12	1	2	5	1
	Card Skimmers	5		44				1	39
	Cyber-Espionage		19	5	1	4	108	98	1
A c t i o n	Hacking	171	43	387	48	89	111	130	30
	Misuse	5	5	26	104	13	8	58	6
	Physical	10	2	46	31	2		11	39
	Social	9	32	372	23	37	109	102	20
	Error	1	19	11	119	10	3	47	12
	Malware	180	26	370	18	42	92	103	24
	Environmental								
A s s e t	Server	175	34	399	123	101	10	100	38
	Media	7	5	10	105	5	1	31	8
	User Dev	174	18	367	25	34	63	109	23
	Person	10	33	372	27	38	109	104	20
	Network			1		2		1	
	Kiosk/Terminal	3		45				1	38
	Embedded								

Volume 1 Figure 10 - Breach pattern/action/asset Table (Source: DBIR 2017, Figure 9)

1.9.1.2 Incident Analysis

> *The 2015 DBIR's analysis of incidents is interesting. As stated in the report, the first four categories in figure 24 [80], in which people play an integral part, represent almost 90% of all incidents. The responsibility is made clear:*

Whether it's goofing up, getting infected, behaving badly, or losing stuff, most incidents fall in the PEBKAC and iD-10T über-patterns. At this point, take your index finger, place it on your chest, and repeat "I am the problem," as long as it takes to believe it. Good - the first step to recovery is admitting the problem. [81]

They also state that:

> *this certainly doesn't diminish the significant challenges faced by defenders, but it does imply a threat space that is finite, understandable, and at least somewhat measurable. If that is indeed the case-and 11 years of data is a pretty strong baseline-then threats may just be more manageable than some of the we-should-all-just-give-up-now-because- our-adversaries-are-superhuman crowd likes to promote. [82]*

The 2016 DBIR shows very similar patterns [83].

In the 2017 DBIR, we learn that "[a]pplication [a]ttacks remains the most prevalent, helped again by a multitude of botnet data that skews the data toward that pattern" [84]. And that without botnets "then Cyber-Espionage would assume the top spot and Web Application Attacks would fall to sixth place." [85] The authors remind us that "the real value of the incident patterns is not in how they compare to each other, but as guidance on what is most likely to negatively impact your organization" [86] (meaning that each organisation must evaluate its posture in relation to the different reported industries).

Incidents leading to confirmed breaches

If we look at incidents leading to confirmed breaches (figure 25 [87]) then the data is slightly different, with POS intrusions accounting for more than a quarter (28.5%) of all incidents leading to breaches. This is not a surprise with the number of huge breaches we've already discussed in section 1.2.1. Crimeware (18.8%), cyber-espionage (18%) and insider misuse (10.6%) and web-app attacks (9.4%) round out the top 5 [88]. We also learn that "in 60% of cases, attackers are able to compromise an organization within minutes" [89]. The 2016 DBIR shows very few changes [90].The 2017 DBIR shows this evolution over time [91] and the authors note:

The triple threat of hacking, malware and social has been on top and trending upward for the last few years, and it does not appear to be going away anytime soon. It represents a potent mixture for cyber-attacks, but at least it is something we can all agree on. We actually did see a decrease in numbers of these three actions in this year's dataset, due (yet again) to the reduction of POS and botnet-driven breaches. [92]

1.9.1.3 Top issues reported in the DBIR

People issues are prevalent and often a key part of a successful attack.

Social (including Phishing) is unsurprisingly still an issue with "23% of recipients now open phishing messages and 11% click on attachments" [93]. This type of social engineering is still as useful as ever and "more than two-thirds of incidents that comprise the Cyber-Espionage pattern have featured phishing" [94]. The 2016 DBIR states that 13% of people tested click on a phishing attachment [95]. I don't believe we're progressing much on that front.

The 2017 DBIR includes a section called "Attack the Humans!" We note that in 2016 "[s]ocial attacks were utilized in 43% of all breaches", that "[a]lmost all phishing attacks that led to a breach were followed with some form of malware, and 28% of phishing breaches were targeted" and that "[p]hishing is the most common social tactic in our dataset (93% of social incidents)" [96].

Insider Misuse, the insider threat (~19% of all attackers), has always been a problem. In 2014, the "top action (55% of incidents) was privilege abuse" [97]. It is interesting to note that most 'abusers' are not IT staff (with developers at 5.6% and system admins at 1.6%), although I wonder if this is not because these users are more technically savvy and not as easily caught (or simply know better). The 2016 DBIR changed the category to "Insider and Privilege Misuse". They found that 77% was action by an insider, 11% by an external attacker, 3% by a partner and 8% included collusion [98]. Financial gain and espionage are identified as the main motivations here [99].

Limiting access, or "least privilege" as information security professionals call it, would help address that risk. These limits and separation of duties are keys to protecting the organization.

And while IT staff may be less likely to abuse privileges, they can still make mistakes: "60% of incidents were attributed to errors made by system administrators- prime actors responsible for a significant volume of breaches and records" [100].

The 2017 DBIR shows again that most misuse is done by insiders (81.6%), but collusion, external and partner actors are also possible (multiple actors amount to 8%) [101]. Similar recommendations are still the norm:

> *The insider threat, while not as common in breaches as external actors, is still very significant, accounting for 15% of breaches (across all patterns, not including errors). The practice of limiting, logging and monitoring internal account usage extends beyond rogue employees.* [102]

Another often forgotten issue is theft through removable devices, thus "organizations should also focus on monitoring designed to capture (and prevent) data transfers or USB usage closer to real time to reduce the potential impact" [103]

Vulnerability management, including patching, is still a huge issue. The report cites the striking statistic that "99.9% of the exploited vulnerabilities were compromised more than a year after the [CVE] was published" [104]. This means that companies are failing to install patches, even annually! I suspect that asset management (a.k.a. accurate system inventories) are partly to blame, at least in my personal experience. Of the top 10 CVE (CVEs are publicly known vulnerabilities), the only recent ones are one from 2012 and one from 2014, with all other 8 dating to 2002 or earlier (over 10 years old!) [105]. But it is not only the older vulnerabilities that are an issue as "about half of the CVEs exploited in 2014 went from publish to pwn in less than a month" [106] (publish to pwn means the period from public disclosure of a vulnerability to there being code available for an attacker to exploit the vulnerability). The 2016 DBIR confirms this trend when it states that "[o]lder vulnerabilities are still heavily targeted; a methodical patch approach that emphasizes consistency and coverage is more important than expedient patching " [107], and so does figure 12 on page 15. "Appendix B: The Patch Process Leftovers" in the 2017 DBIR [108] confirms the previous years' trend when they write that the "findings that aren't patched quickly tend to go unpatched for a long period of time." [109] The authors call these "the leftovers" and "found 12 weeks was where most organizations had completed their patch process through analysis of roughly 116,000 vulnerabilities within organizations. This also aligns with a quarterly patch process." [110] Note that PCI DSS mandates that critical and high risks (risk ranked by the organisation or using CVSS) be fixed within 30 days, with other risk being addressed based on the organisation's patch process.

Their recommendation is to "ultimately, put your risks in context with each other to understand your organization's full attack surface" [111].

Malware (called crimeware in the 2017 DBIR) continues to plague organizations, as "70-90% of malware samples are unique to an organization" (variations in virus families) [112]. It should not be surprising that "malware is part of the event chain in virtually every security incident" [113] Most malware will involve two steps, first " maintaining persistence and staging advanced attacks" and second "capturing and exfiltrating data" [114]. So while we would rather prevent such an attack at its initial stages (using an antivirus, whitelisting, etc.), preventing exfiltration is more critical (this is where tools such as DLP, IPS, as well as others can help). Malware does not have its own section in the 2016 DBIR, but it is covered in a few sections include breach trends [115]. Malware continue to rise, second only to hacking as a threat action that led to a breach [116].

Ransomware is the most visible type of malware observed recently with the May 2017 WannaCry outbreak being its latest poster child. The 2017 DBIR reports that "non-incident data (malware detonations - a sample of 50 million on-the-wire detections), over 99% of malware is sent by either email or web server". [117]. As they clearly point out this is good news:

This means it's coming through your mail server or web proxy where you can take steps to squash it. This dataset of successfully squashed malware supports the data taken from our incident corpus that also shows that almost 80% of crimeware is email-based and drive-by downloads check in at 8%. [118]

These recommendations should be followed (and these should have been implemented years if not decades ago):

Unless your organization mails around software updates, you need to block executables at your email gateway. Disable macro-enabled office documents (https://decentsecurity.com/block-office-macros/), specifically MS Word and Excel, for anyone who doesn't explicitly need it. Stopping malicious JavaScript starts with blocking .js via email and keeping browser software up to date.

Implement a robust malware defense strategy that incorporates client-based malware detection, application whitelisting, sandboxing and network defenses to detect communications from infected hosts.

Prioritize patching vulnerabilities associated with browser exploitation. This includes the browser software, but also plug-ins. [119]

Web Application Attacks are a category that keeps growing. So much risk exists for web applications that it's even got its own specific PCI DSS set of requirements (6.5.*). Some of the attacks of web applications may have ulterior motives as "targeting web servers just to set up an attack on a different target, a tactic known as a Strategic Web Compromise" [120]. The report also adds that "secondary attacks make up nearly two-thirds of Web App Attacks "[121]. The 2017 report "saw a higher number of web application incidents, yet a lower number of breaches" [122]. It appears that attackers are going for PII and credentials with these attacks, since many users reuse passwords on multiple sites. This has little impact on PCI, other than, as stated in the 2017 DBIR "[a]gain, if you are relying on username/email address and password, you are rolling the dice as far as password re-usage from other breaches or malware on your customers' devices are concerned." [123] NIST is in the process of updating its password recommendations [124]. What changes this could bring to PCI DSS is uncertain.

One good news for organizations worried about mobile devices is that they "are not a preferred vector in data breaches" [125] That doesn't mean however that they will not be in the future. No change here in the 2017 report in terms of mobile devices.

The trends continue in the 2016 and 2017 DBIRs; I do agree with the note that "[t]he great complexity of the infrastructure makes web application servers a target for attackers" [126]. Indeed, complexity is the enemy of security.

Denial of Service (DOS) attacks are less interesting for PCI DSS (where confidentiality, not availability is the focus), but we should remember that many attacks have used a simultaneous DDOS (Distributed DOS) attack to overwhelm detection of a compromise (misdirection is the term magicians would use to describe this kind of technique). The 2016 DBIR adds that "DoS attacks are either large in magnitude or they are long in duration, but typically not both" [127]. While bigger and more visible DDOS are reported in the 2017 DBIR (Mirai botnet), the impact for PCI DSS is mostly unchanged.

Physical theft/loss is not surprising and would be almost a non-issue if organizations used disk-level encryption on end-user computers. Disk-level encryption is now a standard feature of enterprise versions of Windows and Mac OSX operating systems. The 2016 DBIR states that "[l]ost assets were over 100 times more prevalent than theft". Again, disk encryption and USB protection would make this a non-issue (at least from a confidentiality perspective). The 2017 report does not show an impact for card data, as Public Sector and Healthcare are the most affected industries [128].

Point-of-sales (POS) intrusions have evolved over the years. The 2015 report mentions that "in 2014, the evolution of attacks against POS systems continued, with large organizations suffering breaches alongside the small retailers and restaurants" [129] with the "most affected industries" being "Accommodation, Entertainment, and Retail" in the 2016 report [130], while Accommodation, Food Services, and Retail were the main targets identified in the 2017 report [131]

- Headline-grabbing remote payment card breaches have shifted from large retailers in 2014 to hotel chains in 2015, and (for the 2017 DBIR at least) "back to being a small business problem". [132]
- Use of stolen credentials to access POS environments is significant, and represents "[a] lmost 65% of breaches" in the 2017 report [133]. 2017 confirms the 2016 trends by writing "[f]ollowing the same trend as last year, 95% of breaches featuring the use of stolen credentials leveraged vendor remote access to hack into their customer's POS environments" [134], hence the increased focus on third-party service providers by the PCI council in PCI DSS 3.2 (see the latter portion of section 1.8.5).
- RAM scraping continues to be omnipresent in 2015 (2016 report), but keylogging malware has a significant role in many POS attacks, being a common method of capturing valid credentials to be used against POS assets; this is similar in 2017.
- Continuing the trend of the last several years, the sprees (single threat Actor, many victims) represented in this data are a byproduct of successful attacks against POS vendors and cannot be attributed to automated attacks targeting poorly configured, internet-facing POS devices [135] ; this does not appear changed in 2017.

1.9.1.4 Breach Costs (Impact)

What about costs? They are one of the hardest thing to quantify and for anyone to agree on. The report cites an average cost of $0.58 per record breached (for all types of records combined: email addresses, medical records, SSN, CHD), while the Ponemon institute provides a value of $201 per record. This a very wide range. I agree with DBIR that it's probably more of a range, with the cost per record likely increasing exponentially with the number of records breached.

The 2016 DBIR adds much more data on breach costs in its "Appendix A: Post-compromise fraud" [136]. They do point to varied prices for PCI, PHI, PII and other non-card financial information for many markets [137] (although those are estimated averages). This data may be helpful in making a business case for security and compliance. The 2017 DBIR does not cover breach costs.

1.9.1.5 Solutions

Threat intelligence is mentioned in the 2015 DBIR as a potential solution [138], but I doubt it is a silver bullet. For threat intelligence to provide good value, it will require more sharing of information between organizations. If you decide to use threat intelligence, I agree with the report that you should "focus on quality as a priority over quantity" [139].

Security is only as strong as its weakest link. So when attacks often follow the pattern:

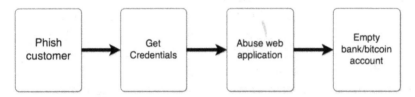

Volume 1 Figure 11 - Attacker Approach [140]

then, we need to make sure that all these steps are protected equally. A 'defense in depth' approach is recommended. More on this in section 1.10.6.

The wrap-up section of the 2015 DBIR provides a good idea of key Critical security controls [141] (CSC) controls that would address incidents that lead to breaches (I've added PCI DSS requirements that overlap, at least in part, with these controls):

CSC	DESCRIPTION	%	CATEGORY	PCI DSS
13-7	2FA	24%	Visibility/Attribution	8.3
6-1	Patching web services	24%	Quick Win	6.2
11-5	Verify need for internet-facing devices	7%	Visibility/Attribution	1.1.7
13-6	Proxy outbound traffic	7%	Visibility/Attribution	1.3.3
6-4	Web application testing	7%	Visibility/Attribution	6.5, 6.6
16-9	User lockout after multiple failed attempts	5%	Quick Win	8.?
17-13	Block known file transfer sites	5%	Advanced	1.2.1
5-5	Mail attachment filtering	5%	Quick Win	N/A
11-1	Limiting ports and services	2%	Quick Win	1.2.1, 1.3.3
13-10	Segregation of networks	2%	Configuration/Hygiene	1.1
16-8	Password complexity	2%	Visibility/Attribution	8.2.3
3-3	Restrict ability to download software	2%	Quick Win	1.2.1, 1.3.3
5-1	Anti-virus	2%	Quick Win	5.*
6-8	Vet security process of vendor	2%	Configuration/Hygiene	12.8

Volume 1 - Table 4 - Verizon Recommended Key SANS Critical security controls with PCI DSS mapping

The report notes that 40% of the CSCs fall into the quick win category. [142]

The 2016 DBIR's wrap-up section [143] does not cover the CSC control like the previous year (nor does the 2017 DBIR). Instead in the 2016 report, key controls are covered in subsections under the headings "recommended controls" (pages 16, 19, 30, 34, 38, 42, 44, 48,51, 54-55, and 59). The 2017 DBIR adds boxes labelled "Things to consider" that are even more generic (but since there's no silver bullet, we need to just follow the recommended best practices outlined in previous years and elsewhere). However, Figure 45 of the 2016 DBIR [144] does provide a nice visual tree structure of what attacks look like (still applicable in 2017).

Again in 2016, Verizon provides very useful insights.

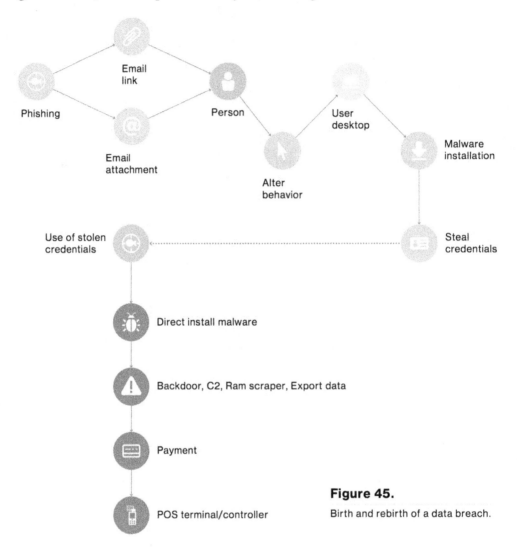

Figure 45.

Birth and rebirth of a data breach.

Volume 1 Figure 12 - 2016 Verizon DBIR "Birth and rebirth of a data breach" [145]

1.9.2 The Verizon 2015 and 2017 PCI Compliance Report

The 2015 PCI Compliance Report [146] covers calendar year 2014 and provides more relevant information for our needs. The report is also very well written and easily accessible as a primer on information security, and I strongly recommend it to my readers. No PCI compliance report was issued in 2016. The 2017 report [147] released in late August 2017 includes data from 2016 but also references 2015. I've updated this section to incorporate the new report. Again in 2017, the Verizon PCI compliance report does not disappoint. I've added commentary for the 2017 report to contrast it to the 2015 one, but I'm also adding new sections strictly for issues brought up by the 2017 report.

Verizon offers both PCI DSS compliance (QSA) and PCI Forensics Investigations (PFI) services. There is a requirement that the investigator of a breach (PFI) cannot be the same company that performed the assessment (QSA) due to an obvious conflict of interest. The group of companies assessed by Verizon QSA business had never been breached and thus served as control group against the breached group investigated by the Verizon PFIs.

A comparison of compliance of requirements between QSA and PFI groups yields interesting correlations (while correlation is not causation, they do provide likely causal factors). The idea here is that requirements that were not functioning properly in breached organizations when compared to control group organizations might just be some of the malfunctioning controls that attackers exploited. Overall in the 2015 report breached organizations were, on average, 36% less compliant than the control group [148]. This is now 42% in the 2017 report and Verizon thinks this may be underreported as PFI's only perform a high-level assessment versus the detailed one by QSA's. [149]

The 2015 report cites a PWC reported statistic that the number of security incidents has increased by an average of 66% per year since 2009 [150]. So in 5 years, this number has increased by a factor of 12, making it much more demanding on organizations to find the proverbial needles in an ever larger haystack.

Verizon then reports that 80% of companies fail when assessed for PCI DSS at an interim stage in the 2015 report (a review held around mid-year, at a different time from when the organization generally validates compliance). So only 20% seem to be able to sustain compliance with the controls they've set in place which, while an increase from 11.1% in 2013 is still fairly, low. Overall, organizations were compliant with 93.7% of controls at the interim stage [151]. The 2017 report shows improvement with 55.4% of organizations achieving 100% compliance at interim validation [152]. We still have a long ways to go

The 2015 report notes 3 main takeaways [153]:

TAKEAWAY 1: COMPLIANCE IS UP - but compliance with requirement 11 (testing) is down to 33% (the lowest of all 12 requirements)

TAKEAWAY 2: SUSTAINABILITY IS LOW - less than a third (28.6%) of companies were found to be still fully compliant less than a year after successful validation

TAKEAWAY 3: DATA SECURITY IS STILL INADEQUATE - current techniques are not stopping attackers - in many cases they aren't even slowing them down.

These appear to still be quite true per analysis of the 2017 report, with takeaway 2 (sustainability or maintaining compliance) being the biggest issue in the 2017 report (more on this in section 1.9.3).

None of these should be a surprise if you follow the news.

Attacks are increasing in complexity. The term APT (Advanced Persistent Threat) is often used to describe the fact that many attacks are not targets of opportunity (though some may be used as part of the overall attack) but are very well funded, long term attacks on targets considered worth breaching. The following paragraph from the report outlines this well:

THE LONG GAME

Data breaches are rarely "smash and grab" affairs. Often criminals will try various types of attack looking for a weak spot. Increasingly this includes attacking the systems of partners and then using their "trusted" access to compromise your systems. Another common tactic is to target less critical systems, say the company intranet, and once in look for ways to "hop" into other systems. So if you leave your payment systems vulnerable to attack, it's not just your customers' card data that you could lose, but just about everything. [154]

Costs of Data Breaches

The costs are very high for breached companies, and the payment card industry as a whole. For a breach, costs can include :

- Fines for non-compliance.
- Notification, card reissuance, and credit monitoring costs for affected parties.
- Forensic investigation and remediation costs.
- Reputational damage, reduced partner and/or consumer confidence and lost business.
- Lower share price and impact on your ability to raise capital.
- Negative impact on user and consumer trust.
- Increased interchange rates charged by banks and/or processors [155]

The 2015 report also cites a survey that says 69% of consumers would be less inclined to do business with a breached organization [156].

Payment innovations and technological approaches

But what about chip cards (EMV), Mobile Payments (Apple Pay, Google Pay, NFC), Bitcoins and other payment technologies? All of these can help reduce attacks, but none are a panacea. Many of these technologies focus on 'card-present' (CP) transactions (in physical stores, requiring merchant participation) and do not address 'card-not-present' (CNP) transactions, including online shopping. This often has the effect of displacing fraudulent activity from 'card present' to 'card-not-present' scenarios rather than stamping it out. An example of this displacement is presented in the report:*"taking Canada as an example, following the introduction of EMV in 2008, the fall in counterfeit and lost/stolen crime has been surpassed by the growth in CNP fraud."* [157]

Mobile device payment technologies such as Apple Pay and Google Payment require a fairly expensive (smartphone) device that not everyone has (or even wants), and device and provider support varies geographically. However, mobile devices provide greater security due to multi (often two) factor authentication (something you have: a soft-token application on the the phone, something you are: your thumbprint, or something you know: a PIN or password) and even leveraging user location. [158]

Many of the same issues will likely affect contactless payments (using a radio-frequency chip on payment cards), as these are limited as they have a lower approved transaction value (which varies geographically and by issuer).

Cryptocurrencies, such as Bitcoins, while increasing in use and even being accepted by some online merchants, still represent only a blip on the radar. And Bitcoins have also seen their fair share of security issues.

Other technologies have been introduced by banks and card issuers (3D Secure, Tokens, Behavioral analytics) and have helped, but alas, cannot eliminate fraud.

All these technologies require that most participants in the PCI model use the technology (called the network effect) to make a dent against fraudulent use. But as these technologies and companies compete on offerings, no one generally supports everything. In addition, the overall volume of credit card payment is still growing and dwarfing the advances by the technological solutions available.

The impact of changes in the IT environment

Mobility, Virtualization, and Cloud Computing have all become standard tools in today's organizations.

Mobility (mobile phones, tablets, as well as laptops) have become prevalent, whether as provided by companies to their employees or as increasing popularity through BYOD (Bring Your Own Device) programs. It should not surprise you that it is easier to control company provided devices than BYOD ones. Tools exist to provide some level of security. And, as mentioned for the DBIR, mobile devices are currently not too much of an issue, but mobile devices should remain on our security radar.

Virtualization is everywhere now, especially since it allows many organizations to reduce costs through server consolidation. But very often, organizations ignore "the potential impact on compliance" [159]. Introspection and snapshots saving memory with CHD to disk are two big issues here. (See section 2.7.1.4 in Volume 2 for more detail, or see the PCI SSC "PCI DSS Virtualization Guidelines" [160] and "PCI DSS Cloud Computing Guidelines" [161]).

I describe 'cloud computing' as simply the marriage of virtualization with third-party hosting providers. It thus multiplies the security and compliance risks of virtualization with those of third-party service providers. These risks are obviously further compounded in cases where the cloud provider also manages CHD storage and encryption keys.

Note that neither the report nor I think that these technologies cannot be used; they must instead just be managed properly. However, some implementations may not be suitable for a PCI DSS environment. [162] "Mobile devices as payment terminals" [163] usage is also growing. But since most of these are not P2PE compliant, they do not reduce scope in anyway. They provide an interesting payment device alternative (often much cheaper), but they also must be secured and often are not.

Is compliance worth it? A look at ROI.

The report mentions that compliance is seen as a "burden" [164] by most organizations, a cost-center and not a profit-center. This leads us to ask what is the ROI (return on investment) provided by compliance, which I would reframe as asking: "what is the ROI of confirming that you have basic information security controls in place". The challenge is: how can you measure the cost of a breach that you avoided?" [165].

The report notes "a strong correlation between compliance and data protection" [166] This is still an issue in the 2017 report, when Verizon clearly states:

> *Note that the PFI dataset typically covers a different caseload of data breaches from one year to the next. That makes the ongoing similarities in compliance trends, with year-over-year comparison of this data correlation, even more striking. It strengthens our finding that breached organizations clearly demonstrate a predictable pattern of behavior.* [167]

Compliance with PCI DSS appears to help reduce "the likelihood" of a breach, by helping identify failures (through testing and monitoring) that can be corrected before they are exploited, and hopefully preventing breaches and their associated costs (fines, investigations, reputation, etc.). Though in order to be effective, root causes of failures, not just the symptoms, must be identified and dealt with. This is akin to having a runny, bloody nose; while we want you to use a tissue to help stop the flow of blood, if you have an underlying condition (say anemia), then fixing that root cause is required so that we prevent the problem from occurring again. For example, the root causes of an unpatched system can be many: not being included on the systems patch list (inventory/asset management issue), having too long a patch cycle that doesn't take risk into account, etc.

The PCI DSS does not ensure security (in all fairness, nothing does), yet I believe that if PCI DSS is used as part of an information security program, it "provides a useful baseline" [168], a large subset of the controls of the information security program.

The value of compliance is hard to measure. That's why I recommend looking at TCO (total cost of ownership) of the required security controls. Most people understand that total costs are divided into fixed costs and variable costs. For PCI DSS, fixed costs are things like developing policies and standards (though some reviews exist, they are much smaller than the initial creation time) and hardening (changing default configurations to a more secure one). Variable costs are all those that include periodic tasks. Appendix C of the report presents the periods specific requirements that need to be performed (some are only identified as 'periodic' which means that an organization must define the periodicity for itself). More often than not, these variable costs are the biggest ones for an organization in the long run. And all those costs generally include infrastructure (a.k.a technology : hardware, software, etc.), services (consulting, assessment, vulnerability scanning, etc.) and staff time.

I've always pushed my clients to look at TCO since what may initially appear to be cheaper (such as putting all systems in one zone and not reducing scope) can actually be more expensive in the long run when variable costs are considered over a number of years.

Page 6 at the bottom of the 2017 report also points in that direction when it states that "[f]or a control system to be effective, controls must be resource-efficient and budget-friendly, and should be reviewed periodically."

SCOPE

The section on scope reduction in the 2015 report starts with the following subtitle: "Scoping is the foundation for compliance" [169]. I could not agree more. In my personal experience, scoping is, at best, misunderstood, which is why I'm dedicating a complete volume to scoping and publishing my scoping model and approach for free online. I believe accurate scoping (and detailed documentation) is the first step towards security and compliance with PCI DSS. More detail on scoping and scope reduction can be found in volume 2.

Reducing scope is required as organizations have limited resources to devote to security. The report agrees when it states that "cutting the DSS scope will result in lower total cost of ownership, make maintenance of security controls easier, and reduce risk by limiting the attack surface" [170]. But scope reduction is not easy as it requires an understanding of both the business needs and the technological environment. Indeed the report adds that "scope reduction may involve fundamental changes to network architecture and to business processes, and it's not always an easy task" [171].

Compensating controls

Compensating controls can be used for most of the PCI DSS requirements if a legitimate business or technical constraint exists. Interestingly, the report cites that 42% of organizations were not able to meet requirement 3.4 (render PAN unreadable, often through encryption) and had to use a compensating control [172]. Some limitations will likely be imposed by a QSA for certain requirements that are already used in an existing compensating control. If you are one of the 42% that cannot meet requirement 3.4, you may have a hard time convincing your QSA that you want to use a compensating control for logging (10.1, 10.2.*, 10.3.*) and monitoring (10.6.*) and other critical requirements.

Compensating controls must go 'above and beyond' [173], meaning that they should be judged to be as strong as the control they are replacing. Because of that reason, they can often become more expensive than the controls they are replacing. They also need to be reviewed annually. You should view compensating controls as temporary measures, areas of higher risk, that require a more permanent solution in the mid to long term. The 2017 report shows that while use of compensating controls has dropped a few percentage points, "[a]bout one-third of organizations (33.8%) found to be fully PCI DSS compliant at interim validation in 2016 would not have reached that goal without the use of a compensating control." [174] This is still very high.

What are the biggest failing controls?

The 2015 report notes that "over 90% of all controls, sub-controls, and testing procedures were passed by 80% of companies" [175]. Those 90% of controls are probably not as interesting as the other 10%. On the same page, the report presents the top 20 testing procedures (TP) with the lowest passing rates in 2014 (a specific PCI DSS requirement consists of one or more testing procedures). These 20 TP cover the following 13 PCI DSS requirements (requirement language has been adapted and summarized for readability):

- 6.2 (1 TP) - Install applicable vendor- supplied security patches
- 6.5.10 (1 TP) - Web application broken authentication and session management
- 11.1 (1 TP) - Test for the presence of unauthorized wireless access points on a quarterly basis
- 11.1.1 (1 TP) - Maintain an inventory of authorized wireless access points
- 11.2.1 (3 TP) - Perform quarterly internal vulnerability scans and rescans as needed
- 11.2.2 (3 TP) - Perform quarterly external vulnerability scans, via an Approved Scanning Vendor (ASV)
- 11.2.3 (3 TP) - Perform internal and external vulnerability scans after any significant changes
- 11.3.1 (1 TP) - Perform external penetration testing annually and after any significant changes
- 11.3.2 (1 TP) - Perform internal penetration testing annually and after any significant changes
- 11.3.3 (1 TP) - Correct exploitable vulnerabilities identified during penetration testing and retest
- 12.6.1 (2 TP) - Educate personnel upon hire and at least annually on security awareness
- 12.8.5 (1 TP) - Maintain information about which PCI DSS requirements are managed by each service provider, and which are managed by the entity
- 12.10.4 (1 TP) - Provide training to staff with security breach response responsibilities

If we further refine this list, we get:

- 6.2 (1 TP) - Patch all systems
- 6.5.10 (1 TP) - Web application authentication / session management issues
- 11.1 (2 TP) - Identify all authorized and unauthorized wireless access points
- 11.2 (9 TP) - Internal and external network vulnerability scans
- 11.3 (3 TP) - Internal and external penetration testing, and verifying fixes.
- 12.6 (2 TP) - Security awareness training of all personnel.
- 12.8.5 (1 TP) - Clear definition of responsibility for PCI DSS requirements between service provider and entity.
- 12.10.4 (1 TP) - Train security breach response staff annually.

So patching (6.2) and vulnerability management (11.2, 11.3) represent 13 of the top 20 missed TP (65%), which seems like a good place to start fixing things.

In the 2017 report, that list has changed slightly to include (among others) :

- POS tampering (9.9.*)
- Vulnerability scanning (11.2.*)
- Penetration testing (11.3.*)
- Hardening (2.*)

Lessons learned.

The following were found to have a high correlation with breached organizations by the 2015 report.

Patching & maintaining security (requirement 6) and logging/monitoring (requirement 10) demand most from an organization as they are frequent periodic processes and not one-time deals (as hardening, requirement 2, is). Compliance for requirements 6 and 10 was 0% for breached companies. The problem with vulnerability management and patching is that it takes time. As stated in the report:

It can take months to fix vulnerabilities in applications:

- Identifying the issue can take time.
- The source code may not be readily available or understood.
- The original developers may no longer be available.
- Coming up with a workaround can take a lot of expertise.
- The languages used may no longer be in common use.
- Fixes can introduce new vulnerabilities. [176]

A reduced scope will help reduce "the patching workload" [177]. Proper initial configuration can also reduce the patching costs. For example, if a (non-needed) web server is disabled during initial installation, then patches for that web server will not have to be installed. This adequate initial configuration, often called hardening, will also help address the risk mentioned that "misconfiguration of systems is actually much more likely to be the cause of a breach" [178]. Remember the 2015 DBIR result that 8 of the top 10 exploited CVE date from 2002 or earlier, and that only one was less than a year old.

The failures in monitoring lead to breaches lasting longer than they should as most organizations learn of breaches "when they receive notification from a law enforcement agency, the card brands, or another third party." [179]

Governance is also a big problem. Anyone who's dealt with multiple organizations has identified those who see PCI DSS compliance as a check-the-box review. I believe that requirement 12, the "security policy" requirement, should really be seen as an "information security program" requirement. An information security program requires active management of information security, including performing regular risk assessments. These governance issues are part of the reason that the PCI SSC introduced the concept of Business-as-Usual (BAU) in PCI DSS 3.0. BAU may lead to future PCI DSS requirements that may be similar to what DESV DE.1 mandates for designated entities to require that management ensures that the information security program is working as expected.

User access controls and authentication are also big issues. This has to be taken alongside the statistic that 20% of attackers are internal or partners. My experience is in line with the report in that roles and accesses tend to be too broadly defined. What requirement 7, "need to know", focuses on is the concept of 'least-privilege' which is interpreted too broadly by organizations. This applies to regular users, but also to privileged users and administrators.

Traceability is key and requires ensuring unique individual accounts. This is supported by the statistic reported from the DBIR that "38% of POS hacking attacks involved stolen credentials" [180]. Individual accounts can help in an investigation. Educating users is also key, as the report notes that "being held accountable increases users' awareness of the value of their credentials and privileged access, meaning they will be more likely to proactively act to protect it" [181].

In some way, with changing IT landscapes, the network perimeter may be broken and "endpoints may not be trusted" requiring other types of "effective access control" [182]. The report calls for "adaptive access controls, authentication mechanisms" [183] and mentions a number of solutions: multi-factor authentication (two is common and required by PCI DSS 3.1 # 8.3), Secure Single Sign-On (SSO), and Privileged Access Management (PAM) systems [184]. The latter, almost a must for large organizations in my humble opinion, not only reduces compliance costs, but also risks (as most high-privilege passwords are never known to an administrator, or even applications). These systems generally also provide the famous AAA services: authentication, authorization (pre-approved or through a ticketing system), and auditing (often even allowing session recording). PCI DSS 3.2 did partly tackle this with the new requirement mandating multi-factor authentication for administrative access to the CDE (8.3.1).

The 2015 report identifies the added risk of administrative accesses when it cites that "analysis of Microsoft Security Bulletins from 2013 by Avecto found that 92% of "critical" vulnerabilities would be mitigated by removing administrative rights across an enterprise" [185].

The report provides added guidance regarding the development of multi-factor authentication:

> *When implementing multi-factor authentication solutions you should be wary of SMS, telephone or email-based solutions. While these can offer a cost-effective way to roll-out multi-factor authentication, many have known vulnerabilities and can be intercepted or even redirected.* [186]

The report also mentions that during many assessments and breaches, network segmentation was found to be ineffective [187]. This fact surely led the PCI SSC to include this testing in requirement 11.3.4 introduced with PCI DSS 3.0, which only became mandatory as of 2015, and thus was not necessarily included in the 2014 assessments performed by QSA. Inefficient segmentation is likely a strong contributing factor in breaches as network perimeter security is generally the first layer in a defense-in-depth model. The report also recommends the use "next-generation firewall application-aware functionality" for better security [188]. Requirement 1.3.5 (which was 1.3.6 in previous versions) changed from "stateful inspection" to "permit only "established" connections into the network" which aligns with this recommendation. This brings to mind multiple questions. Does perimeter security as a main security control still work? If not, what can we do to fix it?

Malware (viruses) are still an issue. The report states that "CHD breaches typically involve a number of techniques, but many culminate in dropping a piece of malware on a high-value system" [189]. This leads many to believe that some major upgrades of requirement 5 are necessary as current solutions do not seem to be working. The DBIR statistics of 70-90% of malware samples being unique alludes to the fact that the task has become much more complex for antivirus solution providers. The report outlines technologies that can help: "more sophisticated technologies that include proactive behavior detection, sandboxing, whitelisting, application control, cloud-enabled threat intelligence, heuristics, and reputation analysis" [190].

Protecting stored cardholder data (Requirement 3) is also an issue, probably in part because organizations keep too much CHD and for too long, though we all hope that efforts in not storing this data or using tokenization will help reduce the issues here. Encryption can help and P2PE solutions should be high on merchant's wish list. My recommendation to companies is to focus on tokenization or truncation (or not keeping data), as it is hard for companies to properly manage encryption keys. As the PCI DSS standard states "Remember, if you don't need it, don't store it!" [191].

Testing systems (requirement 11) was the worst requirement in terms of compliance for both the control group (33%) and the breached group (9%). The conclusions of the report are hard to disagree with: "the lesson is clear: as an industry, breached and non-breached organizations alike, we all need to do better at testing our defenses" [192]. Also remember that testing identifies vulnerabilities that feed into requirement 6, patching and maintaining secure systems.

Finally, 2014 saw many issues with SSL/TLS encryption: heartbleed, poodle, etc. This led to the interim period release of PCI DSS 3.1 in April 2015 which deprecated SSL completely as well as TLS version 1.0. These need to be the sooner the better. A December 2015 update on this topic is now included in appendix A2 of PCI DSS 3.2 under the title "Additional PCI DSS Requirements for Entities using SSL/early TLS". Overall, organizations appear to do well with setting up secure transmission of CHD, but keeping up with encryption standards is where organizations fail [193].

Sustainability of compliance

In order for organizations to sustain their compliance, the report calls for it to be done "by design" or intently by "building sustainability into the functional and operational specifications of the compliance program and reinforcing it through frequent education, training and awareness campaigns" [194]. Change is inevitable. Technology changes, industries change, organizations change. PCI DSS is information security, which addresses risks. This risk approach is what is needed to make the program "resilient" and adaptable to changes. The DESV (appendix A3) pushes designated entities towards that risk approach. The new service providers 10.8.* and 12.11.* partly address this issue, but they're only for service providers.

In order to ensure that we maintain compliance, we must have a way to track how we are doing. One recommendation is to use "metrics" (often called Key Performance Indicators, KPIs) generally presented to management on dashboards. The report breaks down sustainability into 4 areas [195] that should be captured in our metrics:

- Technical - configuration and functionality of system components
- Administrative - mostly documentation (policies, procedures, specifications, logs and written agreements)
- Operational - staff performing processes
- Business - alignment between strategic business objectives, data protection, and compliance objectives

Conclusions of the 2015 PCI compliance report

The 2015 report recommends tackling requirement 6 (Develop and maintain secure systems and applications) followed by requirement 10 (Track and monitor all access to network resources and CHD) [196]. My take is that it depends where your particular organization is failing.

Ultimately, if I regroup the recommendations [197] (and add my personal twist), we get these guidelines/recommendations:

- Accurately document and maintain scope information (including data flows), including as changes occur
- Provide evidence and metrics as a by-product of your regular (BAU) processes
- Log, monitor and test the environment
- Define clear responsibilities and assign accountability
- Manage third-parties

The 2015 report does "call out" twice to the PCI SSC to:

- Set a higher standard for firewalls and replace "stateful-inspection firewalls, a technology that most security professionals consider outdated." which can be bypassed by "Malware and hacker attacks" [198] – PCI DSS 32 changes to 1.3.5 partly addresses this, but ultimately this will evaluated by QSAs, so more guidance is likely needed.

- Provide more clarity on approved scope-reduction techniques in upcoming versions of the DSS so that companies can be clear how they can exclude systems from their DSS scope and compliance workload [199] – The PCI SSC has said they will release scoping guidance in 2016, but as of this writing they have not yet done so.

As the report states "PCI DSS compliance should not be seen in isolation, but as part of a comprehensive information security and risk-management strategy" [200]. Ultimately, security (and remember PCI DSS compliance is about information security) should be considered as any other requirement in everything an organization does. You cannot effectively bolt on security after the fact.

1.9.3 Control Effectiveness in the 2017 report

The 2017 report conveys most of the same elements at issue that were noted in the 2015 report. It focuses more of sustainability of compliance, which requires looking at correctness and effectiveness of controls. Most security professionals I know dislike how many organizations take a "check the box": approach to PCI compliance, what the Verizon 2017 report calls "fire and forget" [201], basically just implementing the control and saying "we're good", and not reviewing if it works even part-time.

Whether PCI DSS controls are sufficient to "provide reasonable assurance that payment card data is secure" [202], the DBIR authors confirmed that "[e]very organization had multiple PCI DSS Key Requirements not in place–including controls that were material to the breach." [203]

The 2017 report does provide a new interesting section on "[t]he lifecycle of PCI DSS controls" [204] that can be helpful.

Effectiveness and correctness are the key issues addressed, as confirmed by the highlighted sentence "Implementation of PCI DSS requirements involves two interdependent aspects: effectiveness and correctness" [205]. This is best covered by pages 8 through 12 in the 2017 report; let's look at them briefly.

Verizon defines "[c]ontrol correctness" as "[a] level of assurance that the security mechanisms of a requirement have been rightly implemented." [206]. A common problem is the afore mentioned "check the box" approach where "organizations will often deem controls to be effective merely by their presence but fail to determine whether they are performing as expected, and at all times" [207]. This effectiveness testing, is what auditors call type 2 testing, or test of operating efficiency. This is what is implied in the new service provider requirements 10.8, 10.8.1, 12.11 and 12.11.1 (see section 1.8.5), by the "BAU" guidance introduced in PCI DSS 3.0, and requirements A3.3.*. Verizon refers to those controls having "resilience" and that "an evaluation of the correctness and effectiveness of a control should be done through direct measurement and reasoning, which will involve an assessment of control design, installation, operation and performance, as well as evaluation of residual risk and control risk." [208]. How to test each control is better addressed at the individual control level, and left to volume 3.

1.10 Where do we go from here? My recommendations

The Verizon reports provide valuable information about what is failing during breaches and offers recommendations for improvements. But the PCI DSS (and the PCI SSC) does not exist in a vacuum. As with any industry, there are different forces pushing to shape where the standard is going. The 5 forces model was proposed by Michael Porter in 1979 in a Harvard Business Review (HBR) article entitled "How Competitive Forces Shape Strategy", and was refined in later years as a tool often used by businesses and consultants in assessing the competitive landscape of an industry. And while I've seen Michael Porter's framework used to analyze the payment card industry from a competitive standpoint [209], I have not seen it used to analyze the PCI DSS standard itself. This is what I will attempt to do now. I'll start by describing the model and the 5 forces influencing the Payment Card Industry and the PCI DSS. Then I'll review the failures identified and review recommendations through that prism.

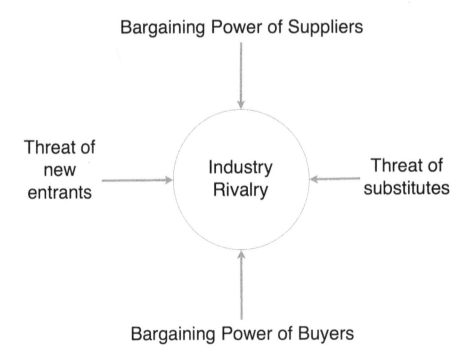

Volume 1 Figure 13 - Porter 5 Forces [210]

1.10.1 Porter's 5 forces

The 5 forces of the model are divided between two threats (from new entrants and substitutes) and two bargaining powers (of buyers and suppliers) that have an impact on the rivalries that exists in an industry.

Porter maintains that those 5 forces shape an industry structure, and that "industry structure determines profitability" [211]. We're reminded of Porter's assertion that "[t]he point of competition is not to beat your rivals. It's to earn profit." [212] A classic example often cited is Apple and the laptops market, where in 2013 Apple was the 6th company in terms of market share but had over 50% of the industry's profits in that same year [213]. Apple is also reported to have 92% of smartphone profits worldwide while selling only 14% of all phones in the first quarter of 2015 [214]. The 5 forces also apply to nonprofits, such as the PCI SSC, and I would also claim it can be applied to the PCI DSS. In the case of nonprofits, they "can do more good because they meet needs more effectively and efficiently" [215]. For the PCI SSC and PCI DSS, this would imply being more effective (better at ensuring the protection of cardholder data) and more efficient (operating at a lower overall costs for the industry as a whole) about its stated mission: to ensure the protection of cardholder data.

The steps [216] involved in industry analysis usually start by looking at product and geography.

Product scope: The product here are standards (mainly the PCI DSS, but also PA-DSS, P2PE, etc.) that are used to ensure the protection of information used for all types of payments, including card-present (in-person) and card-not-present (internet and phone, mostly) transactions.

Geographic scope: The standards are used everywhere globally for most payment (credit, sometimes debit) card payments. Geographically, there are variations on the structures of power. North America is where the card brands have the biggest position of strength (this is where 4 of 5 the founders of the PCI SSC are based), while Europe, due to its laggard attitude towards credit cards, sees more power in its local financial institutions. And while in some markets the standards cover both credit and debit card payments, in many other regions there is strong competition with regional industry organizations that control direct debit payment.

The next step is to look at each participant in the model (some of these could be part of more than one category). We'll also discuss the respective strengths and weaknesses of the forces themselves.

New Entrants

New entrants in our case are new payment methods not currently widely used. They include:

- Mobile (NFC cards)
- Phone payments (Apple Pay, Google Pay, Samsung Pay)
- Application-based payments / loyalty cards (Starbucks)
- Sharing economy applications (Uber, Airbnb)
- Cryptocurrencies, such as Bitcoins
- Merchant Customer Exchange (MCX) (a consortium of more than 50 U.S. retailers with a product called CurrentC, an application linked to debit payments) but that was postponed on June 28, 2016

New entrants face a barrier to entry known as the network effect. In a network effect, the more users participate in a shared system, the more valuable the system becomes (in an exponential fashion). Examples of network effect include: fax machines, social networks, etc. These new entrants need to gain enough market share to become a viable substitute and a threat to the industry, which will come at a high cost in time and money. Size and experience (iTunes & the app store, and Google Play) is why large organizations (Apple, Google) have an advantage over smaller ones. Apple, for example, may target a subset of merchants that are used a vast majority of the time by its users (using the pareto principle also known as the 80/20 rule) and thus gain significant market share.

The strength of the payment card brands is also something that new entrants must face, although Forbes' 2015 "World's Most Valuable Brands" results do have Apple at #1, Google at #3 (#2 in 2017), while Visa is at #30 (#28 in 2017, American Express is #23) [217], [218] (although Apple and Google are not known for "payments").

These new offerings can also put pressure on the industry while reducing or even eliminating the need for PCI DSS. For example, Apple Pay"s use of tokenization reduces the risk for merchants allowing no storing of information (although in memory attacks are still possible). This also applies to Google Wallet, but in both cases rollout varies wildly per regions and countries.

Substitutes

Substitutes include all other forms of payments that are not subject to PCI DSS and the card brands, but are well established in the marketplace, and may not always be seen as direct rivals. They include:

- Cash
- Money orders, postal money orders, certified cheques, cashier's checks and traveler's cheques
- Electronic transfers: Bank (Wire) Transfers, Electronic check (ACH or eCheck), Electronic Funds Transfer (EFT), Western Union
- Direct Debit cards including regional payments options (Interac, M-Pesa)
- Prepaid Cards, Gift Cards (note that some of these are branded by the card brands and not seen as substitutes)

A substitutes' strength varies by type. Cash can work well for card-present transactions, but not for card-not-present. Checks are not accepted everywhere. Debit cards, and cash may be the two biggest substitution threats to PCI. The network effect of being accepted by enough merchants at enough locations is also an important factor for substitutes. Bitcoin and other cryptocurrencies could also be construed as substitutes in some cases, mostly for card-not-present (CNP) transactions.

Buyers

The buyers are the individual cardholders, who can wield a lot of power as a group, basically voting with their wallets. As stated earlier, their incentives are well aligned with the card brands in terms of security, the PCI SSC (and the PCI DSS), as fraud will increase their costs. They will be sensitive however to anything that makes their purchasing more complex or more costly, which may lead them to alternative methods (new entrants or substitutes).

Issuers can also be seen as a form of buyers. Issuers usually ally with only one card brand and will try to use that exclusivity to get more favorable business terms. Issuers can decide not to offer credit cards but only debit cards.

Suppliers

We have multiple subtypes of providers. The first major supplier group is the one that provides technology to the industry. These technology suppliers are already in strong competition between themselves and are very often easily interchangeable. These suppliers sometime provide technical solutions (encryption, tokenization) and will look to push to have their particular implementation recognized (above other solutions if possible).

Another type of supplier are PCI entities (merchants, service providers) that, like buyers, have an option of not accepting a form of payment such as credit cards, although that may come at the expense of a loss of market share due to not accepting the buyer's preferred method of purchasing. The suppliers have very limited leverage over PCI DSS.

Larger PCI entities (who bring a higher risk level to the industry) may have more leverage on fees charged, which the industry could simply move to a system of fines for not meeting security levels (as has been done in the past). In June 2016 in Canada, Walmart is pushing back on fees charged by Visa [219]. This was settled about 6 months later [220]. A final group of suppliers, QSAs, the ones "assessing" the standard, have a power to influence the standard and to judge specific technological implementations. They are often under pressure from their clients to accept less than secure implementation.

Rivalry

The PCI SSC was formed and is managed by the rival card brands: Visa, MasterCard, American Express, Discover, and JCB. To this list of rivals, we must add Diners Card, acquirers, regional payment associations, etc. All of these, while competing for the same market, are in alignment with each other against the type other rivals that affect the industry and the PCI DSS: the attackers (Organized Crime, State Actors) who have an interest in getting their hands on cardholder data. For the PCI DSS, the main rivalry is between the PCI industry and attackers.

Other Non-structural but relevant factors

There are other relevant factors at play here as well [221]:

Government regulations: These tend to be regional but, as in the case of Sarbanes Oxley, they often end up adopted in other regions as well. These potential regulations, a sort of rival, adds pressure on the rival card brands to "protect data" and leads them towards stronger unity, at least as it concerns the stated objective of protecting cardholder data (instead of having it imposed on them by regulators). Investigations by the Federal Trade Commission (FTC) in the USA could lead to changes here (one blogger has covered this extensively) [222].

Technology: (or, changes in) Many of these technologies are offered by suppliers of solutions to the industry (encryption, tokenization, security offerings, segmentation) that tend to make standards less specific as they try to address multiple potential implementations.

Growth: The increase of online shopping and disintermediation can make focusing on card-not-present a viable business for new entrants and substitutes. It can affect these actors' desire to get involved in the marketplace.

Complements: We could place certain technologies (EMV, NFC) as "complements", but I believe we can simply treat them as suppliers of technologies.

Changes in the industry are expensive since many constituents are involved. This pressure from different constituents of the model may be one of the reasons that the standard has changed so little since its creation. Still, changes have occurred and more should be expected.

1.10.2 Porter's 5 forces impact on issues and changes

Let's review the most relevant actors, or participants, affected by the PCI DSS (and other related standards):

Rivals

- PCI SSC - stewards for the PCI DSS and other related standards - goal of increasing security (validated through compliance)
- Card brands - founders and board members of the PCI DSS - goal of increasing security (validated through compliance) and reducing breaches and fraud
- Attackers - they will try to adapt to whatever changes happen within the PCI DSS

Suppliers

- Merchants, Service Providers (including payment processors) - goal of meeting compliance at the lowest costs

- QSAs - Assessors of the current standard - goal of selling security services including compliance validation and charging as much as possible (what markets will bear) often using a leveraged model (using cheaper resources) to increase profits

Buyers

- Cardholders - goal of security and ease of use
- Issuers - goal of increased security and profit

Substitutes

- Cash - merchants can save transaction fees, but there are more risks of robbery
- Debit Card Providers - goal of increased market share

New Entrants

- Phone payments (Apple Pay, Google Pay, Samsung Pay) - goal of increased market share

Additionally, one item that affects all these actors may be the difficulty in getting knowledgeable and experienced security professionals, which are in high demand nowadays.

Previous changes provided by the PCI industry

PCI DSS is often looked at using the People, Process and Technology lens. Most of the changes introduced in the standard have been technological or procedural.

Let's look at the technological first. PCI DSS applies only when there is cardholder data which we must protect, which is why most of the proposed solutions have tried to reduce the amount of information that organizations keep, using solutions such as P2PE and tokenization. With a new version of P2PE just released in June 2015, I can see this being a good option for card-present payments. Adoption of this technology will take time, but as the P2PE standard matures, we should see adoption increase. Tokenization is also pushed forward and helps with cardholder storage (with 42% of merchants and service providers assessed by Verizon having a problem rendering PAN unreadable [223]).

Some or all of these technologies could make the PCI DSS irrelevant if implemented at scale. Remember, fraud will likely always be present. It must simply be kept to low, but acceptable levels.

Some changes have been procedural, though they may have a technological underpinning. Some are to ensure that adequate documentation is produced, such as requirement 1.1.3 introduced in PCI DSS 3.0 and requirements A3.2.* of the recently published DESV and now in appendix A3 of PCI DSS 3.2 (see section 1.8.4), which has been followed by new requirements for service providers only. Others have increased physical security, for example, reviews for potential tampering of POS (Point-of-Sale) terminals (requirements 9.9.*). All these are standard security best-practices.

People is the area where I've seen the fewest changes. And people are often where we find the weakest links in the security chain. The PCI SSC has just introduced new requirements for QSAs (including mandatory certifications), trying to address the issue that not all QSAs are created equal, with some having a very limited understanding of technology used in today's complex IT environments. And with phishing still a very big problem, this is an area where more work needs to occur. PCI DSS 3.2 addressed the risk of phishing of administrators by mandating multi-factor authentication to CDE systems (8.3.1), and also addressed maintaining compliance by ensuring that major changes review the impact on PCI DSS compliance (6.4.6). Although this targets processes and technology, requirements 12.6.* (security awareness) should be improved to address people issues.

1.10.3 Issues and Recommendation Analysis

The PCI SSC released a document called "Best Practices for Maintaining PCI DSS Compliance" in August 2014 that provides general recommendations. This document was updated to version 1.1 in March 2016 [224]. Let's start with these high-level recommendations:

Maintain the Proper Perspective - the goal is protection of cardholder data, compliance is just one way we use to test security; ultimately reducing scope and data retention will help reduce costs and increase security.

Assign Ownership for Coordinating Security Activities - Without adequate funding and authority (often defined as tone-at-the-top), other business requirements will likely take precedence to security. This calls for a watchdog, who will manage a security program (as called for in the DESV and implied by BAU). This is about overall governance of information security within the organization.

Emphasize Security and Risk, Not Just Compliance - This is, to me, the key issue after governance. The alternative to the "check-the-box" model is risk analysis, and I would venture, threat modeling. Threat modeling is an approach for analyzing the security of a system or environment. It boils down to looking at each layer of the system to see how an attacker would target each of them in conjunction and to review the security controls required to adequately defend against attackers. It also allows us to achieve the "defense in depth" approach described in section 1.10.6.

Continuously Monitor Security Controls - As part of the security program (and responding to BAU concerns), this talks about ensuring that processes are being followed and that any degradation of security is identified early and corrected. This is a detective control.

Detect and Respond to Security Control Failures - Another detective control, which ties into all the issues previously identified of "Testing" failures in the Verizon PCI Compliance report. Also added is the often forgotten "root cause analysis" to which I alluded to earlier.

Develop Performance Metrics to Measure Success - This is to ensure that management has visibility into how well security is maintained. It is a feedback loop for governance and a detective control.

Adjust the Program to Address Changes - No organization is static, nor is its operational or technological environment. As things change (people, process or technology), the right people need to be involved to consider the impacts on security. Too often, organizations restructure and sideline the "cost center" that is information security. Other times technological foundational changes (such as using cloud technology) are introduced and those changes do not involve the people who can identify and help resolve the security concerns. Remember (this applies to information security professionals and everyone else), the goal of security should never be of impeding the business from operating, but of finding ways that it be done securely.

1.10.4 Issues of Governance

Adequate governance of the information security program (people) is key to an organization's achievement of its compliance objectives. The role of management is often described as setting up the incentive structure to align the objectives of individuals with those of the organization. But how can we move recalcitrant organizations from a check-the-box mentality to a risk-based approach?

I believe taking a look at the impact Sarbanes Oxley (SOX) had on governance may give us insights for the PCI DSS. One major difference between SOX and PCI is the fact that PCI is an industry standard and does not, by and of itself, bring criminal charges in the way SOX can. And these requirements would also fall more on the card brand side than on the PCI SSC side anyways. Still, I believe incentives are key. But as always the devil lies in the detail.

Since most of the time, management is concerned about profits, I believe some of the answers we seek come from the field of economics. There is a specialty called the Economics of Information Security (there's even an annual conference on this topic which I have attended [225]). Another area which may help is the field of behavioral economics, which has reached the mainstream. Our main economic theories state that human actors will always act rationally, but this has often been proven false. Books by Dan Ariely (*Predictably Irrational*, *The Upside of Irrationality*, , *The Honest Truth about Dishonesty*), nobel-prize winner Daniel Kahneman (*Thinking, Fast and Slow,*) and Michael Lewis (*Moneyball*, made into a movie) all have detailed examples of these failures in judgement. For example, Moneyball shows that baseball scouts' evaluation of players is subjective, flawed, and that players rarely meet the expectations set forth by the recruiters. This field is one of the reasons I feel that using the scientific method, with hypotheses evaluated with data (results, generated for metrics), is the key. Laszlo Bock, Google's SVP People Operations (HR) has a great book [226] that shows Google's data based approach for HR. I believe this can work well with information security and PCI DSS compliance. Such a data-driven approach is, I surmise, what is required to achieve business-as-usual (BAU) (further described in requirements A3.3.* of DESV/Appendix A3). Senior management needs to provide oversight of the information security program and monitor its status through periodic reporting.

Governance is also critical since so many problems encountered are people issues. Authority must come from on high for security and compliance to be maintained. There must also be real consequences (sanctions) for those who bypass security controls. The addition of sanctions, whether as part of the information security policy or not, is necessary in my opinion.

Governance changes have no direct impact on individual buyers (although the might on some issuers), but they do affect suppliers (merchants, service providers) and QSAs. The PCI SSC seems to be pushing governance slowly with the DESV's integration into appendix A3 (as well as new 3.2 service provider requirements derived from it).

1.10.5 Reduction in Scope and Data Retention

Reducing scope and data retention (of CHD) is cited by everyone I know (myself included) as the main environment change that helps organizations achieve and maintain compliance with the PCI DSS. Such changes will, of course, require support from top management (governance issue) since business process changes would likely be required. Particular care must also be taken to ensure that scope creep (increasing the number of systems subjected to PCI DSS requirements) does not occur as can be the case when changes do not take into account the costs born by recurrent requirements (such as patching, logging and monitoring).

My personal experience is that organizations keep information for much more time than is required. I would increase the strictness of requirement 3.1 and ask for business justifications for keeping CHD in all its stored locations based on legal or regulatory justifications. For each of these locations (and expanding from section 4.3 of the RoC reporting template), I would ask and question where requirement 3.4 (render PAN unreadable) is not met including a detailed risk vs cost analysis.

I would also require stronger controls for any information kept longer that a reasonable amount of time (for example, from a few months up to one year). This may mean that this information is temporarily archived to backups, or that older data is moved to other systems where access to this data is further reduced.

Scoping is very misunderstood. Many clarifications are required, which is why I'm dedicating a complete volume (volume 2) to it. DESV/Appendix A3 requirements A3.2.* address a majority of the requirements that I believe are required, including the basis of a proper scope identification process (although this is not mandatory for most organisations). This includes the mandatory data discovery that must be performed periodically as instructed in A3.2.5: Data identified outside its expected location should be treated as an incident and sanctions applied for deviation from approved processes. Here are some questions that should be asked in such a case: why is this data here? If there's a business purpose, why was it not documented in the scope document? Do the systems involved meet security and PCI DSS compliance requirements? I would add the requirement for detailed classification of systems (the model can be any chosen by the organization and deemed acceptable by their assessor). It also includes the requirement for reviewing that changes to scope are evaluated (A3.2.2) and that could lead to scope creep.

We also need increased level of detail for scope information which needs to address ALL connections into the CDE, be they for CHD or not (not all connections need to appear on diagrams, but all should be well documented). A complete scope document will cover all relevant sections of the RoC template (see volume 2, section 2.5.5), and network diagrams (1.1.2), data flow diagrams (1.1.3), business justifications of all connections to the CDE (1.1.6), inventory of all system components (2.4) and their classification (my addition).

I would add a control where, during scope identification, opportunities for scope reduction must be identified and evaluated, especially for "contaminated" systems (systems which do not store, process or transmit CHD but located within the CDE) accessed from outside the CDE. These would include changes in network architecture, locations of systems, and use of scope reducing technologies (P2PE, tokenization, etc.)

All these changes mostly impact suppliers, although I believe that better understood scope and better governance will lead to more efficient operations and reduced costs (and likely more agility) later down the road.

I think the standard needs requirements for increased protection of pre-authorization data, since many attacks have targeted that data, including the use of ram scrapers [227]. These requirements are implicit in requirements 3.2.* and 3.4, but need to be made explicit.

Segmentation / Isolation

Segmentation is a noted issue in scope reduction. The addition of a requirement for testing network segmentation (11.3.4) as part of the annual penetrations tests aimed to fix this gap (increased to every 6 months for service providers in requirement 11.3.4.1). The effects of this new requirement will sadly only be felt in 2016 or later. The Verizon 2017 PCI compliance report does not provide information regarding the effect this new requirement. Requirement A3.2.4 aims to increase this testing to at least twice a year, aligning with firewall rules review (1.1.7). This alignment is important as segmentation configurations are not static. The 2015 PCI compliance report states the problem clearly: "Sustaining the zones' integrity and boundaries requires rigorous enforcement of security standards, policies and procedures to control network and system operations" [228]. Requirement A3.2.4 also calls for testing of any new segmentation technology put in place (a new type of firewall, etc.) prior to being put into production.

Scope reduction changes have no direct impact on individual buyers (although it might on some issuers), but they do affect suppliers (merchants, service providers) and QSAs (less time and money spent on assessments).

1.10.6 Defense in depth

From a technological standpoint, we're dealing with ever more complex IT environments, using a mix of legacy and state-of-the-art technologies (virtualization, web services, cloud, mobile). Attackers use this complexity (which is the enemy of security) to target specific companies using what is referred to as APT (Advanced Persistent Threat). This type of "asynchronous warfare" means that an attacker must only find one way in, and that defenders must defend all access points.

Our general approach to information security, and the one outlined in the PCI DSS, seeks to isolate a network and protect it, which is generally known as perimeter defense (basically creating a hard shell with a mushy inside), which is why a smaller perimeter inside the network (the CDE) is recommended. We also recommend a "defense in depth" approach, meaning multiple layers of security to prevent, slow down and detect attackers, as well as fix and recover after an attack.

In the early 2000s, Microsoft was the poster child for vulnerabilities. The company has made drastic changes to its processes, and while vulnerabilities still arise (complexity is still one key issue), the company is no longer the unenviable holder of the majority of the "top 10 vulnerabilities" [229] (even if they are still important due to their enterprise market size). Microsoft, like many others, have used threat modeling to improve not only their products but also their processes. The Open Web Application Security Project (OWASP) even recommends Microsoft's approach [230] to threat modeling [231]. Mandating threat modeling to identify technical risks as part of the required risk analysis (12.2) would be a good improvement. Threat modeling helps us identify the right controls for our "defense in depth". Threat modeling will take into account the scope documentation in order to cover every potential path within the network. Microsoft's Adam Shostack has written a very good book on how to perform threat modeling in software development that is recommended for the reader wanting to know more [232].

Defense in depth has no direct impact on individual buyers (although it might on some issuers), but they do affect suppliers (merchants, service providers).

1.10.7 Vulnerability Management

While testing is an issue identified by Verizon, the overall issue of vulnerability management, from vulnerability identification to patching, remains the main issue at hand. We need to test more frequently than on a quarterly schedule; at least monthly and maybe even weekly for external ASV scans. Many ASV allow for unlimited scans and this should likely be the norm in the industry. This will put pressure on organizations to actually reduce scope (move systems, close services) to reduce costs. I expect to get push back from such a measure that many will deem too demanding. I'm not advocating that all vulnerabilities be addressed within 30 days, I'm just trying to increase the speed at which vulnerable systems are identified and fixed. This would require updated guidance on risk ranking (6.1) but more so on patching (6.2).

Many vulnerabilities identified are on services that may not be used, but were not closed (2.2.2). The vulnerability analysis should call into question the hardening and installation guides. The "exceptions" identified should be noted as a deviation from process and treated as incidents with potential sanctions (like negative notes on the evaluation of projects that put the systems in place). Again, we're looking to align the incentives (evaluation) with the results we seek (that security be included like any other requirement). Note that this may require that project final evaluations be delayed or spread over a longer period (similar to what is done for CEO compensation over a number of years).

To me, web application security (6.5.*, 6.6) needs to tie back more into vulnerability management. Requirement 6.6 should cover externally facing sites, including those exposed to third-parties through dedicated links, not just publicly accessible. We also still see too many attacks that take advantage of lack of validation of parameters (a simple process to perform), which allows for attacks such as SQL injection (6.5.1). I believe that requirement 6.6 should mandate both (not either, as it currently does) "automated technical solution that detects and prevents web- based attacks" and "Reviewing public-facing web applications via manual or automated application vulnerability security assessment tools or methods". The latter can use free or commercial tools and should include code reviews.

More clarifications from the council on what a "significant change" is (as called for in requirements (11.2.*, 11.3.*, 12.2) is also needed. One blogger has provided a good description [233].

Malware

Malware is an issue and requirement 5 is not passing muster. Many have written on the subject [234]. Requirement 5.1.1 is to "ensure that anti-virus programs are capable of detecting, removing, and protecting against all known types of malicious software". Malware isn't just a Windows issue or a virus issue. Malware is being written and sold to exploit vulnerabilities and is a very profitable industry with some varied gray lines. Whitelisting application technology [235], where usable, should be put in place. To me, malware detection should covered by antivirus solutions, whitelisting and blacklisting applications (many technologies are already available for this purpose), file integrity management and/or change detection (11.5). These all need to be integrated in some fashion, with, at a minimum, using log correlations to better identify threats in a more real-time fashion.

Vulnerability management changes have no direct impact on individual buyers (although it might on some issuers), but they do affect suppliers (merchants, service providers) and QSAs and ASV (more time, effort and money spent by their clients, requiring more staff).

1.10.8 Access control

Access control is a big issue, both from a user and administrator perspective.

From a user perspective, access is overall too broad to systems and often using disparate user directories. I believe that better documentation on roles and accesses/responsibilities is required, and that assessors need to challenge the number of users in roles, as well as the appropriateness of accesses by a role.

Access control for system administrators is a bigger challenge, and one where more controls are required. The risk administrative accesses pose is much higher than that of regular users. The standard needs to mandate the use of separate regular personal accounts and personal administrative accounts (for any high-privilege administrative function). The administrative passwords should have stronger complexity requirements in keeping with the increased risk posed by the role. Note that use of Privileged access management (PAM) systems [236] over centralized jump servers can assist in addressing the administrative access risk. Requirement 8.3.1 added in PCI DSS 3.2 and mandating multi-factor authentication for access to the CDE falls in line with this risk.

Monitoring usage of high-privilege accounts to systems that do not require it (for example, personal computers) should also be added. Use of the wrong accounts is usually due to sloppiness. Reductions in use of administrative rights can help mitigate many critical vulnerabilities [237]. Reliance on password must be diminished as credential reuse [238] is often a key step in a breach. Credentials are often obtained through phishing, other social engineering, guessing or cracking hashes. I was happy to see that the new requirement 8.3.1 addresses my 2015 recommendation of requiring that administrative access to CDE should require multi-factor authentication (8.3).

PCI DSS does not currently mandate the use of hardened management or jump servers ('bastion hosts') and I believe that they should be for administrative accesses. Those boxes are required since "endpoints may not be trusted" [239].

Access control changes have no direct impact on individual buyers (although it might on some issuers), but they do affect suppliers (merchants, service providers).

1.10.9 People Issues

Many people issues are addressed through increased access controls. I believe controls around social engineering and phishing are required, both as a subset of security awareness training (12.6) and included as part of the annual internal penetration test (11.3). The new 8.3.1 partly addresses IT admin phishing but more should likely be done. As Bruce Schneier wrote back in 2000: "Only amateurs attack machines; professionals target people." [240]

Theft and loss of devices can be addressed through mandatory hard-drive encryption on mobile devices (laptops, tablets) maybe as an expansion of requirement 1.4 on the use of personal firewalls.

1.10.10 Process Issues

Many process changes were introduced in version 3.0, including mandating the maintenance of an inventory of all in-scope system components. This is often also called 'asset management', and is still an issue. We need to expand requirement 2.4 to include a process for periodic reconciliation with feedback to other processes that caused the failure in change of asset status.

My 2015 recommendations described next on change management were mostly addressed by the new requirement 6.4.6 of PCI DSS 3.2. The change management process requirements (6.4.5.*) should have the obligation of updating the asset inventory, and the scope information if applicable, as a requirement for approval of changes (6.4.5.2). In urgent cases, a reasonable delay for documentation changes may be given, (that's the role of "urgent change process"), but this should be confirmed or the changes should be reverted. This is about doing things in the correct fashion.

Process changes have no direct impact on individual buyers (although it might on some issuers), but they do affect suppliers (merchants, service providers) and QSAs (more process review, but also better scope inventories allowing for better sampling).

1.10.11 Summary of recommended changes

To sum up, here are the changes I would make to the PCI DSS (2015 recommended changes with comments for the July 2016/PCI DSS 3.2 update):

- Integrate DESV requirements into PCI DSS (maybe as requirement 0) - DESV was included as Appendix A3 but not made mandatory, however some new service provider requirements include the same goals
- Governance
  o Signature by CFO and CEO of AoC (visibility by governance)
  o Mandatory metrics reporting and sign-off by C-level
  o Sanction policy for deviations
- Scope Reduction – The PCI SSC is scheduled to provide scoping guidance in 2016, but has not released anything as June 2016
  o Justification of each storage location and data retention (3.1)
  o Mitigation of information kept longer than "reasonable"
  o Use of DESV/Appendix A3 item A3.2.* as basis for scope identification process
  o Detailed classification of systems within network (1.1.2) and data flow diagrams (1.1.3).
  o Annual review of scope reduction opportunities
  o Protection of pre-authorization data in new explicit requirements (3.2.*, 3.4)
  o Increased review of segmentation (1.1, 1.2, 11.3.4, A3.4)
- Defense in depth
  o Mandate threat modeling to identify technical risks as part of the required risk analysis (12.2)
- Vulnerability Management & Malware
  o Monthly internal vulnerability scans
  o Monthly (even weekly) external vulnerability scans
  o For external facing sites (including to third-parties), mandate both web-attack protection and web-app security review (6.6)
  o Require application whitelisting
  o Integrate management of Anti-virus, whitelisting, file integrity management in centralized vulnerability management
- Access Control
  o Better documentation on user roles and accesses/responsibilities

- o Mandate the use of separate regular personal accounts and personal administrative accounts (for any high-privilege administrative function)
- o Stronger password requirements for administrative accounts
- o Monitor the use of high-privilege accounts to systems that do not require it
- o Multi-factor authentication required for CDE administrative access was added as requirement 8.3.1 of PCI DSS 3.2
- o Mandatory use of jump servers for CDE administrative access
- **People Issues**
  - o Social engineering and phishing included in security awareness training (12.6)
  - o Social engineering and phishing included in annual internal penetration test (11.3)
  - o Mandate hard-drive encryption on mobile devices
- **Process Issues**
  - o Mandate process for periodic reconciliation of inventory (2.4)
  - o Change management process (6.4.5.*) requires update of asset inventory and scope documentation – partly addressed by new requirement 6.4.6 of PCI DSS 3.2

1.11 Parting thoughts – updated September 2017

The initial version of this volume was finalized in July 2015; this section was largely updated in June 2016 and again in September 2017.

The structure of the PCI DSS is basically unchanged since it was created as CISP over 15 years ago. Do I think the structure needs to be changed? Maybe, but only since it seems (in my humble experience) to be so misunderstood. In the 2017 revision, I provide an easier approach in the revised volume 3.

The DESV/Appendix A3 provides a good idea what requirements are likely to be added to future versions of PCI DSS. I actually like the structure of the DESV as the basic structure for the PCI DSS:

- Governance - Create an Information Security Program including PCI DSS compliance (A3.1 - Implement a PCI DSS compliance program)
- A3.2 - Document and validate PCI DSS scope.
- A3.3 - Validate PCI DSS is incorporated into business-as-usual (BAU) activities.
- A3.4 - Control and manage logical access to the cardholder data environment.
- A3.5 - Identify and respond to suspicious events.

I expect the PCI SSC to take a more incremental approach based on changes in the threat landscape (incidents and breaches) around the industry.

For mature organizations, the approach to information security and PCI DSS compliance (including scoping decisions) can (and really should) be performed using a more quantitative approach that takes into account the total cost of the program (TCO). I will touch base more on this TCO approach in volume 3 (Building a PCI DSS Information Security Program), as we look at the detailed requirements which must be put in place for the scope that we will define in volume 2.

End Notes - Volume 1

[1] PCI Resources (2015). PCI DSS Glossary. Retrieved July 24, 2015, from http://www.pciresources.com/pci-dss-glossary.

[2] Privacy Rights Clearinghouse (2015). A database of security breaches from 2005 to the present. Retrieved July 1, 2015, from http://www.privacyrights.org/data-breach/admin/www.mass.gov/dia?order=field_breach_total_value.

[3] Kottasova, Ivana (May 23, 2016). Two Hours and 1600 Fake Credit Cards Later: $13 Million is Gone. CNN Money. Retrieved July 1. 2016, from http://money.cnn.com/2016/05/23/news/bank-fraud-south-africa-japan/.

[4] ZDNet (2015). Anatomy of the Target data breach: Missed opportunities and lessons learned. Retrieved July 1, 2015, from http://www.zdnet.com/article/anatomy-of-the-target-data-breach-missed-opportunities-and-lessons-learned/.

[5] Fortinet (2014). Incident Summary - Target Corp Data Breach - What we, the Industry, know (or think we know). Retrieved July 1, 2015, from http://www.fortinet.com/sites/default/files/whitepapers/Target-Data-Breach-wp-5-2014.pdf.

[6] PCI Security Standards Council (2016). Information Supplement: Third-Party Security Assurance v.1.1. Retrieved July 1, 2016, from https://www.pcisecuritystandards.org/documents/ThirdPartySecurityAssurance_March2016_FINAL.pdf.

[7] Krebs, Bryan (2014). Darknet - Krebs on Security. Retrieved July 1, 2015, from http://krebsonsecurity.com/tag/darknet/.

[8] Quote Investigator (2013). I Rob Banks Because That's Where the Money Is Retrieved July 10, 2015, from http://quoteinvestigator.com/2013/02/10/where-money-is/.

[9] Federal Trade Commission (2015). FTC Files Complaint Against Wyndham Hotels For Failure to Protect Consumers' Personal Information. Retrieved July 1, 2015, from https://www.ftc.gov/news-events/press-releases/2012/06/ftc-files-complaint-against-wyndham-hotels-failure-protect. .

[10] Weatherford, Jack (1997, p.17). The History of Money. New York: Three Rivers Press.

[11] Weatherford, Jack (1997, p.20).

[12] Weatherford, Jack (1997, p.72).

[13] Weatherford, Jack (1997, p.73).

[14] Wikipedia (2011). Usury. Retrieved July 6, 2015, from https://en.wikipedia.org/wiki/Usury.

[15] Weatherford, Jack (1997, p.73).

[16] Weatherford, Jack (1997, p.73-74).

[17] Wikipedia (2011). Usury. Retrieved July 6, 2015, from https://en.wikipedia.org/wiki/Usury.

[18] Wikipedia (2011). Gold standard. Retrieved July 8, 2015, from https://en.wikipedia.org/wiki/Gold_standard.

[19] Weatherford, Jack (1997, p.117).

[20] Weatherford, Jack (1997, p.118-119).

[21] Weatherford, Jack (1997, p.126).

[22] Weatherford, Jack (1997, p.132).

[23] Weatherford, Jack (1997, p.164).

[24] Wikipedia (2011). History of the United States dollar. Retrieved July 8, 2015, from https://en.wikipedia.org/wiki/History_of_the_United_States_dollar.

[25] Wikipedia (2011). Gold standard. Retrieved   July 8, 2015, from https://en.wikipedia.org/wiki/Gold_standard.

[26] Weatherford, Jack (1997, p.226-227).

[27] Weatherford, Jack (1997, p.227).

[28] Government of Canada Publications (2011). Social Insurance Numbers: regulating their use (BP-206E). Retrieved July 6, 2015, from http://publications.gc.ca/Collection-R/LoPBdP/BP/bp206-e.htm.

[29] Forbes (2013). The 10 Biggest Frauds In Recent U.S. History. Retrieved July 6, 2015, from http://www.forbes.com/pictures/eelg45gkdi/1-enron-3/.

[30] PCI Security Standards Council (2015, p.7). Payment Card Industry Data Security Standard - Requirements and Security Assessment Procedures - Version 3.2. Retrieved July 1, 2016, from https://www.pcisecuritystandards.org/documents/PCI_DSS_v3-1.pdf.

[31] PCI Security Standards Council (2012). FAQs. - Retrieved July 7, 2015, from https://www.pcisecuritystandards.org/faq/.

[32] PCI Security Standards Council (2010). Documents Library. Retrieved July 7, 2015, from https://www.pcisecuritystandards.org/security_standards/documents.php.

[33] PCI Security Standards Council (2015, p.5). Payment Card Industry Data Security Standard - Requirements and Security Assessment Procedures - Version 3.2.

[34] Wikipedia (2011). Fortifications of London. Retrieved July 8, 2015, from https://en.wikipedia.org/wiki/Fortifications_of_London.

[35] PCI Security Standards Council (2015). ROC Reporting Template for v3.2. Retrieved July 8, 2015, from https://www.pcisecuritystandards.org/documents/PCI-DSS-v3_2-ROC-Reporting-Template.pdf. .

[36] PCI Security Standards Council (2014). Understanding the SAQs for PCI DSS version 3. Retrieved July 8, 2015, from https://www.pcisecuritystandards.org/documents/Understanding_SAQs_PCI_DSS_v3.pdf.

[37] PCI Security Standards Council (2015, p.18). SAQ Instructions and Guidelines v3.2. Retrieved July 8, 2016, from https://www.pcisecuritystandards.org/documents/SAQ_InstrGuidelines_v3_2.pdf.

[38] Visa Inc. (2015). Merchant PCI DSS Compliance & What Is PCI Compliance? Retrieved July 8, 2015, from http://usa.visa.com/clients-partners/acquirers/data-security/pci-dss-compliance.jsp.

[39] PCI Resources (2015). PCI DSS Book Links. Retrieved July 24, 2015, from http://www.pciresources.com/pci-dss-book-links.

[40] Visa Inc. (2010). Visa International Operating Regulations (PDF). Retrieved July 6, 2015, from http://usa.visa.com/download/merchants/visa-international-operating-regulations-main.pdf.

[41] Visa Inc. (2011). Visa Acquirer Risk Program Standards Guide. Retrieved July 6, 2015, from http://usa.visa.com/download/merchants/AcquirerRiskProgramStandardsGuide_2010.pdf.

[42] Visa Inc. (2000). Cardholder Information Security Program 5.5. Retrieved July 8, 2015, from http://www.21cfrpart11.com/files/library/security/cisp.pdf.

[43] PCI Security Standards Council (2010). Summary of Changes - PCI Security Standards Council. Retrieved July 8, 2015, from https://www.pcisecuritystandards.org/documents/pci_dss_v2_summary_of_changes.pdf.

[44] PCI Security Standards Council (2010, p.10). Payment Card Industry Data Security Standard - Requirements and Security Assessment Procedures - Version 2.0. Retrieved July 8, 2015, from https://www.pcisecuritystandards.org/documents/pci_dss_v2.pdf.

[45] PCI Security Standards Council (2010, p.10). Payment Card Industry Data Security Standard - Requirements and Security Assessment Procedures - Version 2.0. Retrieved July 8, 2015, from https://www.pcisecuritystandards.org/documents/pci_dss_v2.pdf.

[46] PCI Security Standards Council (2013). Summary of Changes from PCI DSS Version 2.0 to 3.0. Retrieved July 8, 2015, from https://www.pcisecuritystandards.org/documents/DSS_and_PA-DSS_Change_Highlights.pdf.

[47] Open Web Application Security Project (2006). Category:OWASP Top Ten Project. Retrieved July 8, 2015, from https://www.owasp.org/index.php/Category:OWASP_Top_Ten_Project.

[48] PCI Security StandardsCouncil (2015). PCI Security Standards Council Revises Date for Migrating Off Vulnerable SSL and Early TLS Encryption. Retrieved January 4, 2016, from https://www.pcisecuritystandards.org/pdfs/15_12_18_SSL_Webinar_Press_Release_FINAL_%28002%29.pdf.

[49] PCI Security Standards Council (2015). PCI DSS Designated Entities Supplemental Validation For use with PCI DSS v3.1. Retrieved July 8, 2015, from https://www.pcisecuritystandards.org/documents/PCI_DSS_v3_DESV.pdf.

[50] PCI Security Standards Council (2015, p.1). PCI DSS Designated Entities Supplemental Validation For use with PCI DSS v3.1.

[51] IIA (2013). The Three Lines of Defense in Effective Risk Management and Control. Retrieved July 8, 2015, from https://na.theiia.org/standards-guidance/Public%20Documents/PP%20The%20Three%20Lines%20of%20Defense%20in%20Effective%20Risk%20Management%20and%20Control.pdf.

[52] PCI Security Standards Council (2017). Blog. What is next for PCI DSS. Retrieved September 15, 2017, from https://blog.pcisecuritystandards.org/what-is-next-for-pci-dss.

[53] PCI Security Standards Council (2017). Blog. Feedback Period: PCI DSS and PA-DSS. Retrieved September 15, 2017, from https://blog.pcisecuritystandards.org/feedback-period-pci-dss-and-pa-dss.

[54] Verizon Enterprise Solutions (2015). 2015 Data Breach Investigations Report (DBIR). Retrieved July 1, 2015, from http://www.verizonenterprise.com/DBIR/2015/.

[55] Verizon Enterprise Solutions (2016). 2016 Data Breach Investigations Report (DBIR). Retrieved September 1, 2017, from http://www.verizonenterprise.com/DBIR/2016/.

[56] Verizon Enterprise Solutions (2017). 2017 Data Breach Investigations Report (DBIR). Retrieved September 1, 2017, from http://www.verizonenterprise.com/DBIR/2017/.

[57] Verizon Enterprise Solutions (2017, p.2). 2017 Data Breach Investigations Report (DBIR).

[58] Verizon Enterprise Solutions (2017, p.ii). 2017 Data Breach Investigations Report (DBIR).

[59] Verizon Enterprise Solutions (2017, p.ii). 2017 Data Breach Investigations Report (DBIR).

[60] Verizon Enterprise Solutions (2015, p.2). 2015 Data Breach Investigations Report (DBIR).

[61] Verizon Enterprise Solutions (2015, p.3). 2015 Data Breach Investigations Report (DBIR).

[62] Verizon Enterprise Solutions (2015, p.5). 2015 Data Breach Investigations Report (DBIR).

[63] Verizon Enterprise Solutions (2016). 2016 Data Breach Investigations Report (DBIR).

[64] Verizon Enterprise Solutions (2016, p.5). 2016 Data Breach Investigations Report (DBIR).

[65] Verizon Enterprise Solutions (2016, p.8). 2016 Data Breach Investigations Report (DBIR).

[66] Verizon Enterprise Solutions (2017). 2017 Data Breach Investigations Report (DBIR).

[67] Verizon Enterprise Solutions (2017, p.3). 2017 Data Breach Investigations Report (DBIR).

[68] Verizon Enterprise Solutions (2015, p.4). 2015 Data Breach Investigations Report (DBIR).

[69] Verizon Enterprise Solutions (2015, p.41). 2015 Data Breach Investigations Report (DBIR).

[70] Verizon Enterprise Solutions (2016, p.7). 2016 Data Breach Investigations Report (DBIR).

[71] Verizon Enterprise Solutions (2017, p.5). 2017 Data Breach Investigations Report (DBIR).

[72] Verizon Enterprise Solutions (2015, p.52). 2015 Data Breach Investigations Report (DBIR).

[73] Verizon Enterprise Solutions (2017, p.6). 2017 Data Breach Investigations Report (DBIR).

[74] Verizon Enterprise Solutions (2017, p.6). 2017 Data Breach Investigations Report (DBIR).

[75] Verizon Enterprise Solutions (2017, p.7). 2017 Data Breach Investigations Report (DBIR).

[76] Verizon Enterprise Solutions (2017, p.7). 2017 Data Breach Investigations Report (DBIR).

[77] Verizon Enterprise Solutions (2017, p.8). 2017 Data Breach Investigations Report (DBIR).

[78] Verizon Enterprise Solutions (2017, p.8). 2017 Data Breach Investigations Report (DBIR).

[79] Verizon Enterprise Solutions (2017, p.8). 2017 Data Breach Investigations Report (DBIR).

[80] Verizon Enterprise Solutions (2015, p.31). 2015 Data Breach Investigations Report (DBIR).

[81] Verizon Enterprise Solutions (2015, p.32). 2015 Data Breach Investigations Report (DBIR).

[82] Verizon Enterprise Solutions (2015, p.31). 2015 Data Breach Investigations Report (DBIR).

[83] Verizon Enterprise Solutions (2016, fig.19, p.23). 2016 Data Breach Investigations Report (DBIR).

[84] Verizon Enterprise Solutions (2017, p.38). 2017 Data Breach Investigations Report (DBIR).

[85] Verizon Enterprise Solutions (2017, p.38). 2017 Data Breach Investigations Report (DBIR).

[86] Verizon Enterprise Solutions (2017, p.38). 2017 Data Breach Investigations Report (DBIR).

[87] Verizon Enterprise Solutions (2015, p.32). 2015 PCI Compliance Report.

[88] Verizon Enterprise Solutions (2015, p.32). 2015 Data Breach Investigations Report (DBIR).

[89] Verizon Enterprise Solutions (2015, p.6). 2015 Data Breach Investigations Report (DBIR).

[90] Verizon Enterprise Solutions (2016, fig.19, p.22). 2016 Data Breach Investigations Report (DBIR).

[91] Verizon Enterprise Solutions (2017, p.5). 2017 Data Breach Investigations Report (DBIR).

[92] Verizon Enterprise Solutions (2017, p.5). 2017 Data Breach Investigations Report (DBIR).

[93] Verizon Enterprise Solutions (2015, p.12). 2015 Data Breach Investigations Report (DBIR).

[94] Verizon Enterprise Solutions (2015, p.12). 2015 Data Breach Investigations Report (DBIR).

[95] Verizon Enterprise Solutions (2016, p.17). 2016 Data Breach Investigations Report (DBIR).

[96] Verizon Enterprise Solutions (2017, p.32). 2017 Data Breach Investigations Report (DBIR).

[97] Verizon Enterprise Solutions (2015, p.42). 2015 Data Breach Investigations Report (DBIR).

[98] Verizon Enterprise Solutions (2016, fig.27, p.36). 2016 Data Breach Investigations Report (DBIR).

[99] Verizon Enterprise Solutions (2016, fig.28, p.36). 2016 Data Breach Investigations Report (DBIR).

[100] Verizon Enterprise Solutions (2015, p.50). 2015 Data Breach Investigations Report (DBIR).

[101] Verizon Enterprise Solutions (2017, p.48). 2017 Data Breach Investigations Report (DBIR).

[102] Verizon Enterprise Solutions (2017, p.49). 2017 Data Breach Investigations Report (DBIR).

[103] Verizon Enterprise Solutions (2017, p.49). 2017 Data Breach Investigations Report (DBIR).

[104] Verizon Enterprise Solutions (2015, p.15). 2015 PCI Compliance Report. Retrieved July 1, 2015, from http://www.verizonenterprise.com/pcireport/2015/.

[105] Verizon Enterprise Solutions (2015, p.16). 2015 Data Breach Investigations Report (DBIR).

[106] Verizon Enterprise Solutions (2015, p.16). 2015 Data Breach Investigations Report (DBIR).

[107] Verizon Enterprise Solutions (2016, p.13). 2016 Data Breach Investigations Report (DBIR).

[108] Verizon Enterprise Solutions (2017, p.64). 2017 Data Breach Investigations Report (DBIR).

[109] Verizon Enterprise Solutions (2017, p.64). 2017 Data Breach Investigations Report (DBIR).

[110] Verizon Enterprise Solutions (2017, p.65). 2017 Data Breach Investigations Report (DBIR).

[111] Verizon Enterprise Solutions (2017, p.66). 2017 Data Breach Investigations Report (DBIR).

[112] Verizon Enterprise Solutions (2015, p.22). 2015 Data Breach Investigations Report (DBIR).

[113] Verizon Enterprise Solutions (2015, p.39). 2015 Data Breach Investigations Report (DBIR).

[114] Verizon Enterprise Solutions (2015, p.39). 2015 Data Breach Investigations Report (DBIR).

[115] Verizon Enterprise Solutions (2016, p.6). 2015 PCI Compliance Report.

[116] Verizon Enterprise Solutions (2016, fig.4, p.8). 2016 Data Breach Investigations Report (DBIR).

[117] Verizon Enterprise Solutions (2017, p.40). 2017 Data Breach Investigations Report (DBIR).

[118] Verizon Enterprise Solutions (2017, p.40). 2017 Data Breach Investigations Report (DBIR).

[119] Verizon Enterprise Solutions (2017, p.41). 2017 Data Breach Investigations Report (DBIR).

[120] Verizon Enterprise Solutions (2015, p.41). 2015 Data Breach Investigations Report (DBIR).

[121] Verizon Enterprise Solutions (2015, p.41). 2015 Data Breach Investigations Report (DBIR).

[122] Verizon Enterprise Solutions (2017, p.57). 2017 Data Breach Investigations Report (DBIR).

[123] Verizon Enterprise Solutions (2017, p.7). 2017 Data Breach Investigations Report (DBIR).

[124] Naked Security (2017). NIST's new password rules – what you need to know. Retrieved September 1, 2017, from https://nakedsecurity.sophos.com/2016/08/18/nists-new-password-rules-what-you-need-to-know/.

[125] Verizon Enterprise Solutions (2015, p.18). 2015 Data Breach Investigations Report (DBIR).

[126] Verizon Enterprise Solutions (2016, p.27). 2016 Data Breach Investigations Report (DBIR).

[127] Verizon Enterprise Solutions (2016, p.57). 2016 Data Breach Investigations Report (DBIR).

[128] Verizon Enterprise Solutions (2017, p.56). 2017 Data Breach Investigations Report (DBIR).

[129] Verizon Enterprise Solutions (2015, p.36). 2015 Data Breach Investigations Report (DBIR).

[130] Verizon Enterprise Solutions (2016, p.35). 2015 Data Breach Investigations Report (DBIR).

[131] Verizon Enterprise Solutions (2017, p.64). 2017 Data Breach Investigations Report (DBIR).

[132] Verizon Enterprise Solutions (2017, p.55). 2017 Data Breach Investigations Report (DBIR).

[133] Verizon Enterprise Solutions (2017, p.55). 2017 Data Breach Investigations Report (DBIR).

[134] Verizon Enterprise Solutions (2017, p.55). 2017 Data Breach Investigations Report (DBIR).

[135] Verizon Enterprise Solutions (2016, p.31). 2016 Data Breach Investigations Report (DBIR).

[136] Verizon Enterprise Solutions (2016, p.66). 2016 Data Breach Investigations Report (DBIR).

[137] Verizon Enterprise Solutions (2016, tbl.4, p.68). 2016 Data Breach Investigations Report (DBIR).

[138] Verizon Enterprise Solutions (2015, p.8). 2015 Data Breach Investigations Report (DBIR).

[139] Verizon Enterprise Solutions (2015, p.11). 2015 Data Breach Investigations Report (DBIR).

[140] Verizon Enterprise Solutions (2015, p.42). 2015 Data Breach Investigations Report (DBIR).

[141] SANS Institute (2009). SANS Institute - Critical Security Controls. Retrieved July 1, 2015, from https://www.sans.org/critical-security-controls/.

[142] Verizon Enterprise Solutions (2015, p.56). 2015 Data Breach Investigations Report (DBIR).

[143] Verizon Enterprise Solutions (2016, p.62). 2016 Data Breach Investigations Report (DBIR).

[144] Verizon Enterprise Solutions (2016, p.62). 2016 Data Breach Investigations Report (DBIR).

[145] Verizon Enterprise Solutions (2016, p.62). 2016 Data Breach Investigations Report (DBIR).

[146] Verizon Enterprise Solutions (2015). 2015 PCI Compliance Report. Retrieved July 1, 2015, from http://www.verizonenterprise.com/pcireport/2015/.

[147] Verizon Enterprise Solutions (2017). 2017 PCI Compliance Report.

[148] Verizon Enterprise Solutions (2015, p.10). 2015 PCI Compliance Report.

[149] Verizon Enterprise Solutions (2017, p.50). 2017 PCI Compliance Report.

[150] Verizon Enterprise Solutions (2015, Introduction Section). 2015 PCI Compliance Report.

[151] Verizon Enterprise Solutions (2015, p.2). 2015 PCI Compliance Report.

[152] Verizon Enterprise Solutions (2017, p.16). 2017 PCI Compliance Report.

[153] Verizon Enterprise Solutions (2015, p.3). 2015 PCI Compliance Report.

[154] Verizon Enterprise Solutions (2015, p.3). 2015 PCI Compliance Report.

[155] Verizon Enterprise Solutions (2015, p.13). 2015 PCI Compliance Report.

[156] Verizon Enterprise Solutions (2015, p.4). 2015 PCI Compliance Report.

[157] Verizon Enterprise Solutions (2015, p.6). 2015 PCI Compliance Report.

[158] Verizon Enterprise Solutions (2017, p.2). 2017 PCI Compliance Report.

[159] Verizon Enterprise Solutions (2015, p.8). 2015 PCI Compliance Report.

[160] PCI Security Standards Council (2011). PCI DSS Virtualization Guidelines. Retrieved July 1, 2015, from https://www.pcisecuritystandards.org/documents/Virtualization_InfoSupp_v2.pdf.

[161] PCI Security Standards Council (2013). PCI DSS Virtualization Guidelines.PCI DSS Cloud Computing Guidelines. Retrieved July 1, 2015, from https://www.pcisecuritystandards.org/pdfs/PCI_DSS_v2_Cloud_Guidelines.pdf.

[162] Verizon Enterprise Solutions (2017). 2017 PCI Compliance Report.

[163] Verizon Enterprise Solutions (2017, p.2). 2017 PCI Compliance Report.

[164] Verizon Enterprise Solutions (2015, p.13). 2015 PCI Compliance Report.

[165] Verizon Enterprise Solutions (2015, p.13). 2015 PCI Compliance Report.

[166] Verizon Enterprise Solutions (2015, p.13). 2015 PCI Compliance Report.

[167] Verizon Enterprise Solutions (2017, p.51). 2017 PCI Compliance Report.

[168] Verizon Enterprise Solutions (2015, p.13). 2015 PCI Compliance Report.

[169] Verizon Enterprise Solutions (2015, p.19). 2015 PCI Compliance Report.

[170] Verizon Enterprise Solutions (2015, p.40). 2015 PCI Compliance Report.

[171] Verizon Enterprise Solutions (2015, p.19). 2015 PCI Compliance Report.

[172] Verizon Enterprise Solutions (2015, p.24). 2015 PCI Compliance Report.

[173] PCI Security Standards Council (2015, p.16). Payment Card Industry Data Security Standard - Requirements and Security Assessment Procedures - Version 3.2.

[174] Verizon Enterprise Solutions (2017, p.18). 2017 PCI Compliance Report.

[175] Verizon Enterprise Solutions (2015, p.18. 2015 PCI Compliance Report.

[176] Verizon Enterprise Solutions (2015, p.47). 2015 PCI Compliance Report.

[177] Verizon Enterprise Solutions (2015, p.47). 2015 PCI Compliance Report.

[178] Verizon Enterprise Solutions (2015, p.33). 2015 PCI Compliance Report.

[179] Verizon Enterprise Solutions (2015, p.59). 2015 PCI Compliance Report.

[180] Verizon Enterprise Solutions (2015, p.49). 2015 PCI Compliance Report.

[181] Verizon Enterprise Solutions (2015, p.51). 2015 PCI Compliance Report.

[182] Verizon Enterprise Solutions (2015, p.9). 2015 PCI Compliance Report.

[183] Verizon Enterprise Solutions (2015, p.9). 2015 PCI Compliance Report.

[184] Verizon Enterprise Solutions (2015, p.9). 2015 PCI Compliance Report.

[185] Verizon Enterprise Solutions (2015, p.9). 2015 PCI Compliance Report.

[186] Verizon Enterprise Solutions (2015, p.54). 2015 PCI Compliance Report.

[187] Verizon Enterprise Solutions (2015, p.1). 2015 PCI Compliance Report.

[188] Verizon Enterprise Solutions (2015, p.29). 2015 PCI Compliance Report.

[189] Verizon Enterprise Solutions (2015, p.11). 2015 PCI Compliance Report.

[190] Verizon Enterprise Solutions (2015, p.11). 2015 PCI Compliance Report.

[191] PCI Security Standards Council (2016, p.37). Payment Card Industry Data Security Standard - Requirements and Security Assessment Procedures - Version 3.2.

[192] Verizon Enterprise Solutions (2015, p.12). 2015 PCI Compliance Report.

[193] Verizon Enterprise Solutions (2015, p.40). 2015 PCI Compliance Report.

[194] Verizon Enterprise Solutions (2015, p.26). 2015 PCI Compliance Report.

[195] Verizon Enterprise Solutions (2015, p.27). 2015 PCI Compliance Report.

[196] Verizon Enterprise Solutions (2015, p.72). 2015 PCI Compliance Report.

[197] Verizon Enterprise Solutions (2015, p.72). 2015 PCI Compliance Report.

[198] Verizon Enterprise Solutions (2015, p.31). 2015 PCI Compliance Report.

[199] Verizon Enterprise Solutions (2015, p.70). 2015 PCI Compliance Report.

[200] Verizon Enterprise Solutions (2015, p.3). 2015 PCI Compliance Report.

[201] Verizon Enterprise Solutions (2017, p.6). 2017 PCI Compliance Report.

[202] Verizon Enterprise Solutions (2017, p.12). 2017 PCI Compliance Report.

[203] Verizon Enterprise Solutions (2017, p.6). 2017 PCI Compliance Report.

[204] Verizon Enterprise Solutions (2017, pp.10-11). 2017 PCI Compliance Report.

[205] Verizon Enterprise Solutions (2017, p.9). 2017 PCI Compliance Report.

[206] Verizon Enterprise Solutions (2017, p.9). 2017 PCI Compliance Report.

[207] Verizon Enterprise Solutions (2017, p.9). 2017 PCI Compliance Report.

[208] Verizon Enterprise Solutions (2017, p.9). 2017 PCI Compliance Report.

[209] PYMNTS.com (2014). Michael Porter's Five Forces And Payments Innovation. Retrieved July 9, 2015, from http://www.pymnts.com/news/2014/a-look-at-how-e-payments-got-to-where-it-is-toda/.

[210] Wikimedia Commons (2014). File:Elements of Industry Structure.svg. Retrieved July 9, 2015, from https://commons.wikimedia.org/wiki/File:Elements_of_Industry_Structure.svg.

[211] Magretta, Joan (2012, p.37). Understanding Michael PorterL The Essential Guide to Competition and Strategy. Harvard Business Press.

[212] Magretta, Joan (2012, p.35). Understanding Michael Porter: The Essential Guide to Competition and Strategy. Harvard Business Press.

[213] WSJ Digits Blogs (2014). As the Mac Turns 30, Apple Ponders 'Post-PC' Era - Digits. Retrieved July 9, 2015, from http://blogs.wsj.com/digits/2014/01/23/as-the-mac-turns-30-apple-ponders-post-pc-era/.

[214] Mashable (2015). Apple iPhone snags 92% of smartphone profits. Retrieved July 16, 2015, from http://mashable.com/2015/07/13/apple-iphone-profits/.

[215] Magretta, Joan (2012, p.31). Understanding Michael Porter: The Essential Guide to Competition and Strategy. Harvard Business Press.

[216] Magretta, Joan (2012, pp.56-57). Understanding Michael Porter: The Essential Guide to Competition and Strategy. Harvard Business Press.

[217] Forbes (2015). The World's Most Valuable Brands List. Retrieved July 10, 2015, from http://www.forbes.com/powerful-brands/list/.

[218] Forbes (2017). The World's Most Valuable Brands 2017: By The Numbers. Retrieved September 1, 2017, from https://www.forbes.com/sites/kurtbadenhausen/2017/05/23/the-worlds-most-valuable-brands-2017-by-the-numbers.

[219] The Canadian Press (Jun 11, 2016). Walmart Canada to Stop Accepting Visa Cards due to ‘Unacceptably’ High Fees. Retrieved July 7, 2016 from http://www.cbc.ca/news/business/walmart-canada-visa-1.3630956.

[220] CBC (2017). Walmart strikes deal with Visa to settle credit card fee dispute. Retrieved September 1, 2017, from http://www.cbc.ca/news/business/visa-walmart-1.3923039.

[221] Magretta, Joan (2012, pp.53-54). Understanding Michael Porter: The Essential Guide to Competition and Strategy. Harvard Business Press.

[222] PCI Guru (2015). FTC. Retrieved July 7, 2016, from https://pciguru.wordpress.com/?s=ftc.

[223] Verizon Enterprise Solutions (2015, p.24). 2015 PCI Compliance Report.

[224] PCI Security Standards Council (2014). Best Practices for Maintaining PCI DSS Compliance. Retrieved July 10, 2015, from https://www.pcisecuritystandards.org/documents/PCI_DSS_V3.0_Best_Practices_for_Maintaining_PCI_DSS_Compliance.pdf.

[225] Workshop on the Economics of Information Security (2009). The Ninth Workshop on the Economics of Information Security (WEIS 2010). Retrieved July 10, 2015, from http://weis2010.econinfosec.org/.

[226] Bock, Laszlo (2014). Work Rules!: Insights from Inside Google That Will Transform How You Live and Lead.

[227] Verizon Enterprise Solutions (2015, p.35). 2015 PCI Compliance Report.

[228] Verizon Enterprise Solutions (2015, p.22). 2015 PCI Compliance Report.

[229] Qualys, Inc. (2010). Top 10 External and Internal Vulnerabilities. Retrieved July 10, 2015, from https://www.qualys.com/research/top10/.

[230] Microsoft (2015). SDL Threat Modeling Tool. Retrieved July 13, 2015, from https://www.microsoft.com/en-us/sdl/adopt/threatmodeling.aspx.

[231] Open Web Application Security Project (2006). Threat Risk Modeling. Retrieved July 13, 2015, from https://www.owasp.org/index.php/Threat_Risk_Modeling.

[232] Shostack, Adam (2014). Threat Modeling : Designing for Security. Indianapolis: John Wiley and Sons Inc.

[233] PCI Guru (2014). Significant Change And Periodic. Retrieved July 18, 2015, from https://pciguru.wordpress.com/2014/12/09/significant-change-and-periodic/.

[234] PCI Guru (2015). Why Requirement 5 Must Change. Retrieved July 13, 2015, from https://pciguru.wordpress.com/2015/04/20/why-requirement-5-must-change/.

[235] SANS Institute (2013). Application Whitelisting: Panacea or Propaganda. Retrieved July 18, 2015, from http://www.sans.org/reading-room/whitepapers/application/application-whitelisting-panacea-propaganda-33599.

[236] Verizon Enterprise Solutions (2015, p.9). 2015 PCI Compliance Report.

[237] Verizon Enterprise Solutions (2015, p.9). 2015 PCI Compliance Report.

[238] Verizon Enterprise Solutions (2015, p.42). 2015 Data Breach Investigations Report (DBIR).

[239] Verizon Enterprise Solutions (2015, p.9). 2015 PCI Compliance Report.

[240] Schneier, Bruce (2000). Schneier on Security. Retrieved July 14, 2016, from https://www.schneier.com/crypto-gram/archives/2000/1015.html#1.

Volume 2 - PCI DSS Scoping

2.1 Volume Introduction

This volume of the book deals with the single most important issue in PCI DSS, namely identifying which people, processes and technologies must be subjected to PCI DSS controls. Details about the required controls for those technologies deemed "in-scope" will be provided in volume 3.

Note: Throughout this book/section, you'll see me use many acronyms (including the already mentioned CHD, PAN, SAD). These are the most relevant ones for this section:

- CHD = Acronym for "Cardholder Data"; consists of the PAN, cardholder name, card expiration date, and sometimes service code
- PAN = Acronym for "Primary Account Number"; the card number printed on the front of the card.
- SAD = Acronym for "Sensitive Authentication Data", it includes the magnetic track information, the PIN or PIN block, as well as the Card-not-present authorization value which we'll refer to as CVV2 but can take any of the following acronyms: CAV2/CVC2/CVV2/CID.
- SPT = An acronym for "Store, Process, or Transmit", meaning that a system or process comes into contact with CHD and/or SAD and is therefore automatically in scope.
- CDE = Acronym for "Cardholder Data Environment", basically what we are trying to protect, which starts with the systems that SPT CHD or SAD but is not limited to these.
- Isolation = There is no possible access between systems.
- Controlled Access = There are limited (restricted) communications possible between systems.
- RoC = Report on Compliance
- Entity = An entity is any organization that has the responsibility to protect card data; for PCI DSS compliance, an entity will be defined as either a merchant or a service provider.

A full glossary is provided at the end of the book and on the companion website.

2.2 Scoping

Ah! Scoping. That so little understood topic central to all of PCI DSS.

The PCI DSS 3.2 standard [1], which runs 139 pages long, devotes exactly 2 pages (pages 10 and 11) to scope, scope validation, and segmentation as a means to reduce scoping, and wireless networks. This may be one of the reasons scoping is so misunderstood.

The Scope definition within the PCI DSS standard (pages 10 and 11) did not change much between versions 2.0 (released in November of 2010) and version 3.0 (released in November of 2013) or version 3.1 (released in April of 2015) or even version 3.2 (released in April of 2016), but the section was restructured and expanded in 3.0, and more examples of in-scope systems were provided. Comparisons between versions can be found on the book's website (http://www.pciresources.com/pci-dss-book-resources/). A new section introduced in June 2015 and called "PCI DSS Designated Entities Supplemental Validation for PCI DSS 3.1" (DESV) [2] also adds requirements that are in lockstep with the standard. DESV was integrated as Appendix A3 of PCI DSS 3.2 and will cease to exist as a separate document.

The PCI SSC has also answered questions through online FAQ, information supplements, presentations (RSA conference 2013) and meetings (annual PCI community meetings). And through all of this, the marketplace's understanding of this topic has been clarified.

The PCI SSC finally released long sought guidance on scoping and network segmentation in December 2016, with minor corrections in May 2017.. This very important document aligns very well with the model and approach I proposed back in July 2015 (and which they were aware of). I've however made one slight change regarding network segmentation that I'll explain shortly in section 2.5.

For this section, I'll be drawing on pages 10 and 11 of the PCI DSS standard and on a few other documents:

- A presentation by the PCI SSC at the RSA conference in 2013 [3] (public) and a similar slides deck from the 2013 PCI community meetings (available to PCI assessors: QSAs, ISAs, PCIPs)
- PCI SSC answers to Frequently Asked Questions (FAQ) [4]

- PCI DSS Designated Entities Supplemental Validation for PCI DSS 3.1 (DESV, released June 2015) - A new set of requirements to increase assurance that an organization maintains compliance with PCI DSS over time, and that non-compliance is detected by a continuous (if not automated) audit process; this set of requirements applies to entities designated by the card brands or acquirers that are at a high risk level for the industry. DESV is now integrated as Appendix A3 in PCI DSS 3.2.
- RoC reporting template
- Information Supplements:
    - Best Practices for Maintaining PCI DSS Compliance (released August 2014 but updated March 2016) [5] (which is in many ways superseded by DESV/Appendix A3)
    - Protecting Telephone-based Payment Card Data (March 2011) [6]
    - Third-Party Security Assurance [7] (released August 2014 but updated March 2016)
    - PCI DSS 2.0 Cloud Computing Guidelines [8] (February 2013)
    - PCI DSS Virtualization Guidelines v2.0 [9] (June 2011)
    - Guidance for PCI DSS Scoping and Network Segmentation (v1.0 December 2016, updated to v1.1 in May 2017) (this supplement will be referred to as the "December 2016 Guidance". [10]

I will also leverage what I was taught when I started performing PCI DSS assessments, extensive but selected readings on the web, discussions with colleagues, and my own work experience, analysis and reflection. I believe this book reflects the general understanding of most practitioners in the field. Relevant references are available on the book's website.

2.3 It all starts with data

Information Security, as its name implies, is about protecting information. This is also the main objective of PCI DSS.

Indeed, the reason PCI DSS applies to any organization is the presence of CHD. If an organization outsources ALL processing, storage and transmission of CHD, then all the organization retains is the obligation to ensure that the third-party service providers it hires are PCI DSS compliant and maintain their compliance with PCI DSS (requirements 12.8.*). This is one way to "reduce scope" and, potentially, compliance costs.

But how can you protect something you don't know you have? This information, or data, must thus first be identified, and a data inventory must be created (and obviously maintained).

The PCI DSS standard actually alludes to this discovery when it talks about scope review: "*The assessed entity identifies and documents the existence of all cardholder data in their environment, to verify that no cardholder data exists outside of the currently defined CDE*"[11]

There are many ways, from manual to automated, to identify information ("data-discovery"). Data Loss Prevention (DLP) tools are often used to automate part of this discovery. They are great at identifying information that follows regular patterns (often expressed under the form and name or a "regular expression", also called regexp or regex) for example, credit card numbers, but no so useful for items such as names which cannot be as easily distinguished from other words. This data discovery is also covered in section 2.5.5.

Note: While PCI DSS only cares about CHD, many organizations often hold more types of data that must be protected. An organization will generally create a data classification that covers all the types of data it holds.

Once identified, we generally start defining types of data (names, addresses, etc.) and then classifying them into buckets (public, sensitive, private, confidential, etc.). In our case, we will use the types as defined in the PCI DSS standard.

Let's start by reviewing what information is in scope, which covers two types of data (any other information is not in scope for PCI DSS - that does not mean that other information should not be protected, just that PCI DSS does not cover or address it).

The first type of data in scope is the Cardholder Data (CHD) and it is the one most often mentioned. It includes the Primary Account Number (PAN), which is the 15 or 16 digit payment card number (credit or debit [12]), the cardholder name, card expiration date and service code (a number rarely mentioned anywhere else). The last 3 elements (name, expiration date, service code) are only in scope if the ("complete") PAN is present (more on this in section 2.6.3).

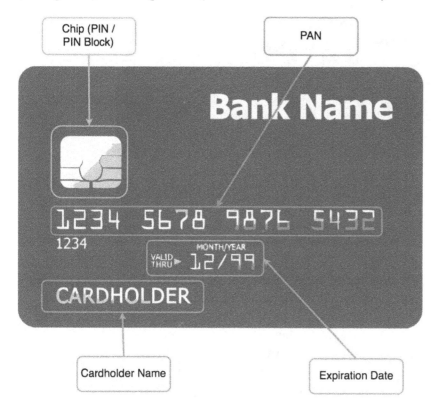

Volume 2 Figure 1 - Rendering of Credit Card (Front)

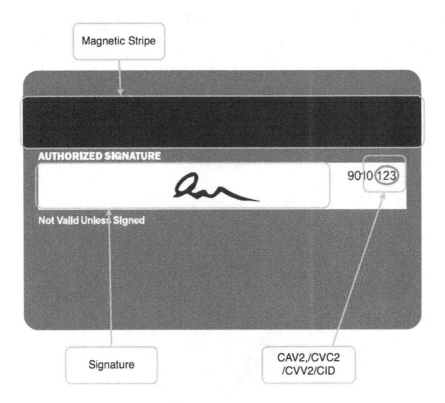

Volume 2 Figure 2 - Rendering of Credit Card (Back)

The other set of data is called Sensitive Authentication Data (SAD) and consists of the information on the magnetic strip (also often called magnetic track), the card-not-present authorization code (3 or 4 digit code printed on the back of the card - except for American Express where it is on the front - and that can bear any of the following names or acronyms: CAV2/CVC2/CVV2/CID), and the PIN or PIN block (if present). SAD must be even more carefully protected than the PAN and other CHD, and that fact is often sadly forgotten (pun intended).

Sensitive Authentication Data (SAD) has more stringent requirements than Cardholder Data (CHD).

	Data Elements	Storage Permitted	Protection Required	Render Unreadable [13]
Cardholder Data (CHD)	Primary Account Number (PAN)	Yes	Yes	Yes
	Cardholder Name	Yes	Yes	No
	Service Code	Yes	Yes	No
	Expiration date	Yes	Yes	No
Sensitive Authentication Data (SAD)	Full Magnetic Stripe Data	No	N/A	N/A
	CAV2/CVC2/CVV2/CID	No	N/A	N/A
	PIN / PIN Block	No	N/A	N/A

Volume 2 Table 1 - PCI DSS data [14]

SAD must not be stored after authorization (even if it remains encrypted), and must be protected (encrypted) if it is stored before authorization. FAQ 1154 [15] confirms these rules. The only exception is for card issuers who need this information to authorize payment transactions. The issuers will need to protect this information and store it encrypted in very few locations. But what is pre-authorization? It is generally used only when either payment systems are non-responsive, or for card-not-present transactions such as postal mail and fax orders. More information on the authorization process can be found in section 1.4.2 of volume 1.

Contrary to popular belief, SAD is not required for recurring payments. This is confirmed by FAQ 1280, including:

Card verification codes/values are used for initial authorization in card-not-present transactions, and are not needed for recurring transactions. Merchants should contact their acquirer (merchant bank) or the payment brands directly, as applicable, for guidance on how to process recurring transactions without storing the prohibited data. [16]

2.4 PCI DSS Scoping explained

I have seen and heard about many ways of classifying systems for PCI DSS or expressing how to go about scoping. The most formal method I have found described out there is in the Open PCI Scoping Toolkit (OPST) [17] (which is not endorsed or approved by the PCI SSC) which was released in 2012, though I only learned of it in 2014. While I agree with the general approach to classifying systems, I have disagreements on the categories in the OPST. I will not discuss the OPST in this volume but you can find my analysis on the book's companion website, at the following link:
http://www.pciresources.com/blog/2016/3/7/a-better-pci-dss-scoping-model-or-the-problems-with-the-opst

The model described here is now available under a Creative Commons license on the book's companion website at http://www.pciresources.com/. (Note: that a similar issue regarding segmentation arises with the PCI SSC December 2016 guidance, more on this in section 2.5).

When I started doing PCI DSS assessments, I learned that there were two types of systems involved: those in the Cardholder Data Environment (CDE) and those connected to it (which is about the extent of what the older PCI DSS 2.0 included in its scoping definition).

The concept of contamination (like a virus, for example the common flu) is often used and is useful to understand that though some systems may not have access to Cardholder Data (CHD), they are still in scope and "contaminated". A viral outbreak in a hospital will cause the hospital to implement control measures (such as isolation) that affect even those not infected; so too does having CHD cause a shared environment to impose controls on entities that may not have this data.

I have also heard, and have myself used, threat modeling, a method by which you try to determine how an attacker would target your infrastructure to get access to your info, and placing the appropriate defenses to prevent, detect and react to such an attack. The threat modeling approach is quite standard in information security, but often requires people or teams that have wide and varied knowledge on all types of attack techniques and information technologies. This approach is implied by the use of systems that *"may impact the security of ... the CDE"*[18] in the scope definition. More on this in section 2.5.2.

All this to say that there are many ways to identify scope and that no one approach is used consistently across the industry. What you need to do in your PCI DSS compliance efforts is to pick one approach you are comfortable with (I will outline my recommendation for one in this book), and formally document how you identified and validated scope. This is key and is and a required part of the compliance process as described in the standard:

At least annually and prior to the annual assessment, the assessed entity should confirm the accuracy of their PCI DSS scope by identifying all locations and flows of cardholder data, and identify all systems that are connected to or, if compromised, could impact the CDE (for example, authentication servers) to ensure they are included in the PCI DSS scope. [19]

I will also identify what you need to document of your scope in section 2.5.5, following the PCI DSS 3.2 ROC reporting template [20].

Approach

Any review of PCI DSS compliance starts with identifying scope. Why is scope so important? Because there are some requirements (monthly patching, daily log monitoring) which are actually expensive for organizations (often more time-consuming and thus greater in human resources costs than in technological ones), and resources being limited, we want to prioritize them appropriately (more in volume 3). There are also risks from a scoping standpoint. Indeed, if we scope too small, we risk not adequately addressing information security threats. On the other hand, if we scope too large, we may not be making the best use of our unfortunately limited information security resources [21] (and finding qualified staff in this field is often difficult as well).

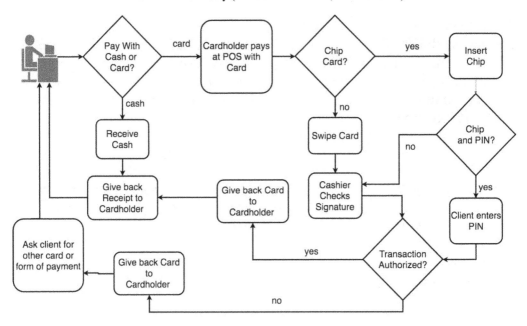

Volume 2 Figure 3 - Sample business process diagram

Identifying scope requires first understanding how cardholder information is processed within the organization. When I perform a PCI DSS readiness assessment, I generally start with business process reviews and their documentation. I would document this by using a standard business process tool (for example Microsoft Visio) but any number of tools can be used; I would then add a textual narrative.

I would also gain an understanding of how these processes get mapped onto the technology in use. In PCI DSS, the resulting diagrams are called Cardholder Data Flow Diagrams and are a new requirement (#1.1.3) as of PCI DSS 3.0 (although they were implied in the scope definition of previous versions).

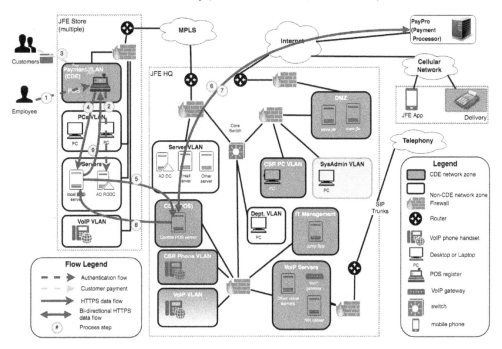

Volume 2 Figure 4 - Sample cardholder dataflow diagram

PCI DSS also calls for complete network diagrams (#1.1.2), and the RoC template identifies at least two diagrams (or sets of diagrams). This includes the high-level network diagram(s) showing the overall architecture of the environment required in section 2.2 [22], which, per the RoC template, must include:

- Connections into and out of the network including demarcation points between the cardholder data environment (CDE) and other networks/zones;
- Critical components within the cardholder data environment, including POS devices, systems, databases, and web servers, as applicable;
- Other necessary payment components, as applicable.

Volume 2 Figure 5 - Sample high-level network diagram (store chain)

Section 4.1 [23] of the RoC template calls for detailed network diagram(s), "to illustrate each communication/connection point between in scope networks/environments/facilities" that must include:

- All boundaries of the cardholder data environment
- Any network segmentation points which are used to reduce scope of the assessment
- Boundaries between trusted and untrusted networks
- Wireless and wired networks
- All other connection points applicable to the assessment

All this information is the bare minimum required to perform proper scoping. Your assessor (QSA, ISA, etc.) may inquire further.

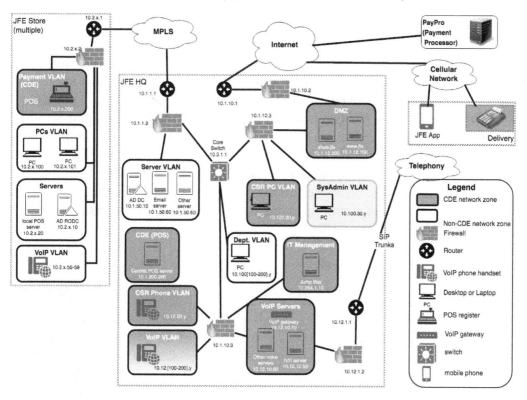

Volume 2 Figure 6 - Sample detailed network diagram (individual store)

2.5 Scoping categories

My approach to scoping, as other approaches do, is used to categorize systems. I initially defined three (3) basic categories that are derived directly from the language of the PCI DSS standard: CDE, connected and out-of-scope. One issue I have with both the PCI SSC Guidance on scoping regards whether segmentation devices (or combinations thereof) constitute CDE systems (my initial contention) or connected systems (PCI SSC, and OPST); I have thus decided to treat segmenting devices as their own category, which I will explain in the revised model. This has no effect on scope, simply on clarity. I'll describe these one-by-one, starting from the inner core that we are trying to protect: the area where we have CHD and/or SAD, the CDE.

2.5.1 First Category: CDE systems

All CDE systems are often called category 1 or type 1 devices. There are 2 different sub-categories in the CDE, but all applicable requirements will apply to all CDE sub-types equally. FAQ #1252 [24] responds to the question "*Do all PCI DSS requirements apply to every system component?* " starting with: "*PCI DSS requirements apply to all system components, unless it is has been verified that a particular requirement is not applicable for a particular system*". We'll refer to this FAQ in volume 3 when discussing how to address all each of the requirements. Generally CDE systems are represented in *red*.

2.5.1.1 CDE/CHD

The Scope of PCI is presented on page 10 of version 3.2 of the standard. The first paragraph states:

> *The PCI DSS security requirements apply to all system components included in or connected to the cardholder data environment. The cardholder data environment (CDE) is comprised of people, processes and technologies that store, process, or transmit cardholder data or sensitive authentication data. "System components" include network devices, servers, computing devices, and applications.* [25]

Let's break this paragraph into its important aspects.

- "*apply to all **system components***" - adding that they "*include network devices, servers, computing devices, and applications.* " - so basically, any type of computer system (hardware, operating system, software, applications) is subject to the requirements.

- "*(CDE) is comprised of people, processes and technologies*" - so, while PCI DSS applies to computer systems, people and processes are also critical (and I recommend, as many others do, taking a business process approach first).
- "*that store, process, or transmit cardholder data or sensitive authentication data*" - what will often refer to as SPT CHD/SAD to summarize. The systems that come into contact with CHD or SAD are the main ones we are trying to protect since they hold, or have access to, the information (the goods) that we are required to protect.

All these systems that SPT CHD/SAD are part, or form the basis, of your CDE (Cardholder Data Environment - the environment in scope for PCI). We'll refer to these as CDE/CHD systems (see table 2 in section 2.5.4 for a summary). The December 2016 Guidance refers to these as "[s]ystem component stores, processes, or transmits CHD/SAD". The OPST calls these type "1a".

2.5.1.2 CDE/Contaminated

In the network segmentation section, the standard states that "*[n]etwork segmentation of, or isolating (segmenting), the cardholder data environment from the remainder of an entity's network is not a PCI DSS requirement*"[26]. Therefore, network segmentation (I will get back to explain what this is in section 2.6.2) is not required other than at the external perimeter of the network. The standard also adds: "[w]ithout adequate network segmentation (sometimes called a "flat network") the entire network is in scope of the PCI DSS assessment". If you do not use segmentation, everything is subject to PCI DSS requirements. Basically, your CDE expands to all systems that are in the same network as your in-scope CDE/CHD systems described above until some segmentation prevents it.

We shall call these systems in the same network zones as CDE/contaminated since there could easily be a transfer of information between systems that are not otherwise restricted (generally by a firewall or other device).

The flu virus analogy works well to explain this concept of "contamination". People with the flu are akin to systems with CHD/SAD. A person in the same room with someone that has the flu runs the risk of becoming infected himself (or herself). This is the same "contamination" principle that was previously described in section 2.4. The December 2016 Guidance refers to these as "[s]ystem component is on the same network segment (for example, in the same subnet or

VLAN) as system(s) that store, process or transmit cardholder data". The OPST calls these type "1b".

2.5.2 Second category: Segmenting (previously called CDE/Segmenting)

The second major category are systems that provide the (generally network) segmentation and prevent "contamination" of CDE systems. Typically, these are firewall devices, but they are not limited to those. These devices are called Segmenting systems (network segmentation will be addressed in section 2.6.2). The scope definition includes an instruction to that effect (and present in previous PCI DSS versions): "If network segmentation is in place and being used to reduce the scope of the PCI DSS assessment, the assessor must verify that the segmentation is adequate to reduce the scope of the assessment." [27]

Note that this function may be accomplished by a combination of devices and systems, but the more complex this gets, the better the documentation your assessor will require.

In the OPST, these would be either "1b": or "2a", thus leading to potential confusion. Without segmenting systems, we cannot have connected systems. Thus, what the PCI SSC December 2016 Guidance calls "System component segments CDE systems from out-of-scope systems and networks", but puts in the connected systems category ("Connected-to or Security-impacting Systems") I will mark at its separate category to prevent any confusion (it is my only disagreement with the PCI SSC document, but this difference is more stylistic than anything else).

This second category is furthermore warranted by the inclusion of a new requirement since PCI DSS 3.0 regarding the testing of segmentation during the required annual internal penetration tests (#11.3.4). Section 3.3 [28] (Network Segmentation) of the PCI DSS 3.2 RoC template adds documentation of this validation of adequate segmentation was performed. Note that the firewall rules that are unrelated to the CDE environment would be out-of-scope. This could happen if the firewall manages the connection point between the CDE and various other network segments. In that case, only the rules that pertain to access to the CDE are in-scope (for review), although it would be a good idea to treat all of them in the same way.

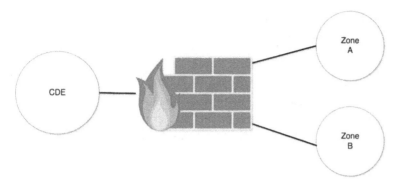

Volume 2 Figure 7 - Image of firewall and 3 network zones (including the CDE)

For example, in the figure 7 diagram, the rules that limit zone A to zone B connections would be out-of-scope for PCI DSS.

Ultimately, unless using a straightforward segmentation device such as a physical firewall, entities you should provide an evaluation that covers requirement 11.3.4 demanding network segmentation penetration testing.

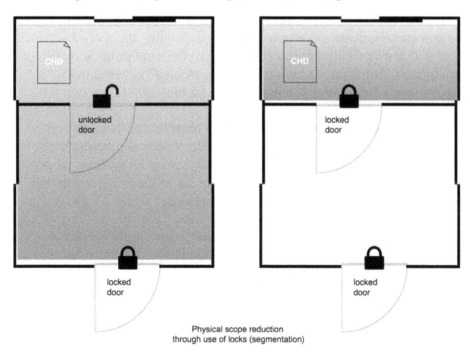

Volume 2 Figure 8 - Physical scope reduction example

2.5.2.1 CDE and Segmenting system analogies

We can understand these categories through a physical security analogy. Imagine there are card numbers (PANs) written down on paper, say on an order form. The document is on a desk in an unlocked room (the room is thus CDE/CHD) within a building. In this case, the complete building (provided it has access control, keys or electronic locks on its outside doors to prevent further "contamination") and the people that have access to get inside the building and the room, are considered "in scope", or capable of accessing the paper form (CDE/contaminated). If we were to put a lock on the door of the room that holds the paper (the lock acts as the Segmenting system), then only the room and the people who can go in the room would be in scope (thus the rest of the building would not become a CDE/contaminated zone). The exterior door lock is still required to protect us from 'untrusted' people. From a security standpoint as well as from a risk perspective, a smaller scope is easier to manage and defend.

2.5.3 Third category: Connected systems

So when does a CDE system contaminate another? Some cases are easier to understand than others. For example, if two systems are in the same network segment and can communicate more or less freely (depending on opened services) then it is clear that contamination can occur (note that the possibility is sufficient to warrant inclusion). But what is required for a "connected" system not to become contaminated? Let's break it down to figure it out.

We know that communication between the systems must be restricted to only those services required for business operations (called "controlled access") according to requirement #1.2.1. Now, we can't always keep all systems we need inside a single zone, or we would be defeating the goals of scope reduction that we should aim for. So what are we to do in these instances?

The standard states that any device that is "connected to the cardholder data environment" [29] (CDE) is in scope since it is not completely isolated. The standard includes in scope any "*[s]ystems that 'may impact the security of' (for example, name resolution or web redirection servers) the CDE*"[30]. This is likely one of the most important lines written on scoping in the standard. This is further addressed on multiple occasions in the 2013 RSA presentation and the 2013 PCI community meetings presentation:

If it can impact the security of the CDE, it is in scope Remember non-CHD systems may be in scope too [31]

and

If an "out-of-scope" system could lead a CDE compromise, it should not have been considered out of scope [32]

Thus, if we are unsure whether or not a system is in scope (as a "connected" system), we should look at whether a compromise of the system could lead to an attack on a CDE system without needing to first compromise another system. If is the case, then this system is in scope. The second subtype of connected systems will partly address this as well.

Getting back to our physical analogy, anybody that can talk to someone in the room could potentially gain access to the CHD information stored on those papers either by getting their hands on it or from someone who has access to that information. Most people worry about theft (or hackers), but the "people" element (in the previously mentioned "people, processes and technologies") is often the weakest link in security. Many of the breaches involve what is called social engineering, or pretexting, which just means convincing someone to give us information (sometimes even system usernames and passwords) or performing actions on our behalf. Phishing (phony emails, the terms comes from "phone" and "fishing", basically fishing for a vulnerable user, often through phone calls) also falls within that category. While I won't delve into the details of these types of attacks, I will provide links to books and articles about this on the book website (www.pciresources.com). Systems that are segmented but not completely isolated from the CDE systems and can communicate with CDE systems without accessing any CHD or SAD through some level of access control become "connected" systems.

In this book, we use isolated to indicate that two systems cannot communicate at all with each other. If communication is limited (note: use of the "any" or "generic" rules are prohibited in PCI DSS), we call it controlled access. The RSA conference presentations confirm this [33]:

- *To be out of scope: segmentation = isolation = no access*
- *Controlled access ≠ isolation*
- *Controlled access:*
  - *Is still access*

- o *Is a PCI DSS requirement*
- o *Does not isolate one system/network from another*
- o *Provides entry point into CDE*
- o *Is in scope for PCI DSS*
    - *Verify access controls are working*
    - *Verify the connection / point of entry is secure*

Connected systems are often referred to as category 2 or type 2 devices. As in the CDE case, there are different types of "connected" devices that present a different level of risk. Let's examine those three subtypes.

2.5.3.1 Connected/Security

There are systems such as user directories (Active Directory, LDAP), patch management systems, vulnerability management systems, several others (this is not an all inclusive list) which provide 'security services'. In our physical analogies, these would be security guards which can issue keys for the room, or it could be cleaning staff that provide services for that room. We can call these connected/security systems. It should not be hard to realize why these are in scope. After all, in the real world, if you could take over the guard station, then you could theoretically walk in to whatever area they are protecting.

The December 2016 Guidance for PCI DSS Scoping and Network Segmentation creates 3 categories of systems that I consider as Connected/Security in a section they call "Connected-to or Security-impacting Systems":

- System component impacts configuration or security of CDE
- System component provides security services to the CDE
- System component supports PCI DSS requirements

I consider that all these types of systems were included initially by my model, but the added clarification from the PCI council is welcomed.

The OPST calls these type "2a".

2.5.3.2 Connected/Communicating Systems

Any system that is 'connected to' the CDE (to CDE systems) is considered a 'connected' system. The exception is systems that are on the 'outside' of Segmenting systems, for example when a Segmenting also affects traffic not related to the CDE such as that described in section 2.5.1.3 and presented in Figure 7.

Some connected systems (that have a connection to CDE/receiving systems) may eventually be ruled out-of-scope, but an evaluation must be formally documented by the organization to determine if PCI DSS applies. It could be of a system receiving information outside the CDE with no possibility of re-entry. For example, say that we have a connected system that receives periodic information transfers initiated from a CDE system and that we have insured that no CHD/SAD is transmitted. The protocol used for data transfer is sftp (part of the SSH suite of applications). The traffic is initiated from the CDE, a file is uploaded to the connected system, and then the connection is closed. Other than returning status messages as part of the protocol, there is no information flowing back to the CDE system. I would contend that the connected system as described here could be ruled out-of-scope since it cannot have an impact on the security of the CDE (although some DLP tool may be warranted). Documentation of the evaluation process should be created, maintained and kept, to be presented to your assessor. The December 2016 Guidance calls these systems "System component directly connects to CDE". The OPST calls these "2b" or "2c"; I don't make the distinction based on flow-direction, but on details of communication.

2.5.3.3 Indirectly Connected

There are also systems that do not have any direct access to CDE systems (they are isolated from the CDE) that are still in scope. Instead, they would generally have access to other connected systems and, through these, could affect the security of the CDE. A classic example would be that of an administrator's workstation which can administer a security device (user directory, etc.), or systems upstream feeding information to connected systems (e.g. patching system, or an http connection as described above). In the case of a user directory, an administrator could potentially grant himself (or others) rights to systems in the CDE and breach the security of the CDE.

Indeed, the standard states that any system that "may impact the security of the CDE" is in scope. We can refer to these systems as connected/indirectly. The December 2016 Guidance calls these systems "System component indirectly connects to CDE". The OPST calls these type "2x".

In our continued analogy, indirectly connected could mean a supply company, such as a food ordering service that, if compromised, could provide with nefarious intent drugged food to the staff or security personnel.

2.5.4 Fourth category: Out-of-scope systems

Finally, any system that is neither a CDE or a connected system is considered out-of-scope for PCI compliance. That system must be completely isolated (no connections whatsoever) from CDE systems, though it may interact with connected systems (and can even reside in the same network zone with connected systems). Do remember, however, if it can affect security of the CDE indirectly through another connected system, that it is a connected system and is therefore in scope.

The December 2016 Guidance for PCI DSS Scoping and Network Segmentation provides 4 tests that must be passed to confirm that a system is out-of-scope (which amount to ensuring that the system does not fall under the previously defined categories):

- System component does NOT store, process, or transmit CHD/SAD => otherwise it would be a CDE/CHD system.
- System component is NOT on the same network segment or in the same subnet or VLAN as systems that store, process, or transmit CHD => otherwise it would be a CDE/contaminated system.
- System component cannot connect to or access any system in the CDE => otherwise it would be a connected/communicating system (although I still contend that some connections could be considered out-of-scope if one can demonstrate they pose no risk, such as pings).
- System component cannot gain access to the CDE nor impact a security control for CDE via an in-scope system => otherwise this is a connected/security or connected/indirectly system.

The OPST calls these category "3".

2.5.5 Categories Summary

To summarize, there are four basic types of systems for PCI DSS purposes. The first group is the Cardholder Data Environment (CDE). The second group is segmenting systems, which are required to enable the other groups. The third group are connected systems, those systems that have some direct or indirect connection into the CDE (which the December 2016 guidance calls "Connected-to or Security-impacting Systems"). The fourth are out-of-scope systems completely isolated from the CDE systems. *For these, always remember that "[s]ystems that 'may impact the security of' (for example, name resolution or web redirection servers) the CDE"[34] are always in scope* or, to put it in other words: "*If it can impact the security of the CDE, it is in scope*"[35].

Classification is key for us so we don't have to apply PCI DSS requirements to all systems.

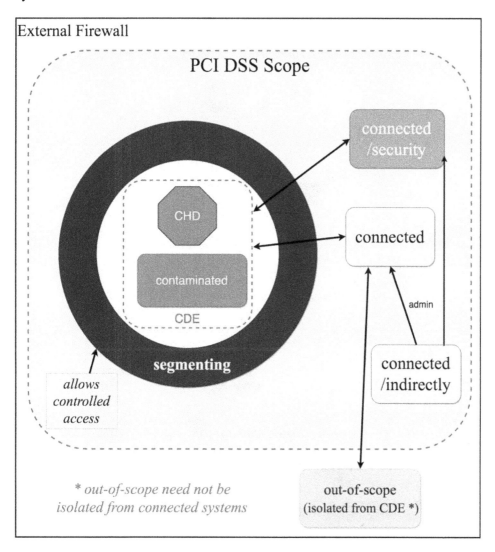

Volume 2 Figure 9 - PCI Scope type diagram

Type	Sub-Type	Segmentation	CHD/SAD	In-Scope
CDE	CHD	None	Yes	Yes
CDE	Contaminated	None	No	Yes
Segmenting		Provides Segmentation	No	Yes
Connected	Communicating	Controlled Access	No	Yes
Connected	Security	Controlled Access	No	Yes
Connected	Indirectly	Indirect Access	No	Yes
Out-of-scope		Isolation	No	No

Volume 2 Table 2 - Classification Categories Summary

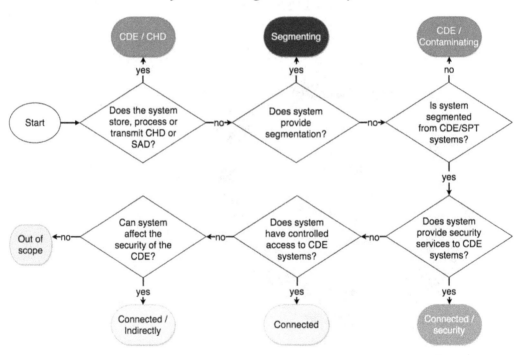

Volume 2 Figure 10 - PCI Scoping Type Decision tree

2.5.6 Scope Identification approach and Scope Documentation

Now that we've described the scope classification model, we need to look at how we must properly document the scope. The approach follows the model closely, with some elements of validation added. Once again, pages 10 and 11 of the standard provide us with the overall approach, while Appendix A3 (DESV [36]) added more guidance of this definition in requirements A3.2.* (DE.2.* in DESV). As we have 2 types of in-scope systems (CDE and connected), we'll be splitting the process in two parts, one for each type.

Part 1 - Identifying the CDE (a four-step process)

Step 1.1 - To identify all systems that store, process or transmit CHD (CDE/CHD systems). These include servers, workstations, appliances, network equipment. The flow of CHD must be documented in diagrams (1.1.3) and detailed textual descriptions need to be produced (RoC #4.2 [37]). The flows and description must cover capture, authorization, settlement and chargebacks.

Step 1.2 - To identify where segmentation occurs (Segmenting systems). Segmenting systems prevent contamination and limit the scope of the CDE. The identified segmented CDE zones are generally represented in red in network diagrams.

Note: any time you implement a new type of segmentation, you should perform segmentation testing as demanded by requirement #11.3.4 and confirm its effectiveness (and fix issues identified) before deploying the new technology into production (also called for in A3.2.4).

Step 1.3 - To identify all other systems within the CDE which are contaminated (CDE/contaminated) systems. This should use the current maintained inventory (required by A3.2.4) but also include a system discovery using scanning tools (ping sweeps are typical here). Any difference with the inventory should be an indication of a failing inventory process and used to review and correct that process. The systems covered include servers, workstations, appliances, network equipment in the same segmented network zones or running under the same Segmenting hypervisors (more on hypervisors in section 2.7.1 on virtualization).

Note: since CDE/contaminated systems bring potential scope reduction opportunities, this step can be used to review if it makes sense to move the system outside the CDE. More on this in volume 3 on TCO (Total Cost of Ownership).

Step 1.4 - Finally, to validate that we do not have other PAN in other systems (A3.2.5 [38]) or locations. This "data discovery" is usually performed using specialized tools (Data Loss Prevention, DLP) but simple 'grep' on Unix/Linux also works. These searches generally use Regular Expressions, but manual discovery may be applicable when few systems are to be reviewed or on systems where such tools may not exist (for example, mainframes). For those who are resource constrained, inexpensive and free options do exist.

The "data discovery" should be performed on any system with the potential of storing PAN; at a minimum, this should cover all systems in the CDE and all connected systems (but really should include all servers, desktops and laptops). If any system is identified with PAN, then the following options are possible:

- Consider the system as a CDE/CHD system and perform anew the previous identification steps
- Migrate the system into the CDE and redo the previous steps
- Securely delete the CHD, and determine why and how PAN was transferred to the system or location to prevent further expansion of scope

In all cases, this should be treated as a security incident per requirement 12.10.*.

Note 1: Version 3.2 of PCI DSS clarified the scope of what should be checked when it added the following line: "*All types of systems and locations should be considered as part of the scoping process, including backup/recovery sites and fail-over systems.* "

Note 2: This is also an appropriate time to review requirement 3.1 and testing procedure 3.1.b to ensure that CHD is destroyed after the approved retention period.

Part 2 - Identify connected systems (a five-step process)

Once the CDE has been properly validated comes the time to identify the remaining in-scope systems.

Step 2.1 - To review all the in-scope firewall (or equivalent equipment implementing the ACLs) rules of Segmenting systems to identify the list of all systems that may connect to the CDE. If the rules are for network ranges instead of individual systems, then using a system discovery tool for the entire range will be required (see step 1.3 of CDE identification). Note that if a rule implies a system that no longer exists, then that rule needs to be removed as required by 1.1.7. The fact that a decommissioning did not remove a system from a firewall ruleset should be treated as an incident and call for a review of the change control process. With the complete list, we will proceed in classifying these systems according to the model.

Step 2.2 - Involves identifying any systems which provide security services, or services that may affect the security of the CDE, and which will be classified as connected/security systems. These include, at a minimum:

- Identity and Directory Services (Active Directory, LDAP)
- Domain Name Systems (DNS), Network Time Systems (NTP)
- Patch management systems
- Vulnerability management systems
- Anti-virus management systems
- File Integrity Management or Change Detection systems
- Performance Monitoring Systems
- Encryption Key Management Systems
- Remote-access (VPN) Systems
- Multi-factor Authentication Systems
- Log Management Systems and Monitoring Solutions (SIEM, syslog, etc.)
- Intrusion Detection Systems/ Intrusion Prevention Systems (IDS/IPS)

Step 2.3 - To identify third-party systems that may be connected to the CDE through some sort of Internet or private link. These systems which are out of your control are also out-of-scope, but the third-party providers must be managed as stated by requirements 12.8.*. Remember that if the connections go through internal network equipment such as routers, then that equipment will still be in scope.

Step 2.4 - To identify connected systems that only receive information and which may (through analysis) be deemed out-of-scope if they pose 'no risk' to the CDE. These systems generally cannot initiate a connection to the CDE and do not have a re-entry to the initiating system (ping or the ICMP protocol may be an exception). This could be the case of a sftp connection, as described earlier. Note that some protocols (DNS, NTP) that might have been deemed as out-of-scope have been used in previous breaches to exfiltrate information. In these cases however, IDS/IPS, DLP or other controls on the CDE connection points or on the initiating system may be more appropriate to monitor for security. The analysis should be thoroughly documented and this documentation must be maintained for review by your assessor (QSA, ISA, etc.).

The remaining systems of the list identified in the first step are simply connected/communicating systems.

Step 2.5 - Finally, to identify systems that are isolated from the CDE but could still affect its security, indirectly through some other connected system. These are obviously classified as connected/indirectly. Often, these are administrative consoles or administrator desktop/laptops.

Additional Guidance

The RoC reporting template [39] gives us more detail of what we must document. Our documentation should include the information in the following subsections of sections 2, 3, 4 of the RoC reporting template. The ones marked as "assessor" are for use by the assessor, not the entity, although the assessor could be internal, either an ISA or someone producing a Self-Assessment Questionnaire (SAQ).

Section		Detail
2	Summary Overview	Title
2.1	Description of the entity's payment card business	
2.2	High-level network diagram(s)	PCI DSS 1.1.2
3	Description of Scope of Work and Approach Taken	Title
3.1	Assessor's validation of defined cardholder data environment and scope accuracy	Assessor
3.2	Cardholder Data Environment (CDE) overview	People, Process, Technology
3.3	Network segmentation	How segmentation is implemented
3.4	Network segment details	All CDE zones and zones containing
3.5	Connected entities for processing	PCI DSS 12.8.*
3.6	Other business entities that require compliance with the PCI DSS	

3.7	Wireless summary	
3.8	Wireless details	
4	Details about Reviewed Environment	Title
4.1	Detailed network diagram(s)	PCI DSS 1.1.2
4.2	Description of cardholder data flows	PCI DSS 1.1.3
4.3	Cardholder data storage	A subset of CDE/CHD systems
4.4	Critical hardware in use in the cardholder data environment	CDE systems and connected/security
4.5	Critical software in use in the cardholder data environment	CDE systems and connected/security
4.6	Sampling	Assessor
4.7	Sample sets for reporting	Assessor
4.8	Service providers and other third parties with which the entity shares cardholder data	PCI DSS 12.8.*
4.9	Third-party payment applications/solutions	PA-DSS
4.1	Documentation reviewed	Assessor
4.11	Individuals interviewed	Assessor
4.12	Managed service providers	Included in-scope or PCI DSS 12.8.*
4.13	Disclosure summary for "In Place with Compensating Control" responses	Assessor
4.14	Disclosure summary for "Not Tested" responses	Assessor

Volume 2 Table 3 - RoC reporting template sections for scope documentation

The subsections marked as "Assessor" would be filled by the assessor during the compliance assessment (RoC or SAQ). The ones marked as "Title" are simply headers.

2.6 Scope Reduction Methods

There are many ways, from simple to complex or business to technical, to reduce scope. The easiest one is always this idea: if you don't need it (information), don't have (or keep) it. You do not have to protect what you do not possess. As the guidance of requirement 3.1 so aptly states: "Remember, if you don't need it, don't store it!" [40].

But if you do need it, some of the methods outlined below can help. Remember however that the devil often lies in the details of the implementation. Your assessor (QSA, ISA, etc.) will have ultimate say on whether an effective scope reduction has been achieved.

Other scope reduction techniques using segmentation such as those required for virtualization will be addressed in the subsequent sections on advanced topics.

2.6.1 Outsourcing to third-party service providers

As I already stated earlier, outsourcing part or all of the CHD handling and processing to a third-party can be an efficient way to reduce scope. Ultimately, outsourcing or not is a business decision, and the compliance costs of keeping it in-house should be included in the total cost analysis decision.

Now, to actually reduce scope, one cannot simply use any third-party service provider (TPSP). If that was not obvious before, it is made abundantly clear in the information supplement [41] provided by the PCI SSC in August of 2014 and updated March 2016. In figure 2 of the information supplement, the due diligence process is presented in the decision tree. If you follow this process, it becomes clear that unless a service provider has either:

- (1) validated and provided evidence of PCI DSS compliance (appearance on a Card Brand service provider list, review of an Attestation of Compliance form or AoC, etc.),
- (2) provided evidence that the entity has validated that it is compliant, or
- (3) provided a reasonable plan to achieve compliance

then the entity should select another TPSP.

Indeed, the supplement also adds: "The use of a TPSP, however, does not relieve the entity of ultimate responsibility for its own PCI DSS compliance, or exempt the entity from accountability and obligation for ensuring that its cardholder data (CHD) and CDE are secure. "[42]

Essentially, you can delegate responsibility to a third-party for tasks, but you cannot outsource your accountability for compliance. Details about the exact PCI DSS requirements of using third-party service providers will be provided in section 3.8.1 of volume 3.

2.6.2 Network Segmentation

Finally, let me address the topic of network segmentation. Network segmentation requires some basic networking knowledge which can be found in the Networking primer in appendix 2. If you have basic networking knowledge (such as of the OSI network model), than you should be good to go. If not, I would strongly recommend reading that primer before going further.

Page 11 of the PCI DSS 3.2 standard provides the basic information regarding the use of network segmentation for scope reduction. The standard is clear on this: *"Without adequate network segmentation (sometimes called a "flat network") the entire network is in scope of the PCI DSS assessment. "[43]* It also states that *"network segmentation can be achieved through a number of physical or logical means. "[44]*

And also that *"to be considered out of scope for PCI DSS, a system component must be properly isolated (segmented) from the CDE, such that even if the out-of-scope system component was compromised it could not impact the security of the CDE. "[45]*

The standard also states that "example of adequate network segmentation" *includes "properly configured internal network firewalls, routers with strong access control lists, or other technologies that restrict access to a particular segment of a network"[46].*

So to consider segmentation to be adequate, we generally look for a device that offers isolation at a layer 3 on the OSI model, which is mostly equivalent to the 'Internet' layer of the TCP/IP model.

OSI Model Layers	TCP/IP Model Layers	Examples
5-6-7	Application	HTTP, FTP, SMTP
4	Transport	TCP, UDP
3	Internet	IPv4, IPv6, ICMP
1-2	Link	Ethernet, DSL, Cable, Wi-Fi, Cellular

Volume 2 Table 4 - TCP/IP Model and OSI Layers

The easiest way to provide this is with a firewall (physical or virtual). Indeed, in mid-size and large-size organizations, this is the recommended approach. But as the network equipment providers' offerings have matured, firewall, routers and switches are presenting many of the same functionalities and all of those could potentially be used for this segmentation purpose. In all cases, the "strong access control lists" (referred to as strong ACLs going forward) is the key to achieving network segmentation using whatever technology is chosen. This implies that, by default, there should be no traffic permitted between the CDE network(s) and other systems, generally called the "deny all" rule (covered in requirement 1.2.1). All traffic must be denied unless it has been formally (and through an authorization process) approved and documented. More on this in section 3.7.1 of volume 3 covering the firewall requirements (1.*).

Some networking equipment does not support strong ACLs. For example, some switches only support inbound VLAN ACLs, meaning they only block incoming connections to a VLAN and not outgoing connections. Those would likely not be adequate.

Other than part of page 11 of the standard, the PCI SSC has issued two FAQ answers regarding network segmentation. The first one (FAQ 1088, What is meant by "adequate network segmentation" in the PCI DSS?) provides much of the guidance used by the industry:

Network segmentation can be achieved through a number of physical or logical means, such as properly configured internal network firewalls, routers with strong access control lists, or other technologies that restrict access to a particular segment of a network.

To be considered out of scope for PCI DSS, a system component must be properly isolated (segmented) from the CDE, such that even if the out-of-scope system component was compromised it could not impact the security of the

CDE. It should be noted that the adequacy of a specific implementation of network segmentation is highly variable and dependent upon a number of factors, such as a given network's configuration, the technologies deployed, and other controls that may be implemented.

Additionally, if segmentation is used to reduce PCI DSS scope, an entity's penetration testing activities (per PCI DSS Requirement 11.3) must include testing of the segmentation controls, to verify they are operational and effective. [47]

The second FAQ (FAQ 1135, Can VLANS be used for network segmentation? [48]) speaks more directly about VLANs but delegates this to your assessor for specific details:

[...] VLANs, or other technologies that restrict access to a particular network segment, the PCI Security Standards Council is not able to offer an opinion about how your organization can achieve adequate network segmentation since it requires an understanding of security features and controls implemented in your environment. We encourage you to contact a Qualified Security Assessor (QSA) to assist in scoping your cardholder data environment and recommend methods specific to your organization to help reduce the scope of your PCI DSS assessment. [49]

Still, your safest compliance bet is to use a firewall type (layer 2 or 3) device for network segmentation, or at least to validate with your assessor, specially for complex or composite network segmentation cases.

2.6.3 PAN Transformations

The PAN is the most important piece of Cardholder Data (CHD), and only with a PAN are cardholder name, expiration date, and service code considered in scope. So what can we do to the PAN to bring it out of scope? This requires understanding the PAN format.

The PAN format follows an international standard, ISO/IEC 7812. The format supports up to 19 digits but the majority of credit card companies use only 16 digits, with the exception of American Express cards which only use 15 digits.

The first 6 digits are known as the Issuer identification number (IIN) which was previously called the Bank Identification Number (BIN). The initial digit of the

IIN describes the industry. Simplifying this list for PCI DSS [50], numbers starting with 4 are generally Visa numbers (though not all such cards bear the Visa logo). Numbers starting with 51 to 55 are for MasterCard, and those starting with 34 or 37 are for American Express. Discover card numbers all start with the number 6 but not all those starting with 6 are allocated to Discover. The IIN is used to route payment information to the proper bank for payment authorization.

Issuing network	IIN ranges	Length
American Express	34, 37	15
Discover Card	6011, 622126-622925, 644-649, 65	16
JCB	3528-3589	16
MasterCard	51-55	16
Visa	4	13, 16

Volume 2 Table 5 - Bank Card Numbers [51]

The next numbers form the individual account number, and the last digit is what we refer to as a check digit (using an algorithm called LUHN), a number calculated from the PAN and used to confirm that the PAN is valid (although it appears that in some cases such as Visa gift cards, the LUHN may not be used).

Let's look at an example. The following Visa number is used in one of their advertisements: 4000 1234 5678 9010

```
4000 1234 5678 9010
**** **                    IIN
        ** **** ***  Account #
                   * Check Digit
```

The 4 at the start indicates this is a Visa card. The IIN is 400012, which in the real world would be assigned to a bank. The individual account number is the next nine digits, 345678901. The last digit, 0, is a calculation of the first 15 digits. The sensitive part of the PAN is part of the account number, and this is what the next section will cover.

2.6.3.1 Truncation (and Masking)

The difference between masking (requirement 3.3) and truncation (one option of requirement 3.4) is presented in FAQ 1146 (What is the difference between masking and truncation?):

Masking is a method of concealing a segment of PAN when displayed or printed (for example, on paper receipts, reports, or computer screens), and is used when there is no business need to view the entire PAN.

Truncation is a method of rendering a full PAN unreadable by permanently removing a segment of PAN data, and applies to PANs that are electronically stored (for example, in files, databases, etc.). For further guidance on truncation formats, please refer to the FAQ "What are acceptable formats for truncation of primary account numbers".

Note that even if a PAN is masked when displayed, the full PAN might still be electronically stored and would need to be protected in accordance with PCI DSS Requirement 3.4. [52]

Thus, PCI DSS defines masking as the operation of hiding parts of a PAN when it is displayed on screens, paper receipts, printouts, etc. (requirement 3.3). Truncation is defined as the permanent transformation in a non-reversible way for usage and storage. The same transformation process can be applied for both masking and truncation, but with different end results.

As stated in the previous section, the account number is sensitive. The IIN is safe and we can easily keep it. Most of you will have seen that most of your receipts include the last 4 digits of the card number, so you can infer that these are safe as well. And this is exactly what requirement 3.3 defines, that "*the first six and last four digits are the maximum number of digits to be displayed*". This could be superseded by card brand requirements or regulatory or legislative requirements as stated in FAQ 1090 [53] ("*What are acceptable formats for masking of primary account numbers (PAN)?* ").

A truncated number is no longer considered a PAN and is non-contaminating (although the system that did the transformation is still in scope since it had the full number). We can use this number (and cardholder name, expiration date, and service code) without fear of contamination and take it out of the CDE. However, masking does not reduce scope but remains a requirement (3.3).

```
4000 1234 5678 9010
**** **            IIN
      ** **** *** Account #
                + Check Digit
4000 12** **** 9010 Max numbers kept for truncation (IIN + Last 4)
```

2.6.3.2 Tokenization

Tokenization is mentioned as one of the options of requirement 3.4 (more on this later) and is referred to as "Index tokens". The guidance for this requirement says: "*An index token is a cryptographic token that replaces the PAN based on a given index for an unpredictable value.* "[54] A token is a surrogate value that replaces the PAN in usage and storage. There are many ways to implement tokenization, but all methods must ensure that an attacker cannot get back to the PAN using the token. The simplest way would use a database to assign each PAN to a random value (format could vary). But this database of values would have to be secured and kept within the CDE. If your particular applications need valid PANs (meaning that the LUHN calculation described earlier for the last digit of the PAN is correct) then you may want to create a tokenisation system using one of the 2 BIN's series reserved for internal use [55] by Visa Europe (much in the same way that RFC 1918 provides internal IP ranges described in the network primer appendix). A sample tokenization application will be provided through the companion website of this book in the fall of 2017.

Other possible implementations, such as ones using cryptography (for example, format preserving encryption or, FPE), also exist in the marketplace, but each organization needs to evaluate if the selected solution is deemed compliant for PCI DSS purposes.

Just like with truncated PAN, we can use a token (from a validated solution) without fear of contamination and take it out of the CDE.

The PCI SSC published an information supplement in 2011 [56], and a draft revision is available to assessors (but has yet to be officialised). A new set of product guidelines [57] (recommendations, not a standard) was released in March 2015. You should consult your assessor before committing to any particular tokenization solution.

2.6.4 Encryption

Encryption is often mentioned by people as a way to reduce scope, but there are many limitations inherent with it. Encryption is one approved way of storing PAN. The resulting encrypted information is still in-scope, as opposed with truncated or tokenized PANs.

2.6.4.1 The PCI DSS FAQ on Encryption

FAQ 1086 (How does encrypted cardholder data impact PCI DSS scope?) provides all the information we need, but this FAQ is often poorly understood. The PCI SSC updated this FAQ during the final revision of the August 2016 revision of the book and this section has been updated based on the August 2016 updated FAQ.

The answer to whether encrypted data is out-of-scope is generally negative if the organization (called entity in the FAQ) can decrypt the information. These following portions of the FAQ make this clear:

Use of encryption in a merchant environment does not remove the need for PCI DSS in that environment. The merchant environment is still in scope for PCI DSS due to the presence of cardholder data. For example, in a card-present environment, merchants have physical access to the payment cards in order to complete a transaction and may also have paper reports or receipts with cardholder data. Similarly, in card-not-present environments, such as mail-order or telephone-order, payment card details are provided via channels that need to be evaluated and protected according to PCI DSS.

Encryption of cardholder data with strong cryptography is an acceptable method of rendering the data unreadable in order to meet PCI DSS Requirement 3.4. However, encryption alone may not be sufficient to render the cardholder data out of scope for PCI DSS. [58]

The new FAQ highlights clear cases where encrypted data in scope:

- *Systems performing encryption and/or decryption of cardholder data, and systems performing key management functions*
- *Encrypted cardholder data that is not isolated from the encryption and decryption and key management processes*
- *Encrypted cardholder data that is present on a system or media that also contains the decryption key*
- *Encrypted cardholder data that is present in the same environment as the decryption key*
- *Encrypted cardholder data that is accessible to an entity that also has access to the decryption key* [59]

Where this gets messier is when a third-party provider is involved in the process (managed provider or not). But this too has been addressed in the updated FAQ:

Where a third party receives and/or stores only data encrypted by another entity, and where they do not have the ability to decrypt the data, the third party may be able to consider the encrypted data out of scope if certain conditions are met. For further guidance, refer to FAQ 1233: How does encrypted cardholder data impact PCI DSS scope for third-party service providers? [60]

The most common case where encryption does work to reduce scope happens when backup tapes are encrypted and sent to an offsite storage provider, while the keys remain with the organization. Since the storage provider does not have the keys, only physical security and inventory management controls (all part of requirement 9) are applicable for the provider.

I have seen many try to argue that a third-party provider (and not the entity) is the one that has access to the keys, processes and clear text data; this may be the case if everything is outsourced, but barring that I would question that assumption. Ultimately however, someone, the entity or the provider (or both), is in scope for the encrypted data and the encryption process and keys.

Stored CHD is subject to the key management requirements (3.4.1, 3.5.*, 3.6.*). These requirements will be described in section 3.7.3.1 of volume 3.

Transmitted CHD must be sent securely on networks not owned by the organization as required in requirement 4.1 [61]. This is often accomplished through TLS connections (SSL, the previous version that became TLS, is no longer considered secure and must be phased out by July 1, 2018. Initially, PCI DSS 3.1 released in April 2015 had put that date at June 30, 2016 but this was changed by an update published by the PCI SSC on December 18, 2015 [62]. These changes were included in appendix A2 of PCI DSS 3.2). Clear text CHD would contaminate the systems they traverse, that portion was already confirmed in section 2.5.1.1. But if a point-to-point TLS connection exists between two systems within the network while traversing other devices (routers, switches), and these devices do not have access to the encryption keys (and certificate) or the encryption process, then what does remain is the ability to capture traffic. Which means that these would not become CDE/CHD systems themselves, but if they could have an impact on security of this traffic they would remain in-scope as either a CDE/contaminated, Segmenting (my preference) or "connected" systems.

This is not the case for a proxy which can inspect the traffic sent; such a device would become a CDE/CHD system since it can decrypt the traffic.

2.6.4.2 Use of P2PE solutions

For transmission of encrypted CHD, there is a special case of an already approved solution to reduce scope which is available to merchants: P2PE. Point-to-point encryption (P2PE) solutions are an already validated solution (by a P2PE QSA) where the provider of the solution (generally a payment processor and/or acquirer) manages all the encryption keys. The application side is fully managed by the provider who also provides payment devices to the merchant as part of the service.

Since the provider manages the keys of the devices that encrypt transaction, then only the provider can decrypt the information. Thus, the traffic from this device does not bring the merchant network into scope. This technology can substantially reduce merchants' compliance costs.

Version 2.0 of the P2PE standard was released in July 2015. As of June 2016, there were only 20 approved solutions available on the PCI council website. As of September 2017, there are 41. We are slowly seeing more solutions emerge. When feasible for an organization, P2PE is one of the best options for reducing scope and therefore compliance costs.

2.6.5 Remote Desktop solutions - One or two steps removed?

The goal here is to reduce scope through the use of a remote desktop environment (MS terminal services, MS Remote Desktop, Citrix, VNC, etc.) often called a VDI (Virtual Desktop Infrastructure). This would be accomplished if we can convert the end user device from a CDE/CHD system to a 'connected' system.

A VDI device receives keystrokes, mouse movements and clicks from the remote user but what is seen on the end-user device is generally sent back as images (the portion of the screen that changes). A study of the RFB (Remote Frame Buffer) technology used for the VNC protocol over a decade ago gave me a glimpse into how this works. There are some complex techniques used to make this more efficient and responsive, but for our purpose, let us consider that other than the keystrokes typed and mouse events from the end-user, everything sent back from the VDI is an image.

There is some debate within the PCI community around exactly what is possible and required to achieve scope reduction with remote desktop solutions. There is no clear consensus and very little information currently available from the council. The one piece of agreed upon info is that a VPN (meaning strong encryption - see encryption primer in appendix 3 for more on this, and two-factor authentication as required in requirements 8.3.* for remote access that "could lead to access to the CDE" - same rule as for connected systems) brings the network "in-between" the two endpoints out of scope, while the individual PC initiating the connection is considered in-scope. Many have taken to say that if such a VPN connection was made and terminated at a remote desktop, then the individual end device would convert to a connected system.

How would an attack work on a VDI connection?

A good way to determine where a VDI and its connected user fall into scope is by going back to the question of whether the systems "*may impact the security of the CDE*"[63], meaning to look at how an attacker would target such a connection.

If an attacker is able to intercept the traffic, then it can do two things. First, it can easily capture the keystrokes sent which, if the VDI is used to input CHD, can get him the information he seeks. Note that capturing the keystrokes, even if they do not have CHD in them, can still give an attacker very valuable information such as usernames and passwords. So the end system must remain in-scope, at least as a "connected" system.

Second, the attacker can capture the images sent back, reconstitute the stream (the protocols used are generally well known), and either manually record the valuable information on the screen or use screen OCR (Optical Character Recognition, the mechanical or electronic conversion of images of typewritten or printed text into machine-encoded text [64]) to grab text and attempt to identify CHD. While this second option is not easily achievable by unskilled attackers (script kiddies), these are not the ones we are most worried about (organized crime and state actors should be our biggest worries).

To determine how the various systems fall into scope, the main factors we need to take into account are:

- whether CHD is present in the process, and if so, the volume of card information (the number of transactions) transferred
- the controls in place which may prevent things such as copy-paste

- the encryption levels between the user system and the remote desktop (default encryption levels for many solutions are not adequate).

There is little debate a VDI works to reduce scope when the user cannot get access to CHD. Thus, such a method generally works well to provide access to administrators (which reduces risks since the desktop used in the VDI is more heavily constrained) provided that they cannot see CHD (which should be stored encrypted, tokenized, hashed or truncated, as per requirement 3.4). But 'live' information can sometimes be seen if an administrator is debugging something through some method which may involve logging (normal log data should still follow the previously mentioned 3.4). Such exceptions should be properly documented (often a ticket system is used to request the administrator perform certain actions and to keep all relevant information) and any temporary logs should be purged when the task is complete (or at least dealt with as per requirement 3.4).

If a VDI user's role includes entering CHD into the VDI via his system then when we generally take the number of transactions into account to determine if we can rule it out of the CDE. If the user inputs a few numbers a day, then such a method as described earlier may be deemed adequate in reducing scope (provided that encryption and other controls are in place). Note that the input system is still in scope as a connected system. But in the case of end-user (input) devices whose primary role is to deal with CHD (think call centers, bank tellers, etc.), then it gets trickier. I would contend that if they do handle many such actions (and that number may vary per QSA) those should always be considered 'CDE/CHD' systems.

Note that accidental access does not generally bring back the end-user in scope, and this should be considered an incident. I've seen cases where a client sent an email containing CHD (unsolicited by the organization), or a system (incorrectly configured) is generating logs with CHD. Unless this was intentional, it should be considered an incident and managed as an exception. The organization still needs to manage the exception and ensure it deletes the offending data as well as attempt to prevent it from occurring again (for example by educating clients as to proper ways to send information).

Ultimately, you need to validate with your QSA if they will accept using VDI such a method for reducing scope, and under what particular conditions (and configurations).

2.7 Advanced Scoping

The PCI SSC publishes many information supplements. Two such guidelines (meaning they are only recommendations) have a major impact on scoping and are interrelated. The "PCI DSS Virtualization Guidelines" was released back in 2011 [65]. And in February 2013, the "PCI DSS Cloud Computing Guidelines" [66] was also released. A new Special Interest Group (SIG) is expected to update the Cloud guidelines turning it into "Cloud Computing" in late 2017 or shortly after. This section defines and condenses what falls into scope according to my understanding of these guidelines (and my expectations going forward).

Since the cloud is basically just a form of outsourced virtualization, we'll delve on virtualization first and then use these same notions for the cloud.

2.7.1 Virtualization

Virtualization allows us to separate systems and applications from the underlying physical hardware. Virtualization has many benefits and few drawbacks. Virtualization allows for more efficient use of hardware as you can share a more powerful machine to run multiple applications independently of each other. It can allow for easy migration of a system to new or more powerful hardware, and even automatic transfer of functions (using synchronization) to a backup system for business continuity and disaster recovery (BC/DR). The downside is that the segmentation within virtualization technologies is often not as clear as with physically separate systems (but as with any technology this is improving over time, such as offering micro-segmentation). This is why virtualization has an impact on PCI DSS scope, mainly on its use of CDE systems.

2.7.1.1 Virtualization Concepts

Virtualization is actually a very old technology that dates back to the mainframe areas of the 1960s where the goal was initially to allow for multiple users, and then multiple customers. IBM was a big proponent of virtualization way before companies like VMware came along and popularized it in the mainstream. Virtualization can also exist for network devices, storage and even memory. As there are so many types and variations of virtualization available, I will mostly address system virtualization in this book.

Virtualization allows for the abstraction of computing resources. There are many approaches to virtualization that we will cover next. Before we get to technical details, I'd like to define a few of the terms that I'll use as they relate to virtualization:

- host : the system (hardware of software) where the hypervisor runs
- hypervisors : the application that allows for virtualization of systems
- VM : acronym for virtual machine, the individual "abstract" system that runs on an hypervisor

2.7.1.2 Hardware vs Software virtualization

Other than mainframe virtualization, hardware virtualization is the most commonly used form in today's infrastructure. The most common hardware virtualization solutions are offered by VMware, Xen (Citrix), and Hyper V (Microsoft). Virtualbox is another option from Oracle (part of the Sun Microsystems acquisition) that has free options but, in my experience, is less used in commercial production environments. Most mainframes also provide some form of virtualization, but those are not covered in this book.

A virtualization solution creates a virtual hardware system called a virtual machine (VM) where an operating system (Windows, Linux, etc.) is installed as it would be on physical hardware.

That VM runs on an application host called a Hypervisor. The hypervisor supports running multiple VMs, limited only by the resources (memory, processor, disk space) that are available. The hypervisor can be run directly on the hardware (and include its own specialized operating system). These are often called "Native", "Standalone" or "Bare Metal". The most common products include VMware ESXi, Citrix Xen and Microsoft HyperV. Native hypervisors are the most common ones used in corporate production environments. On bigger hardware (e.g. farms of blade servers), you can actually have multiple hypervisors running on shared hardware.

The other server hypervisor type is an application that runs on top of an existing operating system as a regular application. This is referred to as a "hosted" hypervisor. Examples include VMware Server and Virtualbox. There are other hypervisor applications that are made to be run on individual computers, but not servers. They include VMware Workstation (Windows, Linux), VMware Fusion (on Mac), Parallels (on Mac).

Whichever hypervisor type is used, similar implications exist in term of virtualization. If we go back to our scoping model, we know that we need to isolate our CDE/CHD systems using Segmenting systems. We can also quickly realise that "connected" systems are not an issue as these can be mixed with out-of-scope systems. So virtualization is only an issue if used for CDE systems.

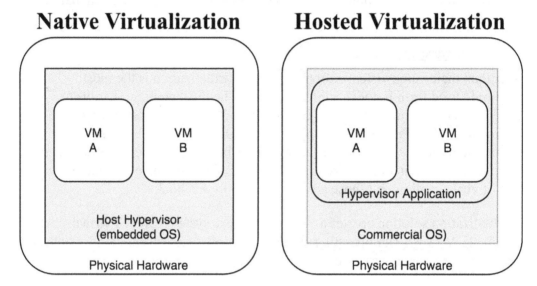

Volume 2 Figure 11 - Native vs hosted virtualization

The basic rules that the PCI DSS virtualization guidelines mentions (they state it more as a "strong recommendation" than an outright obligation) is that CDE system should not be mixed with non-CDE systems ("connected" and out-of-scope) on the same hypervisor. Such a configuration would be called "mixed-mode" and should be avoided. This is because there are known issues, for example escaping from containment and re-entry from one VM to the hypervisor. Re-entry (or escape) may be possible since resources (memory, networking) are shared and full physical segmentation is generally not possible within certain virtualized environments.

Virtualization Re-entry

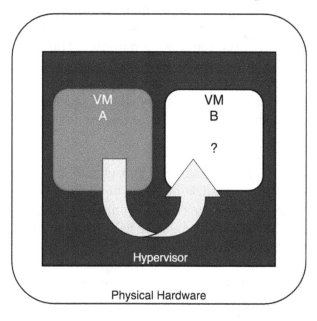

Volume 2 Figure 12 - Virtual Machine re-entry

Let's start with the simplest example, a single hypervisor running 2 VMs. VM A
has CHD so it becomes a CDE/CHD system. The hypervisor, lacking
segmentation from VM A will be contaminated. The hypervisor has some access
to the resources (memory, networking, storage) that it provides for VM A's usage.
The hypervisor can act as the Segmenting device if configured appropriately. VM
B, running on the CDE hypervisor must be treated, per PCI DSS guidelines, as a
CDE/contaminated system since adequate segmentation is hard to demonstrate.
An organization can choose to attempt to prove effective segmentation by
ensuring that the penetration test include the 11.3.4 requirement, but many QSAs
will not accept this. This non-acceptable "mixed-mode" leads to the system being
included in the CDE. The alternative is to ensure that only CDE systems run on
the same hypervisor, and that another hypervisor be used for connected and out-
of-scope systems.

2.7.1.3 Operating-system-level (Container) virtualization

As I wrote the initial version of this section, Docker had become all the rage with developers. This has now increased to include Kubernetes as well (and others), with details on which is better being mostly irrelevant for our purposes. This is also a form of virtualization that has existed for a while. On Unix/Linux, chroot is a well known earlier form of this technology, as well as other 'jail' systems. This type of technology also includes specific platform support for HP-UX (SRP Containers), AIX (WPARs), Solaris (Zones). It is also used for mobile device virtualization (Apple iOS, Android).

The VM equivalents in this case are often called containers. This type of technology is similar to a hosted hypervisor virtualization, but with the difference that it is the underlying host that is shared. This means that all containers share the same version of the host operating system (kernel), but that specific application binaries and configurations can vary per container.

The advantage of such a mode is that it is much lighter weight (on resources) than standard virtualization, but this comes at a cost of even less segmentation. If even one of the containers is a CDE/CHD system, then the whole system (host and containers) must be treated as CDE systems.

Native Virtualization

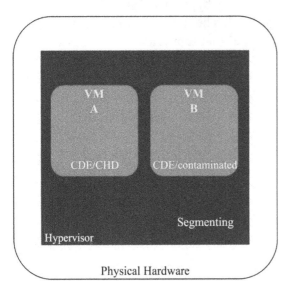

Volume 2 Figure 13 - Virtualization simplest configuration example

Operating System Level Virtualization

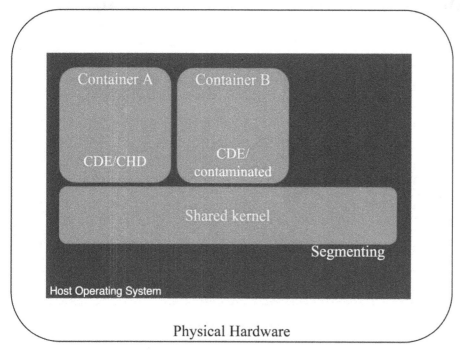

Volume 2 Figure 14 - Operating system level virtualization

Remember that you can create container-based virtualization within hardware or software based virtualization, which can definitely increase complexity, but may help address segmentation issues.

Virtualized web-server containing CDE isolated using hardware virtualization

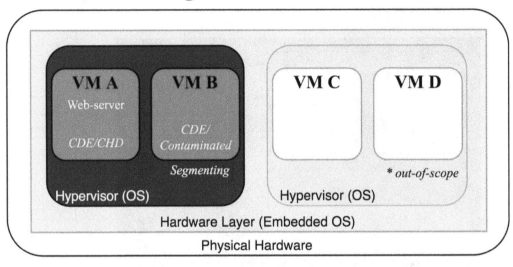

Volume 2 Figure 15 - Virtualized web-server container CDE isolated using hardware virtualization

2.7.1.4 Security considerations in the 2013 Cloud Computing information supplement

While Cloud Computing will be covered in the next section, some elements that apply to virtualization (which is a key component of cloud computing) were presented in the February 2013 information supplement on cloud computing.

Segmentation

The supplement covers segmentation in sections 4.4 through 4.4.3. It clearly states: "*Segmentation on a cloud-computing infrastructure must provide an equivalent level of isolation as that achievable through physical network separation.* "[67] Although cloud computing is mentioned, this is also the litmus test for any virtual environment. So an organization must "ensure that their environment is adequately isolated from the other client environments. [68] In terms of clouds or hosting providers, that assurance is made by the provider, whereas in internal environments this would be validated by the organization. Ultimately however, responsibility that validation has been performed (by someone) rests on the organization demonstrating compliance.

In section 4.4.1, the recommendation is made to use a "*dedicated CDE hypervisor*"[69] to simplify the issue of segmentation (which is made more complex in cloud environments than in private hosting). Dedicating the hypervisor to the CDE systems (no mixed-mode) is also what many QSAs I've spoken to use as minimal guidelines.

Section 4.4.3 details examples of technologies (firewall, switches, routers) but also list a series of controls that organizations should evaluate in virtualization and cloud environments to confirm whether segmentation exists. Some of these can (and likely should) be considered as compensating controls that ensure segmentation. They range from network controls (network segmentation, etc.) to monitoring tools (IDS, DLP) and logical access controls (segregation of duties, two-factor authentication).

Introspection

Introspection is covered in section 6.5.4 [70] of the cloud computing supplement. Introspection is a functionality allowing an hypervisor to control, inspect and monitor the content of one or more of its VMs (memory, hard disk, network traffic, etc.). This functionality is often used for security services on the host. But it can also allow for bypassing logical access controls (requirements 7 and 8) without leaving an evidence of actions performed (requirement 10, logging and monitoring). This can make it hard to achieve the required segmentation if one of the VMs under the hypervisor is a 'CDE/CHD' system. The hypervisor could thus become a 'CDE/CHD' system. For me, the hypervisor running the 'CDE/CHD' VMs will always be at least a 'Segmenting' system for that specific reason.

2.7.2 Cloud Computing

Cloud computing is the logical evolution and combination of server and Internet hosting (which has existed for over 20 years) and virtualization. The February 2013 information supplement by the PCI SSC provides guidelines on what to consider when evaluating the potential use of cloud services in PCI DSS environment. While it was written for version 2.0 of PCI DSS, it incorporates many elements that were later included in version 3.0 and other subsequent information supplements. I'll outline some of the most important things to keep in mind, but I urge the reader to read the 50 page document should they really consider using this type of service. The information supplement also adds clarifications to the virtualization guidelines described in the previous section (and while an update is expected late 2017, I don't expect this to alter my understanding of this issue or have major impacts on this section).

The first element to keep in mind is that a cloud service provider (CSP) is first and foremost a third-party service provider and subject to requirements 12.8.* of PCI DSS. And reminding us that while we can outsource tasks and responsibilities, accountability for compliance remains with the entity. The supplement clearly says this:

> *The allocation of responsibility between client and provider for managing security controls does not exempt a client from the responsibly of ensuring that their cardholder data is properly secured according to applicable PCI DSS requirements.* [71]

For more on this, please review section 2.6.1 and the "Third-Party Security Assurance v1.1" information supplement. As with any portion of this document, the CSP is only in-scope if it is part of the CDE and/or it can affect the security of the CDE or CHD/SAD. If not, I would recommend you still consider the risks of this CSP on your information and environments, but not in-scope for PCI DSS.

As with any technology, not all cloud offerings are created equal. Let's start with a definition. The supplement uses the NIST definition of cloud computing:

> *Cloud computing provides a model for enabling on-demand network access to a shared pool of computing resources (for example: networks, servers, storage, applications, and services) that can be rapidly provisioned and released with minimal management effort or cloud provider interaction.* [72]

There are many deployment models. The main ones being:

- Private cloud - all infrastructure is operated for a single client; this is similar to traditional hosting, but using virtualization
- Community cloud - infrastructure is shared between different clients of a similar type (e.g. industry, use case)
- Public cloud - infrastructure is shared between different clients but open to anyone
- Hybrid cloud - a mix of two or more of the above types

Then we have service models, which have seen more ink:

- Software as a Service (SaaS) - This is simply an application made available generally over the web; Salesforce (a CRM, Customer Relationship Management solution) is often used as an example, but any webmail, portal, etc. also falls into this category.
- Platform as a Service (PaaS) - This is an environment where organizations can create applications and leverage libraries from the provider. Salesforce Force.com platform, Google App Engine, Amazon Web Services are all examples of these.
- Infrastructure as a Service (IaaS) - This is the most similar to a VM (and sometimes actually is one); this is where the customer has the most control over the environment; Examples include Amazon EC2, Rackpace OpenStack, etc.

The difference between the different deployment and service models is who, between the CSP and client, is responsible for which controls. This is the crux of using any service provider and requirement 12.8.5 since PCI DSS 3.0, expressly states that the responsibilities for each of the PCI DSS requirements (CSP, client, shared) must be formally defined. This, and the service provider's compliance with PCI DSS for its in-scope requirements need to be evaluated annually (12.8.4). Appendix C of the supplement gives an example of what a matrix of responsibilities could look like:

PCI DSS Requirement	Responsibility (CSP only, client only, or shared)	Specific coverage/ scope of client responsibly	Specific coverage/ scope of CSP responsibility	How and when CSP will provide evidence of compliance to Client
1.1 Establish firewall and router configuration standards that include the following:				
1.1.1 A formal process for approving and testing all network connections and changes to the firewall and router configurations				
1.1.1 A formal process for approving and testing all network connections and changes to the firewall and router configurations				
1.1.2 Current network diagram with all connections to cardholder data, including any wireless networks				

Volume 2 Figure 16 - PCI DSS Cloud Computing Guidelines - Appendix C

As alluded to earlier, the level of control varies with deployment and service models. For PCI DSS, it would be hard to get any assessor to accept anything but a private cloud as an acceptable deployment model. Some examples may be possible, but I would advise only engaging services from providers that have validated their PCI DSS compliance (most of the big ones already have). This means looking at the different offerings that a provider offers, and picking services that have been validated as compliant. The CSP should have documentation describing which requirements they have certified, and either provide you with a RoC, or be present of payment card approved service provider lists for the specified service offering (see companion website at www.pciresources.com) .

The number of requirements you will be responsible for will vary mostly based on service models. For SaaS, the CSP will likely be on the hook for most of the requirements. Generally the client will have a responsibility for provisioning user accounts, or a subset of requirements 7 and 8. PaaS will likely be somewhere in the middle, where as IaaS will see the CSP covering the least, often physical security (requirement 9), portions of the firewall (requirement 1) and portions of hardening (requirement 2).

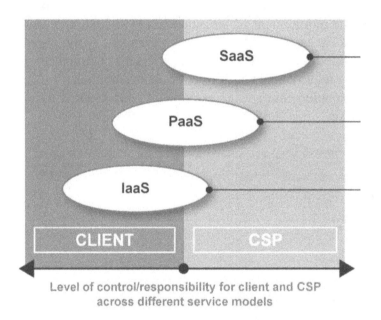

Level of control/responsibility for client and CSP
across different service models

Volume 2 Figure 17 - Cloud level of control/responsibility for client and CSP across different service models [73]

Another way to look at this is from a "stack" perspective, looking at the different layers involved in an application. Appendix B of the supplement presents a sample inventory that partly matches what is presented in figure 2 of the document. In the following table, I show the basic layers about who is generally responsible for each in the 3 service modes and in case of server hosting (not cloud):

	SaaS	PaaS	IaaS	Server hosting
User Management	Client	Client	Client	Client
Presentation - GUI or API	Provider	Client	Client	Client
Application	Provider	Client	Client	Client
Middleware (Solution or Programming Stack)	Provider	Provider	Client	Client
Operating System (OS)	Provider	Provider	Client	Client
Virtual Machine (VM)	Provider	Provider	Client	Client
Virtual Networking	Provider	Provider	Provider / Shared	Provider / Shared
Hypervisor	Provider	Provider	Provider	Provider / Shared
Processing/Memory	Provider	Provider	Provider	Provider
Data Storage	Provider	Provider	Provider	Provider
Network Devices	Provider	Provider	Provider	Provider
Physical facilities	Provider	Provider	Provider	Provider

Volume 2 Table 6 - Example of how control may be assigned between CSP and clients across different service models [74]

All this is great if we are dealing with a single service provider that manages all of their controls. But sometimes these organizations will use service providers themselves. This condition is called nested service-provider relationships. The important thing to remember is to ensure that the nested service provider must also be covered by the requirements. So, as with any contract relationship and technology offering, make sure you check the fine print and account for all the details.

Due to the complexity of achieving segmentation, the first recommendation of the supplement in section 4.5 is to not use cloud computing for any portion of the CDE. This is obviously the safest approach from a compliance standpoint. If you have to use the cloud for the CDE, the supplement recommends (and I would almost say mandates, though these are guidelines and not a standard) using a dedicated physical infrastructure. Ultimately, if you decide to go down the cloud computing path for any use in your CDE, you should confirm with your assessor and keep detailed records of information and opinions given. And please review the guidance of the information supplement.

2.7.3 Converged Infrastructure

More and more we see offerings and usage of a new type of infrastructure from many existing (Cisco, HPE, etc.) and new providers (Nutanix, etc.). Wikipedia describes it as follows:

Converged infrastructure operates by grouping multiple information technology (IT) components into a single, optimized computing package. Components of a converged infrastructure may include servers, data storage devices, networking equipment and software for IT infrastructure management, automation and orchestration. [75]

Some also call it "Hyperconvergence". Most of these mean that in large chassis you will find a mix of networking devices, storage arrays and computing resources tailored to the customer's needs. In a sense, it's the evolution of blade systems with NAS/SANs and networking for better performance. For scoping and network segmentation purposes, the same approach applies but again the devils may lie in the detail. I encourage the reader to check with their assessor and to document their implementation thoroughly.

2.7.4 Serverless computing (APIs)

More organizations are using Cloud-based APIs from the major vendors (Amazon Web Services, Google Cloud Platform, Microsoft Azure) as well as from newer startups. I can definitely see the value for organizations (I am very interested for personal projects), but this is not something that should be considered for anything related to PCI DSS (unless your particular provider has made that particular solution PCI DSS compliant). The boundaries for who is responsible for what are not clear. This does not mean an organization cannot use those services, only that they should not use them for anything PCI DSS related (and that potentially includes connected systems).

2.7.5 Software-Defined Networking (SDN) and virtualized networks

Wikipedia defines SDN as:

an approach to computer networking that allows network administrators to programmatically initialize, control, change, and manage network behavior dynamically via open interfaces[1] and abstraction of lower-level functionality. SDN is meant to address the fact that the static architecture of traditional networks doesn't support the dynamic, scalable computing and storage needs of more modern computing environments such as data centers. This is done by decoupling or disassociating the system that makes decisions about where traffic is sent (the SDN controller, or control plane) from the underlying systems that forward traffic to the selected destination (the data plane). [76]

In a sense, SDN is just an evolution of networking to enable more efficient virtualization, where we separate routing and access rules (control plane) from the actual actions (or decisions, on the data plane). As such, the same controls that apply at the network layer for PCI DSS (mostly in requirement 1) will apply much the same way. Most systems in the SDN infrastructure would be classified as either a segmenting or connected (of the 3 subtypes) system. Such an architecture may require some specific network and data flow diagrams for the SDN architecture (the regular network diagrams would likely be logical), with security built in with the SDN architecture.

2.7.6 Micro-segmentation

Micro-segmentation is another technology that is rising with the evolution of virtualization and the cloud. Micro-segmentation basically means that each individual (virtual) system can have its own personal firewall (at the NIC, Network Interface) and be isolated within its bubble. This can drastically reduce horizontal attacks (attacks between systems in the same network zone or segment). The downside is that ACLs rules can become unwieldy, requiring the use of management console, and of programming APIs. With micro-segmentation (and sometimes SDN), network admins can merge with software developers. This is powerful, but as SpiderMan thought us: "With great power comes great responsibility". I am bullish on this technology improving security, but as with anything, the devil will lie in the details.

2.7.7 Mobile payment devices as terminal

The Verizon PCI compliance report of 2017 covers the ever more present generic mobile payment devices (Apple iPhone and iPad, Android type devices) that are available to merchants to use as payment terminals. For PCI DSS scoping purposes, unless these devices are P2PE (and to my knowledge none support this at the moment), we need to treat them just like any other generic computer, also including requirements 9.9.* covering tampering. Those devices should thus be dedicated to that function alone (meaning you should not install any other application, such as games, email) and adequately locked down. Often these devices will use an additional payment adapter providing a mix of swipe, chip-and-pin, and sometimes even tap-and-pay payments. Both the mobile device and the adapter must follow all PCI DSS requirements. Please check with your assessor to ensure you are doing things in a secure and compliant manner.

2.7.8 Non-covered technologies

In future editions, if there is demand for it, I may choose to cover other advanced topics.

End Notes - Volume 2

[1] PCI Security Standards Council (2016). Payment Card Industry Data Security Standard - Requirements and Security Assessment Procedures - Version 3.2. Retrieved May 31, 2016, from https://www.pcisecuritystandards.org/documents/PCI_DSS_v3-2.pdf.

[2] PCI Security Standards Council (2015). PCI DSS Designated Entities Supplemental Validation For use with PCI DSS v3.1. Retrieved July 2, 2015, from https://www.pcisecuritystandards.org/documents/PCI_DSS_v3_DESV.pdf.

[3] PCI Security Standards Council (2013). RSA Conference - Less is more PCI DSS Scoping demystified. Retrieved July 2, 2015, from https://www.rsaconference.com/writable/presentations/file_upload/dsp-w21.pdf.

[4] PCI Security Standards Council (2015). FAQs. Retrieved July 2, 2015, from https://www.pcisecuritystandards.org/faq/.

[5] PCI Security Standards Council (2014). Best Practices for Maintaining PCI DSS Compliance. Retrieved July 2, 2015, from https://www.pcisecuritystandards.org/documents/PCI_DSS_V3.0_Best_Practices_for_Maintaining_PCI_DSS_Compliance.pdf.

[6] PCI Security Standards Council (2011). Protecting Telephone-based Payment Card Data - PCI ... Retrieved July 2, 2015, from https://www.pcisecuritystandards.org/documents/protecting_telephone-based_payment_card_data.pdf.

[7] PCI Security Standards Council (2016). Information Supplement: Third-Party Security Assurance v1.1. Retrieved May 31, 2016, from https://www.pcisecuritystandards.org/documents/ThirdPartySecurityAssurance_March2016_FINAL.pdf.

[8] PCI Security Standards Council (2013). PCI DSS Cloud Computing Guidelines. Retrieved July 13, 2015, from https://www.pcisecuritystandards.org/pdfs/PCI_DSS_v2_Cloud_Guidelines.pdf.

[9] PCI Security Standards Council (2011). PCI DSS Virtualization Guidelines. Retrieved July 13, 2015, from https://www.pcisecuritystandards.org/documents/Virtualization_InfoSupp_v2.pdf.

[10] Guidance for PCI DSS Scoping and Network Segmentation https://www.pcisecuritystandards.org/documents/Guidance-PCI-DSS-Scoping-and-Segmentation_v1_1.pdf.

[11] PCI Security Standards Council (2016, p.10). Payment Card Industry Data Security Standard - Requirements and Security Assessment Procedures - Version 3.2.

[12] PCI DSS only applies to cards that bear the logo of one of the 5 founding members of the SSC: Visa, MasterCard, American Express, Discover, JCB.

[13] Details will be discussed with "storage" requirement 3.4 in volume 3.

[14] PCI Security Standards Council (2015). Payment Card Industry Data Security Standard - Requirements and Security Assessment Procedures - Version 3.1.

[15] PCI Security Standards Council (2014). FAQ 1154. Public Knowledge Base - Is pre-authorization account data in scope for PCI DSS?. Retrieved July 2, 2015, from https://pcissc.secure.force.com/faq/articles/Frequently_Asked_Question/Is-pre-authorization-account-data-in-scope-for-PCI-DSS/.

[16] PCI Security Standards Council (2014). FAQ 1280. Public Knowledge Base - Can card verification codes/values be stored for recurring transactions?. Retrieved July 2, 2015, from https://pcissc.secure.force.com/faq/articles/Frequently_Asked_Question/Can-card-verification-codes-values-be-stored-for-recurring-transactions/.

[17] (IT Revolution, 2012). Open PCI Scoping Toolkit - IT Revolution. Retrieved July 2, 2015, from http://itrevolution.com/pci-scoping-toolkit/.

[18] PCI Security Standards Council (2016, p.10). Payment Card Industry Data Security Standard - Requirements and Security Assessment Procedures - Version 3.2.

[19] PCI Security Standards Council (2016, p.10). Payment Card Industry Data Security Standard - Requirements and Security Assessment Procedures - Version 3.2.

[20] PCI Security Standards Council (2016). ROC Reporting Template for v3.2. Retrieved May 31, 2016, from https://www.pcisecuritystandards.org/documents/PCI-DSS-v3_2-ROC-Reporting-Template.pdf.

[21] PCI Security Standards Council (2013, p.82). 2013 Community Meetings Assessor Slides.

[22] PCI Security Standards Council (2016, p.10). ROC Reporting Template for v3.2.

[23] PCI Security Standards Council (2016, p.16). ROC Reporting Template for v3.2.

[24] PCI Security Standards Council (2014). FAQ 1252. Public Knowledge Base - Do all PCI DSS requirements apply to every system component?. Retrieved July 2, 2015, from https://pcissc.secure.force.com/faq/articles/Frequently_Asked_Question/Do-all-PCI-DSS-requirements-apply-to-every-system-component/.

[25] PCI Security Standards Council (2016, p.10). Payment Card Industry Data Security Standard - Requirements and Security Assessment Procedures - Version 3.2.

[26] PCI Security Standards Council (2016, p.11). Payment Card Industry Data Security Standard - Requirements and Security Assessment Procedures - Version 3.2.

[27] PCI Security Standards Council (2016, p.11). Payment Card Industry Data Security Standard - Requirements and Security Assessment Procedures - Version 3.2.

[28] PCI Security Standards Council (2016, p.12). ROC Reporting Template for v3.2.

[29] PCI Security Standards Council (2016, p.11). Payment Card Industry Data Security Standard - Requirements and Security Assessment Procedures - Version 3.2.

[30] PCI Security Standards Council (2016, p.11). Payment Card Industry Data Security Standard - Requirements and Security Assessment Procedures - Version 3.2.

[31] PCI Security Standards Council (2013, p.23). RSA Conference - Less is more PCI DSS Scoping demystified.

[32] PCI Security Standards Council (2013, p.27). RSA Conference - Less is more PCI DSS Scoping demystified.

[33] PCI Security Standards Council (2013, p.23). RSA Conference - Less is more PCI DSS Scoping demystified.

[34] PCI Security Standards Council (2016, p.10). Payment Card Industry Data Security Standard - Requirements and Security Assessment Procedures - Version 3.2.

[35] PCI Security Standards Council (2013, p.23). RSA Conference - Less is more PCI DSS Scoping demystified.

[36] PCI Security Standards Council (2015). PCI DSS Designated Entities Supplemental Validation For use with PCI DSS v3.1.

[37] PCI Security Standards Council (2016, p.16). ROC Reporting Template for v3.2.

[38] PCI Security Standards Council (2016, p.8). PCI DSS Designated Entities Supplemental Validation For use with PCI DSS v3.2.

[39] PCI Security Standards Council (2016). ROC Reporting Template for v3.2.

[40] PCI Security Standards Council (2016, p.35). Payment Card Industry Data Security Standard - Requirements and Security Assessment Procedures - Version 3.2.

[41] PCI Security Standards Council (2016). Information Supplement: Third-Party Security Assurance. Retrieved July 2, 2016, from https://www.pcisecuritystandards.org/documents/ThirdPartySecurityAssurance_March2016_FINAL.pdf.

[42] PCI Security Standards Council (2016, p.1). Information Supplement: Third-Party Security Assurance v1.1.

[43] PCI Security Standards Council (2016, p.11). Payment Card Industry Data Security Standard - Requirements and Security Assessment Procedures - Version 3.2.

[44] PCI Security Standards Council (2016, p.11). Payment Card Industry Data Security Standard - Requirements and Security Assessment Procedures - Version 3.2.

[45] PCI Security Standards Council (2016, p.11). Payment Card Industry Data Security Standard - Requirements and Security Assessment Procedures - Version 3.2.

[46] PCI Security Standards Council (2016, p.11). Payment Card Industry Data Security Standard - Requirements and Security Assessment Procedures - Version 3.2.

[47] PCI Security Standards Council (2014). FAQ 1088. Public Knowledge Base - What is meant by "adequate network segmentation" in the PCI DSS?. Retrieved July 2, 2015, from https://pcissc.secure.force.com/faq/articles/Frequently_Asked_Question/What-is-meant-by-adequate-network-segmentation-in-the-PCI-DSS/.

[48] PCI Security Standards Council (2014). FAQ 1135. Public Knowledge Base - Can VLANS be used for network segmentation?. Retrieved July 2, 2015, from https://pcissc.secure.force.com/faq/articles/Frequently_Asked_Question/What-are-acceptable-formats-for-masking-of-primary-account-numbers-PAN/.

[49] PCI Security Standards Council (2014). FAQ 1135. Public Knowledge Base - Can VLANS be used for network segmentation?.

[50] Wikipedia (2011). Bank card number. Retrieved July 2, 2015, from https://en.wikipedia.org/wiki/Bank_card_number.

[51] Wikipedia (2011). Bank card number. Retrieved July 2, 2015, from https://en.wikipedia.org/wiki/Bank_card_number.

[52] PCI Security Standards Council (2014). FAQ 1146. Public Knowledge Base - What is the difference between masking and truncation?. Retrieved July 2, 2015, from https://pcissc.secure.force.com/faq/articles/Frequently_Asked_Question/What-is-the-difference-between-masking-and-truncation/.

[53] PCI Security Standards Council (2014). FAQ 1090. Public Knowledge Base - What are acceptable formats for masking of primary account numbers (PAN)?. Retrieved July 2, 2015, from https://pcissc.secure.force.com/faq/articles/Frequently_Asked_Question/What-are-acceptable-formats-for-masking-of-primary-account-numbers-PAN/.

[54] PCI Security Standards Council (2016, p.40). Payment Card Industry Data Security Standard - Requirements and Security Assessment Procedures - Version 3.2.

[55] Visa Europe (2011).Using the Visa Private BIN Range. Retrieved September 22, 2015, from http://www.visaeurope.com/media/images/12_using_the_visa_private_bin_range_-_best_practice_guide%20110615-73-24720.pdf.

[56] PCI Security Standards Council (2014). Information Supplement: PCI DSS Tokenization_Guidelines. Retrieved July 2, 2015, from https://www.pcisecuritystandards.org/documents/Tokenization_Guidelines_Info_Supplement.pdf.

[57] PCI Security Standards Council (2014). Information Supplement: PCI DSS Tokenization_Guidelines.

[58] PCI Security Standards Council (2016). FAQ 1086. Public Knowledge Base - How does encrypted cardholder data impact PCI DSS scope? Retrieved August 20, 2016, from https://pcissc.secure.force.com/faq/articles/Frequently_Asked_Question/How-does-encrypted-cardholder-data-impact-PCI-DSS-scope?q=1086.

[59] PCI Security Standards Council (2016). FAQ 1086. Public Knowledge Base - How does encrypted cardholder data impact PCI DSS scope?

[60] PCI Security Standards Council (2016). FAQ 1086. Public Knowledge Base - How does encrypted cardholder data impact PCI DSS scope?

[61] PCI Security Standards Council (2016, p.46). Payment Card Industry Data Security Standard - Requirements and Security Assessment Procedures - Version 3.2.

[62] PCI Security StandardsCouncil (2015). Date Change for Migrating from SSL and Early TLS. Retrieved January 4, 2016, from http://blog.pcisecuritystandards.org/migrating-from-ssl-and-early-tls.

[63] PCI Security Standards Council (2016, p.10). Payment Card Industry Data Security Standard - Requirements and Security Assessment Procedures - Version 3.2.

[64] Wikipedia (2011). Optical character recognition. Retrieved July 19, 2015, from https://en.wikipedia.org/wiki/Optical_character_recognition.

[65] PCI Security Standards Council (2011). PCI DSS Virtualization Guidelines.

[66] PCI Security Standards Council (2013). PCI DSS Cloud Computing Guidelines.

[67] PCI Security Standards Council (2013, p.12). PCI DSS Cloud Computing Guidelines.

[68] PCI Security Standards Council (2013, p.12). PCI DSS Cloud Computing Guidelines.

[69] PCI Security Standards Council (2013, p.13). PCI DSS Cloud Computing Guidelines.

[70] PCI Security Standards Council (2013, p.29). PCI DSS Cloud Computing Guidelines.

[71] PCI Security Standards Council (2013, p.1). PCI DSS Cloud Computing Guidelines.

[72] PCI Security Standards Council (2013, p.3). PCI DSS Cloud Computing Guidelines.

[73] PCI Security Standards Council (2013, p.5). PCI DSS Cloud Computing Guidelines.

[74] PCI Security Standards Council (2013, p.10). PCI DSS Cloud Computing Guidelines.

[75] Wikipedia (2011). Converged Infrastructure. Retrieved September 1, 2017, from https://en.wikipedia.org/wiki/Converged_infrastructure.

[76] Wikipedia (2011). SDN. Retrieved September 1, 2017, from https://en.wikipedia.org/wiki/Software-defined_networking.

Volume 3 - Building a PCI DSS Information Security Program

3.1 Volume Introduction

Welcome to volume 3 of this PCI book which leverages the work of volume 2 on how to determine what falls under PCI DSS scope. For details on how the standard came to be, who it applies to, and how and why you should care, please see volume 1.

This volume outlines an approach to compliance of all PCI DSS requirements using a standardized Information Security Program based on industry best practices, including the use of compensating controls when requirements cannot be met *"as stated"*.

The goal of information security should never be to block anything outright, but only to enable users to perform their legitimate business tasks in a secure fashion.

The goal of PCI DSS is to protect cardholder data from theft or unauthorized disclosure. This is our gold standard, the lens through which we will look at the PCI DSS requirements. And while the goal is to protect data, it is accomplished through measures on people, processes and technologies.

Note: Throughout this book/section, you will see me use many acronyms (including the already mentioned CHD, PAN, SAD). These are the most relevant ones for this section:

- CHD = Acronym for "Cardholder Data"; consists of the PAN, cardholder name, card expiration date, and sometimes service code
- PAN = Acronym for "Primary Account Number"; the card number printed on the front of the card.
- SAD = Acronym for "Sensitive Authentication Data", it includes the magnetic track information, the PIN or PIN block, as well as the Card-not-present authorization value which we will refer to as CVV2 but can take any of the following acronyms: CAV2/CVC2/CVV2/CID.
- SPT = An acronym for "Store, Process, or Transmit", meaning that a system or process comes into contact with CHD and/or SAD and is therefore automatically in scope.

- CDE = Acronym for "Cardholder Data Environment", basically what we are trying to protect, which starts with the systems that SPT CHD or SAD but is not limited to these.
- Isolation = There is no possible access between systems.
- Controlled Access = There are limited (restricted) communications possible between systems.
- RoC = Report on Compliance
- Policy = a high-level document identifying the problem addressed by the document, the goals (or objectives), the position of the organization, and assigning responsibilities (technical detail is to be found in procedures) - this document must provide the 'spirit' (as in 'spirit of the law') that individuals will use to ensure that they are meeting the objectives of the organization
- Procedure = these are the ordered steps that are to be followed for any given process (e.g. some form of checklist) - when followed, procedures allow for consistent operations (consistent, not necessarily adequate, complete or optimized)
- Standard = a model that defines how (versus the procedures that address the 'what') things must be done - typically used for configuration standards (i.e. which IP range to use) and device hardening standards
- 'Untrusted' networks = networks not under the control of the organization, often also called "open, public networks" such as the internet
- Issuer identification number (IIN) = previously called the 'Bank Identification Number' (BIN), the full first six digits of the PAN that represent the financial institution
- Identification Number' (BIN) = See Issuer identification number (IIN)
- DMZ (demilitarized zone) = a buffer zone between the internet and the internal network of an organization
- Designated Entities Special Validation (DESV) = PCI DSS Designated Entities Supplemental Validation for PCI DSS 3.1 (DESV) released in June 2015 - new set of requirements to increase assurance that an organization maintains compliance with PCI DSS over time, and that non-compliance is detected by a continuous (if not automated) audit process; this set of requirements applies to entities designated by the card brands or acquirers that are at a high risk level for the industry. DESV is now integrated as Appendix A3 in PCI DSS 3.2.
- Entity = An entity is any organization that has the responsibility to protect card data; for PCI DSS compliance an entity will be defined as either a merchant or a service provider.

A full glossary is provided at the end of the book and on the companion website.

The "PCI DSS Scoping Model and Approach" presented in volume 2 (and published on the www.pciresources.com website) is also required for consultation, as I reference there the different categories.

3.2 The High-Level PCI DSS requirements

The PCI DSS version 3.2 [1] standard released in April 2016 is used going forward in the volume. The PCI DSS 3.1 update published on December 18, 2015 [2] by the PCI SSC and integrated in appendix A2 had previously modified details of section 3.7.4.

Once our PCI DSS scope has been properly defined and hopefully reduced, the next step is to ensure that all 12 PCI DSS requirements and 200+ sub-requirements are met. Some of those requirements may be better met at either system, network or documentation level. I will describe the most appropriate scenarios when discussing each of those requirements.

Within the standard, the 12 PCI DSS high-level requirements are grouped into 6 different objectives that are not numbered. Most experienced professionals in PCI DSS refer to the 12 high-level requirements using a short-name (or description) that I added to table 1.

The 12 high-level requirements organized into these 6 categories provide one approach to structuring an Information Security Program. While this method can work, I prefer a slightly more granular approach.

	Objective / # Requirement	Short Name
	Build and Maintain a Secure Network	
1	Install and maintain a firewall configuration to protect cardholder data	*Firewall*
2	Do not use vendor-supplied defaults for system passwords and other security parameters	*Hardening*
	Protect Cardholder Data	
3	Protect stored cardholder data	*Storage*
4	Encrypt transmission of cardholder data across open, public networks	*Transmission*
	Maintain a Vulnerability Management Program	
5	Use and regularly update anti-virus software	*Antivirus*
6	Develop and maintain secure systems and applications	
	Implement Strong Access Control Measures	
7	Restrict access to cardholder data by business need-to-know	*Need-to-know*
8	Assign a unique ID to each person with computer access	*Authentication*
9	Restrict physical access to cardholder data	*Physical Security*
	Regularly Monitor and Test Networks	
10	Test and monitor all access to network resources and cardholder data	*Logging and Monitoring*
11	Regularly test security systems and processes	*Testing*
	Maintain an Information Security Policy	
12	Maintain a policy that addresses information security	*Policies*

Volume 3 Table 1 - PCI DSS High Level Overview [3]

I will go through all PCI DSS 3.2 requirements in later sections grouping them along related themes, mostly following the high-level requirements, but with small ordering changes to categories and requirements as needed to present a more methodical approach. Those themes are how I would create a PCI DSS Information Security Program for an organization where there are none in place.

3.3 Building a PCI DSS Information Security Program

3.3.1 Where you come from matters

I have worked with and within organizations big and small, and similar patterns often emerge in how they all approach and manage security. Challenges differ depending on the organization type and size. Universities, for example, generally have a decentralized power structure, while big organizations are more top-down in their decision making processes. Risk appetite also has an influence on how you build your information security program.

If you look at any single information security individual, the path (experience) that brought him to his role has a tremendous impact on how he will initially approach security, although this is changing as information security training is more and more incorporated in college level programs.

Some get into information security from a policy/governance side, often through a career or studies in administration or in management of information systems (MIS). It should be no surprise then that those individuals often start with crafting the governance structures, and then the policies. They choose <u>fashion over form</u>.

Others, myself included, come in with a more technical background. This used to be more someone who came up the networking ranks, or the system administrator route. My background was more in application development and system administration, and starting out, practical or technical controls were more my concern: <u>form over fashion</u>. In my first job as an Information Security Officer back in 2001, I taught myself what I needed to know and then configured the Cisco firewall (initially it provided no security), installed a proxy to manage internet traffic, wrote scripts to review (monitor) who went where on the web, etc. All these tasks were, at the time, more important than the policies.

Now neither approach is necessarily favored, as holistic security requires both the governance head and the procedural/technical body to achieve security (and I was the only one performing these tasks, which meant little coordination was necessary).

3.3.2 Information Security Programs are meant to address Risks

With larger organizations or as smaller ones grow and more people get involved with information security, the need for greater/better structure becomes a necessity for coordination purposes. This is where policies and procedures become a means of aligning people with repeatable processes and a shared outcome.

The goal of an Information Security Program should be to protect information (addressing 'confidentiality'). We should also include the protection of systems and infrastructure, which can extend to 'integrity' and 'availability', and include anything that can disrupt a business' activities (vandalism, disgruntled employees, etc).

The most critical thing for the success of an Information Security Program is what we generally refer to as the "tone at the top". Basically, we need the backing and support of the top brass; they must be convinced that protecting this information is important, or we run the risk of having our Information Security Program that reads like a "check the box" type that does not sufficiently address risks. Or as noted leadership trainer John E. Jones said: *"What gets measured gets done, what gets measured and fed back gets done well, what gets rewarded gets repeated"* [4].

The information security risks include what is often referred to as 'cyber security risks' (the technology aspect of information security), which I consider to be a subset of information security since 'cyber security risks' do not include the people and process areas of information security. But ultimately information security risks will be a subset of the risks faced by an organization, which generally include :

- Strategic – risks that would prevent an organization from accomplishing its objectives (meeting its goals).
- Financial – risks that could result in a negative financial impact for the organization (waste or loss of assets).
- Regulatory (compliance) – risks that could expose the organization to fines and penalties from a regulatory agency due to non-compliance with laws and regulations.
- Reputational – risks that could expose the organization to negative publicity.
- Operational – risks that could prevent the organization from working in the most effective and efficient manner or be disruptive to other operations. [5]

Compliance with PCI DSS addresses a regulatory risk, but the controls it requires to be put in place help address many of the other risks faced by the organization as well.

Ultimately, information security is about managing risk. The PCI DSS standard is just more specific about mandatory minimum control requirements than other frameworks. Section 3.5.2 will cover my understanding of what PCI DSS requires in a risk assessment.

3.3.3 Information Security Frameworks

Most comprehensive information security frameworks should be broad enough to support the PCI DSS requirements, though some specific controls and concepts may need to be addressed in the implementation detail.

Several comprehensive frameworks and standards may be used as the basis of an Information Security Program, or to review its completeness. Some of the most common information security frameworks include:

- ISO/IEC 27001/27002 [6] - The international standards have gone through many iterations and were initially derived from British standards derived themselves from UK public sector experience; these standards are often preferred by information security professionals, referenced in section 3.13.
- ITIL [7] (Information Technology Infrastructure Library) - is a set of practices for IT service management (ITSM) that focuses on aligning IT services with the needs of businesses (also derived from British government work); these standards are often preferred by IT professionals.
- COBIT [8] Control Objectives for Information and Related Technology) - a framework created by ISACA for information technology (IT) management and IT governance; ISACA (Information Systems Audit and Control Association) is a nonprofit, independent association that advocates for professionals involved in information security, assurance, risk management and governance; these standards are often preferred by auditors (IT auditors, internal and external auditors), referenced in section 3.14.
- NIST 800 [9] series publications - a series of technical of publications from the NIST (National Institute of Standards and Technology) which are mandatory for most US federal institutions, and often referred to by HIPAA [10] SOX (Sarbanes Oxley [11] and other US based regulations.

In section 3.13, I will map the PCI DSS high-level requirements onto the ISO/IEC 27001/27002 framework and discuss the differences between both. In section 3.14, I will do the same with COBIT 5. All individual controls provided by PCI DSS and other information security frameworks can be classified as:

- preventative
- detective
- corrective

Those three classifications are often referred to as the control triad, a term much used in all types of audits, including financial ones. This is to say that all requirements in PCI DSS (and any decent Information Security Program) will attempt to either:

- prevent non-acceptable behavior (internal or external)
- detect this non-acceptable behavior
- and correct this non-acceptable behavior over time.

3.4 The PCI DSS Information Security Program Structure

The governance of the program, addressed next in this volume, will be key for us to achieve our goals of protecting information. An organization's structure can have drastic impact on the value assigned to protecting information versus other organizational goals. Whatever the reporting structure however, a clear distribution of tasks between the different people involved, internal and external, is required. We'll get back to governance and organizational structure in the next section.

While PCI DSS is divided in 12 high-level requirements, I prefer to start from this basic question, "what are we trying to protect?" and move forward from there (the same approach taken in volume 2 on defining PCI DSS scope). And while I will outline this for CHD and SAD, this approach should work with any type of data.

We start first by identifying the types of data, which form our data classification. PCI DSS does not call for a data classification outright since it has already defined what information requires special care. It does however implicitly allude to it in requirements over data retention and disposal (3.1) and media classification (9.6.*).

3.4.1 Recapping the PCI DSS data elements

The PCI DSS standard and its requirements cover two types of data.

The first type of data in scope is the Cardholder Data (CHD) and it is the one most often mentioned. It includes the Primary Account Number (PAN), which is the 15 or 16 digit payment card number (credit or debit [12]), the cardholder name, card expiration date and service code (a number rarely mentioned anywhere else). The last 3 elements (name, expiration date, service code) are only in scope if the ('complete') PAN is present (more on this in section 2.6.3 of volume 2).

The other set of data is called Sensitive Authentication Data (SAD) and consists of the information on the magnetic strip (also often called magnetic track), the card-not-present authorization code (3 or 4 digit code at the back of the card - except for American Express where it is on the front - and that can bear any of the following names or acronyms: CAV2/CVC2/CVV2/CID), and the PIN or PIN block (if present). SAD must be even more carefully protected than the PAN and other CHD, and that fact is often sadly forgotten (pun intended).

	Data Elements	Storage Permitted	Protection Required	Render Unreadable
Cardholder Data (CHD)	Primary Account Number (PAN)	Yes	Yes	Yes
	Cardholder Name	Yes	Yes	No
	Service Code	Yes	Yes	No
	Expiration date	Yes	Yes	No
Sensitive Authentication Data (SAD)	Full Magnetic Stripe Data	No	N/A	N/A
	CAV2/CVC2/CVV2/CID	No	N/A	N/A
	PIN / PIN Block	No	N/A	N/A

Volume 3 Table 2 - PCI DSS data [13]

Volume 3 Figure 1 - Rendering of Credit Card (Front)

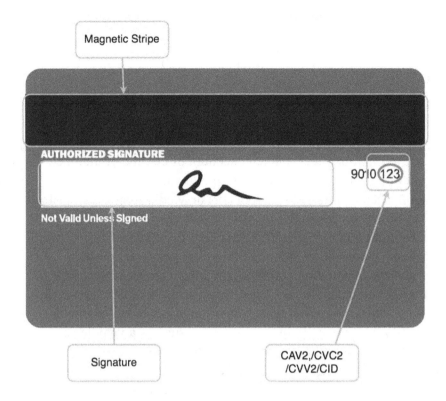

Volume 3 Figure 2 - Rendering of Credit Card (Back)

3.4.2 Data Classification

Most regulatory frameworks identify and classify information much like PCI DSS does. The HIPAA [14] (Health Information Privacy Accountability Act) defines PHI (Patient Health Information) that must be protected. Many privacy laws (state-based in the USA, The Privacy Act [15] and PIPEDA [16] in Canada, the European privacy directives [17] and GDPR [18]) define Personally Identifiable Information (PII), or Sensitive Personal Information (SPI) that must also be protected.

NIST Special Publication 800-122 [19] provides guidance on PII, and references a 2008 GAO (US Government Accountability Office) report to define PII as:

any information about an individual maintained by an agency, including (1) any information that can be used to distinguish or trace an individual's identity, such as name, social security number, date and place of birth, mother's maiden name, or biometric records; and (2) any other information that is linked or linkable to an individual, such as medical, educational, financial, and employment information.

It then goes out to give multiple examples of what this data may include [20]:

- Name, such as full name, maiden name, mother's maiden name, or alias
- Personal identification number, such as social security number (SSN), passport number, driver's license number, taxpayer identification number, patient identification number, and financial account or credit card number
- Address information, such as street address or email address
- Asset information, such as Internet Protocol (IP) or Media Access Control (MAC) address or other host-specific persistent static identifier that consistently links to a particular person or small, well-defined group of people
- Telephone numbers, including mobile, business, and personal numbers
- Personal characteristics, including photographic image (especially of face or other distinguishing characteristics), x-rays, fingerprints, or other biometric image or template data (e.g., retinal scan, voice signature, facial geometry)
- Information identifying personally owned property, such as a vehicle registration number or title number and related information
- Information about an individual that is linked or linkable to one of the above (e.g., date of birth, place of birth, race, religion, weight, activities, geographical indicators, employment information, medical information, education information, financial information).

Now the disclosure or theft of any information from the previous list does not always bring about the same level of risk, or impact to the affected individuals. For example, names, telephone and email addresses are generally considered less sensitive information than bank information or health information. Different types of data will thus have different levels of requirements for 'confidentiality', 'integrity' and 'availability' (often referred to as the C.I.A. triad of information security, with no relation to the 3-letter US agency that shares the same acronym).

And there are countless other examples of data that also requires protection in the myriads of regulated industries out there. Most organizations are subject not just to one, but to multiple of these regulations. It explains why most organizations develop a data classification that will be used to create policies and standards regarding the protection of information identified by these laws and regulations.

3.4.3 Examples of data classification

The number of categories and level of granularity found in data classifications is generally based on what is required by an organization. The adage to make things as simple as can be but never simpler (attributed by some to Albert Einstein [21]) is a good one to follow here.

Military data classification, portrayed in news, books and films, should be familiar to most people, and generally include categories such as 'Top Secret', 'Secret', 'Confidential', etc. [22]

It is very typical to see at least 3 major categories for all organizations: Classified or Restricted, Private and Public. Let's look at these basic ones in more detail.

'Restricted' is information, that if disclosed would cause significant harm to the organization through the risks identified in section 3.3.2. This category can include CHD and SAD (PCI data), Patient Health Information (PHI), more sensitive PII such as Social Security Numbers. It would also include trade secrets (think of the Coca Cola formula or proprietary source code).

'Private' is generally comprised of the internal work products that could have a limited negative impact on the organization if disclosed. This would generally include financial statements, client lists, and less sensitive PII data.

'Public' is information that is widely known and for which disclosure would have little impact on the organization. You may ask why we need a category for this type of information if it does not need protection. The reason is exactly so that you can inform people as to what not to focus energy on protecting (being that all organizations have limited resources, people and money). Already released financial information and press releases are all examples of publicly known information.

Often we'll see these top-line categories further divided; for example, we could have 'Restricted-PCI', 'Restricted-Health', 'Restricted-PII' (including bank data), 'Private-PII' (including emails, telephone) etc. This can allow an organization to define more granular controls that must be put in place for such a category.

To achieve PCI DSS compliance, we need to be able to match CHD and SAD to specific organization data classification categories (which could be simply a category called 'PCI data') all the way to the requirements mandated in policies (see section 3.5.3).

3.5 Governance

The Merriam-Webster dictionary defines governance as *"the way that a city, company, etc., is controlled by the people who run it"* [23].

Any organization with limited resources (pretty much all of them) must make trade-offs to balance between different internal departmental goals (sales vs production). Thus, no matter what area we look at, be that information security, PCI compliance, sales vs production, etc., to whom responsibilities are mandated (what level is this person at in the organization) and what authority this person has demonstrates the value an organization places on that particular area. This is also the case in information security where the role and position of the ultimate person in charge makes a huge difference.

There are many ways that organizations can and have assigned information security responsibilities. Here are a few common ones, starting from the highest level of importance assigned by the organization:

- As a C-level executive responding to the CEO, often under the term CISO (Chief Information Security Officer) or CSO (Chief Security Officer)
- As a director/manager responding to a non-IT C-level executive (the CFO or Chief-Risk Officer (CRO), Compliance chief, etc.)
- As a director/manager responding to the CIO or IT director
- As a manager with limited authority within a convoluted IT department

Obviously the higher the person stands in the organization, then the more visibility senior management, and likely board members, will have into the information security posture. In much the same way, the level of authority given to that individual will be key to the approach taken by the organization to possibly integrate security within all processes (which PCI DSS has included under the term Business-as-usual since version 3.0 [24]). The number of staff dedicated to security functions and their reporting structure is also telling of the importance assigned to this area.

Another item to consider is the department where that function is located. When the person responsible falls under the IT department, there can be some frictions between the rest of IT and Information Security. This kind of friction is inherent in any organization since different departments and roles have different responsibilities and are judged on different things. This is typical of sales (wanting to increase sales) vs production (trying to ensure they can actually produce what is sold) or purchasing, or even finance which may insist on certain levels of profit margins on products. This is normal, and as long as all perspectives are considered appropriately this should not be an issue. This type of friction explains why sometimes Information Security is placed with compliance or risk (not IT) as a 'check' (from checks and balances) to IT. This case can also address issues of separation of duties.

As a personal example, I have worked through conflicts with IT (telecom) in early portions of my career. The telecom engineer's goal was to provide connectivity (focus on availability) while mine was in protecting information through limiting accesses (focus on confidentiality). We both had the interest of the organization at heart, but also had different objectives. The role of our common boss was to be an arbiter when we could not compromise or resolve differences of opinions.

Sometimes the qualities and experience of the person in charge will have an impact on what level that person is placed at: the higher up, the more better communication skills are required (including explaining technical concepts to non-technical people without dumbing them down).

All of these possible role structures have pros and cons and should be considered by organizations based on needs, risk appetite, and skillset when they decide how to structure their organizations and where to assign responsibilities.

3.5.1 Responsibilities for the program

While PCI DSS compliance should not be addressed as an IT problem, it is still very technical (IT) in nature and many responsibilities will fall to technical staff. I generally recommend that one (non-IT) person be in charge of compliance with PCI DSS. If you have a chief compliance function, that would be a likely choice. If not, I would recommend looking at who has the relationship with the entity you need to report your compliance to. For merchants, this entity is your acquirer. For issuers, acquirers and service providers, reporting is made to the card brands (often multiple ones). In a merchant's case, that relationship is often held by the treasury department. So assigning the CFO, the treasury director or manager may work well. This individual does not need to be technically savvy, but would interact with individuals in charge of IT and Information Security (which depending on the organization can be one and the same) and serve as primary point of contact with the entity imposing compliance.

A very small committee may also be employed if assigning a single individual is not feasible, but I still recommend the task be given to a single person if possible. Whatever the case, this relationship is better borne on the business than on the IT side. Remember PCI DSS is a legal, contractual and compliance requirement, not an IT one.

Requirements 12.5.* of PCI DSS mandate assigning information security responsibilities. We also recommend that these fall to a single individual, generally the CISO or CIO. Some of the responsibilities in the sub-requirements can then be delegated, but ultimate accountability should rest with the identified individual. Amongst the responsibilities are:

- developing and maintaining (updating at least annually) information security policies and procedures (12.5.1)
- ensuring monitoring of security alerts (12.5.2)
- implementing security incident response processes (12.5.3)
- administering user accounts (12.5.4), including controls over the addition and termination of users
- monitoring and controlling all access to data (cardholder) (12.5.5)

All of these responsibilities must be documented clearly and approved by management (12.4). Again, while these requirements cover cardholder data, they should still apply in reasonably the same way to all information held by the organization. For service providers, a new requirement (12.4.1, mandatory as of February 1, 2018) mandates the naming of someone responsible for the protection of cardholder data and a PCI DSS compliance program.

3.5.2 (Information Security) Policies (Requirement 12)

The cornerstone of any Information Security Program is proper policies which lead to implementations of procedures and standards. This is why I'm presenting it early in this volume, to show its importance. Policies tell the organization what rules they need to follow. Note that policies, procedures and standards may be found under different names within different organizations (and may include more levels). To align with the PCI DSS standard, we will use the same terminology. One blogger has outlined his own guidance on terminology [25] with which I agree. The following are short definitions that explain what each represents in the context of this book:

- Policy: a high-level document identifying the problem addressed by the document, the goals (or objectives), the position of the organization, and assigning responsibilities (technical detail is to be found in procedures) - this document must provide the 'spirit' (as in 'spirit of the law') that individuals will use to ensure that they are meeting the objectives of the organization
- Procedure: these are the ordered steps that are to be followed for any given process (e.g. some form of checklist) - when followed, procedures allow for consistent operations (consistent, not necessarily adequate, complete or optimized)
- Standard: a model that defines how (versus the procedures that address the 'what') things must be done - typically used for configuration standards (i.e. which IP range to use) and device hardening standards

Your policies may however be the last thing you address as it should reflect the current state of what you are actually doing as an organization. The order used is represented by the typical top-down vs bottom-up approach debate. Ultimately, as long as we arrive at policies, the process to get to them is irrelevant. And obviously, from a risk perspective, it is better to have a consistently followed approach (aka procedure or process) that meets the requirements and addresses the risk, so tackling that first may make more sense. However, you may, as you create or review your information policies and procedures, realize that you have forgotten something in your policies. This would be a good time to update them.

A review of policies is an area where the compliance or internal audit functions of your organization (which can be outsourced if you do not have such a role) can help perform a check function on your information security program.

Policies and their associated/derived procedures, while not as glamourous to IT professionals as the technical aspect of the work, are nonetheless critical elements. They help with personnel changes, from onboarding to people simply going on vacation (I like vacations and prefer this analogy to the *"hit-by-the-bus rule"* which is often mentioned to demonstrate the need for documentation in case an employee does not make it in one day), and they tell us what we should be looking for when assessing the organization.

We often see that issues identified during testing are direct effects of breakdowns in regularly (or not) performed processes. For example, when performing vulnerability scanning on client systems, I often found old vulnerabilities (2 or more year old) that would be addressed by existing patches; often, the affected system had not been properly decommissioned or was not covered by the organizational patch management process.

Since PCI DSS 3.0 and through 3.2, policies and procedures have been distributed amongst each of the 12 high-level requirements (they were previously all within 12.1.1 in PCI DSS 2.0). These specific requirements could still all be included in one or multiple documents, whatever the organization feels fits its needs best, as long as all requirements are covered. Many organizations have a PCI policy that they can update more frequently than other policies.

At a minimum, PCI DSS compliant Information Security Policies (12.1) and Procedures (P&P) should cover assigning responsibilities for :

- PCI compliance - an implied requirement of PCI DSS, but made mandatory in requirement A3.1.* [26] for designated entities [27] (and likely to be covered in future versions of PCI DSS)
- Information security (12.4, 12.5.*) already covered in section 3.5.1
- Managing the firewall type devices (which can include routers and switches) (1.5) a requirement linked to the change control management process
- Managing vendor defaults and other security parameters (2.5) also known as Hardening
- Change control management (6.4, 6.7) including testing and approvals
- Data classification (implied) and data retention (3.1, 3.7)
- Cryptographic key-management policy, processes and procedures (3.5, 3.6, 3.7, 4.3)
- Protecting the transmission of cardholder data (and likely other sensitive data) over networks not under the organization's control (4.3)
- Protecting systems against malware (5.4)
- Vulnerability identification (6.1, 6.7) from vendor sources
- Risk ranking of vulnerabilities (6.1, 6.7)
- Patch management (6.2, 6.7)
- Software Development Life Cycle (SDLC, 6.3, 6.7) including Secure Coding Guidelines and Training (6.5, 6.7)
- Access control, including the use of Role-Based Access Control (7.3)
- Identification and authentication of individual users (8.1.*, 8.2.*, 8.4, 8.5, 8.6, 8.7, 8.8) including user authentication policy for password changes
- Ensuring visitor identification and authorization (9.4.*, 9.10)
- Media (physical and electronic) classification (9.6.*) and management (9.7.*) including media storage (9.5.*) and destruction (9.8.*) (all within 9.10)

- Protecting payment card devices from tampering (9.9.*, 9.10)
- Logging and monitoring of relevant events (10.*, 10.8)
- Wireless network testing (11.1.*, 11.6)
- Vulnerability testing (11.2.*, 11.6) aka performing vulnerability scans
- Network and application penetration testing (11.3.*, 11.6) including network segmentation testing (11.3.4) and corrections of identified vulnerabilities (11.3.3)
- Intrusion detection management (11.4, 11.6)
- Critical changes detection (11.5.*, 11.6)
- Performing risk assessment as required (12.2) covered in section 3.5.2
- Developing and maintaining usage policies for critical technologies (12.3) that pose a high-risk, such as:
  - Remote access and wireless technologies (8.3)
  - Acceptable critical devices and their authorized personnel (12.3.3 / 4) (PCI DSS 3.2 clarified that this meant critical devices, not individual workstations)
  - Mobile devices (laptops, tablets, phones) including BYOD if in-use
  - Removable electronic media, email usage and Internet usage.
  - Never sending unprotected PANs by end-user messaging technologies (4.2)
- Ensuring formal security awareness training of the entity's policies and procedures covering cardholder data security (12.6.*)
- Personnel screening (HR) (12.7)
- Managing PCI Service Providers (12.8.*, 12.9)
- Incident response management (12.10.8)

These policies should be reviewed at least annually, updated when the environment changes (12.1.1) and approved by appropriate level staff in the organization. We will review the specific requirements that must be covered by the policies in section 3.7.

3.5.3 Documenting usage of card information

In order to define and validate scope, as well as assess compliance, we need to maintain basic information. I dedicated a complete volume (volume 2 in this series) to this very important topic and I recommend you review it prior to reading on, if needed.

I generally start with business process flows that show how people in an organization interact with cardholder data (while business process flows are not required by PCI DSS, I recommend that organizations maintain them nonetheless). This is the easiest way to work when initially interacting with non-technical personnel. Those processes often include hardcopy (i.e. paper) as well as electronic information.

Once we have defined processes, we need to map these onto network diagrams into what is referred to as cardholder data flow processes across systems and networks (1.1.3). We obviously also need network diagrams (1.1.2) that provide sufficient levels of detail of what is in-scope.

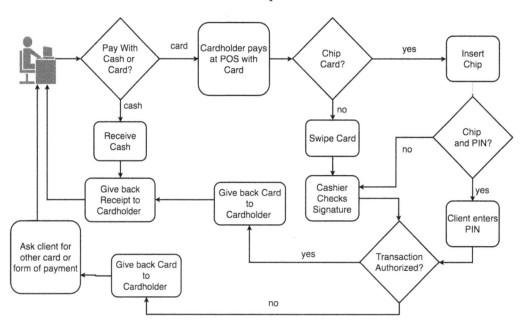

Volume 3 Figure 3 - Sample business process diagram

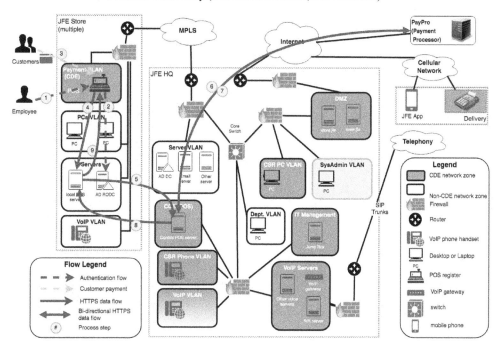

Volume 3 Figure 4 - Sample cardholder dataflow diagram

The RoC reporting template [28] gives us the minimal information that must be produced and maintained. Please see section 2.5 of volume 2 for more detail.

These diagrams should be kept up to date as changes occur. One simple way to make this happen is to ensure that one of the items of the change management processes (for applications, systems and the network) includes the obligation to document the changes affecting PCI DSS, as one requirement for the change to be approved (this would tie in well with the new requirement 6.4.6 introduced in PCI DSS 3.2).

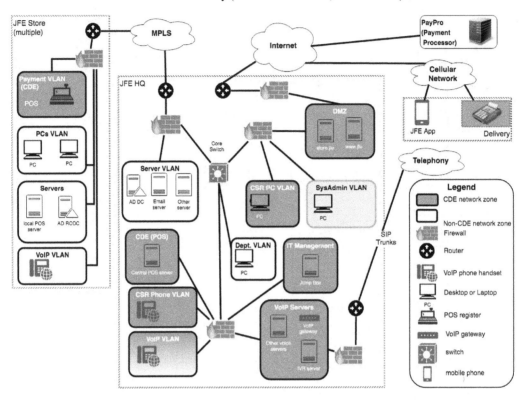

Volume 3 Figure 5 - Sample high-level network diagram (store chain)

PCI DSS 3.0 (in 2013) introduced two new requirements calling for the maintenance of an inventory of all in-scope system components (2.4), and all wireless access-points (11.1) if any wireless networks are in use, regardless of if in-scope. Maintaining an inventory, often called 'asset management', is an area where many organizations fail. But asset management is a key control since you cannot protect what you do not know you have. This is why asset management is required by most regulatory, as well as all information security, frameworks. And many tools (SIEM) that organizations may already have include asset discovery capabilities.

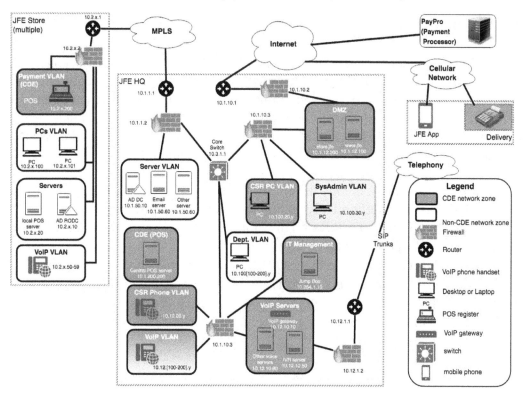

Volume 3 Figure 6 - Sample detailed network diagram (individual store)

The Designated Entity Special Validation (DESV) [29] requirements of June 2015, and incorporated into appendix A3 of PCI DSS 3.2, add further guidance about what an organization must do to 'Document and validate PCI DSS scope' in requirements A3.2.*. A3.2.1 formalizes the scoping requirement from pages 10 and 11 of the standard. A3.2.2.* mandate that upon changes to the environment, and through the change control process, that documentation (network diagrams, cardholder data flows) and controls must be put in place, including performing necessary risk assessments for significant changes (please see section 3.7.11.2 for more detail on what PCI DSS considers significant changes).

3.6 It's all about risk

The PCI DSS standard states it that it *"comprises a minimum set of requirements for protecting account data"* [30] (if you're not meeting those minimal requirements, you're basically not even trying) and implies that it may not be sufficient to ensure security. This claim is the reason for requirement 12.2 to implement a risk assessment process to ensure that all risks are identified, assessed and addressed. The standard provides examples of risk-assessment methodologies:

- OCTAVE [31]: a methodology developed by the Software Engineering Institute (SEI) at Carnegie Mellon University (CMU) and used as part of the CERT Coordination Center (CERT-CC) division of CMU-SEI ('Computer Emergency Response Team', CERT)
- ISO/IEC 27005 [32]: a part of the ISO/IEC 27000 set of standards (including ISO/IEC 27002) that covers Information security risk management
- NIST SP 800-30 [33]: The Guide for Conducting Risk Assessments by the National Institute of Standards and Technology (NIST) aligns well with the other NIST 800 publications.

Indeed, NIST defines the purpose for a risk assessment as follows:

[t]o identify:

(i) threats to organizations (i.e., operations, assets, or individuals) or threats directed through organizations against other organizations or the Nation;

(ii) vulnerabilities internal and external to organizations;

(iii) the harm (i.e., adverse impact) that may occur given the potential for threats exploiting vulnerabilities; and

(iv) the likelihood that harm will occur. [34]

The end result is a determination of risk (i.e., typically a function of the degree of harm and likelihood of harm occurring).

Ultimately, a Risk Assessment (RA) tries to issue a determination about the level of (inherent) risk of a particular product or solution. This risk is due to the exploitation of vulnerabilities by threat sources performing threat events (what we often call threat scenarios). This risk is reduced by the level of protection (and assurance) that controls provide to affect that risk (which can reduce/mitigate or eliminate risks) to a business acceptable residual risk.

As no solution can ever be 100% secure, we look for something that is sufficient to meet the organization's risk appetite (and its legal, contractual and regulatory obligations). In the case of PCI DSS, the RA serves to identify controls that are not mandated by the PCI DSS standard but that may be necessary due to the specifics of the organization's environment.

Still, any methodology that covers the following requirements should be adequate:

- Identifies critical assets, threats, and vulnerabilities
- Results in a formal, documented analysis of risk

Let's investigate those two requirements.

3.6.1 Risk Assessment Requirement 1: Identifies critical assets, threats, and vulnerabilities

How do we identify all <u>assets</u>? The simplest way is through a thorough scope definition as outlined in volume 2. This includes PCI data flow diagrams (1.1.3) and network diagrams (1.1.2), but also a complete inventory of all elements within the in-scope environment (2.4). The RoC reporting template [35] also provides us with more detail about the type of information that we must provide to ensure that everything has been identified. Section 3.6 covers scoping briefly, and volume 2 adds details on how to identify what assets are in scope and how I recommend documenting this.

How do we identify <u>threats</u>? This is where many risk assessments fail in my humble opinion, and where further guidance from the council should be provided. The solution is the use of a discipline called 'Threat modeling', which the Open Web Application Security Project (OWASP) defines for applications (the same can be extended to IT systems and entire network environments):

Threat modeling is an approach for analyzing the security of an application. It is a structured approach that enables you to identify, quantify, and address the security risks associated with an application. Threat modeling is not an approach to reviewing code, but it does complement the security code review process. [36]

OWASP even recommends Microsoft's approach to threat modeling [37] which Microsoft sees as a *"key activity in their Secure Development Lifecycle (SDL)"* [38]. Note that many other organizations provide guidance on threat modeling.

Microsoft's Adam Shostack has written a very good book [39] on how to perform threat modeling in software development that is recommended for the reader wanting to know more. Mr. Shostack describes 3 approaches: focusing on assets, on attackers, or on software.

The focus on assets is what the scoping model and approach of volume 2 is based on. In such a methodology, we focus on 3 things:

- Things attackers want: relatively tangible things such as CHD
- Things you want to protect: the company's reputation or goodwill, or systems like the CDE
- Stepping stones to either of these (connected systems, which can impact security)

This approach is useful for scoping, but a bit less for finding and dealing with identifying threats.

In focus on attackers, security experts may be able to use various types of attacker lists to find threats against a system: government, criminal organizations, etc. This is partly the one used in NIST 800-30 for adversarial threat sources. Given that the attacker has his own motivations (crimes of opportunity, etc.), skills, background, and perspective (and possibly organizational priorities), again this approach may not be the most adequate for identifying threats.

Finally, in focus on software (or systems), we focus on the software being built or a system being deployed. We look at models of architecture, UML diagrams, or even APIs. We look to question and identify assumptions (where understandings differ between models and people). We leverage developers or other IT staff which have an understanding of their environments. This approach is the one Shostack recommends, and which I'll present in the next section (using the STRIDE methodology).

Threat modeling basically has information security professionals try to uncover attack vectors, and then look at which controls (preventive, detective, corrective) are required to eliminate or mitigate risks to a level acceptable by an organization. This acceptable level of risk, called risk appetite, will vary with each organization but is generally influenced by the regulatory environment as well as other business factors.

How do we identify vulnerabilities? This is done through a vulnerability management process which is described in detail in section 3.7.11. This program will include most requirements of 11.*, but also tie back to requirements 6.1 (risk ranking) and 6.2 (patching). Although this type of testing has proven to be an issue for organizations (see section 1.9.2 of volume 1), it is well understood and described in section 3.7.11.

3.6.2 Risk Assessment Requirement 2: Results in a formal, documented analysis of risk

This simply means that everything needs to be documented so that an independent review (for example, your trusted QSA) can review the risk assessment that was performed and the process followed.

3.6.3 Risk Assessment: A proposed formal process based on NIST and Threat Modeling

An overview of NIST SP 800-30 for PCI DSS

NIST defines standards for US government institutions and goes much above and beyond what PCI DSS requires in terms of Risk Assessment. The 800-30 standard mentions that a risk assessment can (and should) be performed at 3 levels:

- Organizational Tier
- Mission/Business Process Tier
- Information System Tier

For PCI DSS, our focus will be at the Information System Tier. Let's go through what a Risk Assessment could look like.

The NIST approach has 4 broad steps, further divided into activities, presented below:

1 – PREPARE : Establish a risk context

- Identify Purpose
- Identify Scope

- Identify Assumptions and Constraints
- Identify Information Sources
- Identify Risk Model and Analytic Approach

2 – CONDUCT : Assess Risk

- Identify Threat Sources
- Identify Threat Events
- Identify Vulnerabilities and Predisposing Conditions
- Determine Likelihood
- Determine Impact
- Determine Risk

3- COMMUNICATE : Respond to Risk

- Communicate Risk Assessment Results
- Share Risk-Related Information

4- MAINTAIN : Monitor Risk over time

- Monitor Risk Factors
- Update Risk Assessment

Let's look at each of the high-level steps.

3.6.3.1 Step 1 - Establish a risk context

For PCI DSS, this is akin to defining scope (People, Process and Technology). I generally describe it as identifying and documenting:

- the People (internal, external)
- performing Business Processes
- using Applications
- running on Systems
- and communicating over Networks
- in physical locations
- involved in the storage, processing or transmission (SPT) of card information (CHD/SAD)
- or that could affect the security of card information (connected).

Note that I'll get back to this definition in the new section (3.15) covering how I now look at PCI DSS controls (rather than the 12 high-level requirements of the standard).

Required scope documentation

For step 1 (and to perform the Risk Assessment), the following scope information is required:

- Cardholder Business Process Diagrams and/or narratives;
- Dataflow Diagrams (1.1.3);
- Network Diagrams (1.1.2);
- Business process narratives (although not mandated - but only implied - by the standard).

3.6.3.2 Step 2 - Phase 2 – Assess Risk

This phase requires us to:

- Identify threat scenarios (risks/threats/vulnerabilities) to the organization's people, processes or technologies – we'll look at two options
- Determine the risk level (likelihood and impact) for each threat scenario

The NIST approach to risk/threat identification

NIST provides a very detailed way of performing this assessment that is probably overkill for smaller and/or less mature organizations, due to its flexibility which can lead to undue complexity.

First we have Threat Sources which can be either:

- Adversarial - an attacker targets the people, processes or technologies
- Not- adversarial: accidental, structural, or environmental

Threat Sources can initiate (for adversarial sources) or occur (in non-adversarial case) Threat Events, which use Vulnerabilities (weaknesses) often leveraging Preconditions (predisposing conditions are facts about systems/environments).

Complexity appears since there can be many-to-many relationships between Threat Sources, Threat Events, and Vulnerabilities, potentially leading to large multidimensional matrices. It can be very hard to strike a balance between the number of source, events, vulnerabilities, and predisposing conditions and the breadth of options. These risks need to be properly identified, so that risk levels can be calculated, and those risks addressed. Are these supposed to be the same for all risk assessments or do we have to redo this work every time? This is not clear. We must remember that NIST provides "guidelines": or recommendations that we must adapt to our situation.

That breadth of options is demonstrated by the number of options in "TABLE E-2: REPRESENTATIVE EXAMPLES - ADVERSARIAL THREAT EVENTS" which runs 6 pages long; the note at the bottom mentions "[w]hile not restricted to the APT as a threat source, the threat events in Table E-2 generally follow the flow of an APT campaign". What is not mentioned is that this list is pretty exhaustive regarding actions that the attackers may take. The first item in table E-2 is "Perform perimeter network reconnaissance/scanning". If you are on the internet, you should expect being consistently scanned. While DDOS and some IPS can help reduce the effect of that specific threat, you can't completely prevent it, and you probably just need to log it for incident response analysis, should it be required later. So this list, while offering good ideas of things that are occurring, is hardly actionable.

Since we know that it is generally the combination of multiple threat events that will lead to a successful attack (APT or opportunistic), we could use these threat events in table E-2 as potential vulnerabilities use the list as a catalog of threats, but instead I prefer using the STRIDE approach.

The STRIDE approach to risk/threat identification

I personally like the STRIDE approach which works well for technical environments, such as in PCI DSS cases, especially with technical staff (developers, network engineers, system administrators, etc.).

Threat modeling is about figuring out what can go wrong so we can address risks appropriately (accept, reduce/mitigate, eliminate, transfer).

STRIDE is a mnemonic, which stands for:

- Spoofing (CSRF) - Pretending to be something or someone other than yourself
- Tampering - Modifying something on disk, on a network, or in memory

- Repudiation - Claiming that you didn't do something, or were not responsible. Repudiation can be honest or false, and the key question for system designers is: what evidence do you have?
- Information Disclosure - Providing information to someone not authorized to see it
- Denial of Service (DoS) - Absorbing resources needed to provide service
- Elevation of Privilege - Allowing someone to do something they're not authorized to do

Adapted from Table 3-1: The STRIDE Threats chapter 3 of Shostack's book [40]

Shostack states that Threat Modeling can be learned, and that is a very good thing (although like anything else, it may be easier for some than others).

The way to do Threat Modeling is to walk through your diagram(s) and look for more threats, using the STRIDE mnemonic. [41]

More guidance is found in Shostack's book.

A high-level example of a risk assessment using this approach can be found in volume 4 for JFE.

Shostack also provides general tips that we should follow:

- start with external entities (including wireless networks); they present a higher risk since internal attacks require physical presence
- Never ignore a threat because it's not what you're looking for right now (write them down and come back to them)
- Focus on feasible threats, not far-fetched ones (Sharknado anyone? versus just a regular hurricane, and most threats addressed through standard controls anyways)

He also provides other advice:

- Validate, Don't Sanitize (sanitization is hard to do well and error prone)
- Trust the Operating System (modern robust operating systems are secure when properly configured and patched regularly) [42]

Risk Calculations (NIST approach)

Once threats have been identified, for each of them we must:

- Calculate Inherent Risk, which is the product of:
  - Likelihood
  - Impact

The basic risk calculation is fairly standard. We can use qualitative or quantitative measures to evaluate risks, each approach having its pros and cons. [43]

We then:

- Determine Control Strength i.e. assurance that controls are

  - well designed
  - operating effectively (type 2 reports) to protect assets [one problem is not all control categories address same events the same way, or likelihood/impact, but if we go down that route we'll make calculations harder]
- Calculate Residual Risk which is whatever risk remains after controls are in place.

Where NIST differs from other methodologies is in the calculations of likelihood and impact.

Likelihood depends on whether threats are adversarial or non- adversarial, which is the product of, for adversarial threats:

- Likelihood of Initiation (adversarial) (Table G-2) : made up of characteristics of associated threat sources, such as:
  - Capability (Table D-3)
  - Intent (Table D-4)
  - Targeting (Table D-5)

And for non-adversarial threats:

- Likelihood of Occurrence (non-adversarial) (Table G-3) : anticipated severity and duration of the event

Either of which gets multiplied by:

- Likelihood of Event resulting in Adverse impacts if it occurs (Table G-4) : takes into account vulnerabilities and preconditions

As for Impact, NIST uses the same simple factor for all threats that focus on business impact (operational, financial, assets).

Remember, NIST is guidance we can therefore implement any methodology that meets the requirements. Ultimately, risk ranking should be consistent with the one defined and used for requirement 6.1 (described later in this volume).

3.6.3.3 Step 3 - Phase 3 – Respond to Risk

Responding means that for each risk identify, we:

- Identify potential corrective actions or control to put in place to address risk
- Evaluate the options and determine the appropriate course of action based on the organization's risk appetite/tolerance
- Implement selected risk responses

3.6.3.4 Step 4 - Phase 4 – Monitor Risk

The list of risks identified should be reviewed periodically to ensure that controls put in place are operating as expected (tying back to what PCI DSS calls B.A.U., Business As Usual, and the new A2 appendix requirements which are currently not mandatory for most entities).

For PCI DSS, this also will be tied to the new requirement 6.4.6 which mandates that such a risk assessment be conducted for new major projects to ensure that PCI DSS compliance is maintained.

3.7 The body of the program

The policies and procedures implemented by the governance arm of the program must meet the PCI DSS requirements. These requirements are explained within the next sub-sections.

3.7.1 Requirement 1 Firewall - Isolating the Cardholder Data Environment (CDE)

The firewall requirement comes first since the first technical layer of information security is generally at the network level, by preventing *"unauthorized access from untrusted networks"* [44]. Firewall functionality can be provided by multiple types of devices, from firewalls themselves to routers and switches, all of which can be physical devices or even virtual ones. The term 'network footprint' (or attack surface, which Microsoft's Adam Shostack, the author of the book Threat Modeling: Designing for Security, calls "trust boundaries") [45] is used to define the limited set of protocols allowed in or out (both are important).

Once scope has been reduced (a standard recommendation but not a PCI DSS requirement), and systems consolidated in the smallest number of (network) areas, we must then work to protect these systems by initially isolating them fully from the rest of the network (also known as 'default deny-all', per requirement 1.2.1) and restricting traffic to only the systems and protocols/ports that are required for business (1.2.1). The business justification of all those protocols/ports open must be documented (1.1.6) and approvals must be granted by personnel independent of the personnel managing the configuration (segregation of duty).

If the organization uses any insecure protocols, then countermeasures must be put in place to protect them and be documented as well (1.1.6). PCI DSS 3.2 removed the definitions of insecure services, deferring to industry standards. It used to state that insecure protocols may include, but are not limited to, FTP, Telnet, POP3, IMAP, and SNMP v1 and v2. Many of these allow the sending of credentials (e.g. usernames and passwords) in clear-text over an unencrypted connection that could allow a well-positioned attacker to intercept the traffic and gain access to these valuable credentials. A 'compensating control' for such a case (ftp, telnet, etc.) could be to run the network connection over an encrypted connection such as a VPN tunnel.

The firewall rules employed should not be generic or apply to all systems. The only exception is where this simplifies implementation for generic services. For example, all CDE systems can send their log information (one-way only) to the centralized log collector system over the syslog port. I also recommend the use of name groups (instead of IP addresses and ranges) within rules to aid in reading the rules.

Here's one simple example of what this documentation could look like.

Source	Destination	Protocols	Action	Business Justification
any	CDE	any	deny	Deny everything not explicitly authorized
CDE	log_server	udp/syslog	allow	Allow CDE systems to send their logs to centralized server
IT_net	CDE_jump	tcp/ssh	allow	Allow IT network systems SSH to the jump server in the CDE

Volume 3 Table 3 - Example of business justification of firewall rules (requirement 1.1.6)

This documentation must tie in to the diagrams described in section 3.6 and 2.5 (of volume 2).

Remember that systems that are connected to 'CDE' systems to via open protocols/ports are 'connected' systems and considered in-scope.

The list of firewall rules must be reviewed at least every six months (1.1.7) to ensure that all rules are still required (which explains why we need to maintain documentation on those rules). Network diagrams (1.1.2) and PCI data flows (1.1.3) will generally also be involved during this review. For larger organizations, tools may be available that tie in with your network devices (including firewalls) and allow you to meet both the objectives of the documentation (1.1.6) and rules review (1.1.7) requirements.

We generally see at least a few different network segments within the network of a PCI compliant organization. At a minimum, we see an externally-facing demilitarized zone (DMZ), the internal network, and an internal PCI zone (called the Cardholder Data Environment, CDE, in PCI terminology). A firewall must be present at each Internet connection and between any DMZ and the Internal network zone (1.1.4).

3.7.1.1 Internet-facing systems in the DMZ

Any internet-facing system should be placed within a special zone usually referred to as a DMZ (1.3.1). The term DMZ comes from the military; it defines a buffer zone between different nations or groups, famously still present between the Koreas (North and South). The DMZ is a less secure zone than the internal network since some of its services are exposed to external attackers (more on internal threats later). This zone generally has a small number of systems performing limited functions. The goal of this intermediate zone is to make an attacker's job more difficult by having them need to subvert a first set of systems with limited access to the internal network.

Only required protocols/ports should be open from the Internet to the DMZ (1.3.2) for both incoming and outgoing traffic (to make exfiltration harder should an attacker ever manage to gain access to this system). Requirement 1.3.3 was removed in PCI DSS 3.2 (and all subsequent 1.3.* requirements were renumbered). Requirement 1.3.3 mandated that there should be no direct connection from the internet to the CDE, but the PCI SSC felt this was already covered by other requirements.

Note that no CHD should ever be stored in the DMZ: it should all be in the CDE (1.3.6), the internal PCI zone. The CDE should not have DIRECT access to the Internet (1.3.4) nor should it be accessible from the internet (1.3). A clarification in the guidance column confirmed that no untrusted external connection should ever terminate outside a DMZ. In fact, for security's sake, standard best practices mandates that most systems in an organization should never access the internet directly, but should go through filtering systems that may restrict access to undesirable sites (undesirable is to be defined by the organization) including filtering for malware or illegal sites. Any filtering system used by in-scope systems is likely contaminated by CHD. In some cases, the filtering solution will allow, through the use of a master certificate, to inspect all traffic that flows through it (in effect, performing a Man-in-the-Middle, or MITM, attack), looking for malware of even exfiltration of data. In such a case, the filtering system should be extremely well-protected and monitored since it will likely be considered a 'CDE/CHD' system.

An organization could have more than one DMZ if they wanted to split zones that come in contact with CHD from others that do not, although this is not a PCI DSS requirement. For example, they could implement a standard DMZ for smtp email gateway and web servers, and another DMZ for proxy systems, and one more for web-facing payment services/systems.

The three remaining 1.3.* requirements are interrelated and a bit more technical, so let me explain them along with some basic networking information. All three seek to protect the organization from Internet-based attacks.

I will use the IPv4 examples as they are simpler to understand than IPv6 (which is slowly replacing IPv4) but the same general concepts apply. A simplified networking primer is available in appendix.

Requirement 1.3.5's language changed in PCI DSS 3.2 to permit only "established" connections into the network but used to refer to *"stateful inspection, also known as 'dynamic packet filtering'"* [46]. This makes it more in-line with Verizon's call in its 2015 PCI compliance report. [47] This serves to protect against an attacker that tries to insert himself into a communication channel that was opened by someone else (say an application). The firewall maintains the 'state' of the connection to ensure this occurs. Most firewalls now meet this standard out-of-the-box. Validation would require the assessor to look at the manufacturer, make and model to confirm this.

Technical description: *This state validation generally occurs at level 3 (network) of the OSI model, usually in the IP (Internet Protocol) implementation of the firewall. Most firewalls perform some type of Network Address Translation (NAT) basically mapping between an external IP address and an Internal IP address. In section 1.9.5 of volume 1, I mention the recommendation of the Verizon 2015 PCI Compliance Report that 'stateful inspection' is not considered strong enough by many information security professionals, at least for external-facing firewalls. The recommendation is to use 'application-aware' firewalls which provide greater protection.* [48]

Requirement 1.3.3 (anti-spoofing measures to detect and block forged source IP) is related to 1.3.5 and generally automatically offered by most firewall devices. An attacker will often attempt to disguise himself as coming from somewhere else to bypass security defenses. We also see forged IP addresses during Denial of Service (DoS) attack. We should ensure that security degrades gracefully during a DoS attack as attackers have managed to hide their tracks during such attacks.

Requirement 1.3.7 asks us to never disclose private IP addresses and routing information to unauthorized parties. This is most often accomplished using

Network Address Translation (NAT) and through the use of network ranges reserved for internal networks (and thus not routable over the general internet).

RFC 1918 has reserved 3 IPv4 ranges reserved for internal networks:

```
10.*.*.*, 192.168.*.* and 172.16.*.* to 172.31.*.*
```

(where * means a number from 0 to 255, or 8 bits).

Note: Microsegmentation, described briefly in volume 2, may make firewall rules a stronger control.

3.7.1.2 Wireless

If any wireless networks are in use within the organization, then firewalls must be in-place between the wireless networks and the CDE (the internal PCI network zone) (1.2.3). Wireless networks are at greater risk since an attacker need not be physically present onsite to access them. In fact, wireless access to networks using specialized antennas can be performed from far larger distances [49]. Only authorized users should be able to get access to the cardholder data environment (CDE) from the wireless network. A safer approach (not mandatory, but something I would recommend) is to have wireless users perform standard remote access (e.g. VPN) into the network in order to access the CDE.

3.7.1.3 Firewall Configuration Standards

Again, on the subject of firewalls (and routers), we mean whichever device is used to provide firewall and network segmentation services, which we would categorize as 'Segmenting' devices.

The organization should have defined a firewall and router standard (1.1) that provides a change process for any network change (1.1.1) including testing the change. This change process can be the generic one used within the organization (and covered in requirement 6.4), but if the required changes affect the PCI DSS scope then security (and compliance, if such a group exists) should have to review and approve the changes, so as to not risk reducing PCI compliance and increasing security risks unknowingly. The new requirement 6.4.6 (mandatory as of February 1, 2018) covered in section 3.7.6.2 addresses this issue. The standard, which could be part of another policy (such as the information security policy), should include descriptions of groups, roles, and responsibilities for management of network components (1.1.5).

Using that standard, the organization should create firewall and router configurations that restrict connections between any in-scope zone and 'untrusted' networks (1.2). The default 'deny-all' should be in there (1.2.1). Guidance clarification in PCI DSS 3.2 confirm that incoming and outgoing rules are covered. 'Untrusted' networks are those not controlled by the organization. The firewall and router configurations should be synchronized (1.2.2), meaning that changes made to them are actually saved and used when the device reboots. Network devices are notoriously not restarted very often and changes made to them can be in memory only (for testing purposes). Requirement 1.2.2 calls for securing and synchronising configurations. Many times, changes are made in memory on firewall devices but are only active as of the time they are entered. If they are not explicitly saved, then the changes may be lost during a reboot.

3.7.1.4 Changes to the CDE

Any change or extension / opening of the PCI network (the CDE) must ensure that security is not degraded. DESV requirement A3.2.2 mandates that those changes be approved, reviewed to ensure risk is managed, required controls are put in place, and that the relevant documentation be updated. Again, the new requirement 6.4.6 (mandatory as of February 1, 2018) covered in section 3.7.6.2 addresses this issue.

Such an extension is exactly what happens when a remote device (i.e. not on the organization network) accesses the CDE. Certain specific additional requirements, described below, apply.

3.7.1.5 Remote Access - Workstations, Desktops, Laptops

Requirement 1.4 mandates a personal firewall for portable (changed from "mobile" in PCI DSS 3.2) devices (not in a fixed location) that may connect remotely to the network or to a network not controlled by the organization (1.4), also called an 'untrusted' network. This would include laptops, tablets, phones, etc., whether employee owned or organization provided.

The goal of this requirement is to protect such devices when they may be connected to a more hostile network environment not controlled by the organization, such as an cafe or airport (or even some home networks). In such networks, malware is often lurking, just waiting for targets to exploit.The value of a personal firewall can be seen with the advent of the WannaCry worm which would have generally been blocked by such a program; it also spread through phishing using email).

It is a good general practice to mandate this on all individual devices, whether or not they are permanently on the network.

While as information security professionals we may debate the risk/reward of employee provided devices (commonly referred to as 'Bring Your Own Device' or BYOD), there is no doubt that this is a trend that is unlikely to recede, and thus it becomes our obligation to protect the organization's information everywhere it is held. A personal firewall is likely not sufficient to protect from threats in such cases, and I would strongly advise looking at security solutions for all mobile devices (employee and organization provided). Those solutions are often categorized as 'Mobile Device Management' (MDM) solutions.

Multi-factor authentication (previously called two-factor) for remote access (8.3.2) is included in requirement 8 (authentication), but it makes sense to tie it to requirement 1. Any remote access (user, administrator, vendor, etc.) that can interact with the CDE in some way, shape or form, can be seen as 'breaching' the CDE 'bubble' (or isolation). This added level in risk is compensated by that second factor which means that two of the following must be used to confirm the user's identity:

o *Something you know, such as a password or passphrase*
o *Something you have, such as a token device or smart card*
o *Something you are, such as a biometric.* [50]

Remember that you must use 2 different categories, as two of the same category (say a password and a PIN) are still considered a single factor (used twice), also note that SMS is not considered a secure second factor. [51]

The goal of authentication is to tie every action back to an individual user; any factor (password, token, certificate, etc.) must be tied to an individual and CANNOT be shared between multiple users (8.6).

PCI DSS 3.2 changed requirement 8.3 by making it a sub requirement numbered 8.3.2, and creating a new requirement overall requirement 8.3 covering all multi-factor authentication. The new requirement 8.3.1 was added mandating multi-factor authentication for administrative (IT) access to the CDE; this new requirement comes after many IT administrators have been targeted by spear phishing attempts.

3.7.2 - Requirement 2 - Hardening

Hardening seems to be new to many organizations but is a basic building block of any Information Security Program. It basically means building default secure configurations for all devices at the offset. This is the systems equivalent to the 'deny all' rule of firewalls, and requires only allowing functions strictly required for business operations (is like reviewing doors and windows in a building to ensure that they work and are secure). It includes disabling (or removing) all default settings and accounts (2.1) and in-addition for wireless networks, changing network passwords, keys and SNMP strings (2.1.1). SNMP, or Simple Network Management Protocol, is a protocol that may return configuration and status of network devices. Once again, this is more dangerous in a wireless environment where an attacker does not need to be physically present.

The way to ensure that all of these default settings are changed is to develop secure configuration standards (2.2). For this purpose, industry-accepted standards have been developed by a number of organizations, including but not limited to:

- Center for Internet Security (CIS) [52]
- International Organization for Standardization (ISO) [53]
- SysAdmin Audit Network Security (SANS) Institute [54]
- National Institute of Standards Technology (NIST) [55]

The standard an organization builds should be based on a trusted industry-accepted standard, or at least validated against them. Certain manufacture recommendations (such as Microsoft and Cisco) may be used if they explicitly address security concerns. For many of my clients, I've recommended that they use one of those source organizations, adopt the standards as-is, and document the differences with the external standard and what reasons justify the deviation. That way, it simplifies the maintenance of those standards over time. For example, an Active Directory standard may call for not reusing 24 last passwords, but due to a specific constraint the organization cannot support more than 12 (which still exceeds PCI DSS requirement 8.2.5). Documentation could look like this:

Configuration Standard: Microsoft Windows Server 2012 SOURCE: CIS Microsoft Windows Server 2012 Exceptions:

Source Section	Recommended Value	Implemented Value	Deviation Justification
1.1.1.5	24	12	System X limitation only supports 12. PCI DSS calls for 4, 12 exceeds this.

The hardening standards include having only one primary function per server (2.2.1) so as to not mix different security roles. The role can be DNS, file storage, database, application, web front end, etc. Note that an individual virtual machine (VM) is seen as one server. The hypervisor running the VM is seen as a server having the hypervisor role. [56]

Only necessary services should be enabled (2.2.2) which means that for insecure services, additional security features must be implemented to address the unsecured portions (2.2.3). For example, telnet and ftp send authentication credential (username and password) through clear-text. What constitutes secure has been delegated to industry standards, and details of secure versions of SSL/TLS are now in appendix A2 of PCI DSS 3.2, which we will cover in section 3.7.4.1. Running those services over a VPN connection may address the clear-text credential issue. Requirement 2.2.4 mandates setting secure default values for all configuration setting. The organization must also remove all unnecessary functionalities (2.2.5). Often, an attacker can use those default (and vulnerable) scripts to nefarious results. One such attack I have myself performed as part of a penetration test is gaining shell (command line) access on a database server using default scripts that came with the software. Had those files been removed, I would have had a harder time gaining access to the machine.

The hardening standards should be reviewed at least annually, and changes should be applied retroactively to all systems currently in production.

Finally, any administrative non-console (i.e. not physical, and by console, we mean the physical console of a system, often found in the data center) access must be encrypted (2.3). This type of access is generally done through properly configured protocols such as Remote Desktop (RDP), ICA or VNC. Again, SSL/TLS is covered in section 3.7.4.1. Encryption is explained in the crypto primer found in the appendix.

So for all types of systems (windows web servers, Linux DNS, etc.) we should include (in one or multiple documents):

- a configuration standard
- a build or installation guide (to meet the requirement)

Often the build guide implies that the organization will create a base hardened operating system (windows, linux, etc.) image that must be used for all new system implementations.

An assessor will review the configuration standards versus the build guide, and industry best practices or manufacturer recommendations, and then sample in-scope systems to see if the proper configuration was applied (most often using tools).

3.7.3 - Requirement 3 - Storage of Cardholder Data

As mentioned in section 3.5.3 (policies) earlier, PCI mandates data retention and disposal policies and procedures (3.1). The retention policy is often included within the data classification policy, or at least references it. The(se) policy(ies) should define time limits for retention with proper justification (mostly laws and regulations), and specifically cover retention requirements for cardholder data. They must also include a process which could be manual or automated, that runs at least quarterly (every 3 months) to identify and delete cardholder data that has passed retention time. Remember that cardholder data can exist in many places including files, databases, and logs (it shouldn't be logged but it could be, etc.). DESV (now appendix A3 of PCI DSS 3.2) requirements A3.2.5.* [57] asks us to implement a *"data-discovery methodology to confirm PCI DSS scope and to locate all sources and locations of clear- text PAN at least quarterly"* [58] (the same frequency as destruction of data) . This discovery could be performed manually, but is better performed using specialized tools that can look for patterns of PAN, including Data Loss Prevention (DLP) or data identification tools. Section 2.5.5 of volume 2 covers this in more detail.

Requirement 3.2 and its sub-requirements cover SAD <u>after</u> authorization. The only entity that can keep SAD is the issuer for its own cards, and it must be adequately protected. SAD pre-authorization data (see section 2.3 and FAQ 1154 [59]) can be kept, but it should be encrypted securely as defined for the PAN in requirement 3.4. SAD includes track data from the magnetic stripe (3.2.1), card verification codes or values (three-digit or four-digit number printed on the front or back of a payment card) (3.2.2), the PIN or PIN-block (3.2.3). The implication is that SAD MUST be destroyed promptly after authorization occurs (or never saved, which is even better).

The next two requirements cover presentation and storage of the PAN. When displaying the PAN, unless you absolutely need the full number (and can justify this as a documented business need), it should be masked (3.3) displaying, at a maximum, the first 6 digits and last 4 digits (something like 4444 44** **** 1234). Look at any payment receipt and you'll see that it only shows the last 4, often so that you can identify within your multiple cards, which one you used. Remember that if you capture a screen containing a full PAN, then it must be stored following requirement 3.4. A clarification in PCI DSS 3.2 of the guidance of requirement 3.3 confirms that only the minimum can be used; if this minimum cannot be met, then compensating controls may be required (see section 3.10).

The PAN's format is 16 digits (15 for AMEX) like the following: 4012 8888 8888 1881

The first digit identifies the brand; generally, 4=Visa, 5=MasterCard, 6=Discover, 3=JCB or AMEX.

The full first six digits represent the financial institution, and are called 'Issuer identification number (IIN)' which was previously called the 'Bank Identification Number' (BIN).

The last digit is a calculation to validate that the full number is valid, a 'check digit' using an algorithm called LUHN.

Requirement 3.4 requires that we *"render the PAN unreadable"*, or not valuable to the attacker. Four ways are identified as acceptable:

- One-way hashes (see the encryption primer appendix for details) - an option that I think should no longer be used as it can likely be brute-forced.
- Truncation (a screen capture of a masked PAN per 3.3 becomes truncated) - truncation is non-reversible.
- Index tokens (tokenisation) - where tokens with unpredictable values replace the PAN - see section 2.6.3.2 of volume 2 for more detail on tokenisation. A sample tokenization application will be provided through the companion website of this book in the fall of 2017.
- Strong cryptography - encryption requirements described further in section 3.7.3.1 "Encryption of Stored Data" below.

In all cases, for the method to be acceptable, it must be impossible for an attacker to reconstitute the PAN.

3.7.3.1 Encryption of Stored Data

Encryption is a complex process; and it is very easy to make mistakes during its implementation. I provide a high-level version of how encryption works in the encryption primer appendix. If you do not have a good understanding of encryption, I suggest you review it before reading this section.

If cardholder data (PAN or SAD) is to be stored encrypted, then multiple requirements must be met. Encryption could be performed at the database table or field level (recommended), file level, or the media can also be fully encrypted, as is the case with some hard drive or tape backup encryption. In the case of encryption performed at the media level (disk or tape), keys must not be associated or managed by the operating system authentication (which would make breaking that layer a single point of failure) but must be managed separately and independently from the local authentication (per requirement 3.4.1). This means that the user would likely have to enter a passphrase (a type of key-encrypting key) manually after logon to get access to the encryption media. See requirement 3.5.3 below for more detail.

Encryption is only as secure as the protection given to its encryption keys, which is why requirement 3.5 mandates developing (and documenting) procedures to protect encryption keys by, amongst other things, restricting access to the smallest number of key custodians necessary (3.5.2). Although that exact number of custodians is not defined, it should be kept to a minimum (a very small number). The keys must also be stored in the fewest possible locations (3.5.4). A new requirement in PCI DSS 3.2, 3.5.1 (which forces renumbering of the other 3.5.* requirements) calls for service provider (although it would be a good idea for any complex environment) to document the cryptographic architecture in use.

The other 3.5.* requirement requires a bit more technical knowledge, which is covered in the encryption primer appendix. Data may be encrypted with either a symmetric cipher such as AES, using a shared-key, or using an asymmetric cipher such as PGP, using a public and a private-key pair (for details see encryption primer). For symmetric ciphers the shared-key must be protected, while for asymmetric ciphers the private-key (which is used to decrypt) must be protected while the public key may be known. Whichever key must be protected, requirement 3.5.3 mandates that secret and private keys be stored in one of the following ways:

- *Encrypted with a key-encrypting key that is at least as strong as the data-encrypting key, and that is stored separately from the data-encrypting key*
- *Within a secure cryptographic device (such as a hardware (host) security module (HSM) or PTS- approved point-of-interaction device)*
- *Or as at least two full-length key components or key shares, in accordance with an industry-accepted method* [60]

A key-encrypting key is just another encryption key (which can use the same cipher). Those key-encrypting keys do not need to be encrypted, just stored securely and separately from the keys they encrypt. A key sharing system used to share these is also often called a key distribution system.

Requirement 3.6 mandates development and documentation of all the relevant key-management processes and procedures for cryptographic keys used for encryption of cardholder data. The processes and their documentation must cover, at the very least, generation of strong cryptographic keys (3.6.1), secure cryptographic key distribution (3.6.2), secure cryptographic key storage (3.6.3), prevention of unauthorized substitution of cryptographic keys (3.6.7), and a requirement for cryptographic key custodians to formally acknowledge that they understand and accept their key-custodian responsibilities (3.6.8). No individual user should generally have access to clear-text versions of the keys, and in such cases where a user may know the key, operations must be managed using split knowledge and dual control (3.6.7), meaning that the key is split between two or more individuals.

Organizations must also provide for the *"retirement or replacement (for example, archiving, destruction, and/or revocation) of keys as deemed necessary when the integrity of the key has been weakened"* or *" keys are suspected of being compromised"* (3.6.5), which also includes defining a 'cryptoperiod' for each cipher and key *"(for example, after a defined period of time has passed and/or after a certain amount of cipher-text has been produced by a given key)"* that will force retirement or replacement (3.6.4). Replacement may also be required if key personnel changes, specially for high-privilege accounts (see section 3.7.8).

3.7.4 - Requirement 4 - Transmission of Cardholder Data

Requirement 4.1 mandates that we must use strong encryption (see the encryption primer in appendix 3) when transmitting cardholder data over open, public networks ('untrusted' networks). Depending on the encryption protocol and algorithm (cipher), some variations of requirements covered in section 3.7.3.1 will need to be in place (see section 3.7.3.1 and the encryption primer in appendix). Some of the main requirements are to validate trusted keys and certificates. The protocol version and encryption strength must also be secure. PCI DSS 3.2 removed the examples of insecure versions (but all versions of SSL and SSH version 1.0 are no longer considered secure) and deferred to industry standards, and placed relevant controls in appendix A2 (covered in the next section). The encryption primer describes the current understanding on the most secure protocols but will defer to the NIST standards, as PCI DSS does, for acceptable strong ciphers.

Since open public networks are outside the control of the organization and a well-placed attacker may be able to intercept and eavesdrop on the communication, we need to secure the communications on networks where we have no control. This can be done by using encrypted communication channels such as VPN (site-to-site or point-to-point) or using dedicated private links.

Open, public networks include, but are not limited to the Internet, wireless networks, and bluetooth connections. For Multiprotocol Label Switching (MPLS) networks, which are often used to provide connectivity between various physical sites (data centers, branches, etc.), the details of the implementation determine whether the network is considered public or private. FAQ #1045 [61] addresses this issue when responding to the question: *"Is MPLS considered a private or public network when transmitting cardholder data?"* It basically asks us if there is any connection to (or entry point from) the open internet:

If the MPLS network contains publically-accessible IP addresses or otherwise provides exposure to the Internet (for example, if an edge router has an Internet port), then it may need to be considered an "untrusted" or a public network.

So, if there is a connection to the internet, then it will be considered an 'open, public network' whereas if no internet connection exists, then it will be considered a 'closed network'.

Wireless networks are at greater risk since an attacker need not be physically present onsite to access them, and must therefore also use strong encryption (4.1.1), which generally means using WPA/WPA2 protocols (also see section 3.7.1.2). The primer goes into more detail on the industry best practices for secure protocols for wireless networks.

The PAN (and SAD) should also never be sent through email, instant messaging, chats and other applications of that nature (4.2). This mandate needs to be placed in a policy somewhere (a logical place is the usage policy described in 12.3.*, but could be any other that is viewed by all users of the organization). DESV A3.2.6.* [62] adds the obligation *"implement mechanisms for detecting and preventing clear-text PAN from leaving the CDE via an unauthorized channel, method, or process, including generation of audit logs and alerts"*, which means this has to go above the policy level to add a technical detective control through some sort of filtering system, which may include Data Loss Prevention (DLP) solutions.

3.7.4.1 SSL/TLS

In version 3.1 of PCI DSS, some protocols were deprecated and organizations still using those need to move to newer secure ones by July 1, 2016 at the latest. As mentioned earlier, the PCI SSC published an update on December 18, 2015 which modified those dates without changing the version of the standard. The date has been pushed back to July 1, 2018 but there are some caveats described in a bulletin [63]:

- TLS 1.1 or greater support (TLS 1.1+) must be offered by June 2016 by "all processing and third party entities – including Acquirers, Processors, Gateways and Service Providers"; which implies that existing merchants are dependent on those entities for migration.
- All new implementations (my understanding is when TLS 1.1+ is available) by these entities must use TLS 1.1+; this applies to newer merchants.
- All entities must use a secure TLS by June 2018 (which will be at least TLS 1.1, but could be a more recent version, as defined by NIST).
- Some exceptions beyond the June 2018 may be available provided one can demonstrate that they are not susceptible to all known exploits for SSL and early TLS, but the bar is set very high and this will likely be enforced by QSAs.

The December 2015 changes have been moved into appendix A2 in PCI DSS 3.2.

3.7.5 - Requirement 5 - Antivirus / Antimalware

Malicious software, or malware, includes but is not limited to viruses, worms, trojans and rootkits. Malicious software has been with us for almost as long as computers have, but their effect has been compounded in a fully networked world (aka the Internet). The Morris worm in 1988, was the first worm identified. And malware has evolved to be not only generic, but at times more targeted at specific organizations with *"70-90% of malware samples are unique to an organization"* (variations in virus families) [64].

Still, the question of whether there really is a need for an antivirus (more anti-malware nowadays) keeps popping up. The Verizon 2015 PCI compliance report confirms that some form of malware is used in the first steps of most successful attacks.

Thus any system vulnerable to malicious software, or malware, needs to have protective software installed (5.1). The software selected should be one recognized by the industry as effective in being able to remove all known malware (5.1.1). These should be centrally managed and end-users should not be able to disable them as a general rule (5.3) (only when a technical reason requires it, authorized by management and then only for as short a period of time as necessary). The software must be kept current (updated so it can detect new malware), scan the systems periodically and generate logs (5.2). Any and all logs generated by the software need to be collected and monitored alongside all other organizational logs as demanded by requirement 10.7 (see section 3.7.10). An alternative to anti-malware is application whitelisting solutions, which allows only vetted applications (generally because they are signed using cryptographic keys) to run, thus preventing (unsigned) malware from running. Application whitelisting may also be less resource intensive on systems. As always, no technology is a perfect solution, which is why we have to maintain multiple layers of controls.

The one part of requirement 5 that may get a different interpretation is of *"commonly affected by malicious software"* (5.1.2). Generally, this has been taken to mean any end-user general purpose operating system such as all versions of Microsoft Windows, Apple's Mac OSX and some desktop usage of Linux. Windows is the one most people think about as it has been targeted more than others since it represents the standard in the business world. Whatever definition you decide to use internally, a new requirement introduced in PCI DSS 3.0 requires that the organization re-evaluate periodically (at least annually) whether these excluded systems warrant the use of anti-malware software (5.1.2) (Windows cannot be considered not affected). For example, an organization that uses Linux or OSX as a desktop may (not necessarily should) consider these to not be commonly affected by malware. It would still need to review whether that claim stands up. Remember that humans (who will use these computers) are often the weakest link in the security chain. The one exception everyone generally agrees about is not requiring antivirus on mainframe and midrange similar types of systems: IBM Z series, IBM P series (AIX), IBM I series (OS/400), HP Non Stop (Guardian), HPUX, etc.

3.7.6 - Requirement 6 - Vulnerabilities, Patching, Change Control and Software and Web Development

As the section title implies, requirement 6 is a hodgepodge of different but related requirements for securing systems and applications.

3.7.6.1 Vulnerability Management

The first portion of requirement 6.1 mandates the creation of a process to identify vulnerabilities using reputable outside sources. For organizations that use mostly components (hardware and software) from very few vendors, this may mean subscribing to mailing lists, newsgroups or RSS feeds (for example, from vendors such Microsoft, Cisco, etc.). The second portion of requirement 6.1 is assigning a risk ranking to all vulnerabilities (from a vendor list, external or internal testing). The latter part of this requirement will also apply to vulnerabilities identified in internally developed software (see 6.3, described shortly). Since not all risks are equal, a vulnerability on an externally-facing system should be riskier than on an internal system, for example. The risk ranking methodology should be based on industry standards and must include a risk level consisting of, at a minimum, high, medium and low rankings. Any vulnerability with a risk level of 'high' or above, should be remediated within one month. We often see risk ranking methodologies using two distinct axes: impact (what could happen if someone exploited this vulnerability) and probability (likelihood). Unless you are an experienced risk professional, please do not create your own methodology but adopt an existing one. There are many industry standards, from CVSS (Common Vulnerability Scoring System, a free and open industry standard for assessing the severity of computer system security vulnerabilities in use since 2004- CVSS is also mandated for external vulnerability scans of requirement 11.2.2), to those provided by SANS, OWASP (Risk Rating [65]) and others. Whichever methodology you use, make sure that your methodology is properly documented and used consistently.

For example, the OWASP Risk Rating methodology uses underlying factors for both likelihood and impact to create an overall risk rating, as described in the table below.

		Overall Risk Severity		
Impact	HIGH	Medium	High	Critical
	MEDIUM	Low	Medium	High
	LOW	Note	Low	Medium
		LOW	MEDIUM	HIGH
		Likelihood		

Volume 3 Table 4 - OWASP Overall Risk Severity Rating from Likelihood and Impact Factors

The OWASP methodology considers 8 likelihood factors and 8 impact factors. Likelihood is further divided into threat agents (related to the attacker) and vulnerability (regarding the vulnerability). Threat agents (attack) factors include skill level, motive, opportunity and size (of group of potential attackers). Vulnerability factors include ease of discovery, ease of exploitation, awareness, and intrusion detection (whether we are well equipped to detect, log and react to an exploitation attempt). Impact is further divided into technical and business impact. Technical impact factors include loss of confidentiality, loss of integrity, loss of availability, and loss of accountability. Business impact includes financial damage (effect on revenue and profit), reputation damage (often to the 'goodwill' effect on the balance sheet), non-compliance (which can have a financial impact), and privacy violation.

Now that you have identified vulnerabilities, you need to address (or remediate) them. Requirement 6.2 (often called *'patching'*) mandates installation of critical patches within one month. PCI DSS 3.2 clarified that this requirement applies to all installed software, including payment applications. Critical patches are those with a high probability of exploitation on a vulnerable system, and high impact if exploited. Patching is an area where I've seen many organizations struggle, especially with a 30 day (month) timeline. This is why a good risk ranking methodology is so important to ensure that adequate patching can be performed in a timely manner. Other less risky vulnerabilities also need to be addressed, but the timeline for these is left to the organization. I've often used 3 months for high vulnerabilities, 6 months for medium vulnerabilities and a year for low vulnerabilities, but each organization needs to make that determination for themselves based on their risk appetite.

3.7.6.2 Change control

Any change to any component must go through a formal change process (6.4) regardless of whether the change is a patch (6.2) identified during the vulnerability identification process (6.1), a configuration or software change, or the testing of systems (11.*). The change control process serves as a check against both insider threats as well as the law of unintended consequences. The law of unintended consequences, which can be compared to the adage that "the road to hell is paved with good intentions", is also augmented by the complexity of systems and applications. Test environments must be different from production ones (6.4.1) and include separation of duties (6.4.2) so that, for example, a developer cannot put code into a production environment (an independent system administrator will generally put this new code into production). In smaller organizations where such separation of duty is not possible due to limited staff, compensating controls should be put in place (see section 3.10). For change control management, compensating controls that could be used might include automatic logging of all changes performed and a review (matching file changes to change control requests) by other departments of the organization (even by non-technical staff). In no case should production data which contains CHD and full PANs be used in testing or development environments (6.4.3). Some test numbers are generally available from payment processors or acquirers. Visa Europe also provided 2 BIN's series reserved for internal use [66], much in the same way that RFC 1918 provides internal IP ranges.

The organization can choose to use random test data or implement a process to sanitize CHD from live data before its use in other environments. Before code is put in production (and the system becomes "active"), any test accounts and data must be removed (6.4.4) from all system components (operating systems, database software, applications, etc.). Hardcoding values within code should never ever be done (for PCI DSS or any other environments). You should always use configuration files (or the registry) both of which are easier to modify.

The documented change control procedures (6.4.5) must include documentation of impact (6.4.5.1), approval by authorized parties (6.4.5.2), functional testing of security impacts (6.4.5.3) and back-out procedures (6.4.5.4) or how to revert back if unforeseen negative impacts occur.

A new requirement of PCI DSS 3.2, 6.4.6 (which must be in place on February 1, 2018), mentioned earlier aims to ensure that an organization maintains its PCI DSS compliance by requiring that on significant changes (see section 3.7.11.2 for definitions), we review PCI DSS requirements and update relevant documentations.

Often emergency change control processes exist which may allow for a verbal authorization first, but mandate proper documentation following the standard/regular process within a very short timeframe (days, not weeks).

3.7.6.3 Software Development Requirements

In an information world, custom developed software is often a business differentiator for organizations. But the focus is generally on functionality and often does not take into account security until much later in the process. If organizations the size of Microsoft and Adobe end up with vulnerabilities, how improbable is it that smaller organizations will not face the same issues? Most pentesters will attest that insecurely coded applications (as well as misconfigured systems) are often the way we manage to penetrate networks and systems. So how does the PCI SSC recommend we address this?

First, an organization must have a Software Development Life Cycle policy and process (6.3) that is based on industry best practices. This can include the standard waterfall process where each phase (requirements analysis, design, implementation, testing, promotion to production) must be finished and approved before moving on to the next one, or even agile development processes (which release to production much faster and often) such as Extreme Programming (XP), Scrum, etc. Information security should be included in all phases of the process (requirements analysis, design, implementation, testing and promotion to production). Note that this applies to all organizations whose software (purchased or internally developed) is used in a PCI DSS environment. All such applications must also meet other PCI DSS requirements for logging, authentication, etc.

Removal of development, test accounts and data must be done prior to release or promotion to production (6.3.1) which is similar to requirement 6.4.4. Code reviews (by an application security expert, or at least a different developer than the one who wrote the code) must be performed to identify potential coding vulnerabilities (6.3.2); code reviews may include automated and manual portions. To identify potential coding vulnerabilities, you must :

- ensure that code reviews are performed by someone other than the author (a qualified internal or external person, knowledgeable about secure coding - also see requirement 6.5.* below)
- verify that secure coding guidelines are followed (also see requirement 6.5.* below)
- verify that recommended corrections are implemented before release
- have code review results reviewed by management as part of the change control process (which is defined in requirements 6.4.*)

This is where buying PA-DSS certified software can help reduce some of those controls. PCI PA-DSS software is software that has gone through an evaluation by a PA-QSA. A PA-QSA is a like a QSA for Software Applications used in a PCI DSS environment. The organization implementing a PA-DSS validated application must follow the implementation guide that comes with the application and place it in a PCI DSS compliant environment. All other 6.3.* and 6.5.* requirements (and possibly 6.6) are taken care of by the PA-DSS certification, simplifying the organization's compliance efforts.

Requirement 6.5 covers basic common web-application coding vulnerabilities. It mandates the development of secure coding guidelines (also required in 6.3.2) and the training of developers on those topics. The training must be updated annually (since threats change), and developers must be retrained annually as well. Sub-requirements closely align to the OWASP top 10 (updated in 2013, just prior to the release of PCI DSS 3.0) and one could say they were at the very least inspired by that list. Other industry standards could be used for the organization guidelines, such as the SANS/CWE top 25 (Common Weakness Enumeration, the top 25 software errors list produced conjunctly between the SANS institute and MITRE Corporation, a not-for-profit company that operates multiple federally funded research and development centers). These requirements cover typical mistakes made by developers that cause easily exploitable vulnerabilities:

- Injection flaws, including SQL injection and others (6.5.1). The flaws are generally caused by non-validated parameters that are sent directly to a subsystem, such as a database or an operating system. In SQL injection for example, this can allow us to bypass authentication or retrieve database information [67].
- Buffer overflows (6.5.2) - typical in compiled languages such as C, C++, Objective-C, Assembler but often not seen in Java and .Net, or some scripting languages. A buffer overflow is another type of improper validation ('bounds

checking'). A buffer (or reserved memory space) of a fixed size is allocated to the application, then a function (such as strcpy in C/C++) is used to copy data that is longer than the buffer and overwrites a part of the memory where code lies.

- Insecure cryptographic storage (6.5.3). Cryptography is complex and implementation mistakes are common. This requirement will cover these issues.

- Insecure communications (6.5.4). This requirement covers usage of encryption (cryptography) for communication to prevent the disclosure of clear-text credentials (username, passwords), session keys, as well as CHD and other sensitive information

- Improper error handling (6.5.5). This requirement covers what I would call 'degrading gracefully' of 'soft fail' errors. Too often, error screens provide debugging information (including file path information) which can be useful to an attacker. A typical example is that when logging, you should never tell a user whether the username or password is incorrect (which can tell an attacker that a user account does exist), but that one of the two is incorrect, for example: "Invalid username and/or password. Please try again.".

Requirement 6.5.6 ties back to the vulnerability identification process (6.1) to ensure that all 'high risk' vulnerabilities identified are addressed (within 30 days as required by 6.1). This can also be a feedback loop that allows improvements of secure coding guidelines.

We then find vulnerabilities in web-applications and application interfaces (for example web-services). These include:

- Cross-site scripting (XSS, 6.5.7). XSS happens when a web-application includes code from different domains and code injected by a malicious user in one domain can access information in another. For example, a company order website integrates an iFrame component for third-party secure payment so that CHD never enters the organization's network. An attacker manages to modify the organization's website and inject XSS code. When the user puts in his payment information, malicious XSS code manages to grab that information and send it to a site controlled by the attacker. Note that the PCI SSC has produced guidance for e-commerce clarification [68] that you should consult.

- Improper Access Control (6.5.8) generally means that some form of permission validation (object reference, URL access) was not performed; this could also cover some insecure web server configuration such as permitting file directory listings.

- Cross-site request forgery, or CSRF (6.5.9) builds upon XSS but targets a comprised authenticated user (a client of the application) to make a request to a vulnerable application.
- Broken authentication and session management (6.5.10) is a new requirement introduced in PCI DSS 3.0. This requirement was added to the OWASP Top 10 2013 version [69]. This requirement just means that the authentication and session system can be easily targeted by an attacker. Attacks of this type can include:
  - o brute-force guessing of credentials if no account locking is present (8.1.6, 8.1.7).
  - o capture (eavesdropping) of credentials not protected by encryption (6.5.4, 8.2.1).
  - o capture of leaked session identifiers (6.5.4) often included in the URL, reused or never timed-out.
  - o other attacks are also likely possible.

As you can probably see, improper validation of input values is one source that leads to many of these issues (and directly tied to 6.5.1, 6.5.2).

These are the minimal required checks to be performed. An organization should review the current threat landscape and identify whether other types of vulnerabilities should be covered within its secure coding guidelines and training.

Since externally-facing web-applications are more and more targeted by attackers, any public-facing (externally outside the organization, connected to the full Internet or just to a limited subset through a network not fully controlled by the organization) are especially at risk. PCI DSS requirement 6.6 gives us two options to address this risk. The first option is to perform an annual security assessment of the application. This is not simply setting up automated vulnerability scans as required by 11.2.*, but more specialized tools with at least some human intervention. I often recommend calling this option web application penetration testing to differentiate it from tools-based vulnerability testing (11.2.*). The second option is to install some form of automated solution that detects and prevents web-attacks. This can mean Web-Application Firewalls, reverse proxies, or other such tools. It goes without saying that if a technological solution is selected, the solution must be kept up to date (6.1, 6.2). In volume 1 (section 1.10.7), I argued that organizations should probably be using both approaches, and not just one of the two. This is still my personal recommendation.

3.7.7 - Requirement 7 - Need to know

In requirement 3.1 we were asked to limit retention of CHD. In 7.1, we are asked to limit access to CHD to only those who absolutely need it. This will include proper separation of duties to prevent collusion, and includes the concept of least privilege (7.1.2), i.e. granting only the minimum level required to perform a function.

Roles must be defined for specific business and IT functions (7.1.1) that specify which system access and which level of access (user, reviewer, administrator, etc.) is required for each role. Often this will come with job description functions and system/application roles assigned to those functions (7.1.3). Granting of roles and permissions must be documented and approved by authorized individuals (7.1.4).

Requirement 7.2 requires implementing one or more Role-Based-Access-Control (RBAC) system(s) with a default of *"deny-all"* (7.2.3) (PCI DSS 3.2 clarified that we can use more than one, which is sometimes warranted when systems cannot use an integrated directory such as dealing with mainframes). A RBAC system simply means that we assign permissions to roles, and roles to users (not permissions to users directly), often through group membership. This reduces the risk that individual permissions will be given that do not belong to an individual, or if that individual changes functions that some permissions not be removed. The RBAC system must cover all components (7.2.1) and assign privileges to individuals (7.2.2) with no shared account used (8.5). Traceability of action is a key objective of PCI DSS (necessary for an investigation should there ever be any form of incident or breach) and requires that roles be assigned to individual accounts, and that no shared accounts be used.

A very good common practice for administrative users is to have dual accounts. Those users will have a regular user account for most functions (email, internet browsing) and an administrative account that is used only for tasks requiring this level of access (not for logging on to their individual workstation). For example, John Doe has a regular 'jdoe' Active Directory (AD) account which he uses to log on to the network and check email, as well as a 'jdoe-a' administrator account which he uses for changes that require administrator privilege. This separation helps reduce risks in the usage of the administrative account. Of course, this implies that some monitoring needs to be in place to ensure that administrators are using administrative accounts only when necessary.

3.7.8 - Requirement 8 - Authentication

In PCI DSS 3.0, multiple sub-requirements of 8.* were moved around to come up with a more logical presentation which I believe helps everyone. This remains unchanged in PCI DSS 3.1 and 3.2. PCI DSS 3.2 clarified that these requirements apply to the entity's employees and third-parties, not to consumers.

Requirements 8.1.* now cover user identification, while 8.2.* cover user authentication requirements.

Authentication procedures must be documented and communicated to all users (8.4) and must include the following:

- Guidance on selecting strong authentication credentials, for example choosing hard-to-guess passwords including no dictionary words or words related to known hobbies (favorite sports team, pastimes)
- Guidance for how users should protect their authentication credentials, for example not writing passwords down (on paper or in a file on the computer)
- Instructions not to reuse previously used passwords (or use the same password for organization and personal accounts)
- Instructions to change passwords if there is any suspicion the password could be compromised, such as who to report this to and the requirement to change your password even if compromise is not confirmed

3.7.8.1 User Identification and Accounts (ensuring traceability)

All users must have a unique identifier (or account) in each in-scope system (8.1.1). No generic or shared accounts are allowed and existing ones must be removed or disabled (8.5). If shared accounts are required due to technical or business constraints, then proper compensating controls must be put in place (covered in section 3.10) to ensure traceability to the individual.

For example, a 'sudo to root' mechanism (where a user logs on as an individual user and then changes to the root account to perform management tasks) with adequate logging and review (of the usage of this shared account by an individual) may be one such compensating control. Specific requirements for accounts used by shared service providers (8.5.1) are described in section 3.8.2.

Procedures must be in place to add, delete and modify user accounts (8.1.2). Terminated users must have their accounts removed <u>immediately</u> (8.1.3). This is an area where I see organizations struggling. To me, terminations are even more critical than granting access to a system, especially if the user is terminated with cause (versus having resigned). Inactive (unused) user accounts must be removed at least every 90 days (8.1.4). If you find that there are many unused accounts at every review then you should likely review which user access roles and membership actually need access (per requirement 7) and uncover why these were not removed more timely. This may have to be dealt with as an incident (12.10.*).

Third-party (called vendors prior to PCI DSS 3.2) accounts are to be enabled only when needed and in use, and should be monitored when used (8.1.5). For remote vendors, monitoring access (and possibly recording) via a jump box is one obvious, but not the only, way to accomplish this. Another could be an administrator initiating a screen sharing session, granting control to the vendor and monitoring what the vendor does (which requires some level of technical understanding by the administrator).

All accounts must be locked after at most 6 failed login attempts (8.1.6) which are potential attacks on the systems and should be investigated as possible incidents (12.10.*, see section 3.8.3). These accounts must be then locked-out out for at least 30 minutes (8.1.7), unless a user whose identity was validated (8.2.2) calls the help desk to reset it (for example, in case of a forgotten password). If a user does not use a system for 15 minutes then the system should be locked and require the user reauthenticate himself to reactivate (8.1.8) (this can be done at the OS level, for example at the Windows lock screen).

3.7.8.2 User Authentication (confirming the identity)

To authenticate the user, the account must be matched with at least one of the following authentifying factors (8.2):

- something you know - a password, passphrase or Personal Identification Number (PIN, in certain cases only)
- something you have - a token (e.g. RSA), a smart card, a smart phone, a certificate installed on a user-assigned computer
- something you are (biometrics) such as fingerprints, iris scans, etc.

If using something you have, the token, card or other device must be tied to an individual account and must not be shared amongst users, both from a procedural and technical standpoint (8.6). There have been reported cases of sharing of an RSA token between support staff by using a webcam to stream the numbers directly to the internet [70]. Convenient yes; insecure and stupid, most certainly.

The credentials (the username/password or other information) must be both stored and transmitted securely in an unreadable fashion (8.2.1). For storage, we're generally looking at a secure and salted hashing function (unless there is a need, reversible encryption should not be used for password storing; in Active Directory this means the option called 'Store passwords using reversible encryption' is not checked). For custom developed applications, this means that password storage must be planned very well and follow industry best-practices [71], [72]. For transmission, this is generally through some transmission encryption such as SSL/TLS (4.1). See the crypto primer in appendix for more details. If passwords or passphrases are used, they must be 'complex' for passwords, this is generally interpreted at being least seven characters long and containing both numeric and alphanumeric characters (8.2.3) (for Active Directory, there is a setting referred to as 'complex passwords'). For passphrases, a similar level of complexity is required, which generally means longer phrases with spaces, punctuation or other special characters and numbers. What constitutes complexity is delegated to NIST standard SP 800-63.

Password or passphrases should be changed every 90 days (8.2.4) and the last four passwords or passphrases employed should not be reused (8.2.5). When an account is created, an initial unique value should be set that must immediately be changed the first time the user logs on (8.2.6). That initial value should be communicated securely to the user (which means by a different communication channel, often on paper or over the phone). Again, validating the user's identity is required before providing him this information or changing his credentials (8.2.2). Note that there has been a debate at NIST on password control rules [73], but I doubt this will affect PCI DSS in the short-term.

Special care must be taken with user accounts with access to databases containing CHD (8.7) to protect and ensure traceability of access to CHD (as required by 10.2.1). Note that on some systems such as mainframes, files may be considered databases and this requirement might apply. Direct access to databases with CHD (per requirement 6.4.3, real PANs are not allowed on test systems) must be restricted to database administrators (DBAs). Application access to databases must be made through special single purpose accounts for the application. End-users must never have direct access to the database. All non-DBA accesses must be through programmatic methods (for example stored procedures, views or specific libraries) to properly control access, ensure adequate logging (10.2.1), and prevent attacks (for example injection attacks as defined in requirement 6.5.1).

3.7.9 - Requirement 9 - Physical security

This requirement is generally the best understood one in all of PCI DSS. This requirement applies to sensitive areas where CHD is transmitted, stored or processed on paper and electronic format. Sensitive areas include data centers, server rooms, call centers, etc., but do not include public-facing (e.g. cashier in store) areas.

All of those sensitive areas require entry controls (e.g. keys, electronic badges) to limit and monitor access physical (9.1). For sensitive areas, we should use video cameras or other access control mechanisms (9.1.1). (PCI DSS 3.2 clarified that we need at least one, but not necessarily both options). The goal is to, yet again, ensure traceability. Video recordings and access logs must be kept for at least 3 months and must be immediately available for review in the event of an incident. I would recommend that physical access logs be centralized along with other logs, as mentioned in section 3.7.10.

Access to network-jacks (which provide connections to the internal network) must be protected (9.1.2). This can be through logical controls (for example, Network Access Control or NAC, which authenticates a device before allowing it to connect to other devices in the network) or physical controls (for example, network-jacks are disconnected by default in a network room, where modification to connections requires physical access that is restricted to authorized personnel as per 9.1 and 9.1.1). Physical access to other network equipment, including to wireless access points, must also be similarly restricted (9.1.3).

Physical access to sensitive areas must be authorized based on job function (as in 7.1.3), with access immediately removed upon termination (like in 8.1.3), and ensuring that access mechanisms (keys, badges) are returned or disabled (9.3).

3.7.9.1 Visitors

Procedures must be put in place to identify and authorize visitors (9.4). Visitors must be authorized and accompanied at all times (9.4.1) when in sensitive areas (defined in section 3.7.9). Visitors must be easily identifiable (for example, using a different badge type) and their access must be limited (9.2, 9.4.2). Visitors must surrender their badge (or if electronic, expiration may be programmed) at the end of the authorized period (9.4.3). A visitor log must be maintained for access to sensitive areas (9.4.4) which contains, at a minimum, the visitor's name and firm, and the organization individual authorizing physical access, as well as relevant dates and times. This visitor log must be kept for at least 3 months.

3.7.9.2 Media Management

For PCI DSS, media can include, but is not limited to, physical media such as paper, as well as electronic media such as CDs/DVDs, hard drives, USB keys, and tape backups. The organization must maintain strict control over all media potentially containing CHD (9.7) with adequate inventory logs (9.7.1) and annual (or more often) inventories. Sensitivity of the data held on the media must be classified (9.6.1), generally based on the organization's data classification policy (3.1), so that strict control of distribution (9.6) can be maintained. This does not mean that a label must be placed on the media identifying *"this media has valuable data"*, which would only help an attacker in determining its value. Labeling means being able to know from the label identifier, often looking at some internal management system, what type of data is on the device. Thus, if a tape backup is lost, we should be able to know what was backed up to that tape (and if it was encrypted or not) to see if an incident must be declared (following requirements 12.10.*).

Media should be sent via secure and traceable means such as a secured courier (9.6.2) and only when approved by someone with appropriate authority (9.6.3), which may be the person performing this task as defined in the procedure. Media should be stored in a physically secure location (9.5), preferably in a secure off-site facility (9.5.1). The organization must perform an annual verification of the site's security (which for a third-party may include a physical visit and/or reviewing of external audit reports). Finally, media, like any data identified in 3.1, should be destroyed when no longer required for business or legal reasons (9.8). Hardcopy (paper) should be shredded, incinerated or made into pulp (9.8.1), and electronic media should be made unrecoverable in an appropriate way (9.8.2). NIST SP 800-88, Guidelines for Media Sanitization, provides useful information for disposing of electronic media.

3.7.9.3 Protection of Point-of-Sale (POS) and other payment devices

Requirements 9.9.* are new requirements introduced in PCI DSS 3.0 (although I had previously instructed my clients to implement such procedures years before the standard came out). These requirements became mandatory as of July 1, 2015.

These requirements apply to card-present transactions, that is when a user presents a physical payment card to a device of some kind (Points-of-sale, kiosks,

ATMs, etc.). Those devices must be protected from tampering and substitution (9.9). Payment card skimmers have a long history, especially in more automated places such as ATMs, gas payments, isolated kiosks. Brian Krebs has documented (and keeps compiling) very interesting examples on his blog [74].

Organizations must keep an up-to-date list of all such payment devices, including make and model, location, device serial number or other unique identifiers (9.9.1). Those devices must be manually inspected for tampering (9.9.2) periodically (I would recommend between daily and weekly depending on how often they are left alone) by personnel who have been trained in what to look for (9.9.3) and their review must be logged somewhere (at its simplest form, on a form like the ones often used to note when bathrooms have been cleaned). This includes validating the identity of any repair person before granting them access to the devices, not installing updates without prior verification, and reporting suspicious behavior to appropriate personnel as a potential incident (12.10.*). No guidance is provided on how long to keep the review logs, but I would recommend to keep those at least 3 months, the same length as physical access logs (9.1.1).

3.7.10 - Requirement 10 - Logging & Monitoring (audit trails)

In the (hopefully very unlikely) event of a breach, we need to be able to identify what happened when, and what was done and by whom, to reconstruct the events that occurred. Logs are critical in that function, and requirement 10.1 mandates audit trails (another term for logs) to link all access to system components to each individual user (traceability), which means that all relevant events must be recorded. Requirement 10.2 is more specific that this must be automated and, at a minimum, cover the following events:

- All individual user accesses to cardholder data (10.2.1) - if access is through programmatic methods (8.7) then the best place to log access may be within that method (without forgetting information required by 10.3.* and described below).
- All actions taken by any individual with root or administrative privileges (10.2.2) (remember no shared accounts!).
- Use of and changes to identification and authentication mechanisms. Any creation, deletion, or change to authentication configuration and any changes to accounts, with a special emphasis on accounts with root or administrative privileges (10.2.5). Multiple failed attempts at logging in (10.2.4) are often

tell-tale signs of an ongoing attack (trying to guess or brute-force account credentials).

- Any access to audit trails (logs, 10.2.3) or Initialization, stopping, or pausing of the audit logs (10.2.6); preventing logging is one of an attackers standard first steps, and erasing them is one of the last (note that adding information to logs and log rotation are common functions).
- Creation and deletion of system level objects (10.2.7); system level objects are those running by the operating system and not an end-user; malware often modifies operating system files so it can take hold on a system.

All logs must include the following level of detail (10.3):

- User name or identifier (10.3.1)
- Type of event (10.3.2)
- Date and time (10.3.3)
- Event action success or failure (10.3.4)
- Source or origination of event (10.3.5)
- Identity or name of affected data, system component, or resource (10.3.6).

Audit trails (logs) should be secured so they cannot be altered (10.5). This generally means that logs are thus sent to an independent and internal centralized log server (10.5.3) for both internal and externally facing servers (10.5.4). Separation of duties from standard system administration functions is generally key to protecting audit trail files from unauthorized modifications (10.5.2), and we often see this through monitoring, centralized logging and incident management functions completely split from system administration functions. Viewing access to logs, since it can contain sensitive information (although should not include any CHD, including no full PAN) must be restricted only to those who require it (10.5.1). On the centralized log server(s), the organization must use either file integrity monitoring or some other change-detection software to detect log data changes (such as pruning) that generate an alert, since an attacker will often perform log destruction in an attempt to hide their tracks (10.5.5).

Logs must be retained for one full year (10.7) with the last 3 months immediately available (more time than physical access logs like camera recordings in 9.1.1). Immediately available can be online, archived or restorable from backups. In other words, immediately means readily available in a few hours, but not days or longer.

Logs must be reviewed (this is the monitoring function) to identify anomalies or suspicious activity (10.6) and the use of tools is not only permitted, but encouraged. This is generally done using SIEM (Security Information and Event Management) tools as manual review of logs is generally too much time-consuming. The proper configuration of those tools (to adjust for false positives and negatives) should be an ongoing periodic task (that periodicity should be defined by the organization). Required reviews (minimum daily) include (10.6.1):

- All security events
- Logs of all system components that store, process, or transmit CHD and/or SAD, or that could impact the security of CHD and/or SAD (generally CDE/CHD, Segmenting and connected/security system)
- Logs of all critical system components (it is up to the organization to define what 'critical' means, but I would include at least all CDE/CHD, Segmenting and connected/security system)
- Logs of all servers and system components that perform security functions (for example, firewalls, intrusion-detection systems/intrusion-prevention systems (IDS/IPS), authentication servers, e-commerce redirection servers, etc.) (generally Segmenting and connected/security system)

Requirement 10.6.2 calls for the periodical review of other logs based on *"the organization's annual risk assessment"* (see section 3.5.2 for the risk assessment). A well known blogger requested clarification [75] through the FAQ process; he was answered in FAQ 1304 [76]. The FAQ states that it *" allows the organization to determine the log review frequency for all other in-scope events and systems that do not fall into those categories"* (those in 10.6.1), so this gives flexibility to the organization. They also clarify that this requirement applies only to in-scope systems. See volume 2 for what constitutes in-scope systems versus out-of-scope ones.

Finally, the standard mentions that any any anomaly or suspicious activity detected must be adequately investigated (10.6.3), potentially instigating the incident management process (12.10.*).

Requirements 10.4.* mandate use of organizational time servers (using the Network Time Protocol, NTP) to ensure that log dates can easily be compared. An organization should maintain a few (but at least two for redundancy) central time servers that are synchronized from industry-accepted time sources (10.4.3) with their time data protected (10.4.2). These servers are sometimes core network switches, routers or Active Directory servers. All critical systems within the organization should be synchronized with these central servers (10.4.1). I would recommend that all (not just in-scope PCI DSS) organizational systems be synchronized as well using the same internal sources.

PCI DSS 3.2 added two other new requirements, 10.8 and 10.8.1, for service providers that must be in place by February 1, 2018. These requirements align with DESV (now appendix A3) requirements A3.3.1 and A3.3.3.1.1. These requirements mandate more testing (to detect failures) of critical security controls (Firewalls, IDS/IPS, FIM, Anti-virus, Physical access controls, Logical access controls, Audit logging mechanisms, Segmentation controls) (10.8) and managing these failures as incidents (10.8.1), expanding the incident management processes (more in section 3.8.3).

3.7.11 Requirement 11 - Testing

Do you prefer finding that hole in your system yourself or would you prefer an attacker to do so? I certainly hope you prefer the former, and this is why testing is crucial.

Requirement 11 is all about proactively looking for vulnerabilities that often stem from a failure in IT processes. For example, did you forget to check a server that is also running XYZ software (which should be patched) and may have vulnerabilities? Your policies do mention that you can't connect an unauthorized device to the network right? Could somebody not have gotten that memo? Or not cared enough to read it? Or felt it got in the way of business? (Note that this may imply the process should be tweaked to balance the business needs with information security).

3.7.11.1 - Testing wireless networks

The first thing the standard asks us to test for is whether an unauthorized wireless network is connected to your network (11.1). This requires identifying all wireless networks and access points (AP) on a quarterly basis (I would recommend a more timely timeframe). Those wireless networks and APs are then compared to the list of authorized AP and networks that you must maintain (11.1.1). This applies even if there is no direct access from the wireless network to the CDE as we're also looking for networks that a user (or an attacker) has connected (against policy) to the internal network. In heavily populated areas, there can be many wireless networks that are not originating from the premises, but from across the street or another floor. Certain tools will help you pinpoint the location of the APs using signal strength so you can rule out false positives (wireless networks present but physically outside your premises and thus not connected to your network). Should you identify an unauthorized network, you should treat this as an incident (11.1.2) and follow your incident response plan (12.10.*). Note that if you implemented technical controls to prevent connection of unauthorized devices to the network, such as NAC also described in section 3.7.9, you could use this as a compensating control that is stronger than what PCI DSS requires.

3.7.11.2 Vulnerability testing

How about that system or application which you forgot about? Requirement 11.2 is here to the rescue. It mandates that we perform internal and external network vulnerability scans on all in-scope systems, at least quarterly and after any significant change. This means that we need to have a process in place to manage these scans. FAQ 1317 [77] provides the following guidance about 'significant changes':

Generally, changes affecting access to cardholder data or the security of the cardholder data environment could be considered significant. Examples of a significant change may include network upgrades, additions or updates to firewalls or routing devices, upgrades to servers, etc.

Thus, a significant change can include: network topology change, a new major change to a system involved in the storage, processing or transmission of CHD, changes in critical technologies such as segmentation of providing security services, etc. One blogger has also provided a more detailed list [78]. Those changes will be covered in the change control process (6.4) and this list should be reviewed by the assessor to determine whether significant changes have occurred, and thus warrant more testing.

The vulnerability scanning process must produce four (plus those for 'significant changes') 'clean' scans per year (clean means with no vulnerabilities identified, or all remediated) for all in-scope systems. This can be achieved by combining multiple scans during the quarterly period (11.2). For example, say an organization has three systems: A, B, and C. During the January 1st scan, A experiences vulnerabilities but B and C do not. The organization remediates the vulnerabilities in A, but when they run the scan on February 1st, systems B and C show new vulnerabilities. While these new vulnerabilities need to be addressed within the applicable timeframe defined in requirement 6.1, the January scan (for systems B and C) and February scan (for system A) can be combined (with proper documentation) to show a 'clean' scan for the period.

Quarterly Internal scans (11.2.1) can be performed by internal qualified individuals using industry recognized tools. All 'high' or higher ranked vulnerabilities (as defined for requirement 6.1) must be remediated within a month. Rescans must be executed to confirm the vulnerabilities were remediated.

Quarterly External scans (11.2.2) must be performed by an Approved Scanning Vendor (ASV) [79]. An ASV is a vendor approved by the PCI council (like for QSA companies) to perform this task. ASVs are more of a commodity service so that they can easily be replaced by another vendor from the list maintained by the PCI SSC [80]. Some ASVs offer a fully automated solution with little involvement from the ASV staff (unless Compensating Controls are needed). Some will also allow for multiple rescans at a flat fee (based generally on the number of IP addresses in-scope). Rescans must be executed to confirm the vulnerabilities were remediated within the appropriate timeframe.

Just in case you forgot, after any significant change to the environment, you must rescan the network (internally and externally) (11.2.3). If such a change occurs, this should also require additional penetration testing (described in the next section).

3.7.11.3 Penetration testing

An organization performing penetration testing must have a well-defined methodology based on industry-accepted standards (11.3). If this task is outsourced to a vendor, that vendor should document its methodology with references to the industry standard and provide it to the assessor validating PCI DSS compliance. The methodology needs to cover all in-scope networks and systems, both externally facing as well as on the internal network. It needs to cover both network testing as well as application testing. Obviously, it needs to be conducted by qualified personnel. These changes to the requirements introduced in PCI DSS 3.0 must be in place since July 1st, 2015. The PCI SSC released guidance on Penetration testing in March 2015 which was updated to version 1.1 in September 2017. [81]

Vulnerability scans are mostly automated tools. They are generally one of the first steps performed during penetration testing. But penetration testing takes it further by using the tester's experience as well as many other specialized tools.

External (11.3.1) and internal (11.3.2) penetration testing must be performed at least annually, or after significant changes are made (see definition in the previous section). Exploitable vulnerabilities must be corrected and then retested to confirm their resolution (11.3.3). A new requirement introduced in PCI DSS 3.0 is that if network segmentation is used (see volume 2 sections 2.5.1.3 and 2.6.2), testing of the effectiveness of the segmentation must be performed (11.3.4) to ensure isolation and adequate access-controls restrictions by someone qualified and independent (segregation of duties). A new requirement for service providers, 11.3.4.1 which must be in place by February 1, 2018, mandates that network segmentation testing be performed every 6 months, tying back to DESV requirement A3.2.4.

My recommendation would be for an organization to have an internal vulnerability scan tool that is used to scan regularly (daily or weekly) all systems (internal and external) to address vulnerabilities in as timely a fashion as possible, based on the level of risk. 3 months is a long time for a vulnerability to be present, especially for systems exposed to the internet (external). Also, please ensure that you keep all relevant documentation demonstrating the work performed.

3.7.11.4 Other detective controls

Another detective control is the requirement for Intrusion Detection Systems (IDS) or Intrusion Prevention Systems (IPS) at the perimeter (Internet and CDE entry points) as well as other critical points in the network infrastructure (11.4). An IPS is an IDS that can also instruct some equipment to automatically block traffic that match a certain network pattern or signature (attacks). Obviously these IDS/IPS systems must be kept up-to-date and the events they generate must be logged and monitored.

A final detective control is the use of change-detection mechanism of modification to critical files (11.5) (often of the Operating System, but also of key applications), which in previous PCI DSS versions was limited to the use of File Integrity Management (FIM) tools. Since version 3.0 of PCI DSS, added flexibility has been provided to use other types of tools, as long as they can be setup to alert appropriate personnel about changes to critical files or configurations. PCI DSS 3.2 removed a loophole used by some when the PCI SSC removed the phrase "within the cardholder environment" in testing procedure 11.5.a (meaning it applies to all in-scope systems). This requirement applies to all CDE systems, as well as where its presence is necessary to detect changes that may affect the security of the CDE (which should mean connected/security systems). Any alert (11.5.1) must be handled through the incident response process (12.10.*) which will confirm whether we are actually dealing with an incident.

3.8 Other Requirements

3.8.1 Third-party service providers (TPSP)

Outsourcing functions to other organizations can be an efficient way for organizations to fulfill business functions it cannot or does not want to perform in-house, whether for costs or capacity reasons.

Now, one cannot simply use any third-party service provider (TPSP). If that was not obvious before, it is made abundantly clear in the information supplement provided by the PCI SSC in August of 2014 and updated in March 2016. In figure 2 of the information supplement, the due diligence process is presented in the decision tree. If you follow this process, it becomes clear that unless a service provider has either (1) validated and provided evidence of PCI DSS compliance, (2) provided evidence so that the entity has validated that it is compliant, or (3) provided a reasonable plan to achieve compliance, then the entity should select another TPSP. Indeed, the supplement also adds:

The use of a TPSP, however, does not relieve the entity of ultimate responsibility for its own PCI DSS compliance, or exempt the entity from accountability and obligation for ensuring that its cardholder data (CHD) and CDE are secure. [82]

Essentially, you can delegate responsibility to a third-party for tasks, but you cannot outsource your accountability for compliance.

So an organization retains the obligation to ensure that the third-party service providers it hires are PCI DSS compliant and maintain their compliance with PCI DSS through a program consisting of policies and procedures (12.8), including performing proper due diligence prior to engaging a TPSP (12.8.3). The program must cover maintaining a list of PCI DSS service providers including a description of the service(s) provided (12.8.1) and monitoring (i.e. validate) the service providers' PCI DSS compliance status at least annually (12.8.4).

When engaging the TPSP and when renewing the contracts, the organization must ensure it has a written agreement from the TPSP that includes *"an acknowledgement that the service providers are responsible for the security of cardholder data the service providers possess or otherwise store, process or transmit on behalf of the customer, or to the extent that they could impact the security of the customer's cardholder data environment"* [83] (12.8.2). PCI DSS 3.0 added a new requirement that ensure that *" information about which PCI DSS requirements are managed by each service provider, and which are managed by the entity"* [84] is properly documented and agreed upon by the organization (the entity) and the TPSP (12.8.5).

PCI DSS 3.0 also introduced requirement 12.9 for service providers (not other entities), which must be in place since July 1, 2015, that ties back to requirement 12.8.2 of the client. The requirement mandates the same written acknowledgement that an entity requires in 12.8.2, this time from the service provider.

3.8.2 Shared service providers requirements

For PCI DSS, 'shared service providers' are PCI service providers who must comply to PCI DSS and that provide services to more than one client. PCI DSS has included requirements for these service providers since version 1.2 released in 2009. Those requirements are not under a number but under appendix 'A' and are mandated within requirement 2.6 (which was moved from 2.4 to 2.6 in the move from PCI DSS 2.0 to 3.0) which requires performing testing of requirements A.1.1 to A.1.4 of the existing Appendix 'A'.

PCI DSS 3.0 introduced a new requirement outside the appendix that also applies only to shared service providers and not other PCI DSS covered entities. Requirement 8.5.1 mandates that shared service providers with remote access to customer's premises must ensure that individual users use different authentication credentials (username and passwords) for different customers. This requirement tries to prevent that if attackers manage to get the credentials for one customer, these cannot be used to attack another customer. A note clarifies that this does not apply for access to infrastructure managed by the shared service provider and that hosts multiple customers. There, one set of credentials for the complete infrastructure may be adequate.

Requirement A.1 simply asks us to protect each hosted environment and data by meeting the four next requirements. The first two requirements cover logical segmentation (it does not have to be physical) between the different entities (organizations) by using different user account or user IDs (A.1.1), and ensuring that an organization does not have privileges that allow it to access another organization's environment (A.1.2). The language of these requirement still appears written for web hosting providers, but will apply equally to all shared service providers. We are then asked to ensure that logging of each environment meets all of the obligations of requirement 10 (see section 3.7.10), including that logs are available to the client and ensuring that they are reviewed per requirement 10.6.* (who reviews the logs must be agreed upon between the shared service provider and its client, but the logs must be available to the client) (A.1.3). Finally, and linked to the previous requirement, the shared service provider must have defined *"processes to provide for timely forensic investigation in the event of a compromise to any hosted merchant or service provider"* (A.1.4), in other words, logs must be readily available as per requirement 10.7 and the shared service provider must have the necessary resources to assist an investigation in case they are needed.

3.8.3 Incident Management

Incident management is a corrective control invoked by a detective control. Sadly, organizations too often learn of most breaches (confirmed incidents) *"when they receive notification from a law enforcement agency, the card brands, or another third party"* [85] and not through the organization's own monitoring.

Requirement 12.10 asks us to create a an incident response plan that is ready *"to respond immediately to a system breach"*. The plan must cover, at a minimum:

- Assigning roles, responsibilities, and communication and contact strategies in the event of a compromise including notification of the payment brands
- Defining specific incident response procedures
- Covering business recovery and continuity procedures (this is the only mention of BC/DR within the whole standard)
- Data backup processes (since backed up data may contain CHD)
- Analysis of legal requirements for reporting compromises (many countries and states have different breach reporting requirements that organizations must adhere to)
- Reference or inclusion of incident response procedures from the payment brands (provided by acquirers to merchants, or from the payment brands themselves for service providers, issuers and acquirers)
- Coverage and responses of all critical system components (it is up to the organization to define what 'critical' means, but I would include at least all CDE/CHD, Segmenting and connected/security system) and further expanded by requirement 12.10.5 to *"Include alerts from security monitoring systems, including but not limited to intrusion-detection, intrusion- prevention, firewalls, and file-integrity monitoring systems"*

The plan must be reviewed and tested at least annually (12.10.2) and all elements of 12.10.1 must be covered during review and testing; it can be done as a tabletop exercise. Specific personnel must be assigned and available at all times (24/7) to respond to alerts (12.10.3) and this personnel must be trained at least annually (12.10.4). Finally, since we know that systems and attacks are not static, the organization must be able to update, evolve and improve *"the incident response plan according to lessons learned and to incorporate industry developments"* (12.10.6). This is often done through post-mortem analysis of events.

PCI DSS 3.2 added two other new requirements, 12.11 and 12.11.1, for service providers that must be in place by February 1, 2018. These requirements align with DESV (now appendix A3) requirements A3.3.3. Similar to requirements 10.8 and 10.8.1, these requirements mandate a documented quarterly review process to confirm that the following PCI DSS related processes are being followed by personnel:

- Daily log reviews
- Firewall rule-set reviews
- Applying configuration standards to new systems
- Responding to security alerts
- Change management processes

3.9 Addressing compliance gaps – prioritization

So, you've done (or had someone do) a readiness assessment or just realized that you are not compliant with certain requirements of the PCI DSS. What are you to do? I mean, can anyone expect you to remediate everything overnight? Do you stop operating until then? Of course not. No business would accept something so drastic. There's an understanding that, since not all things are created equal, some risks are actually greater than others and the controls required to address those risks should follow the risk level. The PCI SSC also understands this. This is why, with version 2.0 of the PCI DSS standard, they started distributing alongside the current version of the standard a prioritized approach to compliance. The version accompanying PCI DSS 3.2 came out about a month after the standard was released.

The PCI DSS Prioritized Approach [86] recognizes that not all issues are equal in terms of risk and that some need to be addressed before others. The PCI SSC has divided the PCI DSS requirements into six different milestones, numbered from 1 to 6. Requirements grouped in Milestone 1 are the ones that reduce risk the most and should be addressed first, while Milestone 6 requirements reduce risk the least and might be addressed later.

The PCI DSS prioritized approach has not generally changed from version 2.0 to 3.0, 3.1 and 3.2.

Table 5 below summarizes the high-level actions and goals of each milestone. The PCI DSS prioritized approach document maps the milestones to each of all twelve PCI DSS requirements and their sub-requirements.

Milestone	Title	Goals
1	Remove sensitive authentication data and limit data retention.	This milestone targets a key area of risk for entities that have been compromised. Remember – if sensitive authentication data and other cardholder data are not stored, the effects of a compromise will be greatly reduced. If you don't need it, don't store it.
2	Protect systems and networks, and be prepared to respond to a system breach.	This milestone targets controls for points of access to most compromises, and the processes for responding.
3	Secure payment card applications.	This milestone targets controls for applications, application processes, and application servers. Weaknesses in these areas offer easy prey for compromising systems and obtaining access to cardholder data.
4	Monitor and control access to your systems.	Controls for this milestone allow you to detect the who, what, when, and how concerning who is accessing your network and cardholder data environment
5	Protect stored cardholder data.	For those organizations that have analyzed their business processes and determined that they must store Primary Account Numbers, Milestone Five targets key protection mechanisms for that stored data.
6	Finalize remaining compliance efforts, and ensure all controls are in place.	The intent of Milestone Six is to complete PCI DSS requirements, and to finalize all remaining related policies, procedures, and processes needed to protect the cardholder data environment.

Volume 3 Table 5 - PCI DSS Prioritized Approach Milestones

PCI DSS Requirements v3.2	Milestone					
	1	2	3	4	5	6
Requirement 1: Install and maintain a firewall configuration to protect cardholder data						
1.1 Establish and implement firewall and router configuration standards that include the following:						
1.1.1 A formal process for approving and testing all network connections and changes to the firewall and router configurations						6
1.1.2 Current network diagram that identifies all connections between the cardholder data environment and other networks, including any wireless networks	1					
1.1.3 Current diagram that shows all cardholder data flows across systems and networks	1					
1.1.4 Requirements for a firewall at each Internet connection and between any demilitarized zone (DMZ) and the internal network zone		2				

Volume 3 Figure 7 - Screenshot of prioritized approach document

The PCI DSS prioritized approach gives us a good idea of which approach to take in achieving PCI DSS compliance. Milestone one is to reduce the amount of information we have and keep on our systems. You don't have to protect what you do not have. This falls in-line with the general recommendation of reducing scope. If you don't need it, don't store it (or collect it in the first place). When we mention that process changes are often the best approach, that would fall directly within this milestone. Note that if there is a business need for the information, you are allowed to keep parts of it (except SAD, covered more in depth in section 3.7.3) provided it is adequately protected. You should however never take the approach *"well I may need it in the future"*. You will almost <u>never</u> need this information (CHD) for this purpose, especially if you are a merchant. Issuers often have to keep more information, but that too should be as limited as possible. The same applies to acquirers and service providers, and to those entities I would classify as "other" (meaning they have CHD but are not necessarily involved in payment processing). Note that this is a general information security recommendation I would provide to all my clients regarding not storing sensitive data (and not just cardholder data) unless you absolutely must. Within milestone one, critical requirements include maintaining network diagrams (1.1.2) and PCI data flow diagrams (1.1.3), managing data retention (3.1, 3.2, 9.8) and performing risk assessments (12.2).

Milestone two relates to protecting the in-scope systems, and ensuring that if ever there was a breach, that you could have enough information so that an investigation would allow for identifying how the breach occurred and who may have been involved. Prevent then detect and investigate/react. Within milestone two, we still find isolating the CDE (1.*), hardening devices (2.* except 2.2.*), securing transmissions (4.*, 8.3, A2), protection from malware (5.*), ensuring physical security (9.*), vulnerability testing (11.2, 11.3), intrusion detection (11.4), managing service providers (12.8.*, 12.9) and incident response (12.10.*). The PCI SSC has also moved up from milestone 4 User Management (most of 8) including Identification (8.1) and Authentication (8.2).

Milestone three covers payment applications. While operating system vulnerabilities are still prevalent, the proportion of vulnerabilities from applications (with web application being especially targeted) has risen to often become the main avenues that attackers target. Many web apps are also often custom-built within organizations by developers that may not have adequate understanding of secure application development. The Open Web Application Security Project (OWASP, found on the web at www.owasp.org) has risen in prominence in large part due to that fact. Within milestone three, we find system hardening (2.2.*), patching (6.2), secure application development (6.3, 6.5.*), change management (6.4), web application security (6.6) and Service Provider requirements (A1).

Milestone four adds monitoring and access control. Monitoring requires logging which is critical to the incident response function of milestone two. Milestone four covers Role-Based Access Control (RBAC, 7.*) and the remaining user management policies and procedures (8.4-8.8), logging (10.*) including synchronizing time (10.4, NTP) and monitoring events (10.6), as well as detecting unauthorized wireless networks (11.1) and critical file changes (11.5).

Milestone five targets stored in-scope data. It covers protecting the PAN (3.3, 3.4, 9.5, 9.6, 9.7), encryption of stored data (3.5, 3.6) and managing visitors (9.2, 9.4).

Finally, milestone six covers all remaining requirements. It covers mostly policies and procedures.

Just because some items are of a lower risk level does not mean that they should not be addressed immediately. Simple changes, often called low-hanging fruit (e.g. easy fixes), should likely be dealt with quickly.

3.10 Compensating Controls

PCI DSS 3.2 covers Compensating Controls (CC) briefly on page 16 and then in Appendix B and C of pages 136 to 138.

On page 16, we have confirmation that all compensating controls must be documented (using the compensating control worksheet of Appendix C), reviewed by the organization, and validated annually by an organization's assessor (internally for self-assessment, or externally by a QSA). The PCI SSC is clear in FAQ 1046 [87] that this validation is a responsibility of the assessor (QSA) and not the PCI SSC itself.

Appendix B is where we get more information on what is required to constitute a compensating control.

Almost all PCI DSS requirements can be addressed using compensating controls if a legitimate business or technical constraint exists preventing meeting the requirement *"as stated"*, but that does not mean organizations should go down that route. The standard mentions that CC must satisfy 3 criteria among the following:

- Meet the intent and rigor of the original PCI DSS requirement.
- Provide a similar level of defense as the original PCI DSS requirement, such that the compensating control sufficiently offsets the risk that the original PCI DSS requirement was designed to defend against.
- Be *"above and beyond"* other PCI DSS requirements. (Simply being in compliance with other PCI DSS requirements is not a compensating control.)
- Be commensurate with the additional risk imposed by not adhering to the PCI DSS requirement.

So compensating controls must go *"above and beyond"* (#3), and *"meet the intent and rigor of the original PCI DSS requirement"* (#1) and basically address any new risk (#4), which means that the bar is set very high indeed.

To see if we are *"above and beyond"* (#3), the standard also asks us to consider that:

- Existing PCI DSS requirements CANNOT be considered as compensating controls if they are already required for the item under review. (Password controls cannot be used for other password requirements, existing logging requirements cannot be used for lack of change detection, etc.)

- Existing PCI DSS requirements MAY be considered as compensating controls if they are required for another area, but are not required for the item under review. (Multi-factor is only mandated for external remote access or administrative access to the CDE, so it can be used internally to compensate for other requirements)
- Existing PCI DSS requirements may be combined with new controls to become a compensating control.

Generally, any new compensating control must bring something new to the table (a non-existing requirement), or increase another control's frequency (from weekly to daily, from daily to real-time, etc.).

Appendix C gives us the template that must be filled (also included in the RoC template and the SAQ formats) by the organization or their assessor for each requirement that is not met (one sheet per requirement). No other format is allowed, although I can see that adding appendixes to this may be helpful in some cases. The template includes six elements that require detailed documentation:

#	Definition	Information Required	Explanation
1	Constraints	List constraints precluding compliance with the original requirement.	
2	Objective	Define the objective of the original control; identify the objective met by the compensating control.	
3	Identified Risk	Identify any additional risk posed by the lack of the original control.	
4	Definition of Compensating Controls	Define the compensating controls and explain how they address the objectives of the original control and the increased risk, if any.	
5	Validation of Compensating Controls	Define how the compensating controls were validated and tested.	
6	Maintenance	Define process and controls in place to maintain compensating controls.	

Volume 3 Table 6 - Compensating Controls Documentation Requirements

Item 1 is a technical or business (often cost-related, but could be regulatory or other) reason why the stated PCI DSS requirement cannot be met. Item 2 is the objective, or risk, that the PCI DSS requirement not met is intended to address; this generally is adapted from the 'guidance' column of the relevant PCI DSS requirement. Item 3 is any new risk not identified by item 2. Item 4 is the detailed list of controls used to compensate for the unmet one. Item 5 details how we validate and test that the CC is operating as expected. Item 6 defines what processes must take place to ensure that no failure in the CC occurs.

3.11 Total Cost of Ownership (TCO) and Return-on-Investment (ROI)

One issue that most experts have happens when they try to explain their domain of expertise to people with a different level of familiarity, mostly because some things become so obvious with experience that we jump over them. I've often been guilty of this, of taking shortcuts in terms of architecture decision. In my case this is due to my ample/extensive experience in IT operations (system administration), software development, information security and IT audit. This section attempts to document a simplified version of my architecture decision thought process.

My thought process tries to reduce both information security risk and compliance costs (measured in hardware, software, but also cost in human resources which over time can be more than the other costs). In that sense, I take into account all the relevant costs to produce a recommendation. My evaluation is based on personal experience in IT.

The basic cost framework taught in business schools is:

Total Costs = Fixed Costs + Variable Costs

Our fixed costs when selecting architecture here include hardware and initial setup costs (including hardening). Note that policies and procedures are fixed costs to the organization that are not impacted by architecture decisions.

Most other PCI DSS requirements are variable costs. Appendix C of the Verizon 2015 PCI compliance report presents the period specific requirements that need to be performed (some are only identified as 'periodic' which means that an organization must define the periodicity for itself). A slightly modified appendix C in the Verizon 2017 PCI compliance report can be used to replace the one I just mentioned. More often than not, these variable costs are the biggest ones for an organization in the long run. And all those costs generally include infrastructure (technology: hardware, software, etc.), services (consulting, assessment, vulnerability, scanning, etc.) and staff time.

All of these requirements involve costs, but depending on the architecture decision, these can vary wildly for each organization. My recommendation is that organizations measure (what cannot be measured cannot be improved) the costs (time and equipment) used to manage all systems and environments that adhere to

PCI DSS requirements and those that must adhere only to organizational requirements. It then becomes possible to say (this is an example, values are made up) that a MS Windows server costs, on average, $1000 per month (base number) and $1450 for PCI compliant ones (including human resource times).

REQ	AREA	DSS 3.0	ACTIVITY	DAILY	WEEKLY	EVERY X MONTHS	ANNUALLY	PERIODICALLY	AFTER CHANGES
	SCOPE MANAGEMENT	All	Confirm all locations and flows of CHD and ensure that they are included in the PCI DSS scope.				A		
1	FIREWALLS AND ROUTERS	1.1.7	Review firewall and router rulesets at least every six months.			6			
2	NONE	-							
3	DATA RETENTION	3.1.b	Identify and securely delete any CHD that's exceeded the defined retention period.			3			
3	CRYPTOGRAPHIC KEYS	3.6.4	Change cryptographic keys that have reached the end of their cryptoperiod.					P	

Volume 3 Figure 8 - Verizon 2015 PCI Compliance Report Appendix C

An organization can now do an apples-to-apples comparison ($ to $) of which solution makes a better sense over a number of years (3, 5, 10, etc.) depending on average duration of systems. While this calculation allows us to compare the TCO of alternative solutions, TCO is not ROI (and since it is hard to quantify the actual monetary risk that compliance addresses, a true ROI is difficult to measure), but it does allow us to make more informed decisions.

3.12 Mappings

In the first edition of this volume (2015) for PCI DSS 3.1, I included a mapping between ISO 27002 and PCI DSS. This is all well and good for Information Security practitioners familiar with ISO 27002, or for those organizations who already have an alignment with this standard, but what about the others? This is why I'm adding a high-level mapping with COBIT 5. I'm also adding my own categorization which I've developed over the previous years and used with clients. I believe this one will make PCI DSS controls more understandable to non-technical personnel.

No mapping is ever 100% correct as the approaches of each framework development teams vary, as do the goals defined by the framework's authors.

This is similar to translating between languages, where a good translation is more an adaptation than a literal translation. There are concepts that are presented differently in different languages. It may be easier to translate between the same family such latin/romance languages, germanic, slavic (russian), but there may yet be local differences. For example, Spanish, Catalan and Portuguese have 2 verbs (ser, estar) for "to be" (representing a permanent or temporary state), whereas like English, French only has one verb (être) and so does Italian (essere).

The same applies here with frameworks. COBIT 5 (and ITIL) are more generic IT frameworks that include elements of Information Security, whereas PCI DSS, ISO 27001/2 are specifically about Information Security.

3.13 Mapping to and Missing ISO/IEC 27002 controls

3.13.1 ISO/IEC 27000 Series

ISO/IEC has created a series of standards in the 27000 series that cover information security under the title *"Information technology -- Security techniques"*. The series includes many documents, with 27001 and 27002 being the most referenced ones. ISO/IEC 27001 is published under the title *"Information security management systems – Requirements"*.

ISO/IEC 27002:2013 is an information security standard published in 2013 by the International Organization for Standardization (ISO) and by the International Electrotechnical Commission (IEC). The title for this standard is *"Information technology -- Security techniques -- Code of practice for information security controls"*.

So ISO/IEC 27001 presents Information Security Program requirements (mostly for audit purposes) while 27002 details the controls that an Information Security Program should include. Both standards share a similar structure.

3.13.2 ISO/IEC 27002 Overview

ISO/IEC 27002 was mostly a renaming of ISO 17799, released in 2005, which was itself the international adoption of the 1995 release of British Standards Institute (BSI) BS7799 of a UK government document. The most recent version of ISO/IEC 27002 came out in 2013 and is referenced as ISO/IEC 27002:2013. This is the version used in the mapping.

The standard includes 5 introductory sections starting at 0

- 0. Introduction,
- 1. Scope,
- 2. Normative references,
- 3. Terms and definitions, and
- 4. Structure of this standard

and then the 14 *"domains"*, described in chapters 5 to 18:

- 5. Information Security Policies

- 6. Organization of Information Security
- 7. Human Resource Security
- 8. Asset Management
- 9. Access Control
- 10. Cryptography
- 11. Physical and environmental security
- 12. Operation Security- procedures and responsibilities, Protection from malware, Backup, Logging and monitoring, Control of operational software, Technical vulnerability management and Information systems audit coordination
- 13. Communication security - Network security management and Information transfer
- 14. System acquisition, development and maintenance - Security requirements of information systems, Security in development and support processes and Test data
- 15. Supplier relationships - Information security in supplier relationships and Supplier service delivery management
- 16. Information security incident management - Management of information security incidents and improvements
- 17. Information security aspects of business continuity management - Information security continuity and Redundancies
- 18. Compliance - Compliance with legal and contractual requirements and Information security reviews

Each of the domains is divided into subdomains and eventually into detailed requirements. For example, the structure for domain 5 *"Information Security Policies"* is:

- 5. Information Security Policies

  - o 5.1 INFORMATION SECURITY POLICY
    - 5.1.1 Information security policy document
    - 5.1.2 Review of the information security policy

3.13.3 ISO/IEC 27002:2013 and PCI DSS 3.2 high-level controls

For this document, I've mapped up to the first dotted number (or subdomain) with a similar high-level structure as PCI DSS 3.2. The mapping was performed to identify related items, and discern where lack of coverage was present.

The following ISO/IEC 27002:2013 domains and subdomains are those used within this mapping:

- 5 Information security policies
  - 5.1 Management direction for information security
- 6 Organization of information
  - 6.1 Internal organization
  - 6.2 Mobile devices and teleworking
- 7 Human resource security
  - 7.1 Prior to employment
  - 7.2 During employment
  - 7.3 Termination and change of employment
- 8 Asset management
  - 8.1 Responsibility for assets
  - 8.2 Information classification
  - 8.3 Media handling
- 9 Access control
  - 9.1 Business requirements of access control
  - 9.2 User access management
  - 9.3 User responsibilities
  - 9.4 System and application access control
- 10 Cryptography
  - 10.1 Cryptographic controls
- 11 Physical and environmental security
  - 11.1 Secure areas
  - 11.2 Equipment
- 12 Operations security
  - 12.1 Operational procedures and responsibilities
  - 12.2 Protection from malware
  - 12.3 Backup
  - 12.4 Logging and monitoring
  - 12.5 Control of operational software
  - 12.6 Technical vulnerability management

- o 12.7 Information systems audit considerations
- 13 Communications security
  - o 13.1 Network security management
  - o 13.2 Information transfer
- 14 System acquisition, development and maintenance
  - o 14.1 Security requirements of information systems
  - o 14.2 Security in development and support processes
  - o 14.3 Test data
- 15 Supplier relationships
  - o 15.1 Information security in supplier relationships
  - o 15.2 Supplier service delivery management
- 16 Information security incident management
  - o 16.1 Management of information security incidents and improvements
- 17 Information security aspects of business continuity management
  - o 17.1 Information security continuity
  - o 17.2 Redundancies
- 18 Compliance
  - o 18.1 Compliance with legal and contractual requirements
  - o 18.2 Information security reviews

The PCI DSS 3.2 summarized controls used in the mapping are:

- 1.1.* Router/Firewall Configuration Standards
- 1.1.1 Router/Firewall Change Process
- 1.1.2 Network diagrams
- 1.1.3 Data flow diagrams
- 1.2.* Firewall between CDE/untrusted
- 1.3.* Firewall between CDE/internet
- 1.4 Personal Firewall for Mobile
- 2 Configuration Management
- 2.1 Change Default Settings
- 2.2.* System Configuration Standards
- 2.3 Encrypt Administrative Access
- 2.4 / 11.1.1 Inventory
- 3.1 Data Retention and Disposal
- 3.2.* No storage of SAD
- 3.3 Mask PAN (display)
- 3.4.* PAN storage

- 3.5.* / 3.6.* Cryptographic Key Management
- 4.1 Encryption in transit (open networks)
- 4.1.1 Secure Wireless Configuration
- 4.2 No PAN in Email, Chat, etc.
- 5.* Antimalware
- 6.1 Vulnerability Management (id & rank)
- 6.2 Patching
- 6.3.* SDLC
- 6.4.* Change Management
- 6.5.* Secure Application Coding
- 6.6 Protect web-facing application
- 7.1.* Define user roles
- 7.2.* RBAC
- 8.1.* User Identification
- 8.2.* User Authentication
- 8.3.1 Multi-factor for administrative access to CDE
- 8.3.2 Multi-factor for remote access
- 8.4 User training on selecting secure passwords
- 8.5 / 8.6 No shared account
- 8.7 Data access Segregation of Duties
- 9.1.* Physical Access Control and Monitoring
- 9.2 / 9.4.* Visitor management
- 9.3 Physical Badge Access
- 9.5.* Physically secure media
- 9.6.* Classify media
- 9.7.* Control media
- 9.8.* Media destruction
- 9.9.* Device Tampering
- 10.1 / 10.2.* / 10.3.* Logging (data access, admin actions)
- 10.4.* Synchronize time clocks (NTP)
- 10.5.* Securing logs
- 10.6.* Log Monitoring
- 10.7 Log Retention
- 10.8 Detect failures of critical security controls (service provider only) (A3.3.1.*)
- 11.1 Identify unauthorized wireless networks
- 11.2.* Vulnerability Testing

- 11.3.* Penetration Testing
- 11.4 IDS / IPS at critical points
- 11.5.* Change Detection Management (FIM)
- 12 Information Security Policy (Program)
- 12.1 Information Security Policy
- 12.2 Risk Assessment
- 12.3.* Acceptable Use Policy
- 12.4 / 12.5.*   Information Security Responsibilities
- 12.4.1 Responsibility for PCI DSS compliance (A3.1.1)
- 12.6 Security Awareness Training
- 12.7 HR Background Checks
- 12.8.* / 12.9 Third-party management
- 12.10.* Incident Response
- 12.11 Quarterly review of PCI DSS processes (service provider only) (A3.3.3)

3.13.4 ISO/IEC 27002:2013 mapping to PCI DSS 3.2

This mapping is not a detailed comparison of every single control (which could not be mapped completely one-to-one anyway), but is performed at a higher level. And since PCI DSS only covers confidentiality and not integrity or availability, there is no overlap over those two elements. The goal of this mapping is to help you identify best practice controls that are not covered by one standard and that you should likely implement as well, or in case you use ISO/IEC 27002 as a basis for compliance with many different regulatory requirements (PCI DSS, HIPAA, Sarbanes Oxley, etc.).

3.13.4.1 ISO/IEC 27002:2013 Domain 5 - Information security policies

This domain contains the policies which map well with PCI DSS requirement 12.1 (and the distributed policies, not the procedures which are covered in domain 12) moved to PCI DSS requirements 1.5, 2.5, 3.7, 4.3, 5.4, 6.7, 7.3, 8.8, 9.10, 10.8, 11.6).

ISO/IEC 27002:2013	PCI DSS 3.2
5 Information security policies	12.1, 1.5, 2.5, 3.7, 4.3, 5.4, 6.7, 7.3, 8.8, 9.10, 10.8, 11.6 Information Security Policies
5.1 Management direction for information security	

3.13.4.2 ISO/IEC 27002:2013 Domain 6 - Organization of information

Domain 6 includes the internal assignment of *"information security responsibilities"* (ISO 6.1) which maps to PCI DSS requirements 12.4 and 12.5.*. These responsibilities must ensure separation of duties (6.1.2). This domain also includes *"mobile devices and teleworking"* (ISO 6.2) which covers PCI DSS requirements 1.4 (Personal Firewall for Mobile Devices), 8.3 (Multi-factor for remote access), 4.1.1 (Secure Wireless Configuration).

ISO/IEC 27002:2013	PCI DSS 3.2
6 Organization of information	
6.1 Internal organization	12.4 / 12.5.* Information Security Responsibilities
6.2 Mobile devices and teleworking	1.4 Personal Firewall for Mobile
	8.3.2 Multi-factor for remote access
	4.1.1 Secure Wireless Configuration

3.13.4.3 ISO/IEC 27002:2013 Domain 7 - Human resource security

Domain 7 is divided into three items: before, during and after employment. Prior to employment (ISO 7.1) maps to PCI DSS requirement 12.7 on having HR perform background checks for new hires. During employment (ISO 7.2) maps to PCI DSS 12.6 (Security Awareness Training), but should also likely include a sanctions policy (not present in PCI DSS and which I call out for in volume 1). Termination and change of employment (ISO 7.3) is not mapped to groups of requirements but to individual PCI DSS requirements 9.3 (Physical access is revoked immediately upon termination), and 8.1.3 (Immediately revoke logical access for any terminated users).

ISO/IEC 27002:2013	PCI DSS 3.2
7 Human resource security	
7.1 Prior to employment	12.7 HR Background Checks
7.2 During employment	12.6 Security Awareness Training
7.3 Termination and change of employment	8.1.3 Immediately revoke logical access for any terminated users
	9.3 Physical access is revoked immediately upon termination

3.13.4.4 ISO/IEC 27002:2013 Domain 8 - Asset management

Asset management allows us to know what we're trying to protect (physical assets as well as data). Subdomain 8.1 (Responsibility for assets) is mapped to our PCI DSS inventory of all in-scope systems (2.4) and wireless access points (11.1.1) but also covers our Acceptable Use Policy (12.3.*). Subdomain 8.2 (Information classification) should include a data classification policy that is missing (or merely implied) from PCI DSS, but does include classifying media (9.6.*). Subdomain 8.3 (Media handling) maps to PCI DSS requirements 9.5.* (Physically secure media), 9.7.* (Control media distribution) and 9.8.* (media destruction).

ISO/IEC 27002:2013	PCI DSS 3.2
8 Asset management	
8.1 Responsibility for assets	2.4 / 11.1.1 Inventory
8.2 Information classification	9.6.* Classify media
8.3 Media handling	9.5.* Physically secure media
	9.7.* Control media distribution
	9.8.* Media destruction

3.13.4.5 ISO/IEC 27002:2013 Domain 9 - Access control

Logical access controls (physical access controls are in domain 11) are fairly well mapped between both standards. Subdomain 9.1 matches with PCI DSS requirement 7.1.* defining user roles. Subdomain 9.2 is mapped to using Role-Based-Access-Control (RBAC) of 7.2.*, ensuring user identification (8.1.*), including unique user accounts (8.5 / 8.6) to ensure traceability, and Changing Default Settings (2.1). Subdomain 9.3 is mapped to PCI DSS requirement 8.2.* (user authentication) and 8.4 (user training on selecting secure passwords). Subdomain 9.4 covers PCI DSS requirement 2.3 to ensure encrypted administrative access to systems.

ISO/IEC 27002:2013	PCI DSS 3.2
9 Access control	
9.1 Business requirements of access control	7.1.* Define user roles
9.2 User access management	7.2.* RBAC
	8.1.* User Identification
	8.5 / 8.6 No shared account
	2.1 Change Default Settings
9.3 User responsibilities	8.4 User training on selecting secure passwords
	8.2.* User Authentication
9.4 System and application access control	2.3 Encrypt Administrative Access

3.13.4.6 ISO/IEC 27002:2013 Domain 10 - Cryptography

The cryptographic controls are fairly well mapped between both standards. This domain maps partly to PCI DSS requirements for PAN storage (3.4.*, also called *"render PAN unreadable"*) when encryption is used, and also covers Cryptographic Key Management (3.5.* / 3.6.*).

ISO/IEC 27002:2013	PCI DSS 3.2
10 Cryptography	
10.1 Cryptographic controls	3.4.* PAN storage
	3.5.* / 3.6.* Cryptographic Key Management

3.13.4.7 ISO/IEC 27002:2013 Domain 11 - Physical and environmental security

Physical security is the oldest form of information security and is also very well mapped between both standards. Subdomain 11.1 (secure areas) is mapped to PCI DSS requirements for Physical Access Control and Monitoring (9.1.*), Visitor management (9.2 / 9.4.*), and Physical Badge Access Controls (9.3). Subdomain 11.2 (equipment) is mapped to protecting payment devices from tampering, as well as 9.1.3 (restrict physical access to network devices) (and potentially 9.1.2).

ISO/IEC 27002:2013	PCI DSS 3.2
11 Physical and environmental security	
11.1 Secure areas	9.1 Physical Access Control and Monitoring
	9.2 / 9.4.* Visitor management
	9.3 Physical Badge Access
11.2 Equipment	9.9.* Device Tampering
	9.1.3 Restrict physical access to network devices

3.13.4.8 ISO/IEC 27002:2013 Domain 12 - Operations security

Domain 12 (operations security) is the biggest of the ISO/IEC 27002:2013 domains, but its mapping is partial. Subdomain 12.1 (Operational procedures and responsibilities) is mapped to the procedures portion of PCI DSS requirements 1.5, 2.5, 3.7, 4.3, 5.4, 6.7, 7.3, 8.8, 9.10, 10.8, and 11.6. Subdomain 12.2 (Protection from malware) is well mapped to the complete requirement 5 of PCI DSS (Protect all systems against malware and regularly update anti-virus software or programs).

Subdomain 12.3 (Backup) is not covered by PCI DSS requirements, nor is 12.7 (Information systems audit considerations). Subdomain 12.4 (Logging and monitoring) is mapped to the complete requirement 10 of PCI DSS as well as 11.5 (Change Detection Management).

Subdomain 12.6 (Technical vulnerability management) is mapped to PCI DSS requirements 6.1 (Vulnerability identification & ranking), 6.2 (Patching), 11.1 (Identify unauthorized wireless networks), 11.2.* (Vulnerability Testing) and 11.3.* (Penetration Testing).

PCI DSS requirements 6.4 (Change control, covered more in detail in section 3.13.4.15) is partly mapped to subdomain 12.5 (control of operational software) and 12.1, as well as 14.2.

ISO/IEC 27002:2013	PCI DSS 3.2
12 Operations security	
12.1 Operational procedures and responsibilities	1.5, 2.5, 3.7, 4.3, 5.4, 6.7, 7.3, 8.8, 9.10, 10.8, 11.6 Procedures
12.2 Protection from malware	5. Antimalware
12.3 Backup	
12.4 Logging and monitoring	10.1 / 10.2.* / 10.3.* Logging (data access, admin actions)
	10.4.* Synchronize time clocks (NTP)
	10.5.* Securing logs
	10.6.* Log Monitoring
	10.7 Log Retention
	11.5.* Change Detection Management (FIM)
12.5 Control of operational software	6.4.* Change Control
12.6 Technical vulnerability management	6.1 Vulnerability Management (id & rank)
	6.2 Patching
	11.1.* Identify unauthorized wireless networks
	11.2.* Vulnerability Testing
	11.3.* Penetration Testing
12.7 Information systems audit considerations	

3.13.4.9 ISO/IEC 27002:2013 Domain 13 - Communications security

Domain 13 (communication security) includes everything regarding network security. Subdomain 13.1 (network security management) maps to multiple PCI DSS requirements including maintaining Router/Firewall Configuration Standards (1.1.*) and Change Process (1.1.1), placing a firewall between the CDE and untrusted internal networks (1.2.*) as well as between the CDE and the internet (1.3.*). It is also mapped to placing IDS / IPS at critical networks points (11.4). Subdomain 13.2 (Information transfer) is partly mapped to PCI DSS requirement 4.2 requiring that no PAN be sent in end-user messaging such as email and chat.

ISO/IEC 27002:2013	PCI DSS 3.2
13 Communications security	
13.1 Network security management	1.1.* Router/Firewall Configuration Standards
	1.1.1 Router/Firewall Change Process
	1.2.* Firewall between CDE/untrusted
	1.3.* Firewall between CDE/internet
	11.4 IDS / IPS at critical points
13.2 Information transfer	4.2 No PAN in Email, Chat, etc.

3.13.4.10 ISO/IEC 27002:2013 Domain 14 - System acquisition, development and maintenance

Domain 14 covers the software development controls of PCI DSS. Subdomain 14.1 (security requirements of information systems) maps to PCI DSS requirements 6.5.* (Secure Application Coding) and 6.6 (Protect web-facing application), and 4.1 (Encryption of data in transit on open networks). Subdomain 14.2 (security in development and support processes) is mapped to the PCI DSS SDLC controls (6.3.*). Subdomain 14.3 (test data) is mapped to some of PCI DSS requirements of change control management (6.4.3, 6.4.4). The new requirement for multi-factor access to CDE system also falls in this category.

ISO/IEC 27002:2013	PCI DSS 3.2
14 System acquisition, development and maintenance	
14.1 Security requirements of information systems	6.5.* Secure Application Coding
	6.6 Protect web-facing application
	4.1 Encryption in transit (open networks)
	8.3.1 Multi-factor for administrative access to CDE
14.2 Security in development and support processes	6.3.* SDLC
14.3 Test data	6.4.3 / 6.4.4

3.13.4.11 ISO/IEC 27002:2013 Domain 15 - Supplier relationships

Domain 15 that deals with suppliers is mapped to PCI DSS requirements covering third-party service provider management (12.8.* / 12.9).

ISO/IEC 27002:2013	PCI DSS 3.2
15 Supplier relationships	12.8.* / 12.9 Third-party service provider management
15.1 Information security in supplier relationships	
15.2 Supplier service delivery management	

3.13.4.12 ISO/IEC 27002:2013 Domain 16 - Information security incident management

Domain 16 (information security incident management) is mapped to PCI DSS requirements 12.10.* (requesting an incident response plan), and requirement 11.1.2 (invoke incident response if unauthorized wireless is found). Failures from monitoring of maintenance of compliance are also addressed here.

ISO/IEC 27002:2013	PCI DSS 3.2
16 Information security incident management	
16.1 Management of information security incidents and improvements	12.10.* / 11.1.2 Incident Response Plan (and 10.8.1 / 12.11.1 for service providers)

3.13.4.13 ISO/IEC 27002:2013 Domain 17 - Information security aspects of business continuity management

Business continuity and Disaster Recovery (BC/DR), like integrity and availability, are not covered by PCI DSS. The only concern slightly related to these is in requirement 12.10.1 to ensure no degradation of confidentiality of CHD in the event of the invocation of BC/DR plans.

Thus an Information Security Program should be reviewed to cover organizational BC/DR needs not mandated by PCI DSS.

ISO/IEC 27002:2013	PCI DSS 3.2
17 Information security aspects of business continuity management	
17.1 Information security continuity	
17.2 Redundancies	

3.13.4.14 ISO/IEC 27002:2013 Domain 18 - Compliance

The compliance domain aligns more with the recently released document Designated Entities Special Validation (DESV). Subdomain 18.1 *"Compliance with legal and contractual requirements"* aligns well with DESV A3.1.* *"Implement a PCI DSS compliance program"*, while subdomain 18.2 *"Information security reviews"* aligns more closely with A3.3.*, *"Validate PCI DSS is incorporated into business-as-usual (BAU) activities"*. Subdomain 18.1 also maps partly to requirement 3.1 of PCI DSS (Data Retention and Disposal Policies). The new service provider requirements also fit in here.

ISO/IEC 27002:2013	PCI DSS 3.2
18 Compliance	
18.1 Compliance with legal and contractual requirements	DESV A3.1.* (designated entities only)
	3.1 Data Retention and Disposal Policies
	12.4.1 Responsibility for PCI DSS compliance
18.2 Information security reviews	10.8 Detect failures of critical security controls (service provider only) 12.11 Quarterly review of PCI DSS processes (service provider only) DESVA3.3.* (designated entities only)

3.13.4.15 PCI DSS 3.2 requirements partially or not covered by ISO/IEC 27002:2013

While ISO/IEC 27002:2013 is a very comprehensive information security framework, there are nonetheless specificities of PCI DSS that are not, or at least not fully, covered by the ISO/IEC standard.

Scope definition is an area that is more specific in PCI DSS. In this area, we identify the following unmapped PCI DSS requirements:

- 1.1.2 Create and Maintain Network Diagrams
- 1.1.3 Create and Maintain Data Flow Diagrams

Management of certain information is also more detailed within PCI DSS 3.2 (and not covered by ISO/IEC):

- 3.2.* No storage of SAD after authentication
- 3.3 Masking of PAN during presentation on screens and receipts
- 8.7 Data Access Controls and Segregation of Duties (including usage of programmatic methods by everyone else but DBAs, partially mapped to ISO/IEC control 6.1.2 Segregation of Duties)

PCI DSS requirements 6.4.* covering change management is mostly addressed by parts of two ISO domains (12 and 14) and the following subdomains:

- 12.1 Operational procedures and responsibilities
- 12.5 Control of operational software
- 14.2 Security in development and support processes
- 14.3 Test data

The PCI DSS requirement covering Risk Assessment (12.2, at least annually and during significant changes) is covered partly in 6.1.5 (information security in project management) but this only covers doing so in projects and does not require annual review of the complete environment as required by PCI DSS. As stated earlier in section 3.5.2 of this volume, the ISO/IEC 27005:2011 standard called *"Information security risk management"* may be employed for these risk assessments.

Finally, the concept of 'hardening' also referred to in PCI DSS as 'System Configuration Standards' (2.2.*) is not covered well by the ISO standard. While we may get some requirements that map partly to some sub-elements, this more procedural and technical portion of the PCI DSS standard is mostly not covered.

3.14 Mapping to and Missing COBIT 5 controls

3.14.1 ISACA and COBIT

ISACA is the creator and maintainer of COBIT

On it's "About ISACA" page, the organization states:

As an independent, nonprofit, global association, ISACA engages in the development, adoption and use of globally accepted, industry-leading knowledge and practices for information systems. Previously known as the Information Systems Audit and Control Association, ISACA now goes by its acronym only, to reflect the broad range of IT governance professionals it serves. [88]

ISACA is one of the largest reference for IT auditors.

COBIT (Control Objectives for Information and Related Technologies) is a "framework for the governance and management of enterprise IT" [89], and is more focused on IT governance than strictly on Information Security (thus competing with ITIL). So when mapping to COBIT, we find that it covers a much broader scope than PCI DSS or even ISO 27002. You can see this in the figure below (photo) that shows a pin board that I used for initial mapping between COBIT 5 (in orange), ISO 27002 (in green), and PCI DSS 3.2 (in yellow) at a high-level. We can see the majority of the PCI DSS requirements map at the bottom central portion of the photo.

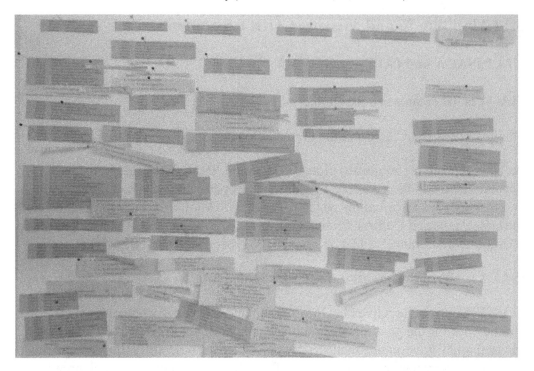

Volume 3 Figure 9 - Photo of pinboard mapping between PCI DSS, ISO/IEC 27002 and COBIT 5

This mapping, along with the ones for ISO 27002 were compared and reviewed with those of the technology group at Desjardins, to both our benefits. I thank the organization and the people involved for their assistance.

3.14.2 COBIT 5 Overview

COBIT 5's fifth principle (not prescriptive) calls for separation of governance (think board of directors) and management (i.e. senior management), as stated on slide 10 of a Introduction PowerPoint presentation:

Principle 5. Separating Governance From Management:

- *Governance ensures that stakeholders needs, conditions and options are evaluated to determine balanced, agreed-on enterprise objectives to be achieved; setting direction through prioritisation and decision making; and monitoring performance and compliance against agreed-on direction and objectives (EDM).*
- *Management plans, builds, runs and monitors activities in alignment with the direction set by the governance body to achieve the enterprise objectives (PBRM).* [90]

Those processes are divided into areas, as shown on the figure below:

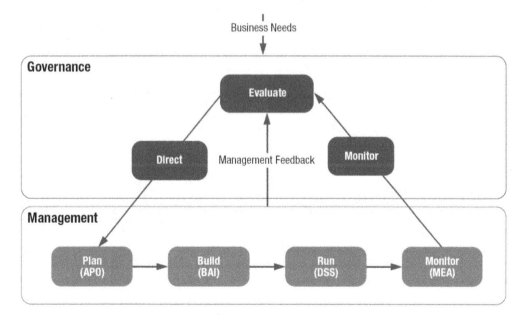

Volume 3 Figure 10 - COBIT 5 Governance and Management Key Areas [91]

Slide 37 describes the "COBIT 5 Enabling Processes":

The COBIT 5 process reference model subdivides the IT-related practices and activities of the enterprise into two main areas–governance and management– with management further divided into domains of processes:

- *The GOVERNANCE domain contains five governance processes; within each process, evaluate, direct and monitor (EDM) practices are defined.*
- *The four MANAGEMENT domains are in line with the responsibility areas of plan, build, run and monitor (PBRM).* [92]

A graphical representation of those processes is presented on the previous slide:

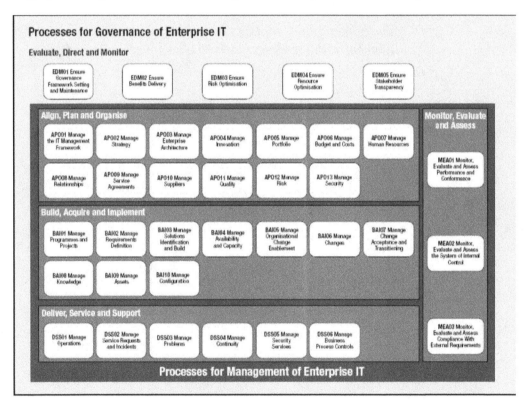

Volume 3 Figure 11 - COBIT 5 Process Reference Model [93]

We therefore have 5 practice areas, one in Governance (EDM, Evaluate, Direct and Monitor) and four in Management:

- Plan (APO, Align, Plan and Organise)
- Build (BAI, Build, Acquire and Implement)
- Run (DSS, Deliver, Service and Support)
- Monitor(MEA, Monitor, Evaluate and Assess)

Each of these 5 areas is further divided in processes where a number is appended to the process acronym. For example, for EDM, this gives us:

Process ID	Process
EDM01	Ensure Governance Framework Setting and Maintenance
EDM02	Ensure Benefits Delivery
EDM03	Ensure Risk Optimisation
EDM04	Ensure Resource Optimisation
EDM05	Ensure Stakeholder Transparency

And finally, these processes are divided into practices, appending a further number preceded by a dot, as is the case for EDM01:

Practice ID	Practice Name	Governance Practice
EDM01.01	Evaluate the governance system.	Continually identify and engage with the enterprise's stakeholders, document an understanding of the requirements, and make a judgement on the current and future design of governance of enterprise IT.
EDM01.02	Direct the governance system.	Inform leaders and obtain their support, buy-in and commitment. Guide the structures, processes and practices for the governance of IT in line with agreed-on governance design principles, decision-making models and authority levels. Define the information required for informed decision making.
EDM01.03	Monitor the governance system.	Monitor the effectiveness and performance of the enterprise's governance of IT. Assess whether the governance system and implemented mechanisms (including structures, principles and processes) are operating effectively and provide appropriate oversight of IT.

Then each practice is composed of activities (similar to test procedures in PCI DSS):

- Analyse and identify the internal and external environmental factors (legal, regulatory and contractual obligations) and trends in the business environment that may influence governance design.
- Determine the significance of IT and its role with respect to the business.
- Consider external regulations, laws and contractual obligations and determine how they should be applied within the governance of enterprise IT.
- Align the ethical use and processing of information and its impact on society, natural environment, and internal and external stakeholder interests with the enterprise's direction, goals and objectives.
- Determine the implications of the overall enterprise control environment with regard to IT.
- Articulate principles that will guide the design of governance and decision making of IT.
- Understand the enterprise's decision-making culture and determine the optimal decision-making model for IT.
- Determine the appropriate levels of authority delegation, including threshold rules, for IT decisions.

I mapped PCI DSS requirements to those 37 different practices. In order to do the mapping, we sometimes went all the way to the activity level, but since no mapping is ever perfect, we'll stay at a high-level in our results.

3.14.3 COBIT 5 and PCI DSS 3.2 high-level controls

For this section, I've used the same high-level structure for PCI DSS 3.2 as was used for ISO 27002. The mapping was performed to identify related items, and discern where lack of coverage was present.

The PCI DSS 3.2 summarized controls used in the mapping are:

- 1.1.* Router/Firewall Configuration Standards
- 1.1.1 Router/Firewall Change Process
- 1.1.2 Network diagrams
- 1.1.3 Data flow diagrams
- 1.2.* Firewall between CDE/untrusted
- 1.3.* Firewall between CDE/internet

- 1.4 Personal Firewall for Mobile
- 2 Configuration Management
- 2.1 Change Default Settings
- 2.2.* System Configuration Standards
- 2.3 Encrypt Administrative Access
- 2.4 / 11.1.1 Inventory
- 3.1 Data Retention and Disposal
- 3.2.* No storage of SAD
- 3.3 Mask PAN (display)
- 3.4.* PAN storage
- 3.5.* / 3.6.* Cryptographic Key Management
- 4.1 Encryption in transit (open networks)
- 4.1.1 Secure Wireless Configuration
- 4.2 No PAN in Email, Chat, etc.
- 5.* Antimalware
- 6.1 Vulnerability Management (id & rank)
- 6.2 Patching
- 6.3.* SDLC
- 6.4.* Change Management
- 6.5.* Secure Application Coding
- 6.6 Protect web-facing application
- 7.1.* Define user roles
- 7.2.* RBAC
- 8.1.* User Identification
- 8.2.* User Authentication
- 8.3.1 Multi-factor for administrative access to CDE
- 8.3.2 Multi-factor for remote access
- 8.4 User training on selecting secure passwords
- 8.5 / 8.6 No shared account
- 8.7 Data access Segregation of Duties
- 9.1.* Physical Access Control and Monitoring
- 9.2 / 9.4.* Visitor management
- 9.3 Physical Badge Access
- 9.5.* Physically secure media
- 9.6.* Classify media
- 9.7.* Control media
- 9.8.* Media destruction

- 9.9.* Device Tampering
- 10.1 / 10.2.* / 10.3.* Logging (data access, admin actions)
- 10.4.* Synchronize time clocks (NTP)
- 10.5.* Securing logs
- 10.6.* Log Monitoring
- 10.7 Log Retention
- 10.8 Detect failures of critical security controls (service provider only) (A3.3.1.*)
- 11.1 Identify unauthorized wireless networks
- 11.2.* Vulnerability Testing
- 11.3.* Penetration Testing
- 11.4 IDS / IPS at critical points
- 11.5.* Change Detection Management (FIM)
- 12 Information Security Policy (Program)
- 12.1 Information Security Policy
- 12.2 Risk Assessment
- 12.3.* Acceptable Use Policy
- 12.4 / 12.5.*   Information Security Responsibilities
- 12.4.1 Responsibility for PCI DSS compliance (A3.1.1)
- 12.6 Security Awareness Training
- 12.7 HR Background Checks
- 12.8.* / 12.9 Third-party management
- 12.10.* Incident Response
- 12.11 Quarterly review of PCI DSS processes (service provider only) (A3.3.3)

3.14.4 COBIT 5 mapping to PCI DSS 3.2

This mapping is not a detailed comparison of every single control (which could not be mapped completely one-to-one anyway), but is performed at a higher level. And since PCI DSS only covers confidentiality and not integrity or availability, there is no overlap over those two latter elements. The goal of this mapping is to help you identify best practice controls that are not covered by one standard and that you should likely implement as well.

3.14.4.1 COBIT 5 – Governance – EDM (Evaluate, Direct and Monitor)

These processes do not map with any of PCI DSS 3.2 controls (nor to ISO). Their focus is on IT Governance, not anything related to Information Security.

COBIT 5 Process ID	COBIT 5 Process	PCI DSS 3.2
EDM01	Ensure Governance Framework Setting and Maintenance	None
EDM02	Ensure Benefits Delivery	None
EDM03	Ensure Risk Optimisation	None
EDM04	Ensure Resource Optimisation	None
EDM05	Ensure Stakeholder Transparency	None

3.14.4.2 COBIT 5 – Management - Plan – APO (Align, Plan and Organise)

Planning processes map to policies and assignment of responsibility of PCI DSS in APO01. Human Resources requirements, APO07 include background checks (12.7). Third-party management (12.8.*, 12.9 from the service provider side) are mapped to APO10. Risk Assessments (12.2) is mapped to Managing Risk (APO12). Finally, the Information Security policies (12.1.*) as well as the Usage Policies (12.3.*, often a subset of the former) are mapped to APO13.

COBIT 5 Process ID	COBIT 5 Process	PCI DSS 3.2
APO01	Manage the IT Management Framework	12.4/12.5.*, 12.10.3, 12.11.*, A3.3.*
APO02	Manage Strategy	None
APO03	Manage Enterprise Architecture	None
APO04	Manage Innovation	None
APO05	Manage Portfolio	None
APO06	Manage Budget and Costs	None
APO07	Manage Human Resources	12.7
APO08	Manage Relationships	None
APO09	Manage Service Agreements	None
APO10	Manage Suppliers	12.8.*, 12.9
APO11	Manage Quality	6.5.*, 12.10.4
APO12	Manage Risk	12.2
APO13	Manage Security	12.1.*, 12.3.*

3.14.4.3 COBIT 5 – Management - Build– BAI (Build, Acquire and Implement)

While 4 of 10 BAI processes (BAI01, BAI02, BAI04, BAI05) have no mapping, we do have some mapping within all other 6. BAI03 is focused on vulnerability management: vulnerability scans (11.2.*) and penetration testing (11.3.*), vulnerability risk ranking (6.1) and patching (6.2) and SDLC controls (6.3) including the web application code review portion of 6.5.*. BAI06 and BAI07 focus on change control (6.4.*) including those for network level changes (1.1.1). BAI08 maps to storage and destruction of CHD. BAI09 maps to inventories (2.4, 11.1.1) and third-party accounts (8.1.5). Finally, system component baselines, or hardening (2.1, 2.2.*, 2.3), are managed with BAI10.

COBIT 5 Process ID	COBIT 5 Process	PCI DSS 3.2
BAI01	Manage Programmes and Projects	None
BAI02	Manage Requirements Definition	None
BAI03	Manage Solutions Identification and Build	6.1, 6.2, 6.3.*, 6.5.*, 11.2.*, 11.3.*
BAI04	Manage Availability and Capacity	None
BAI05	Manage Organisational Change Enablement	None
BAI06	Manage Changes	1.1.1, 6.4.5
BAI07	Manage Change Acceptance and Transitioning	1.1.1, 6.3.1, 6.4.*
BAI08	Manage Knowledge	3.1, 3.2.*, 3.3, 3.4.*, 9.8.*
BAI09	Manage Assets	2.4, 8.1.5, 11.1.1
BAI10	Manage Configuration	2.1, 2.2.*, 2.3

3.14.4.4 COBIT 5 – Management - Run– DSS (Deliver, Service and Support)

DSS processes are where the bulk of the mapping occurs between COBIT 5 and PCI DSS 3.2.

COBIT 5 Process ID	COBIT 5 Process	PCI DSS 3.2
DSS01	Manage Operations	1.5, 2.5, 3.7, 4.3, 5.4, 6.7, 7.3, 8.8, 9.10, 11.6 (procedures), 10.7
DSS02	Manage Service Requests and Incidents	12.10, 12.10.1, 12.10.5
DSS03	Manage Problems	12.10, 12.10.1, 12.10.2, 12.10.6
DSS04	Manage Continuity	None
DSS05	Manage Security Services	1.1.1, 1.1.4-1.1.7, 1.2.*, 1.3.*, 1.4, 3.2.*, 3.4.*, 3.5.*, 3.6.*, 4.1.*, 2.3 5.*, 6.1, 6.2, 6.6 7.1.*, 7.2.*, 8.1.*, 8.2.*, 8.3.*, 8.6 8.4, 8.5.*, 8.7 9.1.*, 9.3, 9.2 / 9.4.* 9.5.*, 9.6.*, 9.7.*, 9.8.*, 9.9.* 10.2.*, 10.3.*, 10.4.*, 10.5.*, 10.6.*, 11.4, 11.5 11.2.*, 11.3.*, 11.3.4.*
DSS06	Manage Business Process Controls	None

DSS01 contains the procedures (not the policies which are covered in domain 12) moved to PCI DSS requirements 1.5, 2.5, 3.7, 4.3, 5.4, 6.7, 7.3, 8.8, 9.10, 10.9, 11.6).

Incident response requirements (12.10.*) are mostly split between DSS02 and DSS03.

DSS04 and DSS06 map to no PCI DSS requirements.

DSS05 is the one where most of the PCI DSS requirements fall (some are partially split with other COBIT practices), including:

- *Network level controls (1.1.1, 1.1.4-1.1.7, 1.2.*, 1.3.*, 1.4)*
- *Shared hosting provider controls (2.6, A1.*)*
- *CHD Storage (3.2.*, 3.4.*)*
- *Encryption Key Management (3.5.*, 3.6.*)*
- *CHD Transmission encryption (4.1.*, A2.*)*
- *Protection against malware (5.*)*
- *Vulnerability Management (6.1) and Patching (6.2)*
- *Protecting web-facing application (6.6)*
- *User roles (7.1.*) and RBAC (7.2.*), User Identification (8.1.*) and Authentication (8.2.*), and Multi-factor authentication (8.3.*, 8.6)*
- *Password guidance (8.4), No shared accounts (8.5.*) and database accesses (8.7)*
- *Physical Access Control and Monitoring (9.1.*), Visitor management (9.2 / 9.4.*), Physical Badge Access (9.3)*
- *Media controls: physically secure (9.5.*), classify (9.6.*), control (9.7.*) and destroy (9.8.*)*
- *Protect payment devices from tampering (9.9.*)*
- *Logging and Monitoring (10.1, 10.2.*, 10.3.*, 10.4.*, 10.5.*, 10.6.*) including IDS/IPS (11.4) and Change Detection Management (FIM) (11.5.*)*
- *Vulnerability (11.2.*) and penetration (11.3.*) testing, network segmentation penetration testing (11.3.4.*)*

3.14.4.5 COBIT 5 – Management – Monitor – MEA (Monitor, Evaluate and Assess)

Monitoring of control status only has limited mapping (currently) to PCI DSS, but this is an area where DESV would map well, and where we may expect to see movement from the industry, with the continued push to B.A.U. "Detect failures of critical security controls" (10.8.*), which in PCI DSS 3.2 is only applicable to service providers, falls within MEA02.

COBIT 5 Process ID	COBIT 5 Process	PCI DSS 3.2
MEA01	Monitor, Evaluate and Assess Performance and Conformance	None
MEA02	Monitor, Evaluate and Assess the System of Internal Control	10.8.*
MEA03	Monitor, Evaluate and Assess Compliance with External Requirements	None

3.14.4.6 PCI DSS 3.2 requirements partially or not covered by COBIT 5

While COBIT 5 has an even broader scope than ISO/IEC 27002:2013, there are nonetheless specificities of PCI DSS that are not, or at least not fully, covered by the COBIT 5 (though less than for ISO).

Scope definition is an area that is more specific in PCI DSS. In this area, we identify the following unmapped PCI DSS requirements:

- 1.1.2 Create and Maintain Network Diagrams
- 1.1.3 Create and Maintain Data Flow Diagrams

"Never send unprotected PANs by end-user messaging technologies" (4.2) might be partly covered elsewhere, but its specific nature means I rather deal with it separately.

"Identifying unauthorized wireless networks" (11.1.*) would be partly covered by COBIT in "Manage network and connectivity security" (DSS05.02), but it would only provide partial mapping in my humble opinion.

Finally, the new requirements to review changes to ensure no loss of PCI DSS compliance (6.4.6), might map partially between change control (BAI07) and the MEA section, but that mapping is partial in all cases.

3.15 The PCI Resources PCI DSS requirements matrix

Throughout the last few years assisting organizations with PCI DSS, I've had to rethink how to most efficiently address how to use the standard for both assessments and remediation (especially to get a quick picture of an organization's compliance).

The result is a matrix structure that classifies all PCI DSS requirements falling within (mostly) one cell of that matrix.

On the vertical axis, we have what I refer to as the stack level (from the bottom):

* Physical Security
* Network Architecture
* Operating System (OS, Generic OS, Network or Appliance embedded OS)
* Application (including middleware, since)
* Data
* User
* Policy
* Governance (organization)

Note: I've seen many variants of this stack often for shared responsibilities models in the cloud, so they should be familiar.

On the horizontal axis, we have the 4 major process areas:

* Scope Management (including the requirements that are specific to PCI DSS)
* Access Control
* Vulnerability Management
* Logging and Monitoring

Note: For PCI DSS, I define scope (People, Process and Technology) as:

* The People (internal, external)
* performing Business Processes
* using Applications
* running on Systems
* and communicating over Networks
* in physical locations

- involved in the storage, processing or transmission (SPT) of card information (CHD/SAD)
- Or that could affect the security of card information (connected).

The same high-level grouping of PCI DSS requirements presented in previous mappings will be used here for the new matrix:

- 1.1.* Router/Firewall Configuration Standards
- 1.1.1 Router/Firewall Change Process
- 1.1.2 Network diagrams
- 1.1.3 Data flow diagrams
- 1.2.* Firewall between CDE/untrusted
- 1.3.* Firewall between CDE/internet
- 1.4 Personal Firewall for Mobile
- 2 Configuration Management
- 2.1 Change Default Settings
- 2.2.* System Configuration Standards
- 2.3 Encrypt Administrative Access
- 2.4 / 11.1.1 Inventory
- 3.1 Data Retention and Disposal
- 3.2.* No storage of SAD
- 3.3 Mask PAN (display)
- 3.4.* PAN storage
- 3.5.* / 3.6.* Cryptographic Key Management
- 4.1 Encryption in transit (open networks)
- 4.1.1 Secure Wireless Configuration
- 4.2 No PAN in Email, Chat, etc.
- 5.* Antimalware
- 6.1 Vulnerability Management (id & rank)
- 6.2 Patching
- 6.3.* SDLC
- 6.4.* Change Management
- 6.5.* Secure Application Coding
- 6.6 Protect web-facing application
- 7.1.* Define user roles
- 7.2.* RBAC
- 8.1.* User Identification

- 8.2.* User Authentication
- 8.3.1 Multi-factor for administrative access to CDE
- 8.3.2 Multi-factor for remote access
- 8.4 User training on selecting secure passwords
- 8.5 / 8.6 No shared account
- 8.7 Data access Segregation of Duties
- 9.1.* Physical Access Control and Monitoring
- 9.2 / 9.4.* Visitor management
- 9.3 Physical Badge Access
- 9.5.* Physically secure media
- 9.6.* Classify media
- 9.7.* Control media
- 9.8.* Media destruction
- 9.9.* Device Tampering
- 10.1 / 10.2.* / 10.3.* Logging (data access, admin actions)
- 10.4.* Synchronize time clocks (NTP)
- 10.5.* Securing logs
- 10.6.* Log Monitoring
- 10.7 Log Retention
- 10.8 Detect failures of critical security controls (service provider only) (A3.3.1.*)
- 11.1 Identify unauthorized wireless networks
- 11.2.* Vulnerability Testing
- 11.3.* Penetration Testing
- 11.4 IDS / IPS at critical points
- 11.5.* Change Detection Management (FIM)
- 12 Information Security Policy (Program)
- 12.1 Information Security Policy
- 12.2 Risk Assessment
- 12.3.* Acceptable Use Policy
- 12.4 / 12.5.*   Information Security Responsibilities
- 12.4.1 Responsibility for PCI DSS compliance (A3.1.1)
- 12.6 Security Awareness Training
- 12.7 HR Background Checks
- 12.8.* / 12.9 Third-party management
- 12.10.* Incident Response
- 12.11 Quarterly review of PCI DSS processes (service provider only) (A3.3.3)

	Scope Management	Access Control	Vulnerability Management	Logging and Monitoring
Governance	12.4.*-12.5.* (A3) Infosec Resp. 12.8.* Third-Party Mgmt A3.2.* Scope Diagrams: 1.1.2 Net. & 1.1.3 Dataflow	12.7 HR BG Checks	12.2 Risk Assessment	10.8.* Detect failures of critical security controls[1]
Policy	12.1.* - Infosec Policy 12.3.* Acceptable Use Policy 4.2 - No PAN 3.1 Data Retention and Disposal	12.6.* - Security Awareness Training 8.4 Train passwords 7.1.* Roles	1.1.*- Router/Firewall Config & Chg 2.1 Chg defaults 2.2.*-2.3 Sys. Config Stds 6.1 Vuln. mgmt 6.4.* Chg Ctrl 11.3.1-11.3.3 Pentests	10.1-10.3.* Logs 10.6.* Monitoring 12.10.* Incident Response
User		8.1.* User ID 8.2.* User Auth 8.5 No shared account		
Data	Store 3.2 SAD, 3.4.* PAN 3.5.*-3.6.* Cryptographic Key Management	8.7 DB SoD		
App	4.1 SSL/TLS, VPN 3.3 Mask PAN	7.2.* - RBAC	6.3 SDLC 6.5.* Secure App 6.6 Protect web apps	10.5.* Secure Logs 10.7 Log Reten.
Operating System	2.4 Inventory	1.4 Personal Firewall	5.* Antimalware 6.2 Patching 11.2.* Vuln. scans	10.4 NTP 11.5 Chg/FIM
Network Architecture	1.1.6 ACL doc. 1.1.7 ACL review (6m) Firewall between: -1.2.* CDE/untrusted -1.3.* CDE/internet 4.1.1 Secure wireless	8.3.* / 8.6 MFA 11.3.4 Segmentation Pentest		11.1 Unauth wireless 11.4 IDS / IPS
Physical		9.1,9.3 Physical Access Control and Monitoring 9.2 / 9.4.* Visitor management 9.5-9.8 Media Ctrls		9.9.* POS Device Tampering

Volume 3 Figure 12 - PCI Resources PCI DSS requirements matrix

A detailed printable version of this will be provided on the book's companion website.

How do you go on using this matrix? I'd recommend going per process area (left to right) and then either top-down or bottom up. Let's do a simple example from the bottom up.

For Scope Management, we can ask:

- Has physical scope been properly defined? Do we have diagrams or clear demarcation of "areas that store, process or transmit CHD/SAD"?
- Has network (architecture) scope been defined? Do we have adequate testing to ensure that network segmentation restrictions are working (11.3.4)?
- Do we have an inventory of all in-scope systems components (2.4)? How do we know that list is complete (e.g. ping sweeps)? Does the list include:
    - all in-scope applications?
    - all in-scope data?
    - all in-scope users and/or departments?

For Access Control, we can ask:

- Has physical access to sensitive areas (data centers, IT, card processing) been adequately restricted? Is access logged?
- Has network access been restricted (firewall and router rules)?
- Has access to operating systems been adequately restricted (user roles including IT administration)?
- Has access to applications been adequately restricted?
- Has access to data been adequately restricted (only directly to DBAs, others through programmatic methods)?

And so on, and so forth

End Notes - Volume 3

[1] PCI Security Standards Council (2016). Payment Card Industry Data Security Standard - Requirements and Security Assessment Procedures - Version 3.2. Retrieved July 13, 2015, from https://www.pcisecuritystandards.org/documents/PCI_DSS_v3-2.pdf.

[2] PCI Security StandardsCouncil (2015). PCI SECURITY STANDARDS COUNCIL REVISES DATE FOR MIGRATING OFF VULNERABLE SSL AND EARLY TLS ENCRYPTION. Retrieved January 4, 2016, from https://www.pcisecuritystandards.org/pdfs/15_12_18_SSL_Webinar_Press_Release_FINAL_%28 002%29.pdf.

[3] PCI Security Standards Council (2015, p.5). Payment Card Industry Data Security Standard - Requirements and Security Assessment Procedures - Version 3.2.

[4] Tom on Leadership (2012). How and Why to Benchmark. Retrieved September 22, 2015, from http://tomonleadership.com/2012/12/10/how-and-why-to-benchmark/.

[5] ISACA (2010). The Basics of Internal Controls. Retrieved September 22, 2015, from http://www.theiia.org/chapters/pubdocs/242/Internal_Controls_Basics_IIA_040709.pdf.

[6] International Organization for Standardization / International Electrotechnical Commission (2014). ISO/IEC 27000 - Information technology -- Security techniques -- Information security management systems. Retrieved September 22, 2015, from http://www.iso.org/iso/catalogue_detail?csnumber=63411.

[7] Wikipedia (2011). ITIL. Retrieved September 22, 2015, from https://en.wikipedia.org/wiki/ITIL.

[8] ISACA (2010). COBIT 5: A Business Framework for the Governance and Management of Enterprise IT. Retrieved September 22, 2015, from http://www.isaca.org/cobit/.

[9] National Institute of Standards and Technology (2007). Special Publications. Retrieved September 23, 2015 from http://csrc.nist.gov/publications/PubsSPs.html.

[10] U.S. Department of Health & Human Services (2009). Health Information Privacy. Retrieved September 23, 2015 from http://www.hhs.gov/ocr/privacy/.

[11] Wikipedia (2011). Sarbanes–Oxley Act. Retrieved September 23, 2015 from https://en.wikipedia.org/wiki/Sarbanes%E2%80%93Oxley_Act.

[12] PCI DSS only applies to cards that bear the logo of one of the 5 founding members of the SSC: Visa, MasterCard, American Express, Discover, JCB.

[13] PCI Security Standards Council (2016, p.8). Payment Card Industry Data Security Standard - Requirements and Security Assessment Procedures - Version 3.2.

[14] U.S. Department of Health & Human Services (2009). Health Information Privacy.

[15] Government of Canada - Justice Laws Website (1985). Privacy Act. Retrieved September 1, 2017, from http://laws-lois.justice.gc.ca/eng/acts/p-21/.

[16] Office of the Privacy Commissioner of Canada (2012). The Personal Information Protection and Electronic Documents Act (PIPEDA). Retrieved September 22, 2015, from https://www.priv.gc.ca/leg_c/leg_c_p_e.asp.

[17] European Commission (2011). Protection of personal data. Retrieved September 22, 2015, from http://ec.europa.eu/justice/data-protection/.

[18] Home Page of EU GDPR. Retrieved September 1, 2017, from http://www.eugdpr.org/.

[19] National Institute of Standards and Technology (2010, p.2-1). Special Publication 800-122 Revision 1, Guide to Protecting the Confidentiality of Personally Identifiable Information (PII). Retrieved September 22,2015, from http://csrc.nist.gov/publications/nistpubs/800-122/sp800-122.pdf.

[20] National Institute of Standards and Technology (2010, p.2-2). Special Publication 800-122 Revision 1, Guide to Protecting the Confidentiality of Personally Identifiable Information (PII).

[21] Quote Investigator (2011). Everything Should Be Made as Simple as Possible, But Not Simpler. Retrieved September 22, 2015, from http://quoteinvestigator.com/2011/05/13/einstein-simple/.

[22] Wikipedia (2011). Classified information. Retrieved September 22, 2015, from https://en.wikipedia.org/wiki/Classified_information.

[23] Merriam-Webster (2005). Definition of governance. Retrieved September 22, 2015, from http://www.merriam-webster.com/dictionary/governance.

[24] PCI Security Standards Council (2015, p.13). Payment Card Industry Data Security Standard - Requirements and Security Assessment Procedures - Version 3.2.

[25] PCI Guru (2015). Policies, Standards And Procedures. Retrieved September 22, 2015 from https://pciguru.wordpress.com/2015/07/02/policies-standards-and-procedures/.

[26] PCI Security Standards Council (2015). PCI DSS Designated Entities Supplemental Validation For use with PCI DSS v3.1. Retrieved July 2, 2015, from https://www.pcisecuritystandards.org/documents/PCI_DSS_v3_DESV.pdf.

[27] Designated entities will be formally identified by their acquirers or the card brands, and is likely to include already breached organizations and those that hold substantial amounts of CHD.

[28] PCI Security Standards Council (2016). ROC Reporting Template for v3.2.

[29] PCI Security Standards Council (2016). PCI DSS Designated Entities Supplemental Validation for Use with PCI DSS v3.2.

[30] PCI Security Standards Council (2015, p.5). Payment Card Industry Data Security Standard - Requirements and Security Assessment Procedures - Version 3.2.

[31] Computer Emergency Response Team (CERT) (2014). OCTAVE - Cyber Risk and Resilience Management. Retrieved September 22, 2015, from http://www.cert.org/resilience/products-services/octave/.

[32] International Organization for Standardization / International Electrotechnical Commission (2014). ISO/IEC 27005 - Information security risk management. Retrieved September 22, 2015, from http://www.iso27001security.com/html/27005.html.

[33] National Institute of Standards and Technology (2012). Special Publication 800-30 Revision 1, Guide for Conducting Risk Assessments. Retrieved September 22,2015, from http://csrc.nist.gov/publications/nistpubs/800-30-rev1/sp800_30_r1.pdf.

[34] NIST (2012). Guide for Conducting Risk Assessments. Retrieved September 1, 2017, from http://nvlpubs.nist.gov/nistpubs/Legacy/SP/nistspecialpublication800-30r1.pdf.

[35] PCI Security Standards Council (2016). ROC Reporting Template for v3.2 Retrieved July 8, 2015, from https://www.pcisecuritystandards.org/documents/PCI-DSS-v3_2-ROC-Reporting-Template.pdf.

[36] Open Web Application Security Project (2008). Application Threat Modeling. Retrieved September 22, 2015, from https://www.owasp.org/index.php/Application_Threat_Modeling.

[37] Microsoft Development Network (2005). Security Development Lifecycle. Retrieved September 22, 2015, from https://msdn.microsoft.com/security/default.aspx?pull=/library/en-us/dnsecure/html/sdl.asp.

[38] Microsoft Development Network (2005). Security Development Lifecycle.

[39] Shostack, Adam (2014). Threat modeling : designing for security. Indianapolis: John Wiley and Sons Inc.

[40] Shostack, Adam (2014). Threat Modeling: Designing for Security. Wiley.

[41] Shostack, Adam (2014). Threat Modeling: Designing for Security. Wiley.

[42] Shostack, Adam (2014). Threat Modeling: Designing for Security. Wiley.

[43] NIST (2012, p.14). Guide for Conducting Risk Assessments.

[44] PCI Security Standards Council (2016, p.19). Payment Card Industry Data Security Standard - Requirements and Security Assessment Procedures - Version 3.2.

[45] Shostack, Adam (2014). Threat modeling : designing for security. Indianapolis: John Wiley and Sons Inc.

[46] PCI Security Standards Council (2016, p.25). Payment Card Industry Data Security Standard - Requirements and Security Assessment Procedures - Version 3.2.

[47] Verizon Enterprise Solutions (2015, p.29). 2015 PCI Compliance Report. Retrieved July 1, 2015, from http://www.verizonenterprise.com/pcireport/2015/.

[48] Verizon Enterprise Solutions (2015, p.29). 2015 PCI Compliance Report.

[49] Wikipedia (2011). Long-range Wi-Fi. Retrieved September 22, 2015, from https://en.wikipedia.org/wiki/Long-range_Wi-Fi.

[50] PCI Security Standards Council (2016, p.69). Payment Card Industry Data Security Standard - Requirements and Security Assessment Procedures - Version 3.2.

[51] Schneier on Security (2016). NIST is No Longer Recommending Two-Factor Authentication Using SMS. Retrieved September 1, 2017, from https://www.schneier.com/blog/archives/2016/08/nist_is_no_long.html.

[52] Center for Internet Security (2003). Retrieved September 22, 2015, from https://www.cisecurity.org/.

[53] ISO - International Organization for Standardization (2015). Retrieved September 22, 2015, from http://www.iso.org/.

[54] SANS Information Security Training (2004). Retrieved September 22, 2015, from https://www.sans.org/.

[55] National Institute of Standards and Technology (2015). " Retrieved September 22, 2015, from http://www.nist.gov/.

[56] PCI Security Standards Council (2015). FAQ 1224. Public Knowledge Base - What does one function per server mean? Retrieved September 22, 2015, from https://pcissc.secure.force.com/faq/articles/Frequently_Asked_Question/What-does-one-function-per-server-mean/.

[57] PCI Security Standards Council (2015, p.8). PCI DSS Designated Entities Supplemental Validation For use with PCI DSS v3.1.

[58] PCI Security Standards Council (2015, p.8). PCI DSS Designated Entities Supplemental Validation For use with PCI DSS v3.1.

[59] PCI Security Standards Council (2015). FAQ 1154. Public Knowledge Base - Is pre-authorization account data in scope for PCI DSS? Retrieved September 22, 2015 from https://pcissc.secure.force.com/faq/articles/Frequently_Asked_Question/Is-pre-authorization-account-data-in-scope-for-PCI-DSS/.

[60] PCI Security Standards Council (2016, p.42). Payment Card Industry Data Security Standard - Requirements and Security Assessment Procedures - Version 3.2.

[61] PCI Security Standards Council (2015). FAQ 1045. Public Knowledge Base - Is MPLS considered a private or public network when transmitting cardholder data? Retrieved September 22, 2015, from https://pcissc.secure.force.com/faq/articles/Frequently_Asked_Question/Is-MPLS-considered-a-private-or-public-network-when-transmitting-cardholder-data/.

[62] PCI Security Standards Council (2015, p.10). PCI DSS Designated Entities Supplemental Validation For use with PCI DSS v3.1.

[63] PCI Security StandardsCouncil (2015). Date Change for Migrating from SSL and Early TLS. Retrieved January 4, 2016, from http://blog.pcisecuritystandards.org/migrating-from-ssl-and-early-tls.

[64] Verizon Enterprise Solutions (2015, p.22). 2015 Data Breach Investigations Report (DBIR). Retrieved July 1, 2015, from http://www.verizonenterprise.com/DBIR/2015/.

[65] Open Web Application Security Project (2008). Category:OWASP Top Ten Project. Retrieved September 22, 2015, from https://www.owasp.org/index.php/OWASP_Risk_Rating_Methodology.

[66] Visa Europe (2011).Using the Visa Private BIN Range. Retrieved September 22, 2015, from http://www.visaeurope.com/media/images/12_using_the_visa_private_bin_range_-_best_practice_guide%20110615-73-24720.pdf.

[67] Open Web Application Security Project (2013). Top 10 2013-A1-Injection. Retrieved September 22,   2015, from https://www.owasp.org/index.php/Top_10_2013-A1-Injection.

[68] PCI Security Standards Council (2013).PCI DSS E-commerce Guidelines. Retrieved September 22, 2015, from https://www.pcisecuritystandards.org/pdfs/PCI_DSS_v2_eCommerce_Guidelines.pdf.

[69] Open Web Application Security Project (2013). Top 10 2013-A2-Broken Authentication and Session Management. Retrieved September 22, 2015, from https://www.owasp.org/index.php/Top_10_2013-A2-Broken_Authentication_and_Session_Management.

[70] The Daily WTF (2014). The Robot Guys. Retrieved September 22, 2015, from http://thedailywtf.com/articles/the-robot-guys.

[71] Open Web Application Security Project (2008). Password Storage Cheat Sheet. Retrieved September 1, 2017, from https://www.owasp.org/index.php/Password_Storage_Cheat_Sheet.

[72] Naked Security (2013). Serious Security: How to store your users' passwords safely. Retrieved September 1, 2017, from https://nakedsecurity.sophos.com/2013/11/20/serious-security-how-to-store-your-users-passwords-safely/.

[73] ISG Research Blog (2017). The Password Debate, and What to Do. Retrieved September 1, 2017, from http://blog.research.isg-one.de/2017/08/24/the-password-debate-and-what-to-do/.

[74] Krebs, Bryan (2014). All About Skimmers - Krebs on Security. Retrieved July 1, 2015, from http://krebsonsecurity.com/category/all-about-skimmers/.

[75] PCI Guru (2014). Requirement 10.6.2 Clarification. Retrieved September 22, 2015, from https://pciguru.wordpress.com/2014/08/08/requirement-10-6-2-clarification/.

[76] PCI Security Standards Council (2015). FAQ 1304. Public Knowledge Base - What devices does PCI DSS Requirement 10.6.2 apply to? Retrieved September 22, 2015, from https://pcissc.secure.force.com/faq/articles/Frequently_Asked_Question/What-devices-does-PCI-DSS-Requirement-10-6-2-apply-to/.

[77] PCI Security Standards Council (2015). FAQ 1317. Public Knowledge Base - What is a

[78] PCI Guru (2014). Significant Change And Periodic. Retrieved September 22, 2015, from https://pciguru.wordpress.com/2014/12/09/significant-change-and-periodic/.

[79] PCI Security Standards Council (2015). Approved Scanning Vendors. Retrieved September 22, 2015, from https://www.pcisecuritystandards.org/approved_companies_providers/approved_scanning_vendors.php.

[80] PCI Security Standards Council (2015). Approved Scanning Vendors.

[81] PCI Security Standards Council (2016). PPenetration testing Guidance v1.1. Retrieved September 1, 2017, from https://www.pcisecuritystandards.org/documents/Penetration-Testing-Guidance-v1_1.pdf.

[82] PCI Security Standards Council (2016, p.1). Information Supplement: Third-Party Security Assurance v1.1. Retrieved July 13, 2016, from https://www.pcisecuritystandards.org/documents/PCI_DSS_V3.0_Third_Party_Security_Assurance.pdf.

[83] PCI Security Standards Council (2016, p.106). Payment Card Industry Data Security Standard - Requirements and Security Assessment Procedures - Version 3.2.

[84] PCI Security Standards Council (2016, p.107). Payment Card Industry Data Security Standard - Requirements and Security Assessment Procedures - Version 3.2.

[85] Verizon Enterprise Solutions (2015, p.59). 2015 PCI Compliance Report.

[86] PCI Security Standards Council (2016). Prioritized Approach for PCI DSS Version 3.2. Retrieved July 1, 2016, from https://www.pcisecuritystandards.org/documents/Prioritized_Approach_for_PCI_DSS_v3-1.pdf.

[87] PCI Security Standards Council (2015). FAQ 1046. Public Knowledge Base - Will the PCI Security Standards Council "approve" my organization's implementation of compensating controls in my effort to comply with the PCI DSS? Retrieved September 22, 2015, from https://pcissc.secure.force.com/faq/articles/Frequently_Asked_Question/Will-the-PCI-Security-Standards-Council-approve-my-organization-s-implementation-of-compensating-controls-in-my-effort-to-comply-with-the-PCI-DSS/.

[88] ISACA (2017). About. Retrieved September 1, 2017, from http://www.isaca.org/about-isaca/Pages/default.aspx.

[89] Wikipedia (2011). COBIT. Retrieved September 1, 2017, from https://en.wikipedia.org/wiki/COBIT.

[90] ISACA (2017, p.31). COBIT 5 Introduction Presentation. Retrieved September 1, 2017, from https://www.isaca.org/COBIT/Documents/COBIT5-Introduction.ppt.

[91] ISACA (2017, p.36). COBIT 5 Introduction Presentation.

[92] ISACA (2017, p.36). COBIT 5 Introduction Presentation.

[93] ISACA (2017, p.36). COBIT 5 Introduction Presentation.

Volume 4 - Hypothetical Case Studies

From Jane's Flower Attic to Jane's Flower Emporium

4.1 Volume Introduction

After over 15 years of information security work, 5 years of doing PCI DSS projects (mostly readiness assessments and remediation assistance) and 2 years after the release of the first 2 volumes of the PCI Resources, I'm happy to announce the release of the next series of guidance.

In the last 4 years, I had the privilege of working with many organizations with varied security and PCI DSS needs. And while I do not strictly focus on PCI DSS but on information security overall, PCI DSS has been the biggest portion of what I've done. The organizations I've worked with range from community banks to very large institutions with over 50,000 employees. I've also worked with merchants of many sizes, as well as a few service providers.

One of the great things about working as a consultant is the variety of issues that one comes in contact with. As I'm moved from doing more audit related work in my Public Accounting / QSA days and more involved not only in readiness assessments but also remediation assistance, I come to see more and more that PCI DSS is not as well understood as we all would like it to be.

I've written this book leveraging all this experience (and the one I gathered during the years prior to doing PCI DSS work) to create simple examples of what maintaining PCI DSS compliance means to different sizes of merchants.

This guidance, while focused on merchants, is nonetheless applicable to any other organizations that are in-scope for PCI DSS.

Picture the journey of Jane Doe, a fictitious entrepreneurial woman that just has a knack for making beautiful flower arrangements. We'll see how her company grows from a small side gig run from her living room, all the way to a mega corporation with many stores nationwide.

For simplicity, all of these examples will be under the actual version of the PCI DSS standard, version 3.2 released in April 2016. We'll see her go through 4 company sizes:

- Jane's Flower Attic (JFA) - section 4.2
- Jane's Flower Boutique (JFB) - section 4.3
- Jane's Flower Chain (JFC) - section 4.4
- Jane's Flower Emporium (JFE) - section 4.5

4.1.1 Assumptions

We'll make the stated assumption that she's running the business in some place in the USA. Since PCI DSS is an international standard, all of these should apply equally. And I'll use Visa (the one I'm most familiar with) as a the card brand working for the bank since it is the biggest of the 5 PCI SSC founding members that enforce compliance (remember that, as written in section 1.7 of volume 1, the PCI SSC only develops the standard and manages the companies that provide audit and other related solutions, while enforcement of the PCI DSS falls to the card brands).

While an organization can define how it structures their quarters for compliance reasons (quarterly periodicity is required for some PCI DSS requirements), all our examples will use calendar-based quarters. Quarter 1 is January through March, 2 is April to June, 3 is July to September, and 4 is October to December.

Much of the knowledge expanded in previous volumes will not be repeated here. Readers are encouraged to consult them for any relevant questions. I'll reference the appropriate sections where applicable.

This volume tries to provide actual real-life examples of how to address PCI DSS. They remain hypothetical since none of the fictitious companies are clients of mine (other than having a professional gardener in my family, I have never served flower companies). But the information is nonetheless based on my experience serving clients of all types and industries.

The PCI council has produced simplified guidance aimed directly at smaller merchants [1] (the initial first 3 size of companies in this volume). I've attempted to align my terminology with the one used in their documents, especially in relation to the names used for payment devices. Here are the definitions of some of the terms used in this volume (also covered in the glossary):

- CARDHOLDER: the individual person to whom a payment card is issued and who pays for products or services using that card

- ISSUER: the entity that issues the card to the cardholder, often (but not limited to) your bank;
- MERCHANT: the entity which receive payments from cardholders for products or services;
- PAYMENT PROCESSOR: the entity that receives payment information from the merchant, authorizes, settles and clears the transaction (can be a bank, but can also be a service provider);
- ACQUIRER: the entity that takes on the financial risk of the merchant transaction (sometimes the acquirer is also a payment processor and the roles are mingled - we will distinguish between these functions);
- CARD BRANDS: the 5 founding members of the PCI SSC that facilitate the payment and settlement (other entities may be involved - for example, in Canada, Interac fulfills that role for debit card payments);
- SERVICE PROVIDERS: an entity that performs some functions regarding to the payment process and/or provides services that may affect the security of the cardholder data.
- A PAYMENT TERMINAL : is the device used to take customer card payments via swipe, dip, insert, tap, or manual entry of the card number. Point-of-sale (or POS) terminal, credit card machine, PDQ terminal, or EMV/chip- enabled terminal are also names used to describe these devices.
- An ELECTRONIC CASH REGISTER (or till) : registers and calculates transactions, and may print out receipts, but it does not accept customer card payments.
- An INTEGRATED PAYMENT TERMINAL : a payment terminal and electronic cash register in one, meaning it takes payments, registers and calculates transactions, and prints receipts.
- A PAYMENT SYSTEM : encompasses the entire process for accepting card payments in a retail location (including stores/shops and e-commerce storefronts), and may include a payment terminal, an electronic cash register, other devices or systems connected to a payment terminal (for example, Wi-Fi for connectivity or a PC used for inventory), servers with e-commerce components such as payment pages, and the connections out to a merchant bank.
- Card-present payment : refer to transactions where the cardholder (the payer) is physically in the presence of the merchant (in the store) and uses his payment card to pay.
- Card-not-present payment : Refer to transactions where the cardholder (the payer) is not physically in the presence of the merchant (in the store), and

'includes (postal) mail (or even fax) order catalog, a phone-based transaction such as airline ticket reservation or very often an online store.

- MOTO or MO/TO : Acronym for "Mail-Order/Telephone-Order".
- POS : Acronym for "point of sale". Hardware and/or software used to process payment card transactions at merchant locations.
- Ethernet : a family of wired computer networking technologies commonly used in local area networks (LAN), metropolitan area networks (MAN) and wide area networks (WAN).
- QSA : Acronym for "Qualified Security Assessor". QSAs are qualified by PCI SSC to perform PCI DSS on-site assessments. Refer to the QSA Qualification Requirements for details about requirements for QSA Companies and Employees.
- ISA : Acronym for "Internal Security Assessor." ISAs are qualified by PCI SSC. ISAs are employees of organizations that help their organizations build their internal PCI Security Standards expertise and strengthen their approach to payment data security, as well as increasing their efficiency in compliance with data security standards.

Let's dig in.

Disclaimer: this volume shows the simplified view of achieved compliance but the information provided and process described are not necessarily sufficient or detailed enough to ensure PCI DSS compliance. The thought process should however be helpful. Diagrams provided are more high-level contextual or logical than detailed and are there to provide an example of how things work. Detailed diagram examples are provided in section 4.7.

Many thanks to Tom Beaupre and Hakim Aliane who provided early comments on the diagram section.

4.2 Jane's journey - Step 1 - A small side business

4.2.1 Jane's Flower Attic (JFA) business

At one point in her life, our Jane decided to start a small business selling flowers.

Why she started the venture is beside the point of our exercise and best left to the reader's imagination.

She actually checked with her country, state and municipal codes and obtained all the right permits (including some form of business incorporation if so required), again outside the scope of our exercise. She opened a business bank account at her local bank where she's been a client for many years. She hired an accountant, either through personal contacts or via her bank.

Initially, she only accepted cash payments and operated with a small cash box. But at one point, maybe around Valentine's day or Mother's day as volume grew, she faced requests to pay with credit cards. Ever wary of doing things right, she went to her bank who set her up with a small payment device (one that supports at least the chip-and-pin standard). The payment device can be used to receive payments in person (card-present) or she can also use to take payments over the phone (card-not-present, TO of the MOTO transactions) and process them manually on the device.

The bank, which also has to adhere to the PCI DSS standard, is also responsible for enforcing other Visa standard, such as the VIOR (Visa International Operating Regulations, mentioned in section 1.7.4 but outside the scope of our exercise here). In our case, the bank is the acquirer for PCI DSS, the company taking on the risk of the financial transaction. It has a deal with a payment processor that we'll call PAYPRO for this exercise (in some cases, the payment processor and the acquirer are one and the same, but we'll keep them separate here).

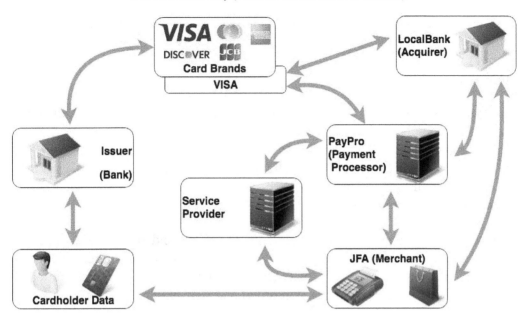

Volume 4 Figure 1 - JFA and The PCI payment model

What guidance does her bank need to provide and what must Jane do to be in good standing?

As an acquirer, Jane's bank is mandated by its affiliated card brands to manage the compliance of its merchants. Among these requirements is ensuring that merchants are compliant with the PCI DSS. Since not all merchants bring forth the same amount of risk, the card brands have defined different levels for different entity types (mainly merchants and service providers) that affect how compliance is reported and demonstrated. All organizations file an attestation of compliance (AoC) alongside one other document. Smaller organizations self-assess using a self-assessment questionnaire (SAQ). Please consult section 4.6 for a detailed comparison of the different merchant SAQs. Large organizations must provide a Report on Compliance (RoC), a point-in-time audit (although the point-in-time requirement may change in the future) by either an external certified QSA company or by an internal ISA (or combination of both).

As part of their compliance efforts, Jane's bank gave her basic guidance about what to do for PCI DSS.

"Jane's Flower Attic" (JFA) is considered a level 4 merchant for PCI DSS as it will receive less than 1 million transactions and no eCommerce transactions per year (level 3 was mostly created for smaller eCommerce merchants [2]). This is definitely reasonable as she's still operating from her living room. The next size of company in section 4.3 will cover Jane opening a boutique in a rented commercial storefront.

Note that some other rules may exist, such as some Visa guidelines that state that some level 4 merchants that receive at least 75% of their transactions in person using an approved payment device may be exempt from PCI DSS compliance altogether [3]. This means that if Jane's clients who pay by credit cards do so mostly in person (75% of the time or more), then Jane may be off the hook for PCI DSS. Her acquirer is who will determine Jane's required compliance path.

But what if Jane mostly takes her orders over the phone and enters them on her payment device? In this case, most of the card payments are considered card-not-present (CNP) telephone orders (the TO of MOTO acronym). For our scenario, let's say she is still mandated to be compliant and look at what she needs to do.

All merchants below level 1 (with some exceptions for level 2 merchants that I will not cover here but that are mentioned section 4.6) are required to provide a self-assessment questionnaire (SAQ) accompanied by the Attestation of Compliance (AoC) to their acquirer (in this case, Jane's bank) annually. Which SAQ is produced depends on what types of payments an organization accepts. The appendix of section 4.6 covers the SAQ selection process and provides more detail regarding SAQs.

Note that while Jane may have a website, she has no eCommerce payment capabilities on it and simply provides telephone contact information (and possibly a physical address).

Since Jane does not accept eCommerce but may accept in-person (card present) and potentially MOTO payments, this removes SAQ A and A-EP which are the eCommerce SAQs. It leaves many other potential options. SAQ C and C-VT are also out since they are for generic computers and non-physical devices. This leaves SAQ B, B-IP or P2PE. SAQ B is for "imprint machines" that dial-out, connecting using the analog phone line (which limits it to one physical location), while SAQ B-IP is for PTS-approved point-of-interaction (POI) devices with an IP connection to the payment processor. This IP (internet protocol) connection could operate via your regular internet provider, or over a cellular network. There can be implications if you're using internal network connections, but we'll forego those for the time being and assume a cellular network connection here since it can allow Jane to charge at the same time she delivers the flower arrangements to her clients (and also ensures that Jane's personal computers or home network are not affected by the payment process). P2PE is a specialized version of SAQ-B-IP for devices which encrypt data at the capture phase (keyed-in, via magnetic stripe, chip card or contactless - also known as tap-and-pay) limiting the risk to the organization; we will not cover this here.

4.2.2 Applying SAQ-B-IP using a cellular network connection to the payment device

Let's take a look at what SAQ-B-IP will mean for a cellular based connection.

SAQ-B-IP includes requirements in 10 of the PCI DSS high-level requirements (5 and 10 are excluded). Using a cellular based connection not connected to any other network system will allow Jane to reduce scope to the single payment device. This means that more controls in section 1 (network controls) can be marked as N/A (Not Applicable). The network diagram (1.1.2) required will be a simple one shown in Figure 4-2; no other network restrictions through firewalls or similar devices are required (1.*) as the device contains. a host-based firewall. Also excluded are wireless network controls (2.1.1, 4.1.1). Since no other devices are in-scope, the hardening section (2.*) is out-of-scope as the device is already considered hardened by the provider. Network segmentation penetration testing (11.3.4) is also not required, nor are vulnerability scans (11.2.*).

However, some controls are still applicable.

Storage controls cover payment forms and include redacting (rendering data unrecoverable through many possible means, such as using special markers, shredding paper, or punching holes through the information) of payment card information once it is no longer necessary (post authorization, 3.2.*, 3.3). This is in the case of telephone payments as card present payments do not require anything other than entry into the device. For any paper documents that are not redacted, controls over physical security of media (i.e. lock & key) must be in place (9.5 to 9.8.*). Physical security of the payment terminal device to protect against tampering are key controls here (9.9.*) and include keeping a list of devices (9.9.1) - easy here since initially Jane only has one payment device- reviewing the device for tampering (9.9.2) - for which her bank surely has given her guidance - that covers the training for detecting tampering (9.9.3).

We also have the policy section (12). For a one-woman shop, this may be creating a single document using the individual requirements as section. Here's an example of what it may look like:

4.2.2.1 JFA Information Security Policy (simplified example)

<Start of JFA Information Security Policy>

Preamble

"Jane's Flower Attic" (JFA) is a LLC corporation established under the state of [STATE] constitution. JFA provides flower arrangements to its clients and receives payment for the services rendered. Payment can be received in cash form, or through a supported payment card. JFA banking services (including payment devices) are provided by Local Bank while payment processing services are provided by PAYPRO.

Glossary

The following PCI DSS terms are used within this policy:

- o *A PAYMENT TERMINAL is the device used to take customer card payments via swipe, dip, insert, tap, or manual entry of the card number. Point-of-sale (or POS) terminal, credit card machine, PDQ terminal, or EMV/chip- enabled terminal are also names used to describe these devices.*
- o *PCI DSS service provider: An entity that performs some functions regarding to the payment process and/or provides services that may affect the security of the cardholder data.*
- o *AoC: Acronym for "Attestation of Compliance". The AoC is a form for merchants and service providers to attest to the results of a PCI DSS assessment, as documented in the Self-Assessment Questionnaire or Report on Compliance.*
- o *SAQ: Acronym for "Self-Assessment Questionnaire". Reporting tool used to document self-assessment results from an entity's PCI DSS assessment.*
- o *RoC: Acronym for "Report on Compliance". Report documenting detailed results from an entity's PCI DSS assessment*

Scope

As JFA uses a payment device provided by Local Bank that is connected using cellular technology provided by CellProv, and that device is not connected to any other system, then the scope of the assessment includes only the payment device. This scope is presented in the following network diagram:

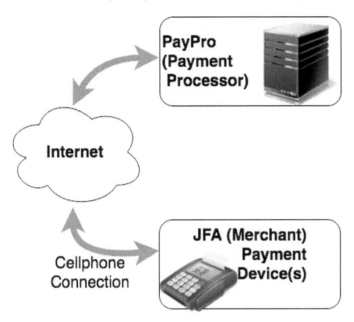

Volume 4 Figure 2 - JFA network diagram

Policy contents

The PCI DSS requirements are outlined next by numerical order, followed by the policy content that will be followed at JCFS.

PCI DSS requirement 12.1 - Establish, publish, maintain, and disseminate a security policy

The objective of this document is to define the policies required by JFA to meet its PCI DSS compliance requirements to Local Bank and the Payment Card Brands (Visa, etc.). JFA has the obligation to ensure that it is protecting cardholder data (also referred to as payment card data or information) from unauthorized disclosure.

PCI DSS requirement 12.1.1 - Review the security policy at least annually and update the policy when the environment changes

JFA has the obligation to ensure that this document is reviewed at least annually, that this review be noted in this section, and that any changes to the environment be assessed to ensure that JFA maintains compliance with PCI DSS. Changes and revisions to this policy are noted next:

JFA Information Security Policy Version History

Date	Person	Information reviewed / changes performed
2016-Jan-15	Jane Doe	Initial version covering PCI DSS 3.1
2016-Nov-31	Jane Doe	Reviewed against changes to PCI DSS 3.2 - no changes required.

PCI DSS requirement 12.3 - Develop usage policies for critical technologies and define proper use of these technologies.

This section defines the usage policy for the payment terminal devices in use at JFA (no other devices are in scope).

PCI DSS 12.3.1 - Explicit approval by authorized parties

Only authorized users as defined in requirement 12.3.5 are allowed access to the payment devices. Payment devices are only to be used for official JFA business.

Devices must be stored in a locked drawer when not in use and periodically reviewed for tampering.

See payment device user guide provided with the payment terminal device for more information on physical device security and periodic review for tampering.

PCI DSS 12.3.3 - Authentication for use of the technology

To use the device, the authorized user must logon using her authentication information: user ID and PIN number. [Volume note: not all devices may require this]

See payment device user guide provided with the device for more information on appropriate usage.

PCI DSS 12.3.5 - A list of all such devices and personnel with access

Only one payment device exists, serial number PD12345678.

Only one approved user exists: Jane Doe (owner and sole employee)

PCI DSS 12.3.9 - Activation of remote-access technologies for vendors and business partners only when needed by vendors and business partners, with immediate deactivation after use

Not applicable (N/A). No remote access is in use.

PCI DSS requirement 12.4 - Ensure that the security policy and procedures clearly define information security responsibilities for all personnel.

As JFA is a one-woman shop, all responsibilities fall on the owner.

PCI DSS requirement 12.5 - Assign to an individual or team the following information security management responsibilities:

PCI DSS 12.5.3 - Establish, document, and distribute security incident response and escalation procedures to ensure timely and effective handling of all situations.

As JFA is a one-woman shop, all responsibilities fall on the owner.

PCI DSS requirement 12.6 - Implement a formal security awareness program to make all personnel aware of the cardholder data security policy and procedures.

As JFA is a one-woman shop, the owner is aware of her responsibilities and confirms her awareness through the review of this policy.

Manage PCI DSS service provider

PCI DSS requirement 12.8 - Maintain and implement policies and procedures to manage service providers with whom cardholder data is shared, or that could affect the security of cardholder data.

PCI DSS 12.8.3 - Ensure there is an established process for engaging service providers including proper due diligence prior to engagement.

JFA has the obligation to ensure that all service providers with whom cardholder data is shared, or that could affect the security of cardholder data are compliant with PCI DSS (such providers will be henceforth defined as PCI DSS service providers).

JFA can only enter into contract with a validated compliant PCI DSS service providers. Acceptable methods of compliance validation are the official PCI SSC Attestation of Compliance (AoC) or the full Self-Assessment Questionnaire (SAQ) or Report on Compliance (RoC).

PCI DSS 12.8.4 - Maintain a program to monitor service providers' PCI DSS compliance status at least annually.

JFA must review the PCI DSS service providers compliance at least annually and update the information in section 12.8.1. If a service provider is deemed non-compliant, then either the service provider must ensure that it will return to compliance, or a replacement must be identified and migrated to. All changes must happen within 3 month of this initial identification.

JFA must maintain the evidence that the review process was performed for 3 years. [volume note: PCI DSS is not explicit in this regard]

PCI DSS 12.8.2 - Maintain a written agreement that includes an acknowledgement that the service providers are responsible for the security of cardholder data the service providers possess or otherwise store, process or transmit on behalf of the customer, or to the extent that they could impact the security of the customer's cardholder data environment.

JFA must ensure that contracts for all service providers identified in section 12.8.1 maintain the acknowledgement of responsibilities required by requirement 12.8.2 of PCI DSS.

PCI DSS 12.8.5 - Maintain information about which PCI DSS requirements are managed by each service provider, and which are managed by the entity.

JFA must ensure that for all service providers identified in section 12.8.1, either the contract or an agreed upon document contain a list of which PCI DSS requirements are covered by the provider and those managed by JFA (including some where responsibilities may be shared).

This can be a simple list of PCI DSS requirement numbers, or a table with columns for JFA and providers (including nested providers if those exist).

12.8.1 - Maintain a list of service providers including a description of the service provided.

List of PCI DSS service providers

Provider	Date Validation Performed	Service Provided
Local Bank	2016-Oct-01	Providing payment device (nested by Payment Device Co.)
PAYPRO	2016-Oct-15	Payment Processing

PCI DSS Requirement 12.10.1 - Incident response plan

JFA has the obligation of maintaining an incident response plan in the unlikely event that cardholder data is breached.

As JFA is a one-woman shop, all responsibilities fall on the owner.

In the event of a compromise, communication is key.

Local Bank has contracted their initial incident response point of contact with their partner payment processor, PAYPRO. The hotline for incidents is 1-800-555-PPRO (7776). PAYPRO is responsible for communication with the card brands.

Local Bank office hours number is 555-1234, and the bank account executive is Mike Smith.

Local Bank and PAYPRO have cell phone contact information for Jane Doe in case of emergency.

Should JFA believe that a breach may have occurred (confirmation is not required), JFA personnel will communicate immediately with the PAYPRO incident hotline.

In the event that JFA is notified of a potential breach, it will work diligently to assist involved in resolving the issue.

Unsolicited electronic cardholder data reception

Covers email, chat, SMS, etc.

No electronic cardholder data is to ever be received or kept. If unsolicited data of this nature is ever received, it is to be considered an exception to the regular process; information regarding this event should be written down or printed and then deleted from any medium (including confirming if electronic trash bins are emptied). One problem with electronic transmissions is that temporary storage occurs and that backups may be made of this information by entities involved in the transmission. For that reason, for any exception where information is received electronically, a registry of this event (which should not include more that the first 6 digits and last 4 of the card number) should be kept on paper only. Information will include at least: date and time, sender information, first 6 digits and last 4 of the card number.

Finally, the sender should be notified that the method they selected to transmit payment information is not secure and they should be instructed as to which secure methods exist (in person or over the phone, but not as voicemail).

<End of JFA Information Security Policy>

But what if the payment device had run through a regular network connection and not a cellular network? We'll investigate this scenario in the next section when Jane opens a small boutique.

4.3 - Step 2 - Jane's Flower Boutique (JFB)

As work starts exploding, Jane is encouraged by her community to expand. She leases a small shop where she can keep more inventory and even hire employees (full or part time, it does not really matter). Her company is now referred to as Jane's Flower Boutique (JFB).

Having a physical site that customers can visit means that Jane should have a payment device always onsite. That device could be a wired device (ethernet) or could be another cellular based device (which would simplify things). Let's say that since Jane needs internet connectivity for her business, the additional cost of the cellular connectivity simply adds costs and she decides to go for an ethernet connected payment device provided by her bank and connected again to PAYPRO. She uses an online accounting system (that acts as an Electronic Cash Register, or virtual point-of-sale system) recommended by her accountant which she accesses using a computer she purchased, but the payment process is handled by the payment device and she just marks the purchase as paid within the sales system. Once payment settlement has been performed (generally after 2 or 3 work days), she (or her accountant) can reconcile the payments with her online accounting software. The payment process is the same as for JFA, as presented in figure 4-1.

The portable payment terminal device that worked for her side gig could still be useful for JFB, especially if Jane wants to offer in-person card payments while delivering her goods; this would require that the device works over a cellular connection. Having the device mobile does open risk that it can more easily be tampered with, but added issues are is still mostly physical security related.

Since the payment device is independent from the register, she will still report using SAQ-B-IP as in the previous case. Other SAQs could also potentially apply. For example, some online accounting software could provide the same functionality as the device through the application and would force her down the path of SAQ-C or SAQ-C-VT, depending on the implementation. But let's stick with SAQ-B-IP here.

Since the payment device is connected to a local network, the network controls are not out-of-scope this time, and our scope will extend beyond the payment device to other devices connected-to or which could affect the security of the payment device or process.

In order to use SAQ-B-IP, we must meet the requirement that the payment device be isolated from other devices on the network by network segmentation (which was a non-issue when we had no other device). Requirement 11.3.4 calls for network segmentation penetration testing. We need to use a device that meets this requirement. The easiest way would be to place the payment device behind a router or firewall which can isolate different network device ethernet ports.

Note: while some will argue that a NAT-router can provide isolation, most cheap ones are not regularly updated, and do not meet all the PCI DSS networking controls.

Leveraging her bank's contact, Jane engages with a local firm used to providing IT (hardware and software) solutions for small and medium-size companies (let's call this company IT-Serv). Although Jane feels comfortable operating the payment device and the sales software, she feels some technical details are beyond her current abilities. IT-Serv agrees to provide periodic services to assist Jane, and serve as her IT department when the need arises. IT-Serv thus becomes a Service Provider to JFB and as part of their agreement, they set up the JFB network. IT-Serv sells JFB a small firewall appliance that they also configure following PCI DSS requirements. They also help her by creating the necessary documentation including a network diagram called for in requirement 1.1.2 of the SAQ and shown next:

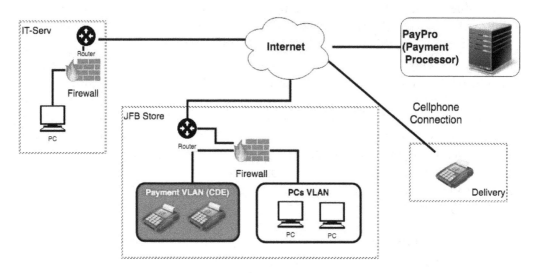

Volume 4 Figure 3 - JFB network diagram

4.3.1 JFB firewall standard

IT-Serv also provides the following firewall standard that addresses multiple requirements:

<start JFB firewall standard>

Preamble

Firewalls are critical devices used in protecting the network and its systems, and ensuring confidentiality, integrity, and availability. This document outlines JFB' stated policy regarding the use of such devices, including procurement, configuration, updates, and testing. This covers PCI DSS requirements but applies to all devices, whether or not in scope for PCI DSS.

Glossary

- o *A PAYMENT TERMINAL is the device used to take customer card payments via swipe, dip, insert, tap, or manual entry of the card number. Point-of-sale (or POS) terminal, credit card machine, PDQ terminal, or EMV/chip- enabled terminal are also names used to describe these devices.*
- o *CDE : Acronym for "Cardholder Data Environment". Basically the area (people, process and technologies) we are trying to protect, which starts with the systems that SPT CHD or SAD but is not limited to these.*
- o *DMZ : Abbreviation for "demilitarized zone." Physical or logical sub-network that provides an additional layer of security to an organization's internal private network. The DMZ adds an additional layer of network security between the Internet and an organization's internal network so that external parties only have direct connections to devices in the DMZ rather than the entire internal network.*
- o *ACL : Acronym for "Access Control List". Provides a list of permissions attached to an object. In networking, an access control list is a set of permissions allowing or denying network traffic between a source and destination connected to the network.*

Procurement

Any firewall used in the network environment must meet the following minimal requirements:

- o *Capable of providing anti-spoofing measures to detect and block forged source IP addresses from entering the network [PCI DSS 1.3.3]*
- o *Permit only "established" connections into the network (i.e. it maintains "state", such as using NAT) [PCI DSS 1.3.5]*
- o *Allow the creation of an isolated network CDE for the placement of payment devices (a separate device can be used to accomplish this)*
- o *Must allow for network access control lists (ACLs), preferably allowing domain names in rules*
- o *Be supported by the manufacturer so that vulnerabilities are patched in a timely manner [PCI DSS 6.1, 6.2]*
- o *Must support secure encrypted administrative connectivity including TLS 1.1 and above (and allowing disabling insecure SSL/early TLS), as well as allowing installation of an externally produced HTTPS certificate and SSH key [PCI DSS 2.3]*
- o *Must support multi factor authentication (MFA) [PCI DSS 8.3.1]*

Configuration

A firewall device must be placed at the network perimeter edge behind the internet router.

If only one firewall is in place, a CDE must be configured on that firewall. A second firewall may be used to create a CDE.

Any payment device must be connected to a CDE on a firewall device, and all default communications must be prevented (default: deny any any). The CDE is a type of internal network zone never accessible from the internet.

[PCI DSS 1.1.4, 1.2]

The initial baseline configuration will follow the manufacturer's recommended best practices if available. It will include at a minimum changing all default credentials, including user account passwords and SNMP strings. [PCI DSS 2.1]

Administrative access will only be allowed from the internal network (no remote access). Administrative access can use SSH or HTTPS. In the case of HTTPS, a TLS certificate signed by an intermediate authority (CA) set up by the IT department will be installed. IT department administrative computers will be configured to support the intermediate authority. Individual administrative accounts must be setup to use multifactor authentication and will be limited to IT support personnel with a need. If technical restrictions prevent individual accounts and shared account are thus used, then a sign-in sheet (which could be paper or electronic) must be maintained for whenever an authorized IT user accesses the administrative console.

[PCI DSS 2.3, 7.1.2, 7.1.3, 8.1.5, 8.3.1, 8.3.2, 8.5]

No wireless device can be connected to the CDE. If a wireless network is required, it should be setup as a secure guest network (WPA2) with no access to the internal networks (only internet access) and its security key (passphrase) updated periodically (monthly recommended). The CDE should only allow authorized outgoing access to the internet, and block all traffic to the internal network and the CDE (use of ACLs).

[PCI DSS 1.2.3, 2.1.1, 4.1.1]

The payment devices in the CDE are to only have authorized outgoing connections that are required for business operations. Unless otherwise justified, this would include only outgoing traffic from the payment devices to the payment processor.

No incoming traffic should be allowed unless a valid documented business justification exists.

[PCI DSS 1.2.1, 1.3, 1.3.4]

CDE firewall rules must be documented, and that documentation updated when changes are required. No insecure services can be used. [PCI DSS 1.1.6]

Updates

- o *JFB' IT staff will monitor for updates to the firewall software through the manufacturer mailing lists. Whenever an update is made available, IT will evaluate the changes to assign a risk ranking using the CVSS base score. [PCI DSS 6.1]*
- o *IT will determine how quickly an update must be installed, but IT will ensure that any update ranked as critical or high risk will be installed as quickly as possible, at least within one month of notification. [PCI DSS 6.2]*
- o *If HTTPS is used for administration, a TLS certificate signed by an intermediate authority set up by the IT department will be updated annually. [PCI DSS 2.3]*

Testing

JFB must ensure the following testing be performed periodically:

- o *Annually, it will contract to have network segmentation penetration testing performed on the firewall device providing the CDE isolation to ensure that communication is not possible. [PCI DSS 11.3.4]*
- o *JFB will contract with an Approved Scanning Vendor (ASV), approved by the Payment Card Industry Security Standards Council (PCI SSC) to provide quarterly external vulnerability of the internet connection. IT will manage the ASV console to schedule and review the results of the scans, as well as conserve copies for filing alongside the SAQ. Note that we expect the scans to show nothing as only outgoing connections should be allowed. [PCI DSS 11.2.2]*

<end JFB firewall standard>

Note: The deadline to use SSL/early TLS for existing implementations is June 30, 2018. Prior to these, mitigations are required (see Appendix A2 of PCI DSS 3.2). New implementations must not use the insecure protocols, which is why we marked as required TLS 1.1 or newer in the example firewall standard. The A2 requirement section for new implementations should be marked as Not Applicable (N/A).

As in the last section, JFB will also need an information security policy. As it would be very similar to the one provided in the last section, we're leaving the limited required changes as an exercise for the reader.

The remaining technical requirements cover mainly the payment device provided by the bank (and are the responsibility of the bank as the service provider for those devices).

They include changing vendor-supplied defaults [PCI DSS 2.1], using strong cryptography and security protocols used to safeguard sensitive cardholder data during transmission over open, public networks [PCI DSS 4.1], masking PAN when displayed [PCI DSS 3.3], updating devices when patches are available [PCI DSS 6.1, 6.2].

4.4 Step 3 - Jane's Flower Chain (JFC)

Let's assume that Jane lives in a decent size city that can support many flower stores. Jane's business is performing so well that she decides to slowly expand to a few stores, forming Jane's Flower Chain (JFC). We'll simplify our work here by looking at the end state and not the growth steps.

In order to provide better service to her customers, Jane contracts with FooPOS systems to get a POS system that ties with the payment processor, PAYPRO and with its merchant bank account offered by its acquirer, Local Bank. A purpose built Point-of-Sale (POS) system, also called an INTEGRATED PAYMENT TERMINAL, can provide easier controls with easier functionality.

Jane decides to retain the services of IT-Serv, but with increased support due to the growth of the company. Because of the new company size, she could ultimately hire her own IT staff but she might require more than 4 to 5 full-time employees to cover separation of duties and vacations (and not all may be used at 100%). Instead, by using IT-Serv she gains access to multiple profiles that can be engaged when needed. She could have a local employee providing coordination, but she decides against it initially, thinking she'll revisit this option periodically.

Jane decides that eCommerce is not something she needs right now, and her new POS system with a payment application allows her to use a SAQ-C which has 112 questions. If she added eCommerce, she would not be eligible for that SAQ and would have to use the catch-all SAQ-D with all 232 questions (though some questions could still be not applicable). The SAQ-D (or complete PCI DSS standard) and/or Report on Compliance (RoC) will be used in another of Jane's endeavours (JFE).

SAQ-C has requirements in all of the 12 high-level requirements. To use SAQ-C, your organization must meet a few conditions:

- Your company has a payment application system and an Internet connection on the same device and/or same local area network (LAN);
- The payment application system/Internet device is not connected to any other systems within your environment (this can be achieved via network segmentation to isolate payment application system/Internet device from all other systems);

- The physical location of the POS environment is not connected to other premises or locations, and any LAN is for a single location only;
- Any cardholder data your company retains is on paper (for example, printed reports or receipts), and these documents are not received electronically; and
- Your company does not store cardholder data in electronic format. [4]

These requirements are similar to SAQ-B-IP used previously. The POS solution must be isolated (first and second bullets) and the branches must be independent and not linked together using an internal network (third bullet, such as an MPLS network). Again there must be no electronic storage, only paper (fourth and fifth bullets). Since our POS combines the sales functionality with the payment processing, we only need to segment it away from any other system that requires connectivity (regular PCs, air conditioning, alarm system, etc.).

Let's see what the network looks like in this configuration (simplified high-level diagram).

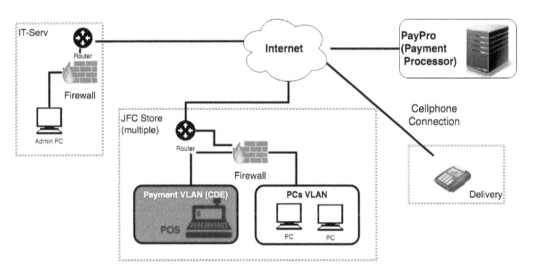

Volume 4 Figure 4 - JFC individual store network diagram

Our PCI DSS scope includes one CDE per branch, including one firewall device to create the CDE (and potentially a second device if we need a separate one as the external firewall) in addition to the POS connected to that network zone. Let's look at the required controls in this case.

4.4.1 Network level controls

Unless otherwise specified, all those controls fall under IT's purview. SAQ-C has fewer controls in the firewall section (requirement 1) than SAQ-B-IP. Gone is the firewall standard [PCI DSS 1.1], but we'll still main the one from JFB. Limiting access to only what services are required for the systems in the CDE to operate [PCI DSS 1.2.1] is still present, whether inbound [PCI DSS 1.3.5] or outbound [PCI DSS 1.3.4]. And wireless network should also be isolated [PCI DSS 1.2.3]. Annual network segmentation penetration testing (11.3.4) are still required, but if the same device type and configuration is in place at all branches (our case), then that test need only be performed in one of the branches. If the IT outsourcer has qualified personnel, they can perform this testing; if not, it must be outsourced.

As we did for JFB in step 2, we'll ensure that the wireless network (if any) is not connected to the CDE [PCI DSS 2.1.1, 4.1.1]. In case wireless networks are in place, we need to maintain an inventory of authorized wireless access points (devices and SSID) [PCI DSS 11.1.1]. Jane decides to leave the wireless guest network decision to individual store branch managers, and have those connected to the internet connection only if managers decide to provide it.

Whether or not wireless networks are in use, JFC must perform (at least) quarterly scans to ensure that no unauthorized wireless networks are connected to the network [PCI DSS 11.1]. This could be performed in many ways, from automated using network controlled devices to using a laptop or a smartphone with a specialized application. Keeping some form of evidence is required. Should an unauthorized connected wireless network be identified (you will likely identify many networks located outside the premise, and thus out-of-scope), you need to invoke the incident response plan [PCI DSS 11.1.2] to react to this event. Jane decides that IT-Serv's staff doing maintenance at stores will perform this scan using tools on their work laptops.

Any "significant change" to the IT infrastructure (not just patches, but changes in devices, applications, providers, etc.) should call for a review of all the SAQ requirements including any assumptions [PCI DSS 6.4.6, new and only mandatory by February 2018]. This forces new ad-hoc vulnerability scans as defined in the testing section [PCI DSS 11.2.3].

Since there are multiple locations, the IT staff will require remote access to the branch networks. All remote access must use multi-factor authentication (MFA)

[PCI DSS 8.3.2], which we already implemented earlier at JFA for administrative access to the firewall devices [PCI DSS 2.3, 8.3.1].

Since IT-Serv provides the IT staff, it is considered an extension of JFC and its staff acting as agents (following the "agency" legal concept). So while IT-Serv is a PCI DSS service provider, its staff are not considered "third parties" for the sake of user accounts, per requirement 8.1.5. Any other remote access third party accounts (for example, FooPOS technical supports) may exist but should be normally disabled unless needed [PCI DSS 8.1.5]. IT decides to instead use screen sharing when third parties need to perform remote access tasks, which meets this requirement.

Let's see what else JFC's IT needs in terms of user account management.

4.4.2 Identification and Authentication controls

A new area added with SAQ-C is how we manage user accounts. While Role-based Access Controls (RBAC) are not mandated in SAQ-C (PCI DSS 7.2.*), some centralized account system can be helpful (LDAP, Active Directory, etc.). IT creates a separate Active Directory (AD) domain for JFC using a hosted provider (Microsoft or other). Each individual user must use an individual account for any system accessed [PCI DSS 8.1.1]. Account lockout lasting at least 30 minutes [PCI DSS 8.1.7] must be forced after at most six failed login attempts [PCI DSS 8.1.6]. A user session must timeout (lock or logoff) after it has been idle for 15 minutes [PCI DSS 8.1.8]. All accounts must be authenticated using either:

- Something you know, such as a <u>password</u> or passphrase
- Something you have, such as a <u>token device</u> or smart card (you can add individual computer certificate tied to an individual user)
- Something you are, such as a <u>biometric</u> (fingerprint reader, etc.) *[PCI DSS 8.2]*

Multi-factor authentication (MFA) implies using two different methods from those three, and not the same factor twice, such as 2 different passwords.

If passwords (or passphrases) are in use, then certain supplemental requirements apply. Passwords must meet complexity requirements, generally meaning minimum password length of at least seven characters and containing both numeric and alphabetic characters [PCI DSS 8.2.3] but any equivalent or higher level works (AD has a setting called "passwords must meet complexity requirements"). Those passwords/passphrases must be changed at least once every 90 days [PCI DSS 8.2.4] and be different from the last 4 the user has handled [PCI DSS 8.2.5].

Because users will likely eventually forget their password and require a reset, when such a reset occurs, the temporary password should be set to a unique value [PCI DSS 8.2.6], meaning you can't just use "Password1" for all users. If the user can see an IT administrator in person, then he can simply enter his new password at that time. For those other cases, IT uses a password manager's random password generator with the "Make Pronounceable" option selected and sets the password to expire upon logon, requiring the user to create a new one. IT must provide a formal security awareness training upon hiring, and annually [PCI DSS 12.6] which will include "authentication policies and procedures" guidance:

- Guidance on selecting strong authentication credentials
- Guidance for how users should protect their authentication credentials
- Instructions not to reuse previously employed passwords
- Instructions that users should change passwords if there is any suspicion the password could be compromised [PCI DSS 8.4]

Security awareness training must also make all personnel aware of the cardholder data security policy and procedures [PCI DSS 12.6].

4.4.3 Physical security controls

Physical security needs to be in place to restrict access to publicly accessible network jacks [PCI DSS 9.1.2] and the location where networking equipment (firewalls, routers, etc.) are located [PCI DSS 9.1.1]. This could be done using a simple key-based door lock mechanism (and a sign-in sheet) or more complex methods such as electronic badges. Door locks are used in JFC's case (with a sign-in sheet inside the locked room). Obviously, only authorized personnel (mainly IT) should have access. Note that the physical location of the POS is not considered a sensitive area as it is required in direct customer interaction.

As in the previous examples, the devices that perform data capture from the physical cards (on the POS system) must be protected from tampering [PCI DSS 9.9.*]. I won't repeat the exact requirements here as they are exactly the same as for JFA and JFB.

Physical security (for example, lock and key) must also cover any media that may contain cardholder data on paper (no electronic storage is allowed for SAQ-C) [PCI DSS 9.5, 9.6.*, 9.7] including the secure destruction of information once it is no longer needed [PCI DSS 9.8.*]. Note that any written sensitive authentication data (card verification code or value in our case) must be redacted (i.e. removed) from paper document once the transaction has been processed [PCI DSS 3.2, 3.2.2]. The track data [PCI DSS 3.2.1] and personal identification number (PIN) or the encrypted PIN block [PCI DSS 3.2.3] are never saved anywhere and only used in the payment authorization process at the POS in JFC branches.

4.4.4 System level controls

For JFC, we have a few types of in-scope devices: firewalls & routers (network devices), POS systems & delivery payment device, and IT administration workstations (connected/indirectly systems per the PCI Resources Scoping Model). All sets of devices serve only one primary function [PCI DSS 2.2.1]. IT will be solely responsible for the network devices and administrative workstations, while it will coordinate with FooPOS regarding the POS systems (FooPOS will be responsible for most of those controls, but remote access may require the assistance of IT for access, as we described earlier).

Both sets of devices must be hardened which means having "vendor-supplied defaults always changed" and "unnecessary default accounts removed or disabled ..." "before installing a system on the network" [PCI DSS 2.1]. For each system type, we need to have documented configuration standards that will determine how systems are hardened [PCI DSS 2.2]. Since these configuration standards must be "consistent with industry-accepted system hardening standards", JFC will adopt one of these as their default standard. Let's say IT picks the Center for Internet Security (CIS) (many others would do as well). IT will configure the device following that standard (which CIS calls a benchmark), and loosen settings as required by the business needs while documenting those deviations from the standard (including the rational). The configuration standards cover removal of unnecessary functionality [PCI DSS 2.2.5] and of unnecessary services, protocols, daemons [PCI DSS 2.2.2]. IT staff have been trained on secure configurations [PCI DSS 2.2.4]. And since IT will not accept insecure protocols, requirement 2.2.3 is met.

Section 3.7.2 of volume 3 shows an example of how deviation from hardening could be documented.

All sets of devices must be patched (at an appropriate frequency, monthly in JFC's case) [PCI DSS 6.2] when vulnerabilities are identified using reputable sources [PCI DSS 6.1] (such as manufacturer mailing lists) that are routinely monitored. A risk ranking for the patches must be in place, but we can default to the standard CVSS unless we have a need for another methodology.

The network devices are not susceptible to viruses, but the POS may be, while the workstations definitely are. Thus requirement 5 is applicable. For those systems that are susceptible, a reputable antivirus must be installed [PCI DSS 5.1, 5.1.1] and updated regularly (I would say at least daily if not hourly) as well as generating and collecting logs in a centralized logging solution [PCI DSS 5.2]. Users should also not be able to disable the anti-malware solution [PCI DSS 5.3]. If the POS is considered "not be commonly affected by malicious software", then we need to periodically (at least annually) review to confirm this assumption still stands (and document our results and rational) [PCI DSS 5.1.2]. A document must be created that explains why these systems are not affected by malware. There is no set format for this document, we just need to ensure it contains a history table to show it has been reviewed annually.

4.4.5 Application level controls

We only have one PCI DSS application, the POS system. Since the FooPOS POS provides the application layer, we need to fill section "Part 2d. Payment Application" in the SAQ. We must follow the manufacturer's implementation guide, which the provider follows since they dispense (in our simpler hypothetical case) all support.

Part 2d. Payment Application

Does the organization use one or more Payment Applications? ☑ Yes ☐ No

Provide the following information regarding the Payment Applications your organization uses:

Payment Application Name	Version Number	Application Vendor	Is application PA-DSS Listed?	PA-DSS Listing Expiry date (if applicable)
FooPOS	1.0.2	FooPOS	☐ Yes ☑ No	
			☐ Yes ☐ No	

Volume 4 Figure 5 - SAQ-C – Part 2d. Payment Application

The POS also takes care of masking the PAN when displayed [PCI DSS 3.3] and that strong cryptography and security protocols used to safeguard sensitive cardholder data during transmission over open, public networks to the payment processor [PCI DSS 4.1]. The same notes regarding secure versions of SSL/TLS mentioned in previous sections apply here and will not be repeated.

4.4.6 Logging and Monitoring

Logging and Monitoring are new functions we did not have to deal with before. All logs from both types of devices need to be reviewed "to identify anomalies or suspicious activity" [PCI DSS 10.6], including a daily review of security related events [PCI DSS 10.6.1], including at a minimum for SAQ-C:

- all actions taken by any individual with root or administrative privileges [PCI DSS 10.2.2]
- Invalid logical access attempts [PCI DSS 10.2.4] (aka login failures)
- Use of and changes to identification and authentication mechanisms [PCI DSS 10.2.5]

PCI DSS 10.6.1 also requires daily review of:

- Logs of all system components that store, process, or transmit CHD and/or SAD
- Logs of all critical system components
- Logs of all servers and system components that perform security functions

Other relevant logs identified by JFC need to be reviewed periodically, but that frequency is up to the risk evaluation of the organization [PCI DSS 10.6.2].

We also must have a "change-detection mechanism" in place for all in-scope systems [PCI DSS 11.5]. The most common (but not the only option) way is to use file-integrity monitoring (FIM) tools. A review of those changes identified must occur at least weekly.

Any exceptions and anomalies identified in all the previously defined monitoring must be investigated [PCI DSS 10.6.3, 11.5.1] and may lead to the invocation of the incident response process [PCI DSS 12.10.*].

The log review will be performed by separate IT staff that do not perform administrative tasks (separation of duties). This is another time where leveraging IT-Serv will reduce costs.

All logs must include sufficiently detailed information including User identification [PCI DSS 10.3.1], Type of event [PCI DSS 10.3.2], Date and time [PCI DSS 10.3.3], Success or failure [PCI DSS 10.3.4], Origination (source) of event [PCI DSS 10.3.5], and Identity or name of affected data, system component, or resource [PCI DSS 10.3.6] (all common in standardized logging systems).

Since the individual stores (sites) are required to be independent for SAQ-C, centralization of logs is not required [PCI DSS 10.5.*], but IT decides to send logs to a centralized system to reduce their management costs (logging from multiple remote systems).

The logs must be retained for one year (but this can include a backup to offline facilities for logs older than 3 months) [PCI DSS 10.7]. While SAQ-C does not mandate centralization of logs, this can simplify the task and assist in ensuring retention. IT-Serv uses a SIEM (Security information and event management) system for all its clients and leverages a separate instance for JFC related tasks.

4.4.7 Testing

Testing only slightly increases with SAQ-C. ASV-conducted quarterly external vulnerability scans are required here as well [PCI DSS 11.2.2], but so are internal scans performed by qualified personnel [PCI DSS 11.2.1] which could be IT-Serv staff. Both may require rescans after fixes are implemented until we get a clean scan per quarter (which can be achieved using combinations of scans from the quarter; see section 3.7.11.2 for more detail).

4.4.8 Governance, Policies, Procedures

SAQ-C includes more policy and procedure requirements than the SAQ-B-IP Information Security policy detailed for JFA.

An Information Security policy that is established, published, maintained, and disseminated to all relevant personnel [PCI DSS 12.1] is again required, ensuring that it is reviewed at least annually and updated when the environment changes [PCI DSS 12.1.1]. The policy is presented to employees during the security awareness training [PCI DSS 12.6.*].

The policy will formally assign [PCI DSS 12.5.1] responsibilities for "Establishing, documenting, and distributing security incident response and escalation procedures to ensure timely and effective handling of all situation"; In this case, Jane is assigned responsibility for the business side including all communications with external parties (bank, card brands), while IT is responsible for all technical aspects (with roles and assignments defined in the incident response plan).

The policy (and/or its detailed procedures) needs to "clearly define information security responsibilities for all personnel" [PCI DSS 12.4]. This includes having all employees follow approved processes, and reporting any suspicious activity (how and to whom). It assigns responsibility to IT of ensuring that any system installed on company network is hardened [PCI DSS 2.5].

The policy also mentions that appropriate usage of company resources is defined in the usage policy, which can be a separate document.

An IT usage policy [PCI DSS 12.3] is created. That policy states the following:

- That access to any JFC system requires the use of an account, that this requires supervisor request (branch managers for regular store employees, or the CEO for all other roles) [PCI DSS 12.3.1, 12.3.2]
- That the policy delegates account guidance to the authentication policy
- That JFC systems are to only be used for JFC business processes [PCI DSS 12.3.5] and that a list of such devices is maintained by IT [PCI DSS 12.3.3]
- That no non-JFC systems may be connected to the JFC network, but that an externally connected guest wifi may be provided by individual stores where employees or customers could connect their own devices (although business comes first and professionalism is expected from all employees) [PCI DSS 12.3.6]
- That remote access is only available for IT staff that have a business need for it, that access will timeout after no more than 10 minutes of inactivity [PCI DSS 12.3.8]
- That remote access of vendors will be performed through screen sharing by IT staff following IT manager approval [PCI DSS 12.3.9]
- That at no time should any debit or credit card number (PAN in PCI DSS terminology) be sent in any electronic medium other than to process a phone payment in the POS [PCI DSS 4.2]; in case the system is down at the time the customer calls, the information should be written on a piece of paper and stored in a secure and locked location and processed later; once processed, the paper should be shredded so the card number be made unrecoverable [PCI DSS 3.4, 9.8.1]

PCI DSS service provider management requirements [PCI DSS 12.8] are the same as for JFA. Our service provider list [PCI DSS 12.8.1] increases to include FooPOS (on top of Local Bank, PAYPRO and IT-Serv) and the hosted Active Directory provider.

The authentication policy [PCI DSS 8.8] describes the requirements that accounts must use:

Accounts

- All accounts will be on Active Directory, unless a technical restriction exists and proper controls are established and approved by management
- Regular account name should be the same for all systems
- Account name must follow the structure [first letter of first name][last name] (for example asmith)
- In case two or more users share the same account name, a sequential number will be appended (for example asmith2)

Passwords [PCI DSS 8.4]

- Passwords must not be any of the last 4 employed by the user
- Passwords should be complex, not easily guessable and not contain any personal information (dates of important personal events, family or pet names, etc.)
- Whenever possible, passphrases are recommended, for example combining unrelated words, numbers and punctuation
- Credentials (passwords) should never be shared, even if requested by IT, as this is likely an attempt to trick the user
- If a user suspects their password may have been compromised, he should call the helpdesk at 1-800-555-HELP to have it reset immediately

Account Permissions [PCI DSS 7.1]

- Roles (Network Administrator, Monitoring, Cashier, Store Manager, etc.) will be defined for personnel with specific responsibilities, limited to only what is strictly necessary to perform job responsibilities [PCI DSS 7.1.2]
- Users will only be assigned to roles and not have further individual accesses assigned [PCI DSS 7.1.3]

Administrative Accounts

- In addition to their regular accounts, IT staff will also have an administrative account with "_a" appended to the account name (for example asmith_a)
- Administrative accounts are to be used only when managing servers and never to logon to a regular workstation (desktop or laptop) (administrative account login will be reviewed by monitoring staff)
- Passwords for administrative accounts must not be the same as the one for an admin's regular account
- No shared administrative accounts are to ever be used; if a technical restriction forces the use of a shared account, then a process to ensure traceability must be put in place and approved by the IT director and business management [PCI DSS 8.5]

Luckily for JFC, there are no technical limitations for using individual accounts.

4.4.9 Incident Response

Finally, Jane and IT will work together to create an incident response plan that meets the confidentiality needs of PCI DSS requirement 12.10.1 (but also covers some integrity and availability issues that are out-of-scope for PCI DSS). Let's create a simplified version:

<start of plan>

JFC Incident Response Plan

In the event of something that affects regular business operations, having a plan can help lessen the impact on the business. While we cannot account for all potential eventualities, most of the required processes defined here will still apply or at least help in such an occurrence.

Potential events considered:

- *Natural disasters such as fire or flooding*
- *Break-in or theft*
- *Network, system, application or other IT compromise, including software issues such as malware (virus) and physical device attached to the network*
- *Hardware failure*

Preventative measures

IT will perform the following regular processes to assist in the recovery and business continuity:

- o *backup configuration of any equipment on the network during installation and whenever changes are made (tracked using the change control process, and audited)*
- o *install backup software on all devices that create information locally (i.e. regular workstations, if any)*
- o *backup all network backups shares*
- o *save all local backups to encrypted tape backups and have these stored offline (note that since no card data is stored, physical storage does not fall under PCI DSS)*

Reporting an event

Most events will occur during business hours and should be reported to the helpdesk at 1-800-555-HELP; outside business hours, you should call to the 24/7 on-call IT emergency phone number at 1-555-5ON-CALL.

The recipient of the call will take detailed notes, starting with the exact date and time and caller information. If the recipient can make a determination as to the type of issue involved, he should do so at this point .

Initial Event analysis

The initial step involves validating this is an issue and determining how critical the event is.

Major business disruption include natural disasters, theft, hardware failure, or potential breach. In the event of major business disruption, senior management must be notified immediately. A list of contact information is maintained and reviewed at least every quarter.

Response to natural disasters and hardware failures

Natural disasters often lead to hardware failures. The general response is to acquire replacement equipment and restore configurations from backups (once physical security can be ensured).

Response to theft

If we suspect a potential breach, then coordination with the police will be required, and notification of senior management must be made by email initially, and by phone during the next business day. In such a case, securing valuable equipment (IT and other) is a priority.

Response to potential breach (hardware of software)

The first step in a potential breach is to ensure we maintain evidence as close to the time this is discovered. IT-Serv's forensics team should be contacted immediately as they will advise the responder of his responsibilities; they may choose to perform tasks themselves.

Once evidence has been gathered, we should follow the same procedures as software issues. Investigation is described later in this document.

Response to software issues

Most software issues will be malware related, but could involve other failures. Since we may not be able to ensure complete eradication of whatever software issue we encountered, we should rebuild systems from scratch. This follows low-level data destruction on hard drives using the IT approved solution, reinstallation of system (preferably from image), hardening and patching, and restoring configuration. Vulnerability scans validating system compliance should be performed before installation on the network.

Investigation of Potential breach

IT-Serv's forensic's team will be responsible to perform a detailed analysis of the evidence gathered. Senior management will be responsible for communication with the local bank, card brands (see Appendix for card brands notification process - not provided in this volume), and external legal counsel. This process is not fully documented as it depends what is identified. Legal counsel will provide recommendations as steps to follow, but the ultimate decision rests with senior management.

<end of plan>

4.5 - Step 4 - Jane's Flower Emporium (JFE)

Here, we'll look at Jane's Flower Emporium (JFE), a large flower store chain (potentially including franchises). At this scale, and due to the fact that not everything is always under central management control, things naturally get more complicated. Indeed, from a compliance standpoint, we're potentially looking at a level 1 merchant (over 6 million payment card transactions per year, meaning over 16,000 per day) which would require an audit by a QSA company (or internal ISA) and potentially as a service provider of the franchisees if certain prescriptions are not taken.

Compared to the 3 previous examples where PCI DSS compliance was the driving factor behind our security programs, JFE is implementing an information security program that will incorporate PCI DSS, but go above and beyond what the standard requires. Like most large organizations, JFE is likely subject to multiple regulatory and contractual requirements. A more comprehensive program will better address the myriad requirements an organization of this size faces, as well as ensure better security and accountability in the long run.

The company is headquartered in the fictional city of Metrocity, but has stores nationwide. Some stores are owned by the company, but others are franchised. All centralized processes, including website and online orders (eCommerce) as well as a customer call center (MOTO), are managed centrally by JFE. All stores follow the same processes, whether they are JFE-owned or franchises (this is a requirement of the JFE franchise agreement). JFE provides all equipment for the stores (including for Card Present payments). Each store has its own merchant ID for payment processing, but all merchant IDs are handled by JFE (otherwise we would likely have corporate serve as service providers those those franchises having merchant accounts). All banking is done with MajorBank, which also serves as the acquirer. As in all previous cases, PAYPRO is the one, only and official payment processor for all transactions in all channels.

Because of all of these business choices, the company cannot use a limited SAQ. Depending on total transaction volume, they will either produce a SAQ-D, or be audited by a QSA company and have a RoC produced (if they reach level 1, and maybe level 2 size depending on some MasterCard requirements). Whatever the reporting results, the requirements are exactly the same and only the reporting format changes (and in case of service provider compliance, a few additional requirements would apply).

Because of the complexity presented here, we'll look at JFE from a business process perspective before looking at its IT. Let's first look at the organization's chart.

4.5.1 JFE Organizational Structure

Our Jane holds the CEO (Chief Executive Officer) and President (of the board) roles for the company she founded. The C-suite is composed of the senior leadership (senior executives) and some more junior ones. For simplicity, I will use the define C-role names within this text instead of assigning hypothetical names.

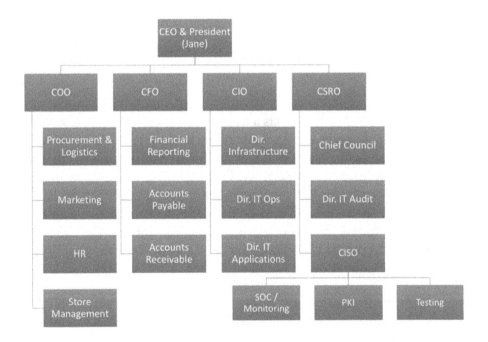

Volume 4 Figure 6 - JFE organization chart

Reporting to the CEO are the COO (Chief Operating Officer), in charge of all business operations from procurement and logistics to marketing, HR and store management, the CFO (Chief Financial Officer) in charge of all financial reporting, accounts payable and receivables, the CIO (Chief Information Officer) in charge of all IT functions, the CRCO (Chief Risk and Compliance Officer) in charge of the Enterprise Risk Program which covers business, financial and even IT risk.

At a junior level, we find the Chief Counsel in charge of legal, the CISO (Chief Information Security Officer) in charge of the IT compliance functions, both reporting to the CRCO. A director of Internal Audit also reports to the CRCO (but is not a junior C-level member).

IT has 3 junior members, the director of Infrastructure (covering networking and telephony, as well as virtualization systems), the director of IT Operations (covering system, application and database administration, as well as the helpdesk), and the director of IT applications (which covers both internal development and external applications).

4.5.2 Best-practice in information security governance - Information security separate from IT

As you may have noticed, information security is not a part of IT, nor does the CISO report to the CIO. The CISO has a dotted-line to the CIO (not shown in figure 6), meaning he has a reporting relationship to the CIO, as his work affects IT directly, but best practices require that some form of adversarial relationship exist between IT and Information Security. IT will most often favor availability (and integrity) over confidentiality, the latter being the main concern of PCI DSS. As the CISO's role goes above and beyond PCI DSS, it serves to have this individual reporting to risk instead of IT (in other organizations, the CISO could report to finance if no risk or compliance function exists; the important thing is having separation of duties).

This means that the information security policy is the responsibility of the CISO, but that other IT policies and procedures will fall under the purview of the CIO's organization. A committee that reviews the policies and procedures will be formed and chaired by the CISO, but include the IT directors. The submitted policies will be approved by the C-suite and/or the board, while IT procedures will be approved by the CIO.

The CISO has other responsibilities that are covered by members of his team rather than IT staff, due mainly to separation of duty issues. We often separate security controls between preventative (like access control), detective (like an IDS) and corrective. Basically, preventative controls are the responsibility of IT (with some requirements definition by the CISO), detective controls are mostly under the CISO, and correctives are shared amongst both group and other stakeholders.

So the CISO's organization has different teams in charge of defining information security policy and managing compliance (including involvement during projects), monitoring for security events (by the SOC, or Security Operations Center), managing the cryptographic infrastructure (the PKI, Public Key Crypto), and performing or coordinating testing (vulnerability scans, penetration testing, web application testing, social engineering, etc.).

4.5.3 Payment transactions

If we get back to payment transaction types, we can see that card present payments will be performed in stores (HQ can contain a store that is managed as any other), but that eCommerce and MOTO transactions are handled in a centralized fashion, though individual stores may be affected as they will receive orders to produce and deliver (but what better way to have a distributed delivery arm that reusing your stores' infrastructure!).

4.5.4 Card present payments in stores and at delivery

Each store is equipped with Point-of-Sales (POS, called an INTEGRATED PAYMENT TERMINAL in the PCI SSC Small Merchant Guidance) systems (one or more, but generally at least two for redundancy) that are provided by FooPOS (as with JFC) and communicate directly with PAYPRO for payment authorization. JFE looked for P2PE integrated payment devices which would have reduced store network scope, but since they found none that met their needs, they proceeded down the regular route. While the payment transactions flow directly to the payment processor, the POS sales function communicate with the centralized POS server at HQ that reflects transactions in JFE's ERP application.

The POS solution part of the ERP suite that JFE uses and that has been certified as a PA-DSS application (which helps simplify compliance). I've written about PA-DSS in section 3.7.6.3:

PCI PA-DSS software is software that has gone through an evaluation by a PA-QSA. A PA-QSA is a like a QSA for Software Applications used in a PCI DSS environment. The organization implementing a PA-DSS validated application must follow the implementation guide that comes with the application and place it in a PCI DSS compliant environment. All other 6.3.* and 6.5.* requirements (and *possibly 6.6) are taken care of by the PA-DSS certification, simplifying the organization's compliance efforts.*

Each store also has a phone system where they can take orders but where they are not allowed to accept card payments through this method.

If a customer wishes to make a card payment, the call is transferred to the centralized call center or the IVR payment solution. The IVR payment solution could be a normal phone system, but in this case JFE opted for a solution that is in-line with the rest of the telephony and that captures and recognizes phone dial tones, removes them from the voice stream and performs the payment processing by calling an API from PayPro.

See figure 4-7 for the network diagram which uses network segmentation and zoning to both reduce PCI DSS scope and increase security.

A customer can also pay during store pickup, or upon delivery as the delivery person is equipped with a portable cellular payment device. The portable payment device used for payment during delivery is not linked to any system, and the transaction information goes to a different merchant ID. A mobile application that allows better logistical coordination provides delivery information and where the payment transaction number is manually captured, as well as allowing to take a photo of the transaction receipt from the payment device (which must be kept 90 days per JFE retention policy) that will be stored in JFE's document imaging solution. The transaction receipt only shows the last 4 digits of the PAN [PCI DSS 3.3], thus it is not considered to contain CHD.

Delivery can be outsourced by individual stores, or in some cities, become a shared service, but in that case this service is still managed by the same department at HQ to ensure that company standards (including information security) are maintained.

4.5.5 Customer Service and MOTO transactions

Customer service falls under the COO's responsibilities under Store Management. Customer service representatives (CSR) mostly handle phone communications with customers using the company's toll-free number: 1-800-555-JANE. Their interactions include both taking orders (MOTO) as well as dealing with (in)satisfaction issues. CSRs also manage customer satisfaction via email, but email is not considered an approved channel for orders. As such, if an email contains order information (with or without payment information), an exception process is invoked with a standard message used in the reply to the customer explaining why this method (email) is not approved (not secure) and how to place an order securely, outlining approved methods. If the email contains card information, this information is eliminated (redacted) before the reply is sent and source emails are deleted immediately after response. All CSR emails are reviewed for quality control purposes and to ensure adherence to this standard. A DLP (Data Loss Prevention) tool also scans incoming and outgoing email messages for card numbers and other sensitive information to ensure sensitive information is not sent through these means. Because of the implementation of these processes and of this well-managed exception process, JFE is able to ensure that its email system remains out of scope for PCI DSS compliance.

Since customers can mention cardholder data during the call with CSRs, this brings the entire VoIP (Voice over IP) telephony system into scope for PCI DSS (analog systems would only require physical security controls, but who still uses analog these days). The VoIP environment consists of multiple networks that are isolated from each other. There are telephone handset networks, one per store and one per floor at HQ. CSRs have their own handset network. Then we have the server network which consists mainly of virtual machines on a separate hypervisor (I covered this in section 2.7.1.4), but also includes equipment that connect to the voice telecommunication providers (the trunk lines). Calls are recorded (for quality control purposes) on one of the servers and stored on the company SAN. Customer Service does not include a voicemail option (though individual users' internal numbers may include a voicemail option).

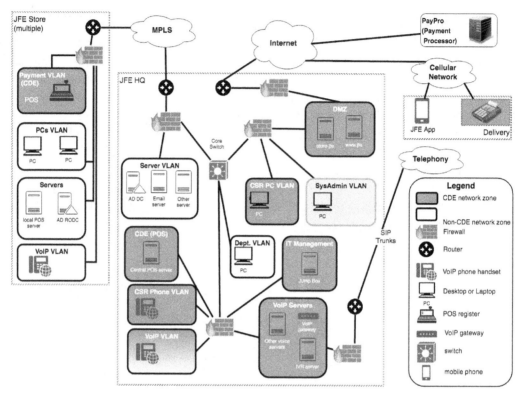

Volume 4 Figure 7 – JFE Network and Telephony Diagram

The order page of the CRM's version of the POS system has a separate tab for entering card information. When the CSR enters this tab, the call recording is automatically paused to prevent the recordings from becoming PCI DSS data. The company initially tried to have CSRs manually pause recordings, but opted for automation after compliance with this order was deemed too low. Since stored calls do not contain card information, these recordings do not fall under PCI DSS compliance for requirement 3.2.* and 3.4 (but the systems are still in-scope since they transmit this data).

4.5.6 eCommerce

eCommerce also falls under the COO's purview, but with IT sharing responsibilities. The website, including the payment portion, is developed by IT Applications (which includes the web development team), maintained by the IT Operations team, but managed by many of the COO's groups. Marketing worries about design and content, while procurement and logistics, and store management also have their roles. CSRs can also interact with the eCommerce system for issues with online orders.

Since JFE wanted a seamless user experience, they opted to use an API on the server side, communicating with PAYPRO, the payment processor. This means that the web server performing these action becomes a CDE system as it (receives first and then) transmits cardholder data. To simplify PCI DSS compliance, JFE has modified the website to have the eCommerce portion run on a different subdomain (store.jfe) than the regular website (www.jfe). Cardholder data is not stored (though caching could occur). Order information is entered in the ERP system using an API to this system but only transaction numbers returned by PAYPRO are stored (no CHD).

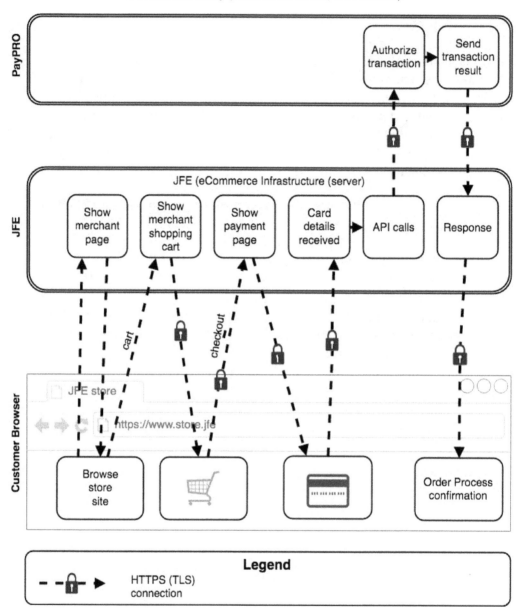

Volume 4 Figure 8 - JFE eCommerce dataflow diagram

4.5.7 The Information Security Program (based on ISO 27002)

The CISO's previous life experiences have taught him that while you can't anticipate everything about the future, planning does help. He likes the quote attributed to General and President Eisenhower that "Plans are useless, but planning is essential" [5].

Understanding that both new requirements will come and that new vectors of attacks will be identified, he fully understands that there is no such thing as 100% security, but that he must manage risk to what the company's risk appetite allows.

As such, he helped build the current Information Security Program based on an existing framework. Previous experience with ISO/IEC 27002 led him to structure it based on the 14 "domains", described in chapters 5 to 18 of the standard (and section 3.12 of volume 3 which he must have leveraged):

5.   Information Security Policies

6.   Organization of Information Security

7.   Human Resource Security

8.   Asset Management

9.   Access Control

10.   Cryptography

11.   Physical and environmental security

12.   Operation Security- procedures and responsibilities, Protection from malware, Backup, Logging and monitoring, Control of operational software, Technical vulnerability management and Information systems audit coordination

13.   Communication security - Network security management and Information transfer

14.   System acquisition, development and maintenance - Security requirements of information systems, Security in development and support processes and Test data

15. Supplier relationships - Information security in supplier relationships and Supplier service delivery management

16. Information security incident management - Management of information security incidents and improvements

17. Information security aspects of business continuity management - Information security continuity and Redundancies

18. Compliance - Compliance with legal and contractual requirements and Information security reviews

He could have gone for other frameworks such as COBIT or NIST that would have worked as well.

Since some requirements of regulations like PCI DSS do not necessarily work well under this framework, he's added a chapter for PCI DSS specific requirements, and he will add another for any other regulations.

Let's look at details of the program that the CISO will have to create, including where responsibilities lie.

<start JFE information security policy structure>

Chapter 5 - Information Security Policies

As mentioned earlier, information security policies are the responsibility of the CISO.

This section only has one subsection: ISO 5.1 Management direction for information security.

As described in volume 3, this chapter covers requirement 12.1 (with 12.1.1 requiring at least annual revisions), as well as policies that were distributed to other requirements when PCI DSS 3.0 came out: 1.5, 2.5, 3.7, 4.3, 5.4, 6.7, 7.3, 8.8, 9.10, 10.8, 11.6. These PCI DSS requirements mention that we must "ensure that security policies and operational procedures are documented, in use, and known to all affected parties for":

- o *2.5: "managing vendor defaults and other security parameters" - falls between ISO 9 (Access Control) for user accounts and 14 (System acquisition, development and maintenance) for most others*
- o *3.7: "protecting stored cardholder data" - falls between ISO 8 (Asset Management), 9 (Access Control), and 10 (Cryptography)*
- o *4.3: "encrypting transmissions of cardholder data" - falls under ISO 10 (Cryptography)*
- o *5.4: "protecting systems against malware" - falls under ISO 12 (Operations security) under section 12.2 (Protection from malware)*
- o *6.7: "developing and maintaining secure systems and applications" - falls between ISO 12 (Operations security), and 14 (System acquisition, development and maintenance)*
- o *7.3: "restricting access to cardholder data" - falls under ISO 9 (Access Control)*
- o *8.8: "identification and authentication" - falls between ISO 6 (Organization of information) for remote access, 7 (Human resource security) for terminations*
- o *and 9 (Access Control) for most elements*
- o *9.10: "restricting physical access to cardholder data" - falls under ISO 11 (Physical and environmental security)*
- o *10.8: "monitoring all access to network resources and cardholder data" - falls under ISO 12 (Operations security) mostly under section 12.4 (Logging and monitoring)*
- o *11.6: "security monitoring and testing" - falls under ISO 12 (Operations security) mostly under section 12.6 (Technical vulnerability management)*

Thus the information security policy will include assignments of responsibilities for:

- o *human resource security (chapter 7) (responsible party: HR)*
- o *asset management (chapter 8) including data classification [PCI DSS 3.1] and media controls [PCI DSS 9.5.* to 9.8.*] as well as Acceptable Use [PCI DSS 12.3.*] (responsible parties: CISO, legal) and maintaining inventories [PCI DSS 2.4, 11.1] (responsible parties: IT Infrastructure, IT Operations)*
- o *access control (chapter 9) which includes defining roles and assigning users to roles (responsible party: COO), and restricting access*

through Role-Based Access Control systems (RBAC) (responsible parties: IT Operations, IT Applications)

o *cryptography (chapter 10) including all encryption key management used for data-at-rest [PCI DSS 3.4 to 3.6.*] and data-in-motion [PCI DSS 4.1] (responsible party: CISO)*

o *physical and environmental security (chapter 11) including access to sensitive areas*

o *where sensitive information or equipment is located [PCI DSS 9.1.*, 9.3], visitor access [PCI DSS 9.2, 9.4] (responsible party: CISO) and protecting devices from tampering [PCI DSS 9.9.*] (responsible parties: CISO, Store Management)*

o *operations security (chapter 12, the largest in ISO) including operational procedures stemming from these policies and change control (responsible party: CIO), malware protection [PCI DSS 5.*] and backups (responsible party: IT Operations),*

o *logging and monitoring (responsible parties: CISO/SOC, CIO), vulnerability management (responsible parties: CISO, CIO), IT auditing (responsible parties: CISO/Internal Audit)*

o *communications security (chapter 13) including appropriately managing firewalls [PCI DSS 1.5] (responsible parties: IT Infrastructure, IT Operations) and information transfers*

o *system acquisition, development and maintenance (chapter 14) including application security [PCI DSS 6.5.*, 6.6, part of 4.1] (responsible parties: CISO, IT Applications), SDLC and QA [PCI DSS 6.4.*] (responsible party: IT Applications)*

o *supplier relationships (chapter 15) including PCI DSS service provider compliance (responsible parties: CISO, procurement)*

o *information security incident management (chapter 16) [PCI DSS 12.10.*] (responsible parties: CISO, legal, CIO)*

o *information security aspects of business continuity management (chapter 17) [not covered by PCI DSS] (responsible parties: CIO, COO, CISO)*

o *compliance (chapter 18) including PCI DSS compliance [PCI DSS A2.1.*, not mandatory for JFE but good practice nonetheless] (responsible parties: CISO, legal, CIO)*

o *PCI DSS specific requirements including scope management and documentation [PCI DSS 1.1.2, 1.1.3, A3.2.*], specific cardholder data storage requirements [PCI DSS 3.2.*, 3.3, 8.7] covered by the data classification.*

Chapter 6 - Organization of Information Security

This chapter covers what we just described in section 4.5.1 and 4.5.2 as roles between the CISO and CIO's organization, and includes 2 sections. First, the internal assignment of "information security responsibilities" (ISO 6.1) which maps to well PCI DSS requirements 12.4 and 12.5.*. These responsibilities must ensure separation of duties (ISO 6.1.2) which were properly done in this case.

For the specific PCI DSS requirements, here are the role assignments:

- o *12.5.1 Establish, document, and distribute security policies and procedures. - CISO*
- o *12.5.2 Monitor and analyze security alerts and information, and distribute to appropriate personnel. - CISO / SOC team*
- o *12.5.3 Establish, document, and distribute security incident response and escalation procedures to ensure timely and effective handling of all situations. - CISO*
- o *12.5.4 Administer user accounts, including additions, deletions, and modifications. - CIO / IT Operations (helpdesk team)*
- o *12.5.5 Monitor and control all access to data. - CISO / SOC team*

Note: I have heard of assessors requiring assignment of these to individuals; I think this is a bad idea because people will change and it is easier to change a role assignee list than a policy or procedure. Ultimately an individual must be in charge, but the responsibility should be assigned to a role or position filled by an individual.

Requirement 12.4 calls to "ensure that the security policy and procedures clearly define information security responsibilities for all personnel". All personnel are expected to follow policies and procedures (and must sign a document to "acknowledge at least annually that they have read and understood the security policy and procedures" [PCI DSS 12.6.2] as part of the Security Awareness training [PCI DSS 12.6.*]. This includes the famous idea that "if you see something, say something" and encourage all users to report deviations and other issues via the proper channels (helpdesk, whistle-blower hotline, etc.)

This domain also includes "ISO 6.2 mobile devices and teleworking" which covers PCI DSS requirements 1.4 (Personal Firewall for Mobile Devices), 8.3.* (Multifactor for remote access and administration), and 4.1.1 (Secure Wireless Configuration), this last one requiring use of "industry best practices to *implement strong encryption for authentication and transmission" of "wireless networks", generally meaning WPA2 enterprise with Active Directory linked accounts.*

Chapter 7 - Human resource security

HR security means ensuring that staff (permanent and temporary employees, contractors, etc.) act in the best interest of the company. It involves evaluating them and conducting background checks [PCI DSS 12.7] during the hiring process, training them during employment (including security awareness [PCI DSS 12.6.] and policies), and ensuring that when they leave the organization, their physical [PCI DSS 9.3] and logical [PCI DSS 8.1.3] accesses are immediately removed, more so if terminated with cause (most employees will not be disgruntled, but how could you determine which will?). For contractual employees, this may be outsourced to another firm which would run equivalent checks.*

Chapter 8 - Asset management

Lack of adequate asset management is such a big problem in organizations that the CIS (Center for Internet Security) CSC (Critical Security Controls) include it as the first two controls on their list:

CSC 1 - Inventory of Authorized and Unauthorized Devices CSC 2 - Inventory of Authorized and Unauthorized Software [6]

The CIS defines the CSC as "a recommended set of actions for cyber defense that provide specific and actionable ways to stop today's most pervasive and dangerous attacks"; basically, some of the key controls we can put in place to protect our organizations.

Responsibility for IT assets falls to the CIO's organization. These include what PCI DSS calls "system components" which they define to "include network devices, servers, computing devices, and applications". An inventory of all "system components" must be maintained and be accurate and cover all IT assets including wireless access points [PCI DSS 2.4, 11.1.1].

Data classification guidance is the responsibility of the CISO and legal, while data retention periods are the responsibility of the CISO, legal, and the various business units who own each type of data [PCI DSS 3.1]. Data classification also applies to applications (and by extension to systems) and applications should have business and IT owners(sometime called "IT custodian") - one of each, again assigned to roles/departments.

Backups of IT systems (configurations, applications, and user data) are the responsibility of IT Operations, which must ensure that data is encrypted when required by the data classification guidelines.

Secure handling of electronic data is the responsibility of IT Operations, while paper documents security is the responsibility of the COO.

Chapter 9 - Access control

Access control is always a key control, and we often find too broad permissions, as well as those which have yet to be removed for users. CSC issues here are lower on the list (but still important): CSC 14 (Controlled Access Based on the Need to Know) and CSC 16 (Account Monitoring and Control).

ISO 9.1 (Business requirements of access control) clearly identifies that the business units, not IT, are the driving force to defining user roles [PCI DSS 7.1.*] and what permissions are assigned to that role (never to an individual - in the worst case you should create a role for one user only). IT and the CISO may assist in role definitions, and the CISO will validate these roles and permissions.

ISO 9.2 (User access management) in medium to large organizations require the use of Role-Based Access Control systems (RBAC) [PCI DSS 7.2.*] such as Microsoft Active Directory or LDAP, managed by IT Operations (Active Directory in our case). No shared accounts are to ever be used because this would reduce traceability of actions; if a technical restriction forces the use of a shared account, then a process to ensure traceability must be put in place and approved by the CISO (examples of such a process includes sudo-to-root, and password vaults).

ISO 9.3 (User responsibilities) includes ensuring that users understand their responsibilities regarding selecting and safeguarding credentials (including passwords) [PCI DSS 7.3, 8.2.3].

ISO 9.4 (System and application access control) is again implemented using the RBAC system (Active Directory here) by placing individuals in appropriate groups, and by having systems configured to use said groups.

Unless a technical restriction exists, all JFE systems and applications must manage permissions through roles implemented as groups within Active Directory. If a restriction exists, an equivalent mechanism must be put in place. Support of the default RBAC mechanism will always be considered a major factor in the selection decision for new systems and applications.

Any remote access connection to a system, whether internal or external, should be encrypted whenever possible, but this is mandatory for any kind of remote administrative access such as SSH, HTTPS web-based, Remote Desktop Protocol (RDP) or similar [PCI DSS 2.3].

Chapter 10 - Cryptography

Cryptography is referenced within the data classification where we determine when encryption is mandatory for data-at-rest [PCI DSS 3.4 to 3.6.] and data-in-motion [PCI DSS 4.1] (even if not required, we could still encrypt), and also covers all encryption key management functions, and administration of any key management system such as HSM (Hardware Security Modules). Cryptography falls under the PKI unit of the CISO.*

Chapter 11 - Physical and environmental security

Protecting physical access to systems is paramount as any system an attacker can reach will likely be breached. These tasks fall mostly on the CISO who owns physical security, but outsources most work to building security including in the Disaster Recovery site. Thus access to secure (sensitive) areas where sensitive information (ISO 11.1, like call centers) or equipment (ISO 11.2, like data centers, data closets) are located [PCI DSS 9.1., 9.3] needs to be restricted to minimal personnel. Visitor access [PCI DSS 9.2, 9.4] should never allow an unaccompanied visitor in a sensitive area, and be able to distinguish a visitor from a regular user.*

Store security requires most of the same controls, but must also include protecting devices from tampering [PCI DSS 9.9.] by periodically reviewing for tampering (such as looking for card skimmers). Guidance will be provided by Storage Management.*

Telecommunication equipment must be physically secured and only accessible with personnel that require such access.

Chapter 12 - Operations security

The largest of the ISO domains has 7 subsections. Preventative controls managed by <u>all of IT</u> include:

- o *ISO 12.1 (Operational procedures and responsibilities) covers the procedures that implement the requirements from the policies*
- o *ISO 12.5 (Control of operational software) including the change control process [PCI DSS 6.4.*]*

IT Operations are in charge of ISO 12.2 (Protection from malware) [PCI DSS 5.] and ISO 12.3 (Backup).*

Detective controls are under the responsibility of the CISO, but may require the CIO team's involvement. They include ISO 12.4 (Logging and monitoring) and ISO 12.6 (Technical vulnerability management). IT audit support (ISO 12.7, Information systems audit considerations) is primarily an IT audit responsibility (under Internal Audit), but may require IT support and CISO involvement.

Chapter 13 - Communications security

Communications, or network security, is ensuring that network access has been limited in order to reduce the risk of unauthorized access. It thus covers network architecture, segmentation and zoning of different systems based on various criteria. Those criteria may include the different classes of data (for example, cardholder data vs. public information) handled or stored by the systems, as well system levels of criticality or controls (for example, externally facing website vs. internal HR application). Those zones or segments are then only allowed to talk to each other over well-defined, monitored and limited access points (generally, specific TCP or UDP ports) through some form of network control device such as a firewall. Communication security thus also covers managing network devices such as firewall, routers, switches, IDS/IPS, but also covers basic virtualization infrastructure so common nowadays. All those functions are the responsibility of IT Infrastructure and IT Operations at JFE. At JFE, all system management is performed by authorized personnel using jump boxes (accessed using multi factor authentication) located in an IT management zone.

Chapter 14 - System acquisition, development and maintenance

More and more vulnerabilities happen at the application level and are not protected by network controls. While only #18 on the CSC top 20 (Application Software Security), these vulnerabilities are often less reviewed than the operating system or middleware layers. Growth of organizations as OWASP (Open Web Application Security Project [7]) demonstrate the importance this chapter represents.

The CISO is responsible for defining basic application requirements from architecture to processes, whether for internally developed or externally acquired applications. This includes having all externally facing web applications placed behind the standard corporate web application proxy filtering solution. Gates exist at all phases of development to ensure that security is included throughout the process (they use a waterfall methodology, but this could be applied in an agile environment as well).

IT Applications is mostly responsible for ensuring that security is included at every step of the SDLC process, including all testing.

Chapter 15 - Supplier relationships

Suppliers have to undergo the equivalent of what we ask from employees in HR security. "Trust, but verify" is our motto. All third parties must undergo a financial solvability check.

All third parties must be evaluated using the rapid-risk assessment third party tool in use to determine if:

- o *If any sensitive information is shared with the third-party (including CHD)*
- o *If the third party can affect the security of sensitive data (for example, if it accesses critical JFE IT resources)*

Any third-party matching any of the previous criteria will undergo a more formal evaluation by the CISO and may have to meet certain requirements, including validation of compliance with certain regulations (such as PCI DSS).

Procurement will maintain a list of all third-parties JFE has relationships with, alongside with a description of their products or services used, and specific requirements (such as PCI DSS compliance).

CISO or IT Audit, as part of the validation of PCI DSS compliance (12.8.4), will review this list annually against a list of payees maintained by Accounts Payable.

Chapter 16 - Information security incident management

Some events may affect regular business operations, and having a plan can help lessen the impact these occurrences on the business. While we can never account for all potential eventualities, the general approach will still apply and will at least assist help lessen their potential impact.

The CISO, working with legal on any regulatory requirements, and with the CIO and the business, will develop an incident response framework following best practices. The framework will be leveraged in the development of specific plans for likely scenarios such as:

- o *Natural disasters such as fire or flooding*
- o *Break-in or theft*
- o *Network, system, application or other IT compromise, including software issues such as malware (virus) and physical device attached to the network*
- o *Hardware failure*

Chapter 17 - Information security aspects of business continuity management

The CISO, working with legal on any contractual requirements, and with the CIO and the business, will define the criticality of each application, and develop alternatives for continuity and recovery that meet the business objectives at a cost that the business feels is acceptable. The BC/DR (Business Continuity/Disaster Recovery) plan will be linked to the incident response framework as incidents will likely be the cause of the invocation of BC/DR. All BC/DR sites will have to meet the same levels of security and ensure no degradation of confidentiality, integrity or availability.

Chapter 18 - Compliance

Legal will assist the CISO in the identification of legal and contractual requirements, as well as with maintaining an inventory of such requirements.

Information security compliance will be the responsibility of the CISO, who will coordinate with Internal Audit to minimize impact to the business, while maximizing the value of the reviews performed. These reviews will include ensuring that information security policies are properly followed and that controls are operating as expected as part of business-as-usual processes (BAU).

Chapter PCI - Specific PCI DSS requirements

PCI DSS has specific requirements that do not align well within the ISO framework.

The CISO is responsible of ensuring that PCI DSS scope is managed and that documentation [PCI DSS 1.1.2, 1.1.3, A3.2.*] is updated as changes to the environment (people, process and technology) are implemented [PCI DSS 6.4.6].

CISO is also responsible to ensure that any cardholder data is only stored when absolutely necessary and according to specific cardholder data storage requirements [PCI DSS 3.2.*, 3.3, 8.7] covered in the data classification.

<end JFE information security policy structure>

4.5.8 JFE's Risk Assessment

The CISO has settled on our recommendations of volume 3 for performing risk assessments using NIST SP 800-30 as the basic risk assessment framework and Threat Modeling (STRIDE) for identifying threats (or vulnerabilities).

4.5.8.1 Step 1 (PREPARE / Establish a risk context)

Step 1 requires us to basically define scope of the environment to risk assess. JFE leverages the scope information it has created including the network diagrams required by PCI DSS (requirement 1.1.2) shown in figure 4-7, and the data flow diagrams (requirement 1.1.3) shown in figure 4-8. JFE also has the descriptions presented in this chapter as business process descriptions. Every time they perform the risk assessment (at least annually), JFE will ensure that the diagrams and description are still valid and up to date. Note that while we'd only need to perform the Risk Assessment on the PCI DSS scope, JFE decides to perform it against all its IT infrastructure.

4.5.8.2 Step 2 (CONDUCT / Assess Risk)

Step 2 allow us to uncover the different threats so they can be addressed. We'll start by going through the STRIDE Threat Modeling approach described in Adam Shostack's book to identify vulnerabilities. As STRIDE is an acronym, let's go through each of the letters in contains and perform the vulnerability identification sub-step to "simply enumerate all the things that might go wrong". [8]

Spoofing is "Pretending to be something or someone other than yourself". Spoofing can be performed on a:

- o Person or role: phishing is one type of risk we can identify here, against regular users [#1], IT administrators [#2] and Call Center personnel [#3] (well- defined policies can help mitigate risks)
- o File: creating a fake copy of a critical file somewhere in the application path (application, configuration, data), for example through malware or another targeted attack [#4] (often mixed with tampering)
- o Network (a machine): externally (for example, hijacking DNS queries [#5]) or internally (for example using ARP poisoning [#6])

Tampering means "modifying something on disk, on a network, or in memory". Tampering can be done to:

- o Files: locally on disk (possibly in conjunction with a spoofing/file) [#7], or even through JavaScript manipulation on a browser [#8]
- o Memory: for example through rootkits or other malware [#9] which don't always require major disk modifications (or hidden ones in cases of rootkits)
- o Network: requires further access than spoofing/networks to perform a Man-in-the-middle (MITM) attack [#10] (ARP poisoning is partly one of these as well, but we're not duplicating entries in the final list)

Repudiation is "claiming that you didn't do something, or were not responsible". Repudiation is associated with evidence of actions (generally logs). This can occur when:

- o You have no logs (thus you can't prove anything): or those logs are insufficient or not traceable to individual end-users [#11]
- o Logs come under attack: garbage is sent to the logs in an attempt to crash/overrun them [#12], or are tampered with (e.g. deleted) when they are not adequately protected [#13]
- o Logs as a channel for attack: using the log system to send links to IT administrators for spear phishing [#14]

Information Disclosure is "providing information to someone not authorized to see it". This can occur through:

- o Network monitoring
- o Directory or filename (for example layoff-letters/adamshostack.docx)
- o File contents
- o API information disclosure

Our threats here include: Insecure web server configurations allowing information leakage [#15], error messages with technical information available to all users [#16], unencrypted communications allowing eavesdropping [#17], improper access controls against critical resources such as cryptographic keys [#18].

Denial of Service (DoS) is "absorbing resources needed to provide service" so they run out. It can be done against:

- o a process
- o a data store
- o a data flow

The biggest network threats are Distributed DoS (DDOS) against external (internet) facing systems (#19), but lack of Quality of Service (QoS) on the internal network [#20] can also cause disruptions. System (process/data store) availability threats are poor dimensioning of systems that become over capacity and unresponsive [#21].

Elevation of Privilege is "allowing someone to do something they're not authorized to do". It can occur due to:

o   Data/code confusion
o   Control flow/ memory corruption attacks
o   Command injection attacks: Improper validation in web apps [#22]

Most other issues will be with either user access control process failure in assignment of permissions (ACLs, such as everyone is admin) (to new hires, change in roles, or terminations) [#23] or through improper role definition (including issues with Separation of Duties, SoD) [#24], or insecure validation of permissions within internally developed applications [#25].

Note that this list is not necessarily exhaustive, but it should give you an idea of how to proceed.

Evaluate Risk and Determine Action Plans

All these risks should be evaluated (risk ranked), but I'll leave this portion of the exercise to the reader.

4.5.8.3 Step 3 (COMMUNICATE / Respond to Risk)

Responding means determining what how to address each risk to either accept it as is, mitigate, eliminate, or transfer it.

We now have 24 different threats that we need to address (some may already be addressed by PCI DSS or other controls, and they are identified below). The recommended additional controls will be presented as options to senior management so that budgets be allocated for their implementation and maintenance, if the business chooses to do so.

#	Threat	Controls Already In Place	Additional Controls recommended
1	Phishing against regular users	Regular users do not have administrative privileges on their workstations	Phishing training, and ongoing phishing testing campaign
2	Phishing against IT administrators	MFA to admin systems (8.3.1)	
3	Phishing against Call Center personnel	Specific procedures to follow & QA	
4	Creating a fake copy of a critical file somewhere in the application	FIM (11.5), Antimalware (5.*)	Application Whitelisting on externally facing and critical servers
5	(Spoofing) Hijacking DNS queries	None	Encrypted DNS internally, OpenDNS externally
6	(Spoofing) ARP poisoning	Network Access Control (NAC)	None needed
7	Tampering with local files on disk	FIM (11.5), Antimalware (5.*)	Real-time monitoring of FIM using SIEM matching to know attacked signatures (updated in near real-time)
8	Tampering JavaScript manipulation on a browser	Workstation hardening including browsers (2.2.*)	Sandboxing of internet browsing using VMs
9	Tampering of memory via rootkits or other malware	FIM (11.5), Antimalware (5.*)	Execute rootkit detection on externally facing servers quarterly

#	Threat	Controls Already In Place	Additional Controls recommended
10	Man-in-the-middle (MITM) attack (Tampering/network)	Use of encryption (https) for all external servers; IDS/IPS flagging and inspecting insecure communications (11.4)	None needed now.
11	Logs are insufficient or not traceable to individual end-users	Periodic testing (sampling) of log generation (e.g. failed login) to SIEM	None needed now.
12	Garbage is sent to the logs in an attempt to crash/overrun them	FIM on centralized log system (?); SIEM provides functionality to detect overruns and alert key staff	None needed
13	(Tampered logs) not adequately protected	Centralized logging (10.5.*), Penetration testing (11.3.*)	None needed
14	Using the log system to send links to IT administrators for spear phishing	See phishing for IT admins, systems are Linux based and not susceptible to directly executed programs	None needed
15	Insecure web server configurations allowing information leakage	Server hardening (2.2.*), Penetration testing (11.3.*)	None needed
16	Error messages with technical information available to all users	SDLC (6.3.*), Secure Coding Guidelines (6.5), Server hardening (2.2.*) includinges debug controls	None needed
17	Unencrypted communications allowing for eavesdropping	Server hardening (2.2.*) includes disabling unencrypted protocols, websites automatically redirect	None needed

#	Threat	Controls Already In Place	Additional Controls recommended
		to HTTPS; IDS/IPS flagging and inspecting insecure communications (11.4)	
18	Improper access controls against critical resources such as cryptographic keys	IT conducts quarterly reviews of access controls of key resources (crypto keys, config files on external servers,etc.)	IA to review process annually
19	(DDOS) against external (internet) facing systems	None	Contract with a DDOS protection provider
20	Internal network Quality of Service (QoS) missing	Network architecture design requirements address QoS using VRFs network segmentation	None needed
21	Poor dimensioning of systems that become over capacity and unresponsive	Monitoring of resources by operations (NOC, SOC)	Annual review of performance (peaks) and growth to ensure capacity planning
22	Improper validation in web apps	SDLC (6.3.*) including code reviews, Secure Coding Guidelines (6.5), Secure Web Application Coding (6.5.*)	None needed
23	User access control process failure in assignment of permissions (ACLs, such as everyone is admin) (to new hires, change in roles, or terminations)	Quarterly Access Control review by all managers	IA to review Access Control process annually

#	Threat	Controls Already In Place	Additional Controls recommended
24	Improper role definition (including issues with Separation of Duties)	Defining user roles (7.1.*), RBAC (7.2.*)	IA to annually review all roles above regular users (those with some form of administrative responsibility)
25	Insecure validation of permissions within internally developed applications	SDLC (6.3.*) including code reviews, Secure Coding Guidelines (6.5), Secure Web Application Coding (6.5.*)	None needed

4.5.8.4 Step 4 (MAINTAIN / Monitor Risk over time)

JFE must perform this exercise annually to identify new threats, evaluate whether changes in controls are required (for any changes in the threat landscape), and verify we should review that the controls that were put in place (both for outside of PCI DSS scope) are working as expected.

End Notes - Volume 4

[1] PCI Security Standards Council (2016). PAYMENT PROTECTION RESOURCES FOR SMALL MERCHANTS. Guide to Safe Payments. Version 1.0 | July 2016. Retrieved July 12, 2017, from https://www.pcisecuritystandards.org/pdfs/Small_Merchant_Guide_to_Safe_Payments.pdf.

[2] PCI Guru (2016). level 3 versus level 4 merchants. Retrieved July 12, 2017, from https://pciguru.wordpress.com/2016/09/09/level-3-versus-level-4-merchants/.

[3] VISA (2015). Small Merchant Security Program Requirements – UPDATE. Retrieved July 12, 2017, from https://usa.visa.com/dam/VCOM/download/merchants/bulletin-small-merchant-security-faq.pdf.

[4] PCI Security Standards Council (2016, p.iii). PCI DSS v3.2 SAQ C, Rev. 1.1. Retrieved July 12, 2017, from https://www.pcisecuritystandards.org/documents/PCI-DSS-v3_2-SAQ-C-rev1_1.pdf.

[5] Wikiquote. Dwight D. Eisenhower. Retrieved July 12, 2017, from https://en.wikiquote.org/wiki/Dwight_D._Eisenhower.

[6] Center for Internet Security (2017). CIS Controls. Retrieved July 12, 2017, from https://www.cisecurity.org/controls/.

[7] Open Web Application Security Project (2006). Retrieved July 12, 2017, from https://www.owasp.org/.

[8] Shostack, Adam (2014). Threat Modeling: Designing for Security. Wiley.

Appendix 1

PCI Resources - PCI DSS Scoping Model and Approach

Source: *http://www.pciresources.com/pci-dss-scoping-model-and-approach/*

The approach and model described here are excerpted from Volume 2 (PCI DSS Scoping) of the PCI Resources book series covering the PCI DSS. Details of the analysis that led to this model, and of other relevant scoping details, can be found in that volume (mostly section 2.5). While PCI DSS Scope covers the people, processes and technologies (PPT), this model will detail mostly the technology portion, the IT system components. People and processes involved should also be covered by organizations.

This model and approach is available under a creative commons licence: Attribution-ShareAlike CC BY-SA (see details on the last page). The volumes in the book series are the intellectual property of their owners and not distributed under this licence. This model approach is the result of Yves Desharnais' thinking and experience with PCI DSS since 2012 (version 2.0). This model is not endorsed or approved by the PCI SSC or anyone else.

It is my hope that opening this model will help everyone agree on what should be in scope, or at least have a reasonable basis for classification and discussion. I believe that this model could also be applied to other data requiring protection, for example, patient health information (PHI) or personally identifiable information (PII). The December 2017 update to version 1.2 of this model is to align with the December 2016 PCI DSS Information Supplement from the PCI SSC and called "Guidance for PCI DSS Scoping and Network Segmentation" (this supplement will be referred to as the "December 2016 Guidance". No changes were made, only clarifications added.

Acronyms

In this model and approach, you'll see me use many acronyms, which I define here:

- CHD = Acronym for "Cardholder Data"; consists of the PAN, cardholder name, card expiration date, and sometimes service code
- PAN = Acronym for "Primary Account Number"; the card number printed on the front of the card.
- SAD = Acronym for "Sensitive Authentication Data", it includes the magnetic track information, the PIN or PIN block, as well as the Card-not-present authorization value which we'll refer to as CVV2 but can take any of the following acronyms: CAV2/CVC2/CVV2/CID.
- SPT = An acronym for "Store, Process, or Transmit", meaning that a system or process comes into contact with CHD and/or SAD and is therefore automatically in scope.
- CDE = Acronym for "Cardholder Data Environment", basically what we are trying to protect, which starts with the systems that SPT CHD or SAD but is not limited to these.
- Isolation = There is no possible access between systems.
- Controlled Access = There are limited (restricted) communications possible between systems.
- RoC = Report on Compliance
- Entity = An entity is any organization that has the responsibility to protect card data; for PCI DSS compliance, an entity will be defined as either a merchant or a service provider.
- DESV = PCI DSS Designated Entities Supplemental Validation for PCI DSS 3.1, a new PCI standard released in June 2015 which is now integrated as appendix A3 of PCI DSS 3.2

Figure 1 - Rendering of Credit Card (Front and Back) showing CHD and SAD

Scoping categories

My approach to scoping, as other approaches do, is used to categorize systems. I initially defined three (3) basic categories that are derived directly from the language of the PCI DSS standard: CDE, connected and out-of-scope. One issue I have with both the PCI SSC Guidance on scoping regards whether segmentation devices (or combinations thereof) constitute CDE systems (my initial contention) or connected systems (PCI SSC, and OPST); I have thus decided to treat segmenting devices as their own category, which I will explain in the revised model. This has no effect on scope, simply on clarity. I'll describe these one-by-one, starting from the inner core that we are trying to protect: the area where we have CHD and/or SAD, the CDE.

First Category: CDE systems

All CDE systems are often called category 1 or type 1 devices. There are 2 different sub-categories in the CDE, but all applicable requirements will apply to all CDE sub-types equally. FAQ #1252 responds to the question "*Do all PCI DSS requirements apply to every system component?* " starting with: "*PCI DSS requirements apply to all system components, unless it is has been verified that a particular requirement is not applicable for a particular system*". We'll refer to this FAQ in volume 3 when discussing how to address all each of the requirements. Generally CDE systems are represented in *red*.

CDE/CHD

The Scope of PCI is presented on page 10 of version 3.2 of the standard. The first paragraph states:

> *The PCI DSS security requirements apply to all system components included in or connected to the cardholder data environment. The cardholder data environment (CDE) is comprised of people, processes and technologies that store, process, or transmit cardholder data or sensitive authentication data. "System components" include network devices, servers, computing devices, and applications.*

Let's break this paragraph into its important aspects.

- "*apply to all **system components***" - adding that they "*include network devices, servers, computing devices, and applications.* " - so basically, any type of computer system (hardware, operating system, software, applications) is subject to the requirements.

- "*(CDE) is comprised of people, processes and technologies*" - so, while PCI DSS applies to computer systems, people and processes are also critical (and I recommend, as many others do, taking a business process approach first).
- "*that store, process, or transmit cardholder data or sensitive authentication data*" - what will often refer to as SPT CHD/SAD to summarize. The systems that come into contact with CHD or SAD are the main ones we are trying to protect since they hold, or have access to, the information (the goods) that we are required to protect.

All these systems that SPT CHD/SAD are part, or form the basis, of your CDE (Cardholder Data Environment - the environment in scope for PCI). We'll refer to these as CDE/CHD systems. The December 2016 Guidance refers to these as "[s]ystem component stores, processes, or transmits CHD/SAD". The OPST calls these type "1a".

CDE/Contaminated

In the network segmentation section, the standard states that "*[n]etwork segmentation of, or isolating (segmenting), the cardholder data environment from the remainder of an entity's network is not a PCI DSS requirement*". Therefore, network segmentation is not required other than at the external perimeter of the network. The standard also adds: "[w]ithout adequate network segmentation (sometimes called a "flat network") the entire network is in scope of the PCI DSS assessment". If you do not use segmentation, everything is subject to PCI DSS requirements. Basically, your CDE expands to all systems that are in the same network as your in-scope CDE/CHD systems described above until some segmentation prevents it.

We shall call these systems in the same network zones as CDE/contaminated since there could easily be a transfer of information between systems that are not otherwise restricted (generally by a firewall or other device). The December 2016 Guidance calls these systems *"System component is on the same network segment (for example, in the same subnet or VLAN) as system(s) that store, process or transmit cardholder data"*.

Second category: Segmenting (previously called CDE/Segmenting)

The second major category are systems that provide the (generally network) segmentation and prevent "contamination" of CDE systems. Typically, these are firewall devices, but they are not limited to those. These devices are called Segmenting systems. The scope definition includes an instruction to that effect (present in previous PCI DSS versions): "If network segmentation is in place and being used to reduce the scope of the PCI DSS assessment, the assessor must verify that the segmentation is adequate to reduce the scope of the assessment."

Note that this function may be accomplished by a combination of devices and systems, but the more complex this gets, the better the documentation your assessor will require.

In the OPST, these would be either "1b": or "2a", thus leading to potential confusion. Without segmenting systems, we cannot have connected systems. Thus, what the PCI SSC December 2016 Guidance calls "System component segments CDE systems from out-of-scope systems and networks", but puts in the connected systems category ("Connected-to or Security-impacting Systems") I will mark at its separate category to prevent any confusion (it is my only disagreement with the PCI SSC document, but this difference is more stylistic than anything else).

This second category is furthermore warranted by the inclusion of a new requirement since PCI DSS 3.0 regarding the testing of segmentation during the required annual internal penetration tests (#11.3.4). Section 3.3 (Network Segmentation) of the PCI DSS 3.2 RoC template adds documentation of this validation of adequate segmentation was performed. Note that the firewall rules that are unrelated to the CDE environment would be out-of-scope. This could happen if the firewall manages the connection point between the CDE and various other network segments. In that case, only the rules that pertain to access to the CDE are in-scope (for review), although it would be a good idea to treat all of them in the same way.

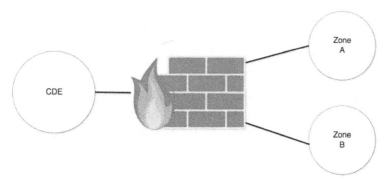

Figure 2 - Image of firewall and 3 network zones (including the CDE)

For example in the diagram above, the rules that limit zone A to zone B connections would be out-of-scope.

Ultimately, unless using a straightforward segmentation device such as a physical firewall, entities you should provide an evaluation that covers requirement 11.3.4 demanding network segmentation penetration testing.

Segmenting systems are generally represented in orange.

Segmentation in virtualization and cloud computing

The "PCI DSS Cloud Computing Guidelines" supplement covers segmentation in sections 4.4 through 4.4.3. It clearly states: "Segmentation on a cloud-computing infrastructure must provide an equivalent level of isolation as that achievable through physical network separation." Although cloud computing is mentioned, this is also the litmus test for any virtual environment. So an organization must "ensure that their environment is adequately isolated from the other client environments. In terms of clouds or hosting providers, that assurance is made by the provider, whereas in internal environments this would be validated by the organization. Ultimately however, responsibility that validation has been performed (by someone) rests on the organization.

In section 4.4.1, the recommendation is made to use a "dedicated CDE hypervisor" to simplify the issue of segmentation (which is made more complex in cloud environments than in private hosting). Dedicating the hypervisor to the CDE systems (no mixed-mode) is also what many QSAs I've spoken to use as minimal guidelines.

For more detail see section 2.7 of Volume 2.

Third category: Connected systems

So when does a CDE system contaminate another? Some cases are easier to understand than others. For example, if two systems are in the same network segment and can communicate more or less freely (depending on opened services) then it is clear that contamination can occur (note that the possibility is sufficient to warrant inclusion). But what is required for a "connected" system not to become contaminated? Let's break it down to figure it out.

We know that communication between the systems must be restricted to only those services required for business operations (called "controlled access") according to requirement #1.2.1. Now, we can't always keep all systems we need inside a single zone, or we would be defeating the goals of scope reduction that we should aim for. So what are we to do in these instances?

The standard states that any device that is "connected to the cardholder data environment" (CDE) is in scope since it is not completely isolated. The standard includes in scope any "[s]ystems that 'may impact the security of' (for example, name resolution or web redirection servers) the CDE". This is likely one of the most important lines written on scoping in the standard. This is further addressed on multiple occasions in the 2013 RSA presentation and the 2013 PCI community meetings presentation:

If it can impact the security of the CDE, it is in scope Remember non-CHD systems may be in scope too

and

If an "out-of-scope" system could lead a CDE compromise, it should not have been considered out of scope

Thus, if we are unsure whether or not a system is in scope (as a "connected" system), we should look at whether a compromise of the system could lead to an attack on a CDE system without needing to first compromise another system. If is the case, then this system is in scope. The second subtype of connected systems will partly address this as well.

In this methodology, we use isolated to indicate that two systems cannot communicate at all with each other. If communication is limited (note: use of the "any" or "generic" rules are prohibited in PCI DSS), we call it <u>controlled access</u>. The RSA conference presentations confirm this:

- *To be out of scope: segmentation = isolation = no access*
- *Controlled access ≠ isolation*
- *Controlled access:*
  - *Is still access*
  - *Is a PCI DSS requirement*
  - *Does not isolate one system/network from another*
  - *Provides entry point into CDE*
  - *Is in scope for PCI DSS*
    - *Verify access controls are working*
    - *Verify the connection / point of entry is secure*

Connected systems are often referred to as category 2 or type 2 devices. As in the CDE case, there are different types of "connected" devices that present a different level of risk. Connected systems are generally represented in yellow. Let's examine those three subtypes.

Connected/Security

There are systems such as user directories (Active Directory, LDAP), patch management systems, vulnerability management systems, several others (this is not an all inclusive list) which provide 'security services'. In our physical analogies, these would be security guards which can issue keys for the room, or it could be cleaning staff that provide services for that room. We can call these connected/security systems.

The December 2016 Guidance for PCI DSS Scoping and Network Segmentation creates 3 categories of systems that I consider as Connected/Security in a section they call "Connected-to or Security-impacting Systems":

- System component impacts configuration or security of CDE
- System component provides security services to the CDE
- System component supports PCI DSS requirements

I consider that all these types of systems were included initially by my model, but the added clarification from the PCI council is welcomed.

The OPST calls these type "2a".

Connected/Communicating Systems

Any system that is 'connected to' the CDE (to CDE systems) is considered a 'connected' system. The exception is systems that are on the 'outside' of Segmenting systems, for example when a Segmenting also affects traffic not related to the CDE such as that described in the Segmenting section and presented in Figure 2.

Some connected systems (that have a connection to CDE/receiving systems) may eventually be ruled out-of-scope, but an evaluation must be formally documented by the organization to determine if PCI DSS applies. It could be of a system receiving information outside the CDE with no possibility of re-entry. For example, say that we have a connected system that receives periodic information transfers initiated from a CDE system and that we have insured that no CHD/SAD is transmitted. The protocol used for data transfer is sftp (part of the SSH suite of applications). The traffic is initiated from the CDE, a file is uploaded to the connected system, and then the connection is closed. Other than returning status messages as part of the protocol, there is no information flowing back to the CDE system. I would contend that the connected system as described here could be ruled out-of-scope since it cannot have an impact on the security of the CDE (although some DLP tool may be warranted). Documentation of the evaluation process should be created, maintained and kept, to be presented to your assessor. The December 2016 Guidance calls these systems "System component directly connects to CDE". The OPST calls these "2b" or "2c"; I don't make the distinction based on flow-direction, but on details of communication.

Indirectly Connected

There are also systems that do not have any direct access to CDE systems (they are isolated from the CDE) that are still in scope. Instead, they would generally have access to other connected systems and, through these, could affect the security of the CDE. A classic example would be that of an administrator's workstation which can administer a security device (user directory, etc.), or systems upstream feeding information to connected systems (e.g. patching system, or an http connection as described above). In the case of a user directory, an administrator could potentially grant himself (or others) rights to systems in the CDE and breach the security of the CDE.

Indeed, the standard states that any system that "may impact the security of the CDE" is in scope. We can refer to these systems as connected/indirectly. The December 2016 Guidance calls these systems "System component indirectly connects to CDE". The OPST calls these type "2x".

Fourth category: Out-of-scope systems

Finally, any system that is neither a CDE or a connected system is considered out-of-scope for PCI compliance. That system must be completely isolated (no connections whatsoever) from CDE systems, though it may interact with connected systems (and can even reside in the same network zone with connected systems). Do remember, however, if it can affect security of the CDE indirectly through another connected system, that it is a connected system and is therefore in scope.

Out-of-scope systems are generally represented in green. The December 2016 Guidance for PCI DSS Scoping and Network Segmentation provides 4 tests that must be passed to confirm that a system is out-of-scope (which amount to ensuring that the system does not fall under the previously defined categories):

- System component does NOT store, process, or transmit CHD/SAD => otherwise it would be a CDE/CHD system.
- System component is NOT on the same network segment or in the same subnet or VLAN as systems that store, process, or transmit CHD => otherwise it would be a CDE/contaminated system.
- System component cannot connect to or access any system in the CDE => otherwise it would be a connected/communicating system (although I still contend that some connections could be considered out-of-scope if one can demonstrate they pose no risk, such as pings).
- System component cannot gain access to the CDE nor impact a security control for CDE via an in-scope system => otherwise this is a connected/security or connected/indirectly system.

The OPST calls these category "3".

Categories Summary

To summarize, there are four basic types of systems for PCI DSS purposes. The first group is the Cardholder Data Environment (CDE). The second group is segmenting systems, which are required to enable the other groups. The third group are connected systems, those systems that have some direct or indirect connection into the CDE (which the December 2016 guidance calls "Connected-to or Security-impacting Systems"). The fourth are out-of-scope systems completely isolated from the CDE systems. For these, always remember that "[s]ystems that may impact the security of (for example, name resolution or web redirection servers) the CDE"are always in scope or, to put it in other words: "If it can impact the security of the CDE, it is in scope".

Classification is key for us so we don't have to apply PCI DSS requirements to all systems.

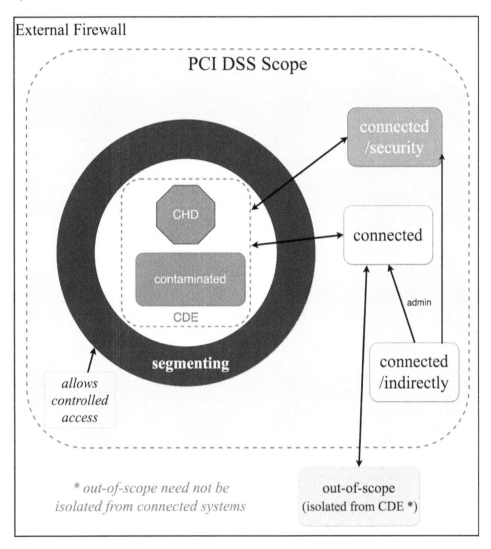

Figure 3 - PCI Scope Type Diagram

Type	Sub-Type	Segmentation	CHD/SAD	In-Scope
CDE	CHD	None	Yes	Yes
CDE	Contaminated	None	No	Yes
Segmenting		Provides Segmentation	No	Yes
Connected	Communicating	Controlled Access	No	Yes
Connected	Security	Controlled Access	No	Yes
Connected	Indirectly	Indirect Access	No	Yes
Out-of-scope		Isolation	No	No

Table 1 - Classification Categories Summary

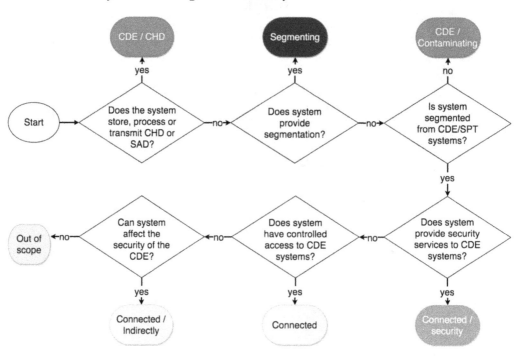

Figure 4 - PCI Scoping Type Decision tree

Scope Identification approach and Scope Documentation

Now that we've described the scope classification model, we need to look at how we must properly document the scope. The approach follows the model closely, with some elements of validation added. Once again, pages 10 and 11 of the standard provide us with the overall approach, while Appendix A3 (DESV) added more guidance of this definition in requirements A3.2.* (DE.2.* in DESV). As we have 2 types of in-scope systems (CDE and connected), we'll be splitting the process in two parts, one for each type.

Part 1 - Identifying the CDE (a four-step process)

Step 1.1 - To identify all systems that store, process or transmit CHD (CDE/CHD systems). These include servers, workstations, appliances, network equipment. The flow of CHD must be documented in diagrams (1.1.3) and detailed textual descriptions need to be produced (RoC #4.2). The flows and description must cover capture, authorization, settlement and chargebacks.

Step 1.2 - To identify where segmentation occurs (Segmenting systems). Segmenting systems prevent contamination and limit the scope of the CDE. The identified segmented CDE zones are generally represented in red in network diagrams.

Note: any time you implement a new type of segmentation, you should perform segmentation testing as demanded by requirement #11.3.4 and confirm its effectiveness (and fix issues identified) before deploying the new technology into production (also called for in A3.2.4).

Step 1.3 - To identify all other systems within the CDE which are contaminated (CDE/contaminated) systems. This should use the current maintained inventory (required by A3.2.4) but also include a system discovery using scanning tools (ping sweeps are typical here). Any difference with the inventory should be an indication of a failing inventory process and used to review and correct that process. The systems covered include servers, workstations, appliances, network equipment in the same segmented network zones or running under the same Segmenting hypervisors (more on hypervisors in section 2.7.1 on virtualization).

Note: since CDE/contaminated systems bring potential scope reduction opportunities, this step can be used to review if it makes sense to move the system outside the CDE. More on this in volume 3 on TCO (Total Cost of Ownership).

Step 1.4 - Finally, to validate that we do not have other PAN in other systems (A3.2.5) or locations. This "data discovery" is usually performed using specialized tools (Data Loss Prevention, DLP) but simple 'grep' on Unix/Linux also works. These searches generally use Regular Expressions, but manual discovery may be applicable when few systems are to be reviewed or on systems where such tools may not exist (for example, mainframes). For those who are resource constrained, inexpensive and free options do exist.

The "data discovery" should be performed on any system with the potential of storing PAN; at a minimum, this should cover all systems in the CDE and all connected systems (but really should include all servers, desktops and laptops). If any system is identified with PAN, then the following options are possible:

- Consider the system as a CDE/CHD system and perform anew the previous identification steps
- Migrate the system into the CDE and redo the previous steps
- Securely delete the CHD, and determine why and how PAN was transferred to the system or location to prevent further expansion of scope

In all cases, this should be treated as a security incident per requirement 12.10.*.

Note 1: Version 3.2 of PCI DSS clarified the scope of what should be checked when it added the following line: "*All types of systems and locations should be considered as part of the scoping process, including backup/recovery sites and fail-over systems.*"

Note 2: This is also an appropriate time to review requirement 3.1 and testing procedure 3.1.b to ensure that CHD is destroyed after the approved retention period.

Part 2 - Identify connected systems (a five-step process)

Once the CDE has been properly validated comes the time to identify the remaining in-scope systems.

Step 2.1 - To review all the in-scope firewall (or equivalent equipment implementing the ACLs) rules of Segmenting systems to identify the list of all systems that may connect to the CDE. If the rules are for network ranges instead of individual systems, then using a system discovery tool for the entire range will be required (see step 1.3 of CDE identification). Note that if a rule implies a system that no longer exists, then that rule needs to be removed as required by 1.1.7. The fact that a decommissioning did not remove a system from a firewall ruleset should be treated as an incident and call for a review of the change control process. With the complete list, we will proceed in classifying these systems according to the model.

Step 2.2 - Involves identifying any systems which provide security services, or services that may affect the security of the CDE, and which will be classified as connected/security systems. These include, at a minimum:

- Identity and Directory Services (Active Directory, LDAP)
- Domain Name Systems (DNS), Network Time Systems (NTP)
- Patch management systems
- Vulnerability management systems
- Anti-virus management systems
- File Integrity Management or Change Detection systems
- Performance Monitoring Systems
- Encryption Key Management Systems
- Remote-access (VPN) Systems
- Multi-factor Authentication Systems
- Log Management Systems and Monitoring Solutions (SIEM, syslog, etc.)
- Intrusion Detection Systems/ Intrusion Prevention Systems (IDS/IPS)

Step 2.3 - To identify third-party systems that may be connected to the CDE through some sort of Internet or private link. These systems which are out of your control are also out-of-scope, but the third-party providers must be managed as stated by requirements 12.8.*. Remember that if the connections go through internal network equipment such as routers, then that equipment will still be in scope.

Step 2.4 - To identify connected systems that only receive information and which may (through analysis) be deemed out-of-scope if they pose 'no risk' to the CDE. These systems generally cannot initiate a connection to the CDE and do not have a re-entry to the initiating system (ping or the ICMP protocol may be an exception). This could be the case of a sftp connection, as described earlier. Note that some protocols (DNS, NTP) that might have been deemed as out-of-scope have been used in previous breaches to exfiltrate information. In these cases however, IDS/IPS, DLP or other controls on the CDE connection points or on the initiating system may be more appropriate to monitor for security. The analysis should be thoroughly documented and this documentation must be maintained for review by your assessor (QSA, ISA, etc.).

The remaining systems of the list identified in the first step are simply connected/communicating systems.

Step 2.5 - Finally, to identify systems that are isolated from the CDE but could still affect its security, indirectly through some other connected system. These are obviously classified as connected/indirectly. Often, these are administrative consoles or administrator desktop/laptops.

Additional Guidance

The RoC reporting template gives us more detail of what we must document. Our documentation should include the information in the following subsections of sections 2, 3, 4 of the RoC reporting template. The ones marked as "assessor" are for use by the assessor, not the entity, although the assessor could be internal, either an ISA or someone producing a Self-Assessment Questionnaire (SAQ).

Section		Detail
2	Summary Overview	Title
2.1	Description of the entity's payment card business	
2.2	High-level network diagram(s)	PCI DSS 1.1.2
3	Description of Scope of Work and Approach Taken	Title
3.1	Assessor's validation of defined cardholder data environment and scope accuracy	Assessor
3.2	Cardholder Data Environment (CDE) overview	People, Process, Technology
3.3	Network segmentation	How segmentation is implemented

Section		Detail
3.4	Network segment details	All CDE zones and zones containing
3.5	Connected entities for processing	PCI DSS 12.8.*
3.6	Other business entities that require compliance with the PCI DSS	
3.7	Wireless summary	
3.8	Wireless details	
4	Details about Reviewed Environment	Title
4.1	Detailed network diagram(s)	PCI DSS 1.1.2
4.2	Description of cardholder data flows	PCI DSS 1.1.3
4.3	Cardholder data storage	A subset of CDE/CHD systems
4.4	Critical hardware in use in the cardholder data environment	CDE systems and connected/security
4.5	Critical software in use in the cardholder data environment	CDE systems and connected/security
4.6	Sampling	Assessor
4.7	Sample sets for reporting	Assessor
4.8	Service providers and other third parties with which the entity shares cardholder data	PCI DSS 12.8.*
4.9	Third-party payment applications/solutions	PA-DSS
4.1	Documentation reviewed	Assessor

Section		Detail
4.11	Individuals interviewed	Assessor
4.12	Managed service providers	Included in-scope or PCI DSS 12.8.*
4.13	Disclosure summary for "In Place with Compensating Control" responses	Assessor
4.14	Disclosure summary for "Not Tested" responses	Assessor

Table 1 - RoC reporting template sections for scope documentation

The subsections marked as "Assessor" would be filled by the assessor during the compliance assessment (RoC or SAQ). The ones marked as "Title" are simply headers.

References:

This model draws on pages 10 and 11 of the standard and on a few other documents:

- A presentation by the PCI SSC at the RSA conference in 2013 [1] (public) and a similar slides deck from the 2013 PCI community meetings (available to PCI assessors: QSAs, ISAs, PCIPs)
- PCI SSC answers to Frequently Asked Questions (FAQ) [2]
- PCI DSS Designated Entities Supplemental Validation for PCI DSS 3.1 (DESV, released June 2015) - A new set of requirements to increase assurance that an organization maintains compliance with PCI DSS over time, and that non-compliance is detected by a continuous (if not automated) audit process; this set of requirements applies to entities designated by the card brands or acquirers that are at a high risk level for the industry. DESV is now integrated as Appendix A3 in PCI DSS 3.2.
- RoC reporting template
- Information Supplements:
  - Best Practices for Maintaining PCI DSS Compliance (released August 2014 but updated March 2016) [3] (which is in many ways superseded by DESV)
  - Protecting Telephone-based Payment Card Data (March 2011) [4]
  - Third-Party Security Assurance [5] (August 2014)
  - PCI DSS 2.0 Cloud Computing Guidelines [6] (February 2013)
  - PCI DSS Virtualization Guidelines v2.0 [7] (June 2011)
  - PCI DSS Information Supplement: Guidance for PCI DSS Scoping and Network Segmentation [8] (December 2016)

[1] (RSA PCI DSS Scope, 2013). less is more pci dss scoping demystified - RSA Conference. Retrieved July 2, 2015, from https://www.rsaconference.com/writable/presentations/file_upload/dsp-w21.pdf.

[2] (PCI SSC FAQs). FAQs - PCI Security Standards Council. Retrieved July 2, 2015, from https://www.pcisecuritystandards.org/faq/.

[3] (2014). Best Practices for Maintaining PCI DSS Compliance. Retrieved July 2, 2015, from https://www.pcisecuritystandards.org/documents/PCI_DSS_V3.0_Best_Practices_for_Maintaining_PCI_DSS_Compliance.pdf.

[4] (2011). Protecting Telephone-based Payment Card Data - PCI ... Retrieved July 2, 2015, from
https://www.pcisecuritystandards.org/documents/protecting_telephone-based_payment_card_data.pdf.

[5] (2016). Third-Party Security Assurance v1.1 - PCI Security Standards. Retrieved May 31, 2016, from
https://www.pcisecuritystandards.org/documents/ThirdPartySecurityAssurance_March2016_FINAL.pdf.

[6] (2013). PCI DSS Cloud Computing Guidelines - PCI Security ... Retrieved July 13, 2015, from
https://www.pcisecuritystandards.org/pdfs/PCI_DSS_v2_Cloud_Guidelines.pdf.

[7] (2011). Virtualization Guidelines - PCI Security Standards Council. Retrieved July 13, 2015, from
https://www.pcisecuritystandards.org/documents/Virtualization_InfoSupp_v2.pdf.

[8] (2017). December 2016 PCI council scoping guidance vs PCI Resources model - PCI Resources. Retrieved January16, 2017, from
https://www.pcisecuritystandards.org/documents/Guidance-PCI-DSS-Scoping-and-Segmentation_v1.pdf.

Version History

Version	Author	Description	Date
1.0	Yves Desharnais	Initial release	July 2015
1.1	Yves Desharnais	Clarifications, Formatting and Update to PCI DSS 3.2 and other PCI SSC updated documents	July 2016
1.2	Yves Desharnais	Clarifications and changes related to PCI DSS Information Supplement: Guidance for PCI DSS Scoping and Network Segmentation	December 2017

Author:
> Yves Desharnais, 8850895 CANADA INC.
> Email: info@pciresources.com
> Website: www.pciresources.com

Appendix A2 - Network Primer

A2.1 Appendix Introduction

Networks are central to many of the controls of PCI DSS. Networks also form the first technical security layer, while operating systems form the second layer, and applications the third.

This primer will cover the basic protocols and technologies including TCP/IP, Ethernet, DSL, cable and wireless networks.

The internet, a network of networks, has grown so much and become so mainstream that most of us cannot imagine going back to pre-internet days. From home and business phone-lines (DSL) and television cable (coaxial cables) connections, to optical fiber, local Wi-Fi and cellular (2G, 3G, 4G/LTE, etc.) connections, we are more interconnected every passing day.

The Internet started as a project called the ARPANET developed under funding by DARPA, the US Defense Advanced Research Project Agency, in the late 1960s. ARPANET included the development of the TCP/IP stack that is at the core of the Internet, whichever lower level network connectivity technology is in use.

A2.1.1 The Open Standards Interconnect (OSI) network model

To understand networking, we often refer to a conceptual model called the OSI network model which consists of 7 layers built on top of each other. We'll describe them briefly as we refer to these going forward. This model is an approximation of what happens in most networking technologies, but is close enough to gain an understanding of any networking technology. TCP/IP will be described and linked back to this model.

Let's start at the bottom and work our way up.

Data Type	#	Layer	Function
Data	7	Application	Access point to network services
	6	Presentation	Manages encryption and decryption of data as well as converting between different formats
	5	Session	Manages interhost communication and sessions between different applications
Segments	4	Transport	End-to-end connection and flow control. The notion of ports is at this layer
Packet / Diagram	3	Network	Determines data flow and logical addressing (IP addresses)
Frame	2	Link	Physical addressing (MAC address)
Bit	1	Physical	Binary signal transmission

Appendix A2 - Table 1 - The 7 OSI layers

Level 1 is physical hardware, where the low level electrical (phone lines, coaxial cable, fiber optic, etc.) or wireless (cellular, Wi-Fi) operations occur. Level 1 works at the bit level (a bit is the basic unit of information in computing and has two possible values: 0 or 1). Think of someone who knows which way to package information, such as using envelopes or appropriate boxes.

Level 2 is the data-link layer that basically provides a point-to-point connection, essentially to the next system that it has a direct connection to. Level 2 works with groups of bits generally called a frame. Think of the employee that only knows the people sitting next to him and no one else.

Level 3 is the network layer. This is where routing (the process of selecting the best path to follow) occurs between different hosts. Think of someone who can pick the best route to get to any city.

Level 4 is the transport layer. Built on top of the routing layer of level 3, the transport layer allows us to send packets of information reliably. Think of someone who can deliver a package to a specific building in a city.

Levels 3 and 4 are often used together, as are levels 5, 6 and 7, or they can be interchangeable. This is described in the next section, covering the TCP/IP model.

Level 5 is the session layer supposed to manage "state" between devices, for example, clients and servers.

Level 6 is the presentation layer. It includes all kinds of translation between character sets (ASCII, EBCDIC, Unicode), compression and encryption/decryption.

Level 7 is the application layer and what the end-user generally interacts with.

To help remember their order, layers 7, 6 and 5 are often referred to as the "APS" layers (application, presentation, session). Think of someone who can deal with the content of the package received and send an appropriate response.

Most applications that users interact with are on levels 5 through 7.

A2.1.2 TCP/IP

The TCP/IP model is simpler than the OSI network model. Layers in the TCP/IP "stack" combine a few of the OSI model layers.

The link layer is a combination of the first two layers (1 and 2) of the OSI model into the type of network connection used. Most of you will have heard the term MODEM (for MOdulator, DEModulator). A modem provides the conversion from information provided at level 3 down to level 2 and 1, so it can be transmitted over some form of medium over long distances.

These 2 first layers could be provided by phone line (DSL) connections (usually terminated with a 4 cable connector called RJ11), Ethernet connections (RJ45), cable (coaxial) connections, or wireless connections (any of the Wi-Fi, Bluetooth, cellular - Edge, 3G, or LTE). Older technologies such as token-ring networks would also fall under that level.

We are generally less concerned with level 1 and 2 from a security standpoint, as network switches are the most susceptible network devices for these types of attacks. Some attacks do exist at those levels. They are partly protected using physical security controls, and through level 3 protections at the perimeter of the network. This is one of the reasons that we require a minimum of security controls at level 3 for PCI DSS network segmentation.

The Internet and transport layers are basically one level of the OSI layer model each, and are the ones we use the most in our network security controls.

The Internet layer in the TCP/IP stack is the refers to the IP layer, which assigns one (or multiple) IP address(es) to devices. There are 2 versions of IP currently used: IP version 4 (IPv4), still mostly in use, dates back to 1981, and support roughly 4.3 billion IP addresses (2^{32} exactly, due to its use of 32-bit addresses); and IP version 6 (IPv6), which is very slowly being integrated in the internet, published in 1998 in order to add more potential devices by using 128-bit addresses. Most examples given in this primer will use IPv4 addresses, which are generally shown as 4 numbers between 0 and 255 separated by dots, such as 10.11.12.255. This will be covered in more detail in the next section.

The Internet layer also includes the ICMP (Internet Control Message Protocol, commonly used by the "ping" application). Layer 3 generally deals with "packets" of data which contain both routing information (think of the subject, sender, recipient of an email) and the content (think of the message and attachments).

Also included in this layer is the Internet Group Management Protocol (IGMP), a protocol used to "multicast" or send information to multiple recipients at once. IGMP is mostly used for multimedia streaming and thus not useful for PCI DSS security controls. We will therefore not delve into IGMP further.

The transport layer of the TCP/IP stack is also the transport layer, or layer 4, of the OSI model. This layer builds upon the Internet layer, generally on top of the IP protocol previously described. Two protocols stand out: the UDP and TCP protocols. They add reliability over the IP protocol. Layer 4 also introduces ports that are generally assigned to services. Ports are 16 bits long ($2^{16} = 65536$ possibilities). Ports start at 0 and end at 65535. Ports less than or equal to 1024 are considered reserved ports (to operating system processes) but that distinction is not that critical any more.

UDP (User Datagram Protocol) dates back to 1980. UDP is a stateless protocol, meaning that all requests received are treated independently from each other. UDP offers no guarantee of delivery (no certainty the information, or packets, will be received at all) or that information will be received in the same order it is sent. While this may be an issue in some cases, the upside is that this offers a higher performance than the other model, TCP. UDP works well for applications with many clients, such as streaming of media (audio and video).

On the other hand, TCP (Transmission Control Protocol) is the first part of the TCP/IP name. Most of the protocols we interact with operate over TCP/IP. TCP is a stateful protocol, meaning that a connection must first be established, and that we have assurance that data will be received in the same order it is sent. This is handled directly by the TCP protocol, allowing applications to unload themselves from that responsibility. Imagine a client asks for information over a TCP connection. The information that the server wants to send to the client in this case is split into 4 packets called A,B,C and D. The server will then work to send each of the packets to the client. The packets are numbered so that the client can reconstitute them in the same order. Say the client receives packets A,D,C (in improper order and missing packet B), the client will re-request packet B from the server and will ensure that the application received the proper A,B,C,D order, or an error message will display should the connection prove unreliable. This reliability condition is critical for most transactional processing on the Internet.

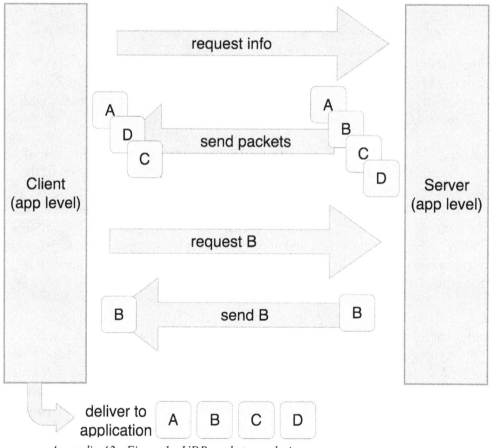

Appendix A2 - Figure 1 - UDP packet reordering

The application layer of the TCP/IP stack combines layers 7, 6 and 5 of the OSI model (the "APS" layers). This layer includes most protocols we interact with.

TCP/IP Model Layer	Examples	#	OSI Model Layer
Application	HTTP, FTP, SMTP	7	Application
		6	Presentation
		5	Session
Transport	TCP, UDP	4	Transport
Internet	IPv4, IPv6, ICMP	3	Network
Link	Ethernet, DSL, Cable, Wi-Fi, Cellular	2	Link
		1	Physical

Appendix A2 – Table 2 - The TCP/IP vs OSI layers

A2.1.3 IPv4 Networks

IP version 4 is the main protocol in use today. IP addresses in version 4 consist of 4 bytes, where a byte is 8 bits, and thus the IP address has 32-bits. Each byte can be represented as a number from 0 to 255 (256 possibilities). Those addresses are generally presented separated by dots as in the example 192.168.1.1. This address in binary format (bits) is 11000000.10101000.00000001.00000001. This will be relevant shortly.

There are subsets of IP addresses that are reserved for internal networks and defined in RFC 1918 [1]. These addresses cannot be routed to the Internet, and should not be, since most organizations share portions of these. The 3 basic ranges are: 192.168.*.*, 10.*.*.* and 172.16.*.* to 172.31.*.*, with "*" being any value from 0 to 255, and the last range starting with 172 and having the second digit being between 16 and 31 inclusively. Since these addresses are not routable on the Internet, we often see the use of Network Address Translation (NAT) as a way to communicate. NAT is a means by which a system that has an Internet routable address (typically a router or firewall) serves as an intermediary between our internal and external systems, and keeps track of which ports it uses for each connection (always initiated by the internal system). This tracking of ports is called "stateful inspection" or "dynamic packet filtering" and prevents someone else from using the established connection.

NAT is very common in today's households Internet connections (and in enterprises), though most people have no idea this is even happening (nor do they really need to know). 192.168.1.1, within the first range mentioned, is the default IP address for most home routers.

These reserved ranges are defined in a standard called Address Allocation for Private Internets (RFC 1918). 3 different ranges are defined:

- 192.168.*.* (256*256=65,536 possibilities)
- 10.*.*.* (256*256*256~=16 million possibilities), and
- 172.16.*.* to 172.31.*.* (16*256*256~=1 million possibilities).

This RFC is mentioned in requirement 1.3.7 of PCI DSS 3.2 (1.3.8 in v.3.1).

Subnetworks and Netmasks

A subnet is a logical subdivision of the whole IP network range. A subnet keeps the first digits (bits actually) of an IP address. The most common network range subdivision is when only the last byte of the IP address changes, called a class C (more later on this). The last byte, or last 8 bits, would be the one that is allowed to be changed. So, in our example, 192.168.1.2, only the last number 2 can change and assume a value from 0 to 255. We call netmask the portion that does not change in the IP address. In this case, the netmask would become 255.255.255.0, or 11111111.11111111.11111111.00000000. You may also encounter the network range presented in the form /24 (where 32 total bits - 8 mask bits = 24 netmask bits) as in 192.168.1.1/24. These are all equivalent. This subnet example is for a byte (or 8 bit), but a subnet can be of any bit length from 1 to 32 (where 32 bit subnets only include 1 IP address).

Different network segments (on local networks and the internet) are communicated and their traffic is connected using a series of networking equipments which includes hubs, switches, routers, and firewalls. Those network segments (or subnets) are what we isolate using networking equipments to protect systems from unauthorized access.

Before subnets were introduced in 1993, classful networks were used and the nomenclature of classes is still sometimes used today. Classes (A, B, C, D, E) were allocated to some organizations in those early days.

Class A networks have a netmask of /24, so only the first byte is fixed, but only the first 128 values (0 to 127) were allocated and the other 128 options were left for other classes. For example, IBM still has all the IP addresses with 9.*, and AT&T has 12.*. Class B networks have a netmask of /16 and thus can have 65,536 IP addresses (2^{16}). Class C networks have a netmask of /8 and only allow for 256 different addresses (2^8). Class D and E are specialized classes. Class D are used for multicast, which allows us to send packets of information to multiple recipients. Class E are reserved for future addressing modes [2].

Class	Leading bits	Size of network number bit field	Size of rest bit field	Number of networks	Addresses per network	Start address	End address
A	0	8	24	128 (2^7)	16,777,216 (2^{24})	0.0.0.0	127.255.255.255
B	10	16	16	16,384 (2^{14})	65,536 (2^{16})	128.0.0.0	191.255.255.255
C	110	24	8	2,097,152 (2^{21})	256 (2^8)	192.0.0.0	223.255.255.255
D (multicast)	1110	not defined	not defined	not defined	not defined	224.0.0.0	239.255.255.255
E (reserved)	1111	not defined	not defined	not defined	not defined	224.0.0.0	255.255.255.255

Appendix A2 - Table 3 - IPv4 Network Classes

A2.1.4 TCP/IP Protocol Examples

There are thousands of protocols running over TCP/IP. The standardized ones are described in an RFC, or Request For Comments, a publication from the Internet Engineering Task Force (IETF), the organization that creates the voluntary standards that underpin the Internet. Some of those protocols are almost as old as the Internet itself. SMTP (Simple Mail Transfer Protocol), the protocol used to send email between different servers, was defined in 1982 and though it has received some updates since then, it remains very close to its original definition. We'll go through some of the most common and important ones, namely HTTP and FTP. But first, let's look at standard tools of another protocol: ICMP.

A2.1.4.1 Ping and traceroute

This is the one example that does not use the TCP and IP protocols, instead using the ICMP of the Internet layer (level 3 of the OSI model). ICMP is used within local networks, though local in this case may mean long distances. ICMP messages are generally used to diagnose problems. The ping application is the most commonly used of the tools using the ICMP protocol, and its name is derived from the naval term used when sonar tries to identify vessels (boats and submarines) by sending a frequency that bounces back on vessels and is detected back at the sender.

The ping tool is used to determine whether a remote device (host) is reachable and to diagnose the connection. Failure to respond by the remote host can be caused by a network failure or by the host being turned off, for example. A ping command from the command line generally takes the IP address as parameter. Here are two examples of commands pinging devices on my home network:

```
$ ping 192.168.1.1
PING 192.168.1.1 (192.168.1.1): 56 data bytes
64 bytes from 192.168.1.1: icmp_seq=0 ttl=64 time=6.069 ms
64 bytes from 192.168.1.1: icmp_seq=1 ttl=64 time=2.267 m
```

In the first example, we can see that the device is responding to our requests. We see a response time with each request that can assist us in determining the speed of our connection.

```
$ ping 192.168.1.100
PING 192.168.1.100 (192.168.1.100): 56 data bytes
Request timeout for icmp_seq 0
```

In the second example, we get a timeout (meaning no request). In this scenario, this answer is explained by the fact that there is no device at that particular address on my home network. If I knew there were such a device, I would have to investigate why I could not connect to it.

I think most people can quickly see the value of such a tool. But the ICMP protocol can allow us to do much more. The traceroute program makes great use of ICMP. In the first example, you may have noticed a parameter called 'ttl' in the response. TTL, or time-to-live, is a counter that gets decremented every time we hit a hop (a network device in the path, such as a switch or router). Here is an example connecting to a Google DNS server:

```
$ traceroute 8.8.8.8
traceroute to 8.8.8.8 (8.8.8.8), 64 hops max, 52 byte packets
1 controlpanel.home (192.168.1.1) 2.366 ms 1.668 ms 3.010 ms
2 206.248.154.121 (206.248.154.121) 14.977 ms 18.483 ms 15.259 ms
3 ae2_2110-bdr03-tor.teksavvy.com (69.196.136.41) 14.282 ms 14.426 ms 14.055 ms
4 72.14.211.14 (72.14.211.14) 14.162 ms 13.926 ms 14.037 ms
5 72.14.239.75 (72.14.239.75) 13.930 ms
  72.14.236.97 (72.14.236.97) 15.187 ms
  72.14.235.187 (72.14.235.187) 14.593 ms
6 google-public-dns-a.google.com (8.8.8.8) 14.185 ms 14.429 ms 26.004 ms
```

We see that the traceroute program allowed for a maximum number of 64 hops (this is configurable). Then we see a series of lines numbered 1 to 6, meaning it took us 6 hops to get to the server. The way everything works is that we send a series of ICMP requests with a TTL of 1 and then increment until we get a response from the server. This is because the time-to-live when it reaches 0 returns a message to the sender that the last hop was IP W.X.Y.Z.

So our program sent an ICMP packet with TTL=1 with destination 8.8.8.8. The first hosts it encountered, my home router at 192.168.1.1 (local IP address), decremented TTL to 0 and then since 0 had been reached, returned a message to my computer that destination had not been reached. The program then sent a second ICMP packet with a TTL of 2 this time. The TTL got decremented at my home router (to 1) and then was sent to the next hop, one of my Internet provider's servers. The server also decremented the TTL and, having reached 0, sent the reply back to the program. This process continues until the maximum TTL is reached, or the destination is reached. In our case, the latter occurs after 6 of 64 attempts. The traceroute program, similar to the ping program, can help us diagnose a communication problem, but this time highlighting a network path that may be slower or unavailable.

A2.1.4.2 Hypertext Transfer Protocol (HTTP)

The Hypertext Transfer Protocol (HTTP) is one of the most important protocols in use today, both from an end-user and an application perspective. HTTP was initially created in the early 1990s to support the World Wide Web (WWW or the web). The WWW was created by Tim Berners Lee's team at CERN (the French acronym of the European Organization for Nuclear Research). That team also invented the HTML language used for web pages. While in use for the web, HTTP is also used by applications and systems to communicate with each other. Version 1.0 of HTTP was introduced in 1996, and version 1.1 in 1999. Version 2.0 was just released in 2015, and can be seen as a wrapper over version 1.1, adding new functionality but allowing for good backward compatibility with the 1.1 version.

HTTP works in a request-response manner. The connection can be established for every request, or kept-alive for a time, and thus re-used, since version 1.1. The requests come in the form of a verb an URI. The basic verbs developed for version 1.0, and still in use today, are GET, POST and HEAD. Version 1.1 added 5 more verbs: OPTIONS, PUT, DELETE, TRACE and CONNECT. GET is the simplest form and is used to request a path.

The first line of the requests follow this form:

```
VERB URI HTTP/version
```

VERB is the verb. URI refers to the path of the local resource being requested. Version is one of the supported versions. Other lines may be included in the request specifying options (called headers in the HTTP protocol).

For example, the request:

```
GET /page/ HTTP/1.0
```

Here, We are requesting the resource at "/page/" on the local server using version 1.0 of HTTP and the GET verb. The server will return a response starting with a line including the version (1.0), a status code (200) and status message (OK), such as:

```
HTTP/1.0 200 OK
```

The positive response in this case would then be followed by the requested resource formatted according to the standard.

Let's use a common (but very simplified) example. A user accesses his home computer to browse a site on the Internet that is hosted on a Linux server. He opens a web browser (Chrome, IE, Firefox, Safari, etc.) and types in a web address (a URL). On the client system, the browser opens an HTTP connection at layer 7 (http). The request flows to layer 6 where character changes may be made, and then to layer 5 (the OSI is approximation of reality, and in this case nothing is done for layer 5). The client system then initiates a reliable layer 4 TCP connection to the server. TCP calls IP at layer 3 to send the packets to the host identified. This information is sent to the next host for routing over an Ethernet (layers 1-2), which is the user's Internet modem (DSL, cable, cellular, etc.).

The server receives the information which flows back up through levels 1, 2, 3, and 4, and is received by the HTTP server which operates the layers 5, 6, and 7. The server then identifies whether the request resource is present, and replies to the client accordingly. The response flows back to the end user.

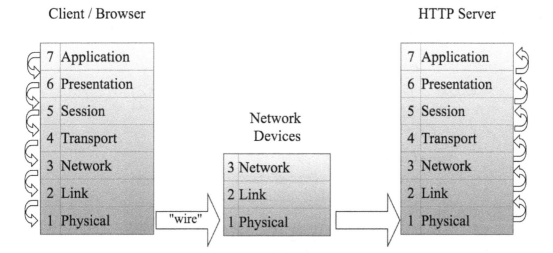

Appendix A2 - Figure 2 - HTTP communications through network layers

Now all of this happens very fast, with the performance issues (bottleneck) generally happening between layers 1-3 as other layers are performed on the local system (host/device).

2.8.4.3 File Transfer Protocol (FTP)

File Transfer Protocol (FTP) is another early protocol of the Arpanet that was initially created in 1971, but reviewed multiple times [3]. FTP runs over TCP/IP and normally uses TCP port 21 (although any port can be used). FTP can operate in two modes: active and passive. In both cases, the client contacts the server on its main port. The user will generally respond to server request to provide credentials (username and password) although some systems can allow for anonymous connections (no password necessary). FTP is considered an insecure protocol since the password is sent unencrypted (also called "in the clear") over the main connection (thus failing PCI DSS requirement 8.2.1). The two different modes are applicable when file transfers are initiated by the client. For active mode to work, the client must be reachable over the Internet. This generally precludes the use of internal networks. In active mode, the client opens a port and sends the server a command telling it to connect to that port. In passive mode, the client requests that the server open a port and the client then connects to that port. The file transfer occurs on that "data" channel and not on the main "control" connection which is used to send commands from the client and responses from the server (tcp port 20 is the default port in passive mode).

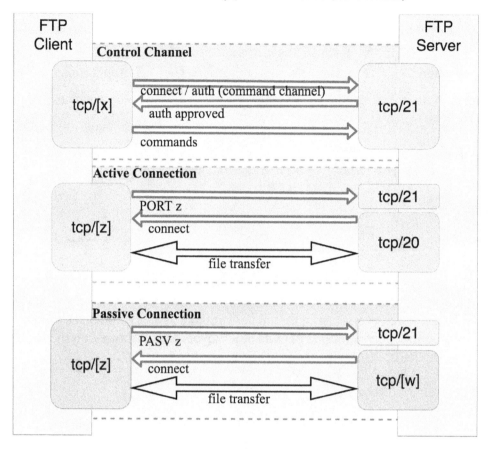

Appendix A2 - Figure 3 - FTP protocol

A2.1.5 Network Segmentation Requirements for PCI DSS

To summarize, we have the following network layers for TCP/IP:

OSI Layer	TCP/IP Layer	Protocol Examples
7,6,5	(APS) Applications	HTTP, FTP, etc.
4	Transport	TCP, UDP
3	Internet	IPv4, IPv6, ICMP
2,1	Link	Ethernet, DSL, Cable, Wi-Fi, Cellular

Appendix A2 - Table 4 - TCP/IP Model Summary

Understanding how those layers work helps us understand what PCI DSS may consider adequate network segmentation. As we've seen, layers 1 and 2, while they have issues can be generally protected at layer 3. It is important to remember that specific implementations within particular networking equipment may not all offer the same level of security. For that reason, we must perform network segmentation testing as required by #11.3.4 to ensure that attacks against layers 1 but mostly 2 are properly contained by our specific implementation. For PCI DSS, we accept layer 3 segmentation that includes strong ACL's, and that has been adequately tested by well-trained experts.

More information can be found for free on the Internet regarding how networks function. The reader is encouraged to read further if he needs further information.

End Notes - Appendix A2

[1] Groot, G. (1996). RFC 1918 - Address Allocation for Private Internets. Retrieved from https://tools.ietf.org/html/rfc1918.

[2] Deering, S. (1989). RFC 1112 - Host extensions for IP multicasting - IETF Tools. Retrieved from https://tools.ietf.org/html/rfc1112.

[3] Postel, J. (1985). RFC 959 - FILE TRANSFER PROTOCOL (FTP). Retrieved from https://www.ietf.org/rfc/rfc959.txt.

Appendix A3 - A primer on encryption

A3.1 What is encryption?

So what is encryption and why should you care?

Encryption is all around all of us, and most of us do not even realise it. We use it whenever we do online shopping (hopefully), or access the biggest free email providers (gmail, hotmail/outlook, yahoo, others). It's securing information on our phones and our computers, both personal and business. Encryption keeps information safe. It's gotten to the point that Arthur C. Clarke so famously described as *"any sufficiently advanced technology is indistinguishable from magic"*.

Figure 1 - The lock icon on https://www.google.com on Chrome and Firefox under a Mac

A few years back in another job, I initially considered creating a small course called *'encryption for auditors'*. This is the evolution of this initial idea. It presents an accurate, but simplified (meaning not all details are presented) explanations on the matter.

This document is just an overview of cryptography. It will not make you a cryptographer, or a cryptographic engineer. A cryptographer designs (and evaluates) cryptographic algorithms, while a cryptographic engineer designs solutions using cryptography. One can do both, but these are very complex functions and, as with many things, the devil often lies in the details.

Cryptography, the science of encryption, is a very complex science that requires strong mathematical bases. This primer will not go into the mathematics, but will give you the basics of how encryption is used in IT environments for meeting security requirements such as those in PCI DSS.

I encourage users that wish to understand encryption more in depth (including the math) to review books and online courses. Users of cryptography, like with most fields of science, get to enjoy the fruits of the scientists (in this case, the cryptographers) without all of the hard work.

The Merriam-Webster dictionary defines encryption as:*"to change (information) from one form to another especially to hide its meaning"*. The science of encryption is called cryptography. Webster's definition for cryptography is a bit clearer:*"the process of writing or reading secret messages or codes"*. Wikipedia gives us a clearer description still:*"In cryptography, encryption is the process of encoding messages or information in such a way that only authorized parties can read it. Encryption does not of itself prevent interception, but denies the message content to the interceptor"*.

So encryption is one way we use to protect information from unauthorized people, even if they can get a hold of the message. To encode such a message, some sort of key is required. This is akin to being around a group speaking another language. Without the*'key'*, in this case understanding of the language, the speakers can say anything they want and we cannot gain any information of what is being said. This was exactly what the US military leveraged during World War II. The Navajo people and their language were used to exchange secret messages that the enemy could not understand (neither could regular US military personnel) [1].

The easiest definition to agree on, is that strong encryption is the process of securing information so that it can only be viewed by someone with the right key. Someone without the key can do nothing with the information (we'll cover the one attack, brute forcing, a little later).

A3.2 Encryption basics

Reading most security standards, you will hear of two cases of encryption: for data being transmitted, referred to as encryption of data-in-motion, and for data stored, referred to as encryption of data-at-rest.

There are generally two processes in encryption.

- Encryption takes an input, the message, and through a key and a specific algorithm, generates an output, which we call cipher-text.

- Decryption takes the cipher-text as input, alongside the decryption key and algorithm, generates the original message as output.

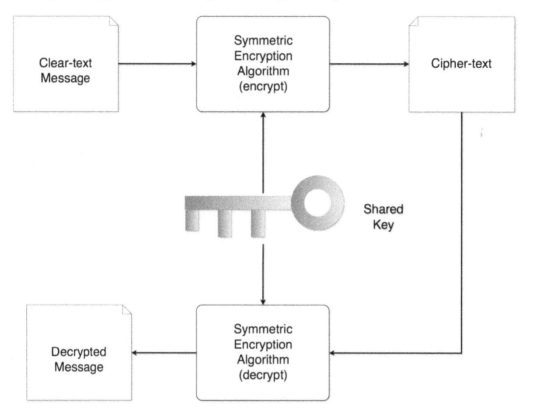

Appendix A3 - Figure 2 - Basic Symmetric Encryption Process

In cryptography, the algorithm used is called a 'cipher', and the resulting encrypted text is called 'cipher-text'.

In both cases, the algorithm, or cipher, used is generally publicly known, has been vetted by the cryptographic community over years, and its strength lies in the key(s) used. The example of the AES standard describes this well. In 1997, NIST created a contest to replace an aging cipher called Triple-DES (more in section 3.13.3.1), created in the 1970s. Cryptographers worldwide were to present for selection their cryptographic algorithms, or cipher, over the following months. Then, during the next couple of years cryptographers evaluated and tested the proposed algorithms. Finally, based on all this evaluation, one cipher was selected out of the five remaining ones. The winning cipher, Rijndael, was announced on October 2, 2000, and then approved in 2001. AES is now one of the most used ciphers out there, and recent computer chips even include specific computer instructions to facilitate its use.

Keys, just like passwords, need to be *'strong'*, meaning hard to guess. For keys, this means the sufficiently large key length (generally measured in bits, 0/1 pairs) and a lot of *'randomness'*. Randomness is one of those details generally understood but harder to define and that we will not delve into here. Suffice to say, randomness is required.

A3.3 Ciphers, cryptographic algorithms

Ciphers can be categorized in several ways.

One type of category is whether we are working on files or network communication. If dealing with fixed size blocks of data, usually for files, we use what we call <u>block ciphers</u>. If working with a continuous stream of information, as in the case of any network communications, then we use a <u>stream cipher</u>.

A second more useful categorization for our purposes is as cryptographic primitives. There are basic cryptographic functions (called primitives) that we need to understand before going forward. I'll go over the three most common ones: symmetric cryptography, asymmetric cryptography and hashing functions.

A3.3.1 Symmetric cryptography

Symmetric, as in *'the same viewed both ways'*, refers to the fact there is only one single key used for both encryption and decryption. This is why we often refer to it as private-key or shared-key encryption. This means that the key must be shared between the various people (or processes) that have access to the information (or message). And we all can understand that the more people know of something, the less secret it is likely to remain. See figure 10 for a representation of symmetric cryptography.

The most known and commonly used symmetric ciphers are: DES, 3DES (also called Triple-DES, TDES, which uses 3 DES iterations with 3 different keys), AES, Blowfish and Twofish.

A3.3.2 Asymmetric cryptography

The other type of cryptography is asymmetric encryption, meaning the use of different keys, and is also referred to as public-key cryptography. Two keys are generally used. They are usually referred to as the public key and the private key. The private key is to be kept very secret by its owner, and the public key is shared with everyone else. Those two keys are mathematically related to each other and this allows the algorithm to work; the mathematical details vary per algorithm. But the private key must be extremely well guarded. Generally, this means that a message encoded with one key can be decrypted with the other key (they are interchangeable); this property will be useful in the examples presented at this end of this section. Now, you may say to yourself, it seems that asymmetric is more secure since less people will have the keys so it should be easier to protect. You would be right. The downside to asymmetric cryptography is that it is vastly slower than its symmetric counterpart. You'll see in the examples below that we actually often use all three forms of primitives, leveraging the strengths that each provides.

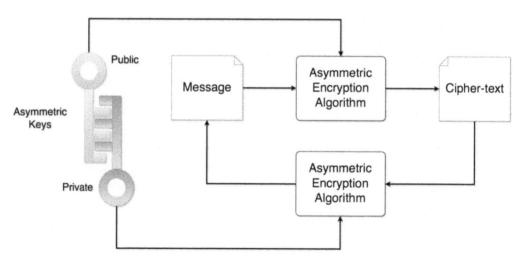

Appendix A3 - Figure 3 - Asymmetric cryptography

The most famous asymmetric ciphers are RSA and Diffie-Hellman. Elliptic-curve ciphers are also currently gaining traction.

A3.3.3 Hashing functions

Hashing functions, unlike symmetric or asymmetric functions, are irreversible. They are also often called *'one-way functions'*. That is, there is no decryption process involved with them. It is not possible to recalculate the input from the output. A hashing function takes an input message of any length (very small to very big), and through an algorithm, generates an output of a specific length to an algorithm. The output is always the same for a defined input. But if even only one character changes in the input message, the output will be completely different. We call this process *'hashing'*, or say that the value is *'hashed'* or that we get the *'hash'* of the value.

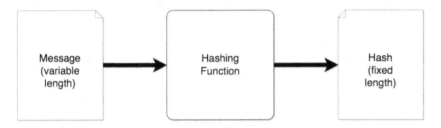

Appendix A3 - Figure 4 - Hashing functions

Some of the most common hashing algorithms include MD5 and the SHA series such as SHA-1, SHA-256 . Here are a few examples for the message *'password'* (without the quotes):

Algorithm	Lengths (bin)	Hash of *'password'*
MD5	128	5f4dcc3b5aa765d61d8327deb882cf99
SHA-1	160	5baa61e4c9b93f3f0682250b6cf8331b7ee68fd8
SHA256	256	5e884898da28047151d0e56f8dc6292773603d0d6aabbdd62a11ef721d1542d8

Appendix A3 - Table 1 - Example of different hash values for 'password'

A3.4 Usage of cryptographic primitives

The usage section is here to help you understand real world examples of cryptography.

A3.4.1 Usage: secure storage of passwords

Storing passwords *"in clear-text"* or unencrypted should never be done. If any attacker were to get access to the systems, then they would have those passwords, and they could do anything as if they were you (impersonation). Hashing functions are the cryptographic primitives generally used for storing passwords. When you set your new password to a system, that password is then hashed and that hash is saved. When you try to log in again, the password you entered is hashed and compared to the hashed version stored. That way, your password is never stored in clear-text (that an attacker could see and then use to impersonate you). This is why most audit controls for passwords will use the language "passwords are stored using non-reversible encryption". 'Non-reversible encryption' is another word for hashing functions, a one-way function.

Hashing functions, like any cryptographic functions, are of varying strength depending on the algorithm in use. And depending of the use case (passwords, file integrity) different algorithms can be used.

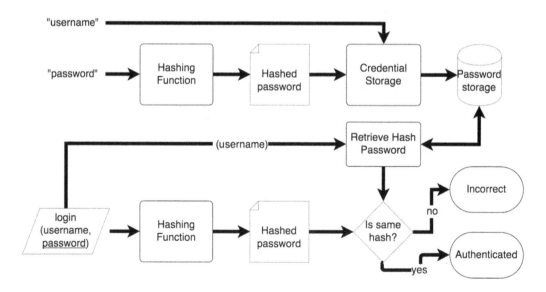

Appendix A3 - Figure 5 - Password storage and validation

Now remember how I mentioned that passwords should be hashed? Or that it is not possible to recalculate the input from the output? Well both are true, but also have their limits. And that can be a problem if we simply use the algorithms (although some algorithms are better than others) for typical password values. Say we decide to store passwords using MD5 (MD5 should no longer be used for most things, we're using it as an example only here). I create the password *'Password23'*. This gives us a hash of *'37f2b0b7eff2cd34bb5cbd77c14d4850'*. While *'Password12'* gives us a hash of *'08f5b04545cbf7eaa238621b9ab84734'*. Anybody can calculate these since everyone knows the algorithm. And therein lies the issue. If a system used in multiple (think millions) of systems worldwide were to use the same worldwide function, then the hash for a specific password would always be given the same hash.

Thus, an attacker targeting systems like these could calculate the hash of all possible permutations (or variations of all possible characters) of passwords and store these in a big database. If he gets access to a system with these hashes, all he now has to do is look in that very big database for the hash and he could retrieve the password. We call such a process brute-forcing, meaning the attacker actually had to calculate all the values to get back at the password. Precomputed tables like the ones I described are called *'rainbow tables'* in information security. And many of these are already made by attackers and available for download (some at a fee). So what are we to do about this? Well that's where we can make an attacker's life harder by adding what we call a *'salt'*. A *'salt'* is a fixed value that will be prefixed to the input message so that the hash output is changed.

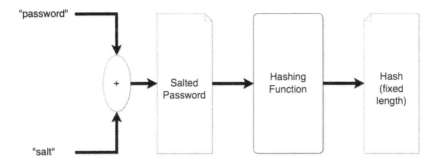

Appendix A3 - Figure 6 - Diagram of salted hash process

The value of a *'salted'* hash is that precomputed data for that hash may not exist and may make the attack much harder for an attacker who will have to perform the brute-forcing himself.

One can also use multiple iterations of the hashing algorithm to make an attacker's job more difficult. Some algorithms are more demanding and make this an almost impossibility for almost all attackers, unless insecure passwords are used (but that is a topic for another day).

A3.4.2 Usage: Transmitted (or Stored) Data - example OpenPGP

Pretty Good Privacy, or PGP, was an application created by Phil Zimmermann in 1991 for encrypting data that was to be transmitted. The OpenPGP standard was born out of this application and is now used not only in PGP (owned by Symantec) but also by the GnuPG application, as well as others.

The OpenPGP standard uses the basic primitives we've just learned about, plus a few others. It starts by compressing the message. A session key, a one-time-only secret key, is then generated. The session key is a symmetric (shared) key which, using a symmetric cipher, to encrypt the compressed message will result in secure cipher-text. The session key is then encrypted with the asymmetric public-key of the recipient, meaning that only the recipient (who is the only one with the private-key) can decrypt the session key and decrypt the cipher-text.

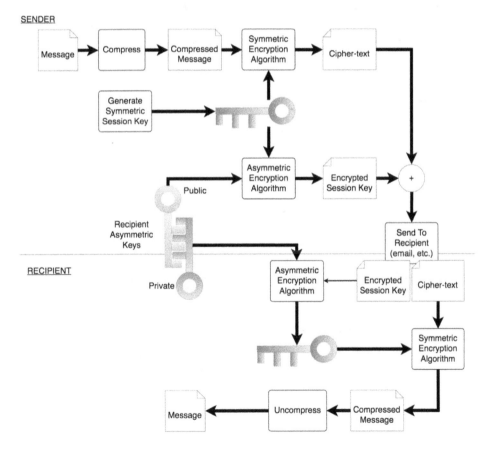

Appendix A3 - Figure 7 - PGP encryption and decryption processes

A3.4.3 Usage: Digital Signatures - OpenPGP

OpenPGP can also be used to create digital signatures. Digital signatures allow one to prove that they actually sent a message. For this purpose, we need two primitives: asymmetric encryption and hashing functions.

So how do we do it? Well, we first take the message to be sent and calculate a hash using a secure and well-defined hashing function. We thus get a small piece of text, the hash. We then encrypt this hash using our private-key, and send both the message and the digital signature together to the recipient. Now, I know this is not the standard process, but bear with me a minute. The two keys are reversible in nature. Thus, what we encrypt with the private-key can be decrypted with the public-key. Since the public-key is available to anyone, such an encryption is not secure, but that is exactly the point. Anyone who gets the message can calculate the hash themselves, and compare it by decrypting (with the public key) the value received. If they are the same, then we know it was sent by the legitimate sender (as long as the sender managed to keep his private-key secure).

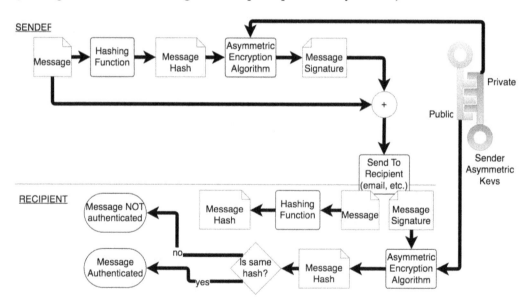

Appendix A3 - Figure 8 - Digital signatures using PGP

A3.4.4 Sent Data - HTTPS (SSL/TLS)

Hypertext Transfer Protocol Secure (HTTPS) is a protocol that allows encryption when transmitting data on the web. It is the most used encryption protocol in use today. You've all seen it when the lock icon appears in the site address you are visiting (see figure 9 for an example).

HTTPS is actually the use of the web protocol, HTTP, over the SSL/TLS protocol. SSL was created in the mid 1990s by Netscape (which later became the Mozilla and maker of Firefox web browsers) to secure connections and prevent eavesdropping and tampering by man-in-the-middle (MITM) attacks. In a MITM attack, someone in the middle acts as a middle-man and can eavesdrop and even modify the information sent. TLS is the evolution of SSL as an independent standard. TLS 1.0 would have been SSL 3.1. SSL has not been updated since 1996. SSL (all versions) and TLS 1.0 are considered insecure and more recent versions of TLS should be used (for more, see section 3.7.4.1 and appendix A2 of PCI DSS 3.2).

Now we know how to use encryption to keep data safe, but how do we know that somebody is not intercepting our information? This is why we use SSL/TLS certificates. A certificate is an electronic document to prove, through digital signatures, ownership of a public key.

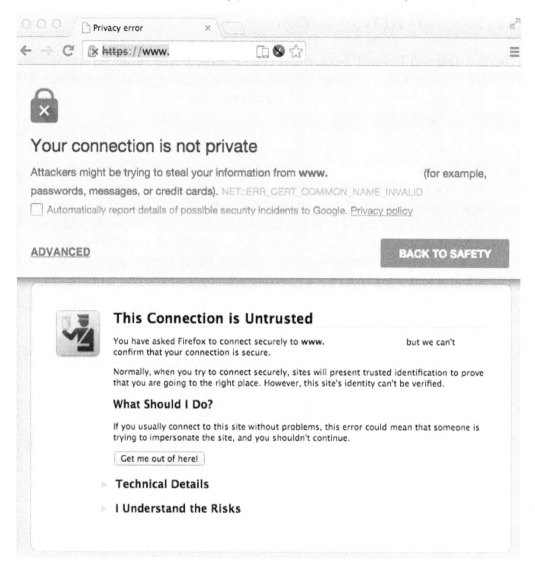

Appendix A3 - Figure 9 - SSL/TLS certificate errors in Chrome and Firefox

The process of negotiation is called the SSL handshake (an agreement on how to communicate securely, presented graphically in figure 10). A user starts a connection using a web browser (some applications also do this) transparently to the server, and the browser and server negotiate some details of which version of SSL/TLS and which ciphers to use. The server then returns its SSL/TLS certificate. This certificate includes a public-key for asymmetric cryptography. The certificate is validated by the browser. This can include matching the name of the server (i.e. a certificate for www.yahoo.com should not be used for a www.google.com site), whether the certificate has expired (valid dates), and its ownership (more on the validation of ownership a little later on). If the certificate is valid, everything continues as expected. If there's something wrong, the browser generally presents a warning message or page (see example in figure 9).

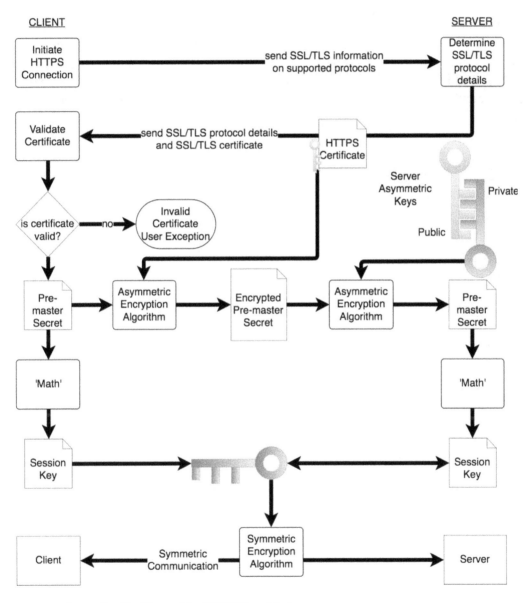

Appendix A3 - Figure 10 - HTTPS handshake

In some cases, the server can also request a certificate from the client and validate it in much the same way. The browser generates a pre-master secret that it encrypts with the server certificate's public key and then sends it to the server. The server decrypts the pre-master secret using its certificate private-key. That pre-master secret, through a series of mathematical steps, is converted to a symmetric session key by both the browser and the server. These two finalize the handshake and secure communication can then begin using the session keys for encryption. You may notice that when you start a connection to an encrypted website (https) the connection often seems sluggish, but later feels much faster. This is simply because the handshake requires slower asymmetric encryption and other calculations, while the latter part uses the faster symmetric encryption and the session key.

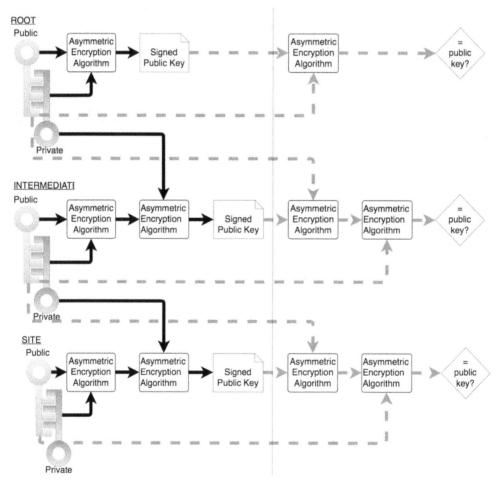

Appendix A3 - Figure 11 - Certificate chaining

Now back to certificate validation. To confirm the ownership of the certificate, we need to get someone to vouch for it. But how can someone know all of the websites and validate their certificates? No one can. What happens is that we have organizations called certificate authorities (CA) to aid us in that. CAs are organizations that are already recognized by browsers as trusted authorities. They form the 'root' of the certificate process. Each web browser stores 'root' certificates for authorities it trusts (there are issues with this model, but until the industry as a whole addresses it, we will not address it here).

A CA signs the certificate (basically the public-key) of a site (using a process similar to the PGP digital signature process described in section 3.13.4.3) using the CA's private-key (see figure 19 for a graphical representation of this process). There can even be a chain of those certificates with many intermediate CAs, in which case there will be a series of signed public-key certificates with each level signing the next level. In order to validate a site's certificate (this process is presented on the right-hand side of figure 19), we first retrieve the 'chain' of certificates and start validating the signatures in the sequence. This is generally performed starting at the root certificate and working towards the site's certificate, but the important task is to confirm that the chain has not been broken and that all signatures are as expected.

Secure Ciphers (Algorithms)

So which algorithms should I use? That is something that will vary over time. Worldwide, the US National Institute of Standards in Technology, or NIST, is recognized as the source of what is acceptable cryptography. Most security standards (including PCI DSS) defer to NIST, as will I.

Summary Table

Primitive	Other Names	Keys	Reversible?	Speed
Symmetric	Private-key	One: shared	Yes	Fast
Asymmetric	Public-key	2: Private and Public	Using other key	Slow
Hash function	One-way function	None	No, only using brute-force	Fast

Appendix A3 - Table 2 - Summary of cryptographic primitives

End Notes - Appendix A3

[1] Nez, Chester and Judith Schiess Avila (2011). Code Talker: The First and Only Memoir by One of the Original Navajo Code Talkers of WWII. Berkeley: San Francisco. .

Appendix A4 - An introduction to the Merchant Self-Assessment Questionnaire (SAQ) selection process

A4.1 Appendix introduction

This section is applicable to merchants only, as service providers must use the complete service provider SAQ-D (or a RoC, if required). SAQs are applicable to merchants with lower transaction volumes. Specific card brand compliance programs vary but generally level 1 merchants are described as those with over 6 million transactions per year. Level 1 merchants will always produce a RoC (Report on Compliance) and never use a SAQ (Self-Assessment Questionnaire). Level 2 merchants are generally those with between 1 and 6 million transactions per year. Visa requires that those only provide a SAQ [1]. The acquirer has authority to determine at which level an organization stands and what document it must provide to demonstrate compliance. Generally, only very large vendors (and those who were breached and elevated directly to level 1) must produce a RoC, which is an audit by an approved vendor, a QSA (Qualified Security Assessor) company (or internal ISA). Merchants should confirm with their acquirer to determine how they should demonstrate compliance.

An organization that receives money from card payments is never completely off the hook from PCI DSS compliance, but its compliance (and reporting) requirements can be reduced through the use of a simpler SAQ. The easiest way to identify which SAQ is applicable to a merchant is to use the flowchart on the last page (section "Which SAQ Best Applies to My Environment?") of the "Assessment Questionnaire Instructions and Guidelines" document. [2] But even that flowchart throws off many people.

As described in volume 1, PCI DSS defines 2 types of payment transactions: Card Present, and Card Not-Present. And Card Not-Present ones can be further divided in 2 types of transaction: eCommerce and MOTO (an acronym which stands for Mail Order/Telephone Order). These 3 types of transactions will help determine which SAQ to select; it can also allow an organization determine what it must change (from a business process point of view) to move to a simpler SAQ.

Table 1 is a compilation of the most important elements of SAQ selection. The factors that determine which SAQ is required are the transaction types an organization accepts (Card Present, eCommerce, MOTO). Those SAQ cannot be combined; if more than one is required, SAQ-D must be selected. Each SAQ also includes a list of requirements that must be met (all of them) or the SAQ cannot be used.

PCI DSS 3.2 Merchant SAQ Options

SAQ	Description	Card Present	eCommerce	MOTO	# Controls	Notes
A	Card-not-present merchants (e-commerce or mail/telephone-order); that have fully outsourced all cardholder data functions to PCI DSS compliant third-party service providers, with no electronic storage, processing, or transmission of any cardholder data on the merchant's systems or premises. Not applicable to face-to-face channels.	No	Yes	Yes	21	All functions outsourced to PCI third-parties. No web redirect possible (although some providers may be able to collect information and transfer it back to merchant).
A-EP	E-commerce merchants who outsource all payment processing to PCI DSS validated third parties, and who have a website(s) that doesn't directly receive cardholder data but that can impact the security of the payment transaction. No electronic storage, processing, or transmission of cardholder data on merchant's systems or premises. Applicable only to e-commerce channels.	No	Yes	No	150	Only eCommerce through web redirect.
B	Merchants using only: • Imprint machines with no electronic cardholder data storage; and/or • Standalone, dial-out terminals with no electronic cardholder data storage. Not applicable to e-commerce channels.	Yes	No	Yes	38	In person or MOTO only.
B-IP	Merchants using only standalone, PTS-approved payment terminals with an IP connection to the payment processor with no electronic cardholder data storage. Not applicable to e-commerce channels.	Yes	No	Yes	62	In person or MOTO only.
C-VT	Merchants who manually enter a single transaction at a time via a keyboard into an Internet-based, virtual payment terminal solution that is provided and hosted by a PCI DSS validated third-party service provider. No electronic cardholder data storage. Not applicable to e-commerce channels.	Yes	No	Yes	62	In person or MOTO, all using Virtual Terminal.
C	Merchants with payment application systems connected to the Internet, no electronic cardholder data storage. Not applicable to e-commerce channels.	Yes	No	Yes	112	In person or MOTO, all using POS or payment application.
P2PE	Merchants using only hardware payment terminals included in and managed via a validated, PCI SSC-listed P2PE solution, with no electronic cardholder data storage. Not applicable to e-commerce channels.	Yes	No	Yes	24	In person or MOTO, all using P2PE device.
D	SAQ D for Merchants: All merchants not included in descriptions for the above SAQ types.	Yes	Yes	Yes	232	Catch-call, more flexible but more controls to meet.

Appendix A4 - Figure 1 - PCI DSS 3.2 Merchant SAQ

As an aside, I had one university client that used simpler SAQs internally for smaller departments (cafeteria, coffee shops, bookstore) which each smaller department had to fill. They then compiled responses to produce a university-wide SAQ-D.

From the table, you can see a description of the SAQ (from the PCI SSC documentation), notes that I've added, but also a column with a number of controls ("# Controls" column). We can see that SAQ-D has 232 controls (that are further divided in test procedures) that must be met while SAQ-A only has 21. This is because a simpler SAQ means that we have a smaller scope. In volume 3 section 3.11, I covered my thinking on "Total Cost of Ownership (TCO)" wanting to focus on the overall cost to the organization of the compliance program (meaning looking at all control costs) and not just the number of questions to answer.

Let's look at the different SAQs.

A4.2 eCommerce SAQs

SAQ-A and SAQ-A-EP are geared for those organizations that accept eCommerce payments, and are generally considered level 3 merchants [3]. Any organization that accepts eCommerce payments must use one of the SAQ-A, or SAQ-D if these cannot be used.

Use of these two SAQs requires that an organization not accept an in-person payment (card present) also referred to as "face-to-face" channels.

A4.2.1 SAQ-A

SAQ-A is the simplest of all SAQs as it requires that all PCI DSS functions be outsourced to PCI DSS compliant service providers. This can include MOTO transactions (call center functions, lockbox, etc.) but all completely outsourced. Even the website must be fully outsourced. Web redirect is not possible in SAQ-A, but is available in SAQ-A-EP described in the next section.

SAQ-A requires that "all elements of the payment page(s) delivered to the consumer's browser originate only and directly from a PCI DSS validated third-party service provider(s)". This includes images, stylesheets, executable resources (for example, javascript) and any other files. So if the look and feel of that page is modified, the required files must come from third-party sites and not the organization's website. Often, developers will use third-party CDNs (Content Delivery Networks) for well known resources. One example, is the use of the jQuery javascript library (jquery.com) which is offered by many CDNs (https://code.jquery.com/, https://cdnjs.com/libraries/jquery/, https://developers.google.com/speed/libraries/). The problem is that these CDNs, while hopefully secure, are not necessarily compliant with PCI DSS, and JavaScript resources, since they execute on the end-user's browser, could be used to perform many different attacks. This is why we must have compliance (which is stated confirmation that a minimal set of information security controls are in place and operating as expected). SAQ-A's questions cover hardening systems (2.1), user identification and authentication (8.*), physical security of media (9.5.* to 9.8.*), managing PCI DSS third-party providers (12.8.*) and having an incident response plan (12.10.1). The other risks have been transferred to the third-party service providers.

A4.2.2 SAQ-A-EP

SAQ-A-EP is for organizations that only accept eCommerce payments (no MOTO or in person), but may host their own website, and redirect to a third-party payment provider for the payment portion of the order (The website can still be outsourced, but then the hosting provider is subject to PCI DSS requirements as a service provider). As such, the organization's website is considered a "connected" system and is in-scope for PCI DSS, even though it never comes into contact with cardholder data as it could "affect the security of the payment transaction and/or the integrity of the page that accepts the consumer's cardholder data" by redirecting to a malicious website.

We can see that the number of questions that must be answered (150) is not that much lower than the catch-all (232) SAQ-D. Still, because no cardholder storage is done, the risk has been greatly reduced. It is easier to identify which controls are not under the organization's purview. Since no electronic cardholder data is received by the organization, then requirements 3.1 and 3.4 to 3.6.* are not applicable and not present in this SAQ. The sections on SDLC (Software Development Lifecycle, 6.3.*) and related separation of duties (6.4 to 6.4.4) are also out. So is RBAC (Role-based Access Controls, 7.2.*) and database admin controls (8.7), many physical security controls, wireless network controls, the need to perform a risk assessment (12.2), implementing a usage policy (12.3.*), HR background checks (12.7) and the bulk of the incident response plan controls (12.10.2 to 12.10.6).

In January 2017, the PCI SSC released very good updated ecommerce guidance [4] that describes various approaches to implementing eCommerce with their pros and cons. I advise the readers involved in eCommerce to read this document thoroughly.

All other (non SAQ-D) SAQs cannot be used for eCommerce.

A4.3 Physical payment devices

The SAQ-B and SAQ-C series, as well as SAQ-P2PE differ in the devices used and the type of connectivity to the payment processor. All of those SAQs can allow for both in-person and MOTO transactions (but no eCommerce) with different degrees of risk reduction (between 24 and 112 questions to answer). All of them do not allow electronic storage of cardholder data (CHD) but can allow storage of physical documents with cardholder data (although once no longer needed, this information should be redacted in an unrecoverable manner).

The SAQ-B series and P2PE cover the use of physical payment devices; this generally includes merchants (brick-and-mortar and/or MOTO) that use sales systems which do not include integrated card payments, but that allow capture of a transaction number from a physical device for financial and accounting reconciliation purposes. SAQ-C series cover computer-based payment applications including virtual terminals, and will be covered in the next section.

If an organization's provider can facilitate a P2PE certified solution (device and service, published on the PCI council approved devices site [5]), this would provide the largest reduction in scope. P2PE, Point-to-Point encryption, means that the data entering the device (keyed-in, via magnetic stripe, chip card or contactless - also known as tap-and-pay) will be encrypted at the capture point and only be decryptable by the provider at the other end, meaning that the company's network will not come into scope. This is why this SAQ only has 24 questions that need answering. The questions cover data storage on paper (remember, no electronic storage) including physical security of media, protecting the payment devices from tampering (9.9.*) and governance or policy controls (12.*). If P2PE is not an option, one of the two SAQ-B's may be applicable.

The difference between SAQ-B and SAQ-B-IP is the way the device connects to the payment processor. SAQ-B is connected through analog connectivity (i.e. not over the internet), such as a phone line modem (and yes, these are still quite common in my experience for smaller or older shops). The IP in SAQ-B-IP is for

"Internet Protocol", meaning the devices use some form of internet connection; that connection can be through your company's regular internet connection (isolated from other systems), through a separate network connection (achieving isolation), or even through cellular network connectivity. The latter allows cafes and restaurant to bring the device to the patrons and have them pay without the card ever being out of their customers' sight, further reducing the risk of card fraud. As of 2017, this is starting to be more common in the USA, but has been a feature in canadian stores for a few years now. It could also allow a delivery person to perform card present transactions instead of having to use MOTO transactions. SAQ-B only has 38 questions covering the same controls as P2PE, but adding protection of PAN (3.3, 4.2), defining employee roles (7.1.*), usage policy (12.3.*). SAQ-B-IP has 62 questions and adds (to the ones in SAQ-B) some network controls (1.*, 4.1, A2 if using older TLS and SSL), hardening (2.*), patching (6.1, 6.2), user access controls (8.*), vulnerability scans (11.2.*) and network segmentation penetration testing (11.3.4).

A4.4 Computer based payment applications

Finally, merchants who do not use physical payment terminals but instead use regular computer-based systems may be able to use the SAQ-C series. This is again applicable for card-present (in person, face-to-face) or MOTO transactions with no eCommerce and no electronic cardholder data storage. The simplest way here is to use a virtual terminal provided by the payment processor and fill out SAQ-C-VT which has only 62 questions. A virtual terminal is generally a minimal website where an employee logs on (authenticates himself) and enters cardholder data one at a time for processing. The data may be temporarily visible (i.e. not masked) during data entry, but once submitted, the information is masked as per PCI DSS requirements.

The PCs connecting to the virtual terminal application must be isolated from the rest of the network. SAQ-C-VT controls are very close to those of SAQ-B-IP and include anti-malware controls (5.*) but not vulnerability scans (11.2.*).

SAQ-C has 112 questions and applies to those merchants whose POS (Point of Sale) is a computer system (called INTEGRATED PAYMENT TERMINAL in the Small Merchant guidance [6]). This often requires the involvement of many providers (hardware, operating system, application, payment processors). The POS must be isolated from the rest of the network. A subset of all of the 12 requirements of PCI DSS must be performed. The goal of SAQ-C is to provide a balance between payment application flexibility and PCI DSS compliance requirements.

End Notes - Appendix A4

[1] VISA (2015). Small Merchant Security Program Requirements – UPDATE.

[2] PCI Security Standards Council (2016, p.18). SAQ Instructions and Guidelines v3.2. Retrieved July 12, 2017, from https://www.pcisecuritystandards.org/documents/SAQ-InstrGuidelines-v3_2.pdf.

[3] PCI Guru (2016). level 3 versus level 4 merchants.

[4] PCI Security Standards Council (2017). PCI DSS Information Supplement: Best Practices for Securing E-commerce. Retrieved July 12, 2017, from https://www.pcisecuritystandards.org/pdfs/best_practices_securing_ecommerce.pdf.

[5] PCI Security Standards Council (2017). PCI Point-to-Point Encryption (P2PE)tm Solutions. Retrieved July 12, 2017, from https://www.pcisecuritystandards.org/assessors_and_solutions/point_to_point_encryption_solutions.

[6] PCI Security Standards Council (2016). PAYMENT PROTECTION RESOURCES FOR SMALL MERCHANTS. Guide to Safe Payments. Version 1.0 | July 2016. https://www.pcisecuritystandards.org/pdfs/Small_Merchant_Guide_to_Safe_Payments.pdf.

Appendix A5 - PCI DSS Scope Diagram Guidance v.1.0 for PCI DSS 3.2

A5.1 PCI DSS Scope Diagram Guidance Introduction

Many firms produce PCI DSS diagram guidance internally for their assessors, and sometimes for their clients, but treat it as trade secrets and do not share it openly. I've seen a few versions of these throughout the years. I believe that providing open guidance will help the industry improve its security. It is my hope that feedback received from the community will improve this guidance over time. This guidance was produced for PCI DSS 3.2 but will be updated periodically.

A5.2 Preamble

Properly documenting PCI DSS scope is often referred to as requirement 0 of PCI DSS; and in my experience scoping is at best misunderstood. This lack of understanding led to the PCI Resources PCI DSS scoping model and approach which I made available to all for free in July 2015, and further updated in July 2016. I'll reference that model in this guidance document. You can find the latest version here: http://www.pciresources.com/pci-dss-scoping-model-and-approach/ (also available there in a convenient PDF format) The PCI council (PCI SSC) released guidance on scoping and network segmentation on December 9, 2016 which was considered in this document.

PCI DSS 3.2 has 2 requirements, 1.1.2 and 1.1.3, that call for diagrams to be produced by the entity (for PCI DSS, an entity is any organization that has the responsibility to protect card data; for PCI DSS compliance, an entity will be defined as either a merchant or a service provider). These diagrams can be created by the entity (internally) or the assessor could do it for them. The important thing is that they are created and maintained.

In addition to requirements 1.1.2 and 1.1.3, the scope section of PCI DSS 3.2 mentions that:

At least annually and prior to the annual assessment, the assessed entity should confirm the accuracy of their PCI DSS scope by identifying all locations and flows of cardholder data, and identify all systems that are connected to or, if compromised, could impact the CDE (for example, authentication servers) to ensure they are included in the PCI DSS scope. [1]

Other guidance can be found by following the scope section (A3.2.*) requirements of Designated Entity Special Validation of Appendix 3 (A3) of PCI DSS 3.2.

Ultimately proper scope definition means that an assessor must be able to understand how PCI (cardholder) data (and other relevant data flows such as authentication) flows from users performing business processes using applications, running on systems and communicating over the different network segments located in different physical locations. The required diagrams must meet this <u>intent</u>.

This scope is also required to confirm an accurate inventory of system components (2.4) and relevant third-parties (12.8.*) so we can ensure all requirements are met for all components (at the network, system and application levels). This will also ensure accurate testing, including penetration testing (11.3.*) and network segmentation penetration testing (11.3.4) on devices providing isolation of CDE networks. Diagrams are also required to be able to perform adequate risk assessments (requirement 12.2).

A5.3 Scope diagram requirements

The PCI DSS standard includes the two (2) previously mentioned requirements for diagrams (testing procedures are omitted here) [2].

PCI DSS Requirements	Guidance
1.1.2 Current network diagram that identifies all connections between the cardholder data environment and other networks, including any wireless networks	Network diagrams describe how networks are configured, and identify the location of all network devices. Without current network diagrams, devices could be overlooked and be unknowingly left out of the security controls implemented for PCI DSS and thus be vulnerable to compromise.
1.1.3 Current diagram that shows all cardholder data flows across systems and networks	Cardholder data-flow diagrams identify the location of all cardholder data that is stored, processed, or transmitted within the network.

	Network and cardholder data-flow diagrams help an organization understand and keep track of the scope of their environment, by showing how cardholder data flows across networks and between individual systems and devices.

Thus, each entity is tasked with maintaining 2 sets of diagrams: network diagrams and data flow diagrams. I use sets because there can be as many as needed to meet the intent of the requirements; indeed, a post by an Optiv blogger [3] talks about 5 levels of diagrams (though how many exactly should be dependent on each organization). The approach is to start from a high-level contextual diagram and add as many other diagrams as needed.

The PCI DSS 3.2 ROC reporting template provides further guidance. Here are the relevant section titles extracted from its table of content (organized by diagram type):

- Network diagram information
    - 2.2 High-level network diagram(s)
        - 3.3 Network segmentation
        - 3.4Network segment details
        - 3.5 Connected entities for payment processing and transmission
        - 3.7 Wireless summary
        - 3.8 Wireless details
    - 4.1 Detailed network diagram(s)
        - 4.4 Critical hardware and software in use in the cardholder data environment
        - 4.7 Service providers and other third parties with which the entity shares cardholder data or that could affect the security of cardholder data
        - 4.8 Third-party payment applications/solutions
- Data flow diagrams
    - 4.2 Description of cardholder data flows
    - 4.3 Cardholder data storage

If you look at this list, you can easily see that we have a minimum of 2 sets of network diagrams that must be included (intermediate levels are also possible):

- high-level network diagrams (2.2)
- detailed network diagrams (4.1)

As a reminder, PCI DSS only defines two types of in-scope systems: CDE (cardholder data environment) and connected (connected are only possible in the presence of effective network segmentation). Everything else is out-of-scope for PCI DSS.

So, we have 3 sets of diagrams. Let me detail the requirements that must be covered by each set (you can use this list as a checklist to validate your diagrams):

- **High-level network diagrams**: to understand the entity's networking topography, showing the overall architecture of the environment being assessed, and how it connects to untrusted networks (those not under the entity's control, such as the internet)

    o Include all relevant network segments (both wired and wireless) where we find CDE and connected systems (with enough detail such as VLAN numbers and, potentially, IP ranges or a way to map it to ranges)
        ▪ networks that store, process and/or transmit CHD (CDE)
        ▪ networks that do not store, process and/or transmit CHD, but are still in scope (segments containing connected systems that may also include out-of-scope systems)
        ▪ networks confirmed to be out of scope
    o Connections into and out of the network including demarcation points (devices that provide network segmentation) between the CDE and other networks/zones (connected, out-of-scope, untrusted)
    o Critical components within the CDE, including POS devices, systems, databases, and web servers, as applicable
    o Other necessary payment components, as applicable
    o Connected entities for payment processing and transmission, including service providers and other third parties with which the entity shares cardholder data or that could affect the security of cardholder data (i.e. third parties and managed service providers)
    o Data center facilities where any of the previously identified components are hosted
- **Detailed network diagrams**: to illustrate each communication/connection point between in scope networks/environments/facilities

- o ROC Guidance: Ensure the diagram(s) include enough detail to clearly understand how each communication point functions and is secured. (For example, the level of detail may include identifying the types of devices, device interfaces, network technologies, protocols, and security controls applicable to that communication point)
- o All boundaries of the cardholder data environment
- o Any network segmentation points which are used to reduce the scope of the assessment
- o Boundaries between trusted and untrusted networks (connectivity, generally external networks)
- o Wireless and wired networks
- o All other connection points applicable to the assessment
- o Every system contained in each CDE segment, as well as the following critical systems (some of which may still be CDE systems)
  - Critical Hardware
    - Type of Device (for example: firewall, server, IDS, etc.)
    - Vendor Make/Model
    - Role/Functionality (often through use of icons and legends)
  - Critical Software
    - Name of Software Product
    - Version or Release
    - Role/Functionality (often through use of icons and legends)
- o Third-party payment applications/solutions
- o Data center facilities where any of the previously identified components are hosted
- **Cardholder Data flow diagrams**: to understand what data flows through which systems (and networks) – often, assessors ask clients to create business process diagrams (i.e. non technical) to describe how CHD is captured, stored (application level), shared or transmitted, and disposed. Business areas understand this easily. After this, we need to ensure that this is mapped over the applications, systems, networks and data center locations.
  - o These must be overlaid over the network diagrams, or allow the assessor to easily see how they map over those (this often requires sitting down business owners, developers and network folks together)
  - o They must cover the following data flows (generally using legends):

- Capture (refers to the specific transaction activity of data capture or entry into the network)
- Authorization
- Settlement
- Chargeback
- Other as applicable (for example, authentication should be included)
- For each type of data flow, the following information must be ascertained (often using legends on diagrams):
    - Types of CHD involved (for example, full track, PAN, expiry)
    - Describe how cardholder data is transmitted and/or processed and for what purpose it is used (protocols, etc.)
    - I recommend accompanying the diagrams with narratives for each flow
- Cardholder data storage locations
- Legends should be present
- Note that sometimes having multiple diagrams for different flows (on top of the same diagrams) helps for legibility and maintainability of those diagrams
- Data center facilities where any of the previously identified components are hosted

A5.4 Updates and validation of the consistency of the diagrams

All diagrams must be reviewed (some evidence of reviews must be kept) at least annually and when the environment changes significantly (both diagram requirements call for diagrams to be "kept current"). Requirement 6.4.6 introduced in PCI DSS 3.2 and which will become mandatory after January 31, 2018, calls for "documentation updated as applicable" "upon completion of a significant change".

It is the assessor's responsibility to ensure the consistency and completeness of the diagram sets. A particular validation of the network diagrams are called for by two (2) testing procedures (1.1.4.b and 1.1.4.c) of requirement 1.1.4 to ensure that the network diagrams are "consistent with the firewall configuration standards" defined in requirement 1.1. The firewall rules defined in requirement 1.1.6 and reviewed per requirement 1.1.7 should also be in locked step.

A5.5 Legends and color coding

There are no specific requirements for using specific colors, so that detail is left to the entity (organization). What should be visually clear is what systems and network segments are CDE and connected systems. One common way is to use colors such as red for CDE systems and network, orange or yellow for connected systems or network, and green for anything out of scope (which is the color scheme I used in my model).

There should be a legend identifying icons and links on all the diagrams even if there are captions below the elements. The protocols linking system and network components need to be identified on the diagrams (forexample, HTTPS, SFTP, TLS). Data flow diagrams should also indicate what elements of cardholder data (PAN, encrypted PAN, Expiration date, etc) are sent over each data flow.

A5.6 Sample diagrams

The example diagrams are for a merchant with stores connected via an MPLS private network (only accessible to the merchant) offered by a network service provider (internet connections would be possible, but are not shown here). To simplify compliance, telephony in stores is using standard analog lines and are not integrated in a networked-telephony system (this often forgotten can of worms is subject for other guidance). We are also not including any virtualization. These diagrams are but one possible representation. Styles may vary. Required content, much less so.

A5.6.1 Sample High-Level Diagram

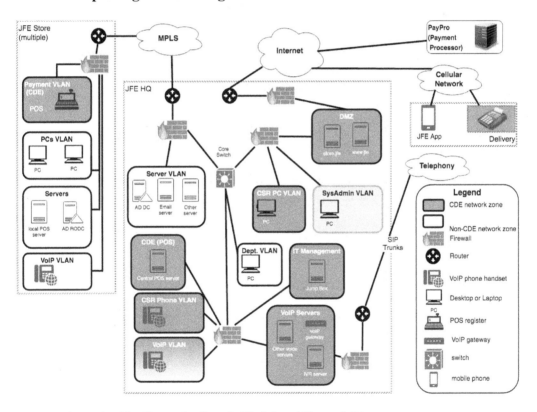

Appendix A5 - Figure 1 – Sample High-Level Network Diagram

A5.6.2 Sample Detailed Network Diagram

The IP addressing scheme here is adapted from one that was in use at a previous employer over 10 years ago. In that scheme, the HQ was using 10.1.0.0/16 and branches were in 10.2. x.0/24 where X was a number assigned to each branch.

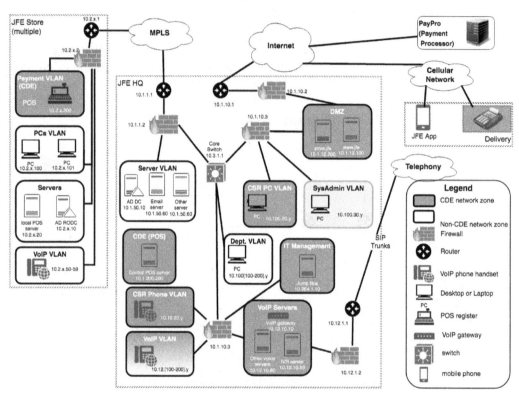

Appendix A5 - Figure 2 – Sample Detailed Network Diagram

A5.6.3 Sample Data-Flow Diagram

The data-flow diagrams (1.1.3) add flow information on top of the detailed network diagram. Elements that are irrelevant may be omitted. This example is for "capture" at a store, where the customer's payment is processed. Other diagrams would be required in a real-world example. I often recommend that a textual narrative accompany the data flow diagrams (it ensures accurate understanding of the process).

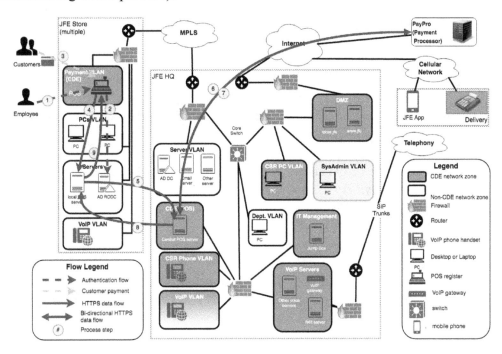

Appendix A5 - Figure 3 – Sample Dataflow Diagram

Textual narrative of process/dataflow

Steps in the diagram:

- o *Employee logs in to the Point-of-Sale (POS).*
- o *User is authenticated to local Active Directory (AD) RoDC (which connects to the main AD servers if user information is not already present in the AD RoDC).*
- o *Employee processes the customer's order and asks the customer to input his payment card in the payment processing device of the POS.*
- o *Payment information is sent encrypted from the payment device to the local POS server.*
- o *Payment information is sent encrypted from the local POS server to the central POS server across the different network devices in-between (if the central POS server is not accessible, the local server could be configured to communicate with the payment processor directly as in step 6).*
- o *The central POS server sends the encrypted payment information to the payment processor.*
- o *The payment processor sends transaction confirmation information to the central POS server.*
- o *The central POS server sends the information back to the local POS server.*
- o *The local POS server sends the information back to the POS, and the employee hands the customer his receipt (or in case the payment was not approved, deals with the issue).*

A5.7 Complex cases

Sadly, we encounter many cases where things are not as simple as suggested in this document. While I cannot provide all possible examples, I do want to touch on points colleagues have raised regarding this.

A5.7.1 Authentication, Authorization and Auditing

PCI DSS includes requirements for user identification (PCI DSS 8.1.*), authentication (PCI DSS 8.2.*) and authorization (PCI DSS 7.*). Information security often refers to these as AAA, Authentication (including identification), Authorization and Auditing. Auditing is part of requirement 10 in PCI DSS.

For simple environments, we can expect these authorizations are directly included in data flow diagrams. More complex environments may require specific diagrams that fully document authentication and other AAA functions for both privileged and non-privileged users in a logical and network/physical format.

A5.7.2 Composite network segmentation cases

Most times network segmentation is accomplished through a simple mechanism such as layer 2 or 3 (see the OSI network model for details on these layers) device such as a firewall or router (hence, the firewall configuration standards of requirement 1.1) which could be a physical or virtual device (slightly more complex).

Due to business or technical constraints some entities use a combination of processes and technology to achieve the equivalent segmentation. These cases are often not clearly documented and may require very detailed diagrams.

For example, an entity uses a web appliance that accepts end-user connections, performs XML transformation, routing and authentication, where many of these tasks are performed at different levels of the OSI model in between layers 2 through 7. Providing exact guidance for such a case is complex and we'd recommend you confirm with your assessor as this falls outside the scope of this guidance (at this time).

End Notes - Appendix A5

[1] PCI Security Standards Council (2016, p.10). Payment Card Industry Data Security Standard 3.2. Retrieved May 31, 2016, from https://www.pcisecuritystandards.org/documents/PCI_DSS_v3-2.pdf.

[2] PCI Security Standards Council (2016, p.10). Payment Card Industry Data Security Standard 3.2.

[3] Optiv (2011). PCI DSS and the Network Diagram. Retrieved July 12, 2017, from https://www.optiv.com/blog/pci-dss-and-the-network-diagram.

Glossary

Term	Description	Source
AAA	Acronym for "authentication, authorization, and accounting". Protocol for authenticating a user based on their verifiable identity, authorizing a user based on their user rights, and accounting for a user's consumption of network resources.	PCI
Access Control List	Provides a list of permissions attached to an object. In networking, an access control list is a set of permissions allowing or denying network traffic between a source and destination connected to the network.	Author
ACL	Acronym for "Access Control List".	Author
Acquirer	The entity that takes on the financial risk of the merchant transaction (sometimes the acquirer is also a payment processor and the roles are mingled - the volumes distinguish between these functions).	Author
AoC	Acronym for "Attestation of Compliance". The AoC is a form for merchants and service providers to attest to the results of a PCI DSS assessment, as documented in the Self-Assessment Questionnaire or Report on Compliance.	PCI
APT	Acronym for "Advanced Persistent Threat". An 'advanced persistent threat'(APT) is a set of stealthy and continuous computer hacking processes, often orchestrated by human(s) targeting a specific entity. An 'APT' usually targets organizations and/or nations for business or political motives.	Wikipedia
ASV	Acronym for "Approved Scanning Vendor." Company approved by the PCI SSC to conduct external vulnerability scanning services.	PCI
ATM	Acronym for "Automatic Teller Machine".	Author

Term	Description	Source
Authorization	In the context of access control, authorization is the granting of access or other rights to a user, program, or process. Authorization defines what an individual or program can do after successful authentication. In the context of a payment card transaction, authorization occurs when a merchant receives transaction approval after the acquirer validates the transaction with the issuer/processor.	PCI
Automatic Teller Machine	An ATM, also known as an Automated Banking Machine (ABM), is an electronic machine that allows a bank cardholder to withdraw cash without the assistance of a cashier.	Author
Bank Identification Number	The first four to six digits of a credit card. The Bank Identification Number (BIN) is also called Institution Identification Number (IIN).	Author
BAU	Acronym for "business-as-usual." BAU is an organization's normal daily business operations.	PCI
BIN	Acronym for "Bank Identification Number".	Author
Card brands	The 5 founding members of the PCI SSC that enforce the PCI DSS within the PCI industry, and facilitate the payment and settlement.	Author
Card Production	Card Production is a standard developed and maintained by the PCI SSC that covers the requirements that payment card producers (which can be issuers) must implement.	Author

Term	Description	Source
Card Verification Code or Value	Also known as Card Validation Code or Value, or Card Security Code. Refers to either: (1) magnetic-stripe data, or (2) printed security features. (1) Data element on a card's magnetic stripe that uses secure cryptographic processes to protect data integrity on the stripe, and reveals any alteration or counterfeiting. Referred to as CAV, CVC, CVV, or CSC depending on payment card brand. The following list provides the terms for each card brand: • CAV - Card Authentication Value (JCB payment cards) • CVC - Card Validation Code (MasterCard payment cards) • CVV - Card Verification Value (Visa and Discover payment cards) • CSC - Card Security Code (American Express) (2) For Discover, JCB, MasterCard, and Visa payment cards, the second type of card verification value or code is the rightmost three-digit value printed in the signature panel area on the back of the card. For American Express payment cards, the code is a four-digit non embossed number printed above the PAN on the face of the payment cards. The code is uniquely associated with each individual piece of plastic and ties the PAN to the plastic. The following list provides the terms for each card brand: • CID - Card Identification Number (American Express and Discover payment cards) • CAV2 - Card Authentication Value 2 (JCB payment cards) • CVC2 - Card Validation Code 2 (MasterCard payment cards) • CVV2 - Card Verification Value 2 (Visa payment cards)	PCI

Term	Description	Source
Card-not-present payment	Refers to transactions where the cardholder (the payer) is not physically in the presence of the merchant (in the store), and 'includes (postal) mail (or even fax) order catalog, a phone-based transaction such as airline ticket reservation or very often an online store.	Author
Card-present payment	Refers to transactions where the cardholder (the payer) is physically in the presence of the merchant (in the store) and uses his payment card to pay.	Author
Cardholder Data	The main data covered by PCI DSS. Consists of the PAN, cardholder name, card expiration date, and sometimes service code. See Sensitive Authentication Data for additional data elements that may be transmitted or processed (but not stored) as part of a payment transaction.	PCI
Cardholder Data Environment	Basically the area (people, process and technologies) we are trying to protect, which starts with the systems that SPT CHD or SAD but is not limited to these.	Author
Cardholders	The individual person to whom a payment card is issued and who pays for products or services using that card	Author
CDE	Acronym for "Cardholder Data Environment".	Author
CHD	Acronym for "Cardholder Data".	PCI
CISP	Aconym for "Cardholder Information Security Program". A program created by Visa's in 1999 and that served as the foundation for the PCI DSS.	Author
Clearing	Clearing is the process of matching (called reconciliation in accounting terms) merchant bank (which is generally the acquirer) and issuer transactions.	Author

Term	Description	Source
Controlled Access	In the context of network segmentation for PCI DSS, the configuration that allows only limited (restricted) communications possible between systems.	Author
Critical Security Controls	SANS top 20 recommended security controls	Author
CSC	Acronym for "Critical Security Controls".	Author
CVE	The Common Vulnerabilities and Exposures (CVE) system provides a reference-method for publicly known information-security vulnerabilities and exposures. (See zero-day vulnerabilities for the contrary).	Wikipedia
CVV, CVV2	See "Card Verification Code or Value" for more detail.	PCI
DDOS	Acronym for "Distributed Denial of Service" attack. A DDOS attack is a DOS attack where the attack source is more than one-and often thousands-of unique IP addresses.	Wikipedia
DESV	PCI DSS Designated Entities Supplemental Validation for PCI DSS 3.1 (DESV) - A new set of requirements to increase assurance that an organization maintains compliance with PCI DSS over time, and that non-compliance is detected by a continuous (if not automated) audit process; this set of requirements applies to entities designated by the card brands or acquirers that are at a high risk level for the industry.	Author
DLP	Acronym for "Data Loss Prevention". Data loss prevention (DLP) solution is a system that is designed to detect potential data breach / data ex-filtration transmissions and prevent them by monitoring, detecting and blocking sensitive data while in-use (endpoint actions), in-motion (network traffic), and at-rest (data storage).	Wikipedia

Term	Description	Source
DMZ	Abbreviation for "demilitarized zone." Physical or logical sub-network that provides an additional layer of security to an organization's internal private network. The DMZ adds an additional layer of network security between the Internet and an organization's internal network so that external parties only have direct connections to devices in the DMZ rather than the entire internal network.	PCI
DOS	Acronym for "Denial of Service" attack. A DOS attack is an attempt to make a machine or network resource unavailable to its intended users, such as to temporarily or indefinitely interrupt or suspend the services of a host connected to the Internet.	Wikipedia
DR/BC	Acronym for "Disaster Recovery/Business Continuity". Disaster recovery (DR) involves a set of policies and procedures to enable the recovery or continuation of vital technology infrastructure and systems following a natural or human-induced disaster. Disaster recovery focuses on the IT or technology systems supporting critical business functions,as opposed to business continuity, which involves keeping all essential aspects of a business functioning despite significant disruptive events. Disaster recovery is therefore a subset of business continuity.	Wikipedia
DSS	Acronym for "Data Security Standard". See PCI DSS.	Author
EMV	Acronym for "Europay MasterCard Visa". EMV equipped payment cards use a small chip to store cardholder data more securely than a magnetic track. EMV is a technical standard for smart payment cards and for payment terminals and automated teller machines which can accept them.	Wikipedia

Term	Description	Source
Exfiltration	Used by some 'computer security' practitioners in place of 'data theft', to mean an unauthorized release of data from within a computer system or network (data or files extracted from borders of a computer operations center [Source: OPM Director Katherine Archuleta Testimony])	Wikipedia
FTP	Acronym for "File Transfer Protocol." Network protocol used to transfer data from one computer to another through a public network such as the Internet. FTP is widely viewed as an insecure protocol because passwords and file contents are sent unprotected and in clear text. FTP can be implemented securely via SSH or other technology. See S-FTP.	PCI
HIPAA	The 1996 Health Insurance Portability and Accountability Act holds requirement for the establishment of national standards for electronic healthcare transactions and national identifiers for providers, health plans, and employers.	Wikipedia
Host	For virtualization, the system (hardware of software) where the hypervisor runs.	Author
HTTP	Acronym for "hypertext transfer protocol." Open internet protocol to transfer or convey information on the World Wide Web.	PCI
HTTPS	Acronym for "hypertext transfer protocol over secure socket layer." Secure HTTP that provides authentication and encrypted communication on the World Wide Web designed for security-sensitive communication such as web-based logins.	PCI
Hypervisor	The application that allows for virtualization of systems.	Author

Term	Description	Source
IDS	Acronym for "intrusion-detection system". Software or hardware used to identify and alert on network or system anomalies or intrusion attempts. Composed of: sensors that generate security events; a console to monitor events and alerts and control the sensors; and a central engine that records events logged by the sensors in a database. Uses system of rules to generate alerts in response to detected security events. See IPS.	PCI
IIN	Acronym for "Institution Identification Number".	Author
Institution Identification Number	The six digits of a payment card as defined in the ISO/IEC 7812 standard.	Author
IPS	Acronym for "intrusion prevention system." Beyond an IDS, an IPS takes the additional step of blocking the attempted intrusion.	PCI
ISA	Acronym for "Internal Security Assessor." ISAs are qualified by PCI SSC. ISAs are employees of organizations that help their organizations build their internal PCI Security Standards expertise and strengthen their approach to payment data security, as well as increasing their efficiency in compliance with data security standards.	PCI
ISO	In the context of industry standards and best practices, ISO, better known as "International Organization for Standardization" is a non-governmental organization consisting of a network of the national standards institutes.	PCI
Isolation	In the context of network segmentation for PCI DSS, the configuration that allows no possible access between systems.	Author
Issuer	The entity that issues the card to the cardholder, often (but not limited to) your bank.	Author

Term	Description	Source
IT	Acronym for "Information Technology". Information technology (IT) is the application of computers and telecommunications equipment to store, retrieve, transmit and manipulate data, [1] often in the context of a business or other enterprise.	Wikipedia
Malware / Malicious Software	Software or firmware designed to infiltrate or damage a computer system without the owner's knowledge or consent, with the intent of compromising the confidentiality, integrity, or availability of the owner's data, applications, or operating system. Such software typically enters a network during many business-approved activities, which results in the exploitation of system vulnerabilities. Examples include viruses, worms, Trojans (or Trojan horses), spyware, adware, and rootkits.	PCI
Merchant	The entity that receives payments from cardholders for products or services.	Author
MOTO or MO/TO	Acronym for "Mail-Order/Telephone-Order".	PCI
NAT (Network Address Translation)	Aaka network or IP masquerading. Change of an IP address used within one network to a different IP address known within another network, allowing an organization's internal addresses to be only visible internally, and external addresses that are only visible externally.	PCI
NERC	Acronym for "North American Electric Reliability Corporation". The organization which manages information security standards for electrical energy companies, and the name of the main standard produced.	Author

Term	Description	Source
NFC	Acronym for "Near field communication". In the payment context, NFC allow payments to be performed simply by placing the payment card with the NFC chip close to the payment reader (no need to swipe the magnetic track or insert the chip).	Author
NIST	Acronym for "National Institute of Standards and Technology." Non-regulatory federal agency within U.S. Commerce Department's Technology Administration.	PCI
Organization	In the context of the PCI Resources book volumes, any entity subject to the PCI DSS and that may include, business and not-for-profits.	Author
OSI Network Model	The Open Standards Interconnect (OSI) network model is a conceptual model which consists of 7 layers built on top of each other.	Author
P2PE	Point-to-Point Encryption (P2PE) is a standard developed and maintained by the PCI SSC that allows scope reduction through the use of encrypted transmission on payment terminals where the merchant cannot decrypt the information.	Author
PA-DSS	Acronym for "Payment Application Data Security Standard". A standard maintained by the PCI SSC that provides controls over an application used in the environment of an organization that stores, processes or transmits cardholder data or sensitive authentication data.	Author
PAN	Acronym for "primary account number" and also referred to as "account number." Unique payment card number (typically for credit or debit cards) that identifies the issuer and the particular cardholder account.	PCI

Term	Description	Source
Payment processor	The entity that receives payment information from the merchant, authorizes, settles and clears the transaction (can be a bank, but can also be a service provider).	Author
PCI	Acronym for "Payment Card Industry".	PCI
PCI DSS	Acronym for "Payment Card Industry Data Security Standard". A standard maintained by the PCI SSC that provides controls over the environment of any organization that stores, processes or transmits cardholder data or sensitive authentication data.	Author
PCI SSC	Acronym for "Payment Card Industry Security Standard Council." The PCI SSC was formed by the card brands, and manages information security standards to help protect cardholder data.	Author
PFI	Acronym for "PCI Forensics Investigator". PFIs are qualified by PCI SSC to perform PCI DSS forensic investigations in case of cardholder data breaches.	Author
PIN	Acronym for "personal identification number". Secret numeric password known only to the user and a system to authenticate the user to the system. The user is only granted access if the PIN the user provided matches the PIN in the system. Typical PINs are used for automated teller machines for cash advance transactions. Another type of PIN is one used in EMV chip cards where the PIN replaces the cardholder"s signature.	PCI
PTS	Acronym for "PIN Transaction Security". PTS is a set of modular evaluation requirements managed by PCI Security Standards Council, for PIN acceptance POI terminals. Please refer to www.pcisecuritystandards.org.	PCI
Ping sweeps	In computing, a ping sweep is a method that can establish a range of IP addresses which map to live hosts.	Wikipedia

Term	Description	Source
POS	Acronym for "point of sale". Hardware and/or software used to process payment card transactions at merchant locations.	PCI
Primary Account Number	The card number printed on the front of the card.	Author
PWN	Pwn is a slang term derived from the verb own, as meaning to appropriate or to conquer to gain ownership.	Wikipedia
QSA	Acronym for "Qualified Security Assessor". QSAs are qualified by PCI SSC to perform PCI DSS on-site assessments. Refer to the QSA Qualification Requirements for details about requirements for QSA Companies and Employees.	PCI
QSAC	Acronym for "Qualified Security Assessor Company." A QSAC company is a firm qualified by PCI SSC to perform PCI DSS on-site assessments. See QSA for more information.	Author
RAM-scraper	A type of malware program that grabs information that flows through an electronic device's memory.	Author
Regular Expressions	A regular expression (abbreviated regex or regexp and sometimes called a rational expression) is a sequence of characters that define a search pattern, mainly for use in pattern matching with strings, or string matching, i.e. 'find and replace'-like operations.	Wikipedia
Report on Compliance	Report documenting detailed results from an entity's PCI DSS assessment.	PCI
RoC	Acronym for "Report on Compliance".	PCI
S-FTP	Acronym for Secure-FTP. S-FTP has the ability to encrypt authentication information and data files in transit. See FTP.	PCI

Term	Description	Source
SAD	Acronym for "Sensitive Authentication Data".	PCI
SANS	Acronym for "SysAdmin, Audit, Networking and Security". An institute that provides computer security training and professional certification. (See www.sans.org.)	PCI
SAQ	Acronym for "Self-Assessment Questionnaire". Reporting tool used to document self-assessment results from an entity's PCI DSS assessment.	PCI
Sarbanes Oxley	The Sarbanes-Oxley Act of 2002, is a United States federal law that set new or expanded requirements for all U.S. public company boards, management and public accounting firms.	Wikipedia
Sensitive Authentication Data	Includes the magnetic track information, the PIN or PIN block, as well as the Card-not-present authorization value which we will refer to as CVV2 but can take any of the following acronyms: CAV2/CVC2/CVV2/CID.	Author
Service provider	An entity that performs some functions regarding to the payment process and/or provides services that may affect the security of the cardholder data.	Author
Settlement	Payment of the outstanding balance owed by the issuer to the acquirer, and later the merchant.	Author
SIEM	Security information and event management (SIEM) is a term for software products and services combining security information management (SIM) and security event management (SEM).	Wikipedia
SIN	A social insurance number (SIN) is a number issued in Canada to administer various government programs, including the administration of the Canada Pension Plan and Canada's varied employment insurance programs, and for tax reporting purposes.	Wikipedia
SOX	Acronym for "Sarbanes Oxley".	Author

Term	Description	Source
SPT	An Acronym for "Store, Process, or Transmit", meaning that a system or process comes into contact with CHD and/or SAD and is therefore automatically in scope for PCI DSS.	Author
SQL Injection	Form of attack on database-driven web sites. A malicious individual executes unauthorized SQL commands by taking advantage of insecure code on a system connected to the Internet. SQL injection attacks are used to steal information from a database from which the data would normally not be available and/or to gain access to an organization's host computers through the computer that is hosting the database.	PCI
SSL	Acronym for "Secure Sockets Layer". Industry standard that encrypts the channel between a web browser and web server. Now superseded by TLS. See TLS.	PCI
SSN	In the United States, a Social Security number (SSN) is a nine-digit number issued to U.S. citizens, permanent residents, and temporary (working) residents.	Wikipedia
Third-Party Service Providers	In the context of the PCI Resources book volumes, any entity subject to the PCI DSS and that may include, business and not-for-profits.	Author
TLS	Acronym for "Transport Layer Security". Designed with goal of providing data secrecy and data integrity between two communicating applications. TLS is successor of SSL.	PCI
TPSP	Acronym for "Third-Party Service Providers".	Author
Virtual machine	The individual "abstract" system that runs on an hypervisor.	Author
VM	Acronym for "virtual machine". A VM is an emulation of a particular computer system.	Wikipedia

Term	Description	Source
Zero-day vulnerabilities	A zero-day (also known as zero-hour or 0-day) vulnerability is an undisclosed and uncorrected computer application vulnerability that could be exploited to adversely affect the computer programs, data, additional computers or a network. It is known as a "zero-day" because once a flaw becomes known, the programmer or developer has zero days to fix it.	Wikipedia

The column "source" identifies the origin of the terms in this glossary.

- "Author" refers to terms defined by the author of this book.

- "PCI" refers to definitions adapted from the PCI SSC documents, mainly the PCI DSS Glossary (https://www.pcisecuritystandards.org/documents/PCI_DSS_Glossary_v3-2.pdf).

- "Wikipedia" refers to definitions adapted from the wikipedia website.http://www.pciresources.com/http://www.pciresources.com/